"*Beyond Talent: Creating a Successful Career in Music* provides practical advice to budding musicians in an easy-to-follow format."—*Arts Management*

"Real-life experience is reflected here, not just from the author but from the numerous examples provided by real musicians, from résumés and Web pages to anecdotes and sample contract. . . . This book will help people create more opportunities for themselves, and provide guidance for people to shape their musical careers in more realistic and successful ways."—Jeffrey Snedeker, *The Horn Call*

"*Beyond Talent* is full of valuable information for students as well as professionals . . . Many compliments to Angela Beeching and to Oxford University Press for publishing this fine book."—Kathleen Chastain, Clinical Assistant Professor of Flute and Wind Chamber Music, Oberlin Conservatory of Music

"I recommend this book highly to anyone who wants to give a young artist a fighting chance to build a career."—Keith Hatschek, Director, Music Management Program, Conservatory of Music, University of the Pacific

"This is a terrific book for college-age and other young musicians who are serious about their careers. It is the best resource I've seen for young and developing musicians!"—Harriet Schwartz, College of Fine Arts Career Consultant, Carnegie Mellon University

"*Beyond Talent* supports the dream of a career in music while laying out the nuts and bolts of what it takes to make that happen. That's a delicate line that we walk—how to support students' passions and commitment to music but also prepare them for the substantial non-musical elements in career development. This book offers a refreshing and direct approach." —Janis Weller, Chair, Liberal Arts, McNally Smith College of Music

"The students were truly inspired by it . . . They told me on a regular basis that it was one of the best books they had ever read. . . . I would highly recommend *Beyond Talent* to anyone teaching a course that deals with life in the real world for music majors after they graduate."—Diane Roscetti, Professor of Music, California State University, Northridge

D0206192

"The title of this book gives just a glimpse of the breadth of information that is actually included. Author Angela Myles Beeching is director of the Career Services Center at the New England Conservatory, and it is clear that she draws from her personal experience advising hundreds of musicians in all aspects of their careers. Although the book is written primarily for musicians aspiring for full-time professional performing careers, the chapters include practical tips and guidelines that can also be applied to music teachers, composers, and freelancers. . . . This book could easily be used as a textbook for a group of musicians to discuss, ponder, and creatively experiment with promoting their own music making and creating their own 'career paths.' "—*American Music Teacher*

"*Beyond Talent* is a wonderfully helpful book for the professional future of any young musician. Beeching writes clearly and comprehensively. Her book is a must for the library of any professional musician."—Robert Freeman, former Dean, College of Fine Arts, the University of Texas at Austin

"Career specialists and students are hungry for this information. When it is packaged as clearly, concisely, and entertainingly as this book is, it is easy to imagine its addition to the shelves."—Simone Himbeault Taylor, Director, Career Center, University of Michigan

"An excellent manual for musicians at all levels. Full of practical advice and important information, simply presented, easily understood and ready to use."—Janet Bookspan, Stage Director and Performance Coach

BEYOND

TALENT

Creating a Successful Career in Music

Second Edition

Angela Myles Beeching

OXFORD
UNIVERSITY PRESS

2010

OXFORD
UNIVERSITY PRESS

Oxford University Press, Inc., publishes works that further
Oxford University's objective of excellence
in research, scholarship, and education.

Oxford   New York
Auckland   Cape Town   Dar es Salaam   Hong Kong   Karachi
Kuala Lumpur   Madrid   Melbourne   Mexico City   Nairobi
New Delhi   Shanghai   Taipei   Toronto

With offices in
Argentina   Austria   Brazil   Chile   Czech Republic   France   Greece
Guatemala   Hungary   Italy   Japan   Poland   Portugal   Singapore
South Korea   Switzerland   Thailand   Turkey   Ukraine   Vietnam

Published by Oxford University Press, Inc.
198 Madison Avenue, New York, New York 10016

www.oup.com

Oxford is a registered trademark of Oxford University Press.

Library of Congress Cataloging-in-Publication Data
Beeching, Angela Myles.
Beyond talent : creating a successful career in music / by Angela Myles Beeching. — Rev. 2nd ed.
p. cm.
Includes index.
ISBN 978-0-19-538259-4
1. Music—Vocational guidance. I. Title.
ML3795.B42 2010
780.23—dc22 2009019134

Resources are available online at www.oup.com/us/beyondtalent
Oxford Web Music 🎵
For more information on Oxford Web Music, visit www.oxfordwebmusic.com

12
Printed in Canada
on acid-free paper

Prelude to the Second Edition

This expanded edition is packed with new musician profiles, fresh perspectives, and updated, streamlined information. Special emphasis is placed on music entrepreneurship, audience engagement, and the use of online tools. To address these issues and more, this new edition of *Beyond Talent* offers scores of new resources and ideas plus a comprehensive online companion guide with video clips, articles, and hyperlinks connecting readers to a sampling of the best online music resources; see http://www.oup.com/us/beyondtalent.

Preface

It takes more than talent to succeed in music. Maybe it always has, but today's musicians need to be more creative than ever when it comes to their careers, cultivating an entrepreneurial approach to connecting with audiences and creating value in their communities. Musicians need to use the full range of their skills in making a place for themselves in the changing profession. This book is designed to show you how to take charge of your future; it's all about putting *you* in the driver's seat.

As director of the Career Services Center at New England Conservatory, one of the world's top music schools, I've advised hundreds of talented music students, alumni, staff, and faculty. In addition, I have worked with scores of other professional musicians at national arts conferences and workshops. I have counseled classical, jazz, world, and some pop musicians on a range of career issues.

The work is fascinating: consulting with musicians on everything from recording, commissioning, and online promotional projects to launching performance series and new ensembles. I've advised musicians whose goals were to become orchestral players, college music faculty, general managers of opera companies, studio musicians, film composers, and more.

In doing this work, I've found that even established artists find it difficult to get practical information on the business side of the profession. Many musicians need guidance on managing their careers, on how to promote themselves and turn dreams into reality. Mostly, people need help thinking through their goals and coming up with workable action plans. Unfortunately, many musicians don't get the advice and information they need to succeed, and consequently, they fail to establish themselves professionally. This doesn't have to happen to you.

Is This Book for You?   ◆

Are you curious about creating a niche for yourself in the music profession? Are you interested in how other musicians have found their paths? Would you like to set goals and accomplish them? If so, this book is for you.

Successful musicians tailor-make their own career paths, and these paths typically require an entrepreneurial and individual approach. There's no one-size-fits-all formula for success: each musician makes his or her own way. This book includes a wide range of ideas, suggestions, and examples to help you create your own path to success.

What This Book Includes   ◆

Drawing on my years of experience as a music career counselor, educator, and cellist, this book offers concrete, detailed information to help musicians make their way in the professional marketplace. It is seasoned with the accumulated wisdom of clients, colleagues, and mentors: the musicians, artist managers, concert presenters, and music educators with whom I have consulted over the years.

Each chapter contains background information, specific how-to directions, and real-life stories. All the examples are real, although in some cases I've changed the names and a few of the details to safeguard people's privacy. There are exercises for creating long-term and short-term goals and suggested practical steps for achieving them.

Some of the information and suggestions may be new to you. The more familiar material may help you evaluate your strategies, or confirm your good habits. Some of the information may seem like rocket science, whereas other sections cover commonsense approaches and good manners—the kinds of things we can all use an occasional reminder about.

This book explains how to do the following:

- Find and create performance opportunities
- Produce professional-quality promotional materials
- Attract media attention to build your reputation and audience
- Raise funds for your music projects
- Enhance your performance work as needed with supplementary, satisfying employment
- Design your own career success plan to reach your long-term goals

How Is This Book Organized?   ◆

As much as possible, topics are presented in a first-things-first, step-by-step basis. For instance, how to create promotional materials is discussed before how to book performances. So, although chapters can certainly be read on their own or out of order, the book is designed to take the reader through a linear, career-mapping process. Taking the journey from chapter 1 to the end should help you develop perspective and a more holistic approach to advancing your career.

Where Do the Musician Examples Come From?   ◆

This book is full of examples of real musicians solving real issues in their careers. For the examples that come from confidential career advising, I've altered names but left the stories in tact. You will also find other examples, not requiring anonymity, in which musicians' stories include their actual names.

These "example" musicians work in a range of genres and serve to illustrate an array of career challenges and solutions. There is much that musicians can learn from the innovation and creativity of artists outside their genre, and often the best ideas are generated by examining an issue from alternative vantage points.

Bonus Item: The Dirty Secret about Career Planning   ◆

Before proceeding further, I want to come clean about a problem with the concept of career planning. It's a problem inherent to books such as this and to the profession of career counseling. It's blasphemous for me to admit, but the real way people go through life is *not* with a handy map and directions. They don't usually set goals and plan carefully and work systematically toward success. Why? Because there's so much in life that we cannot control and so much of our career direction depends on exploration. Life is fluid, and so are careers.

In reality, we go through life as though there *were* no path, as though we were in a dense forest and simply making our way as best we can. An idea leads to a conversation, a connection, a project, and through the course of these projects our career path emerges. It's often only in looking back over years that we can fashion a story line out of our own history. In hindsight, we can see how the projects connected, and how our goals and interests drove us to various choices and opportunities. But in the present, the path is all too often impossible to discern. It's impossible to see clearly the cause and effect of all the choices we make, small and large, each day. But our choices are the essential "stuff" of which our projects, career paths, and lives are made.

Career counselors advocate making plans, writing down goals, exploring opportunities, and taking practical steps toward completing projects. I say and write these things and I believe them . . . *to a degree.*

We *pretend* that life will work logically, that action A will lead to outcome B. But everyone knows that life almost never works according to plan. You can't account for luck or for being in the right or wrong place and time. There's also your personal life and your health—these in many ways determine the course of a career. And there's the fact that any one of our projects can take us away from our original plan, take us off course, and lead us to a new goal, a new path. That's what makes life fascinating—you don't get to know in advance how things will turn out. It's all a big gamble.

Here's my own story: I started playing the cello at age 8 and was hooked. I wanted nothing more than to play music. I won scholarships throughout school and as a graduate student thought that the be-all and end-all would be to get a tenure track college teaching job so I could teach and perform. I got a doctorate, won several fellowships, and had two different tenure track positions teaching cello, first in California and then in New York. But I found that once I'd reached my goal—to get one of these jobs—that my life wasn't quite as I'd imagined it. I found I needed to do something else. If someone had told me at age 20 or age 30 that I would end up running a music career center and publishing a career guide—and that I'd love this work—I would have called that person crazy. But life throws surprises at us, and this keeps things interesting. If life went according to plan, we'd all be bored.

So yes, I advise musicians to set goals and make plans, because there *are* practical ways to get from point A to point B in your career. But realize that your life—the good stuff—is all about the journey. Stay flexible because your goals and plans will change as you explore your options.

Tricks of the Trade   ◆

On my desk at work I have a useful tool for career counseling. It's a magic wand. And, sitting on top of my computer monitor, there's a plastic tiara for the really tough days. With my magic wand I wish I could make people's dreams come true, give them the lucky break they need, and create the life work they want. But the reality is that we each have to find our own way. At least we don't have to do it alone. In life, we all get to learn from our mistakes and we get many opportunities to both learn from and help one another.

In a sense, this book is my magic wand to you: my best advice and perspective. The world needs music and musicians, and it's your responsibility to find a way to put your talents to good use.

Acknowledgments

First, I want to thank my agent Ann Rittenberg and my editor Suzanne Ryan for their much appreciated guidance and patience. And I especially want to thank this constellation of terrific readers, friends, and quoted advisors, appearing here in alphabetical splendor.

Liam Abramson
Andy Appel
Stephen Beaudoin
Robert Besen
John Blanchard
Howard Block
Sarah Bob
Janet Bookspan
Eric Booth
Josh and Donna Brietzer
Mark Broschinsky
Kathy Canfield
Claire Chase
Carrie Cheron
Nancy Christensen
Afton Cotton
Susan Dadian
Adrian Daly
Katie DeBonvillle
Ed Donahue
Eric Edberg
James Falzone
Catherine Fitterman

Jack Garrity
Ellen Goldensohn
John Greer
Kevin Harris
Freddie Hart
Josh Hoekwater
Pat Hollenbeck
The JP Prose Writers' Group!
Jeffrey James
Rani Katsenelenbogen
Sarah Lee
Tanya Maggi
Patrick Maxfield
Michael McGrade
Rick McLaughlin
Tom Meglioranza
Derek Mithaug
Casey Molino Dunn
Jennifer Morris
Lior Navok
Lisa Nigris
Deborah Obalil
Barbara Owens

Eric Platz
Gwen Powell
Steve Procter
Barbara Raney
Jean Rife
Omar Roca
Sebastian Ruth
Chokdee Rutirisari
Nancy Shear
Laurie Shulman
Toni Sikes
Pamela Slim
Peter Spellman
John Steinmetz
Dan Swenson
Kelland Thomas
Brenda Ulrich
Ginevra Ventre
Steve Wogaman
Judith Ciampa Wright
Jacob Yarrow
Phillip Ying

Contents

BEYOND

TALENT

1

Mapping Success

"This is such an exciting time in the world of music—musicians and institutions are re-examining and redefining who they are, what they do, what they want to do, and what is important in their lives."—Adrian Daly, Dean, Cleveland Institute of Music

What is it you dream of? For some musicians, it's performing with the world's best orchestras or with great opera companies. Some musicians want to record and tour with their own ensembles; some wish to create multimedia works involving music, dance, theater, and technology. Others dream of directing major arts institutions, writing music for film and video games, performing on Broadway, or teaching music at the college level. As you read this, you're probably reflecting on your own particular dream career. Having the dream is great, but what comes next?

Musicians often attribute career success to fate or destiny. They say it's a matter of being in the right place at the right time, getting "discovered," or just being lucky. Unfortunately, this kind of thinking leads to a passive approach: to simply letting things happen as they will. My goal is to fundamentally change this thinking and promote the idea that *you* are the person in charge. *You* are the architect of your future. Through your attitude and actions, you can determine your luck and success.

Today's Musicians Profiled: Success Redefined ◆

What characterizes the newest generation of musicians? What kinds of successful careers are they creating for themselves? Here are a few examples of not-so-traditional approaches.

Cellist Matt Haimovitz garnered national media attention several years ago when the *New York Times* ran a piece about his unorthodox national tour—solo cello recitals played in rock clubs, coffeehouses, and even a pizza parlor. He had become frustrated with the traditional concert experience and missed seeing his generation in the audience. He wanted to reach out to new audiences with the music he was passionate about—from J. S. Bach to living composers to his own arrangements of rock standards. He has championed performing in nontraditional venues; for his "Anthem" tour of American works, Haimovitz performed Jimi Hendrix's improvisational version of *The Star-Spangled Banner* and recorded it live at former New York City's punk palace CBGB. Shortly after his initial forays into alternative spaces, Haimovitz hired a former singer-songwriter to find and book appropriate clubs for more extensive tours in support of his latest projects.

In 2000 he and composer Luna Pearl Woolf founded an indie classical label, Oxingale Records, and since then have released over 15 albums encompassing a wide range of artists and genre-blending collaborative works. Recent projects include *After Reading Shakespeare,* featuring literary-themed solo cello suites by three Pulitzer Prize–winning American composers. Haimovitz has toured the album in over forty cities, including exclusive appearances at Borders bookstores as part of "Borders on the Road." Oxingale has also launched a YouTube channel featuring his performances and on the label's website (http://www.oxingale.com), fans can download free ringtones of Matt's signature cellistic pyrotechnics.[1]

Here is an example of another music career path with a different focus: ICE, the International Contemporary Ensemble (http://www.iceorg.org), is a flexible group of thirty musicians who play everything from duos to chamber orchestra works, multimedia pieces using extended techniques, non-Western instruments, as well as improvisatory and electroacoustic works.

Claire Chase, flutist and cofounder of ICE, wrote about her experience as a musician-entrepreneur in 2008:

> When I formed ICE in Chicago the summer after I graduated from Oberlin, I had no money, no business experience, very few contacts in

the area. I produced our first concert on a budget of $605, which was exactly the amount of my first check working for Wolfgang Puck Catering Company.

Seven years later, we have given more than 250 concerts, including the world premieres of over 400 new works, and we have two solvent companies in Chicago and New York (with California coming soon), four albums on the way this season, and upcoming tours in three continents.

Our generation of young musicians, despite the economic challenges that we face, is experiencing an unprecedented freedom. We can do anything we want to do. We can produce our own concerts, release our own albums, create our own communities and our own movements, and we don't need a lot of money to do this. We just need great ideas, we need a spirit of adventure, and we need each other (thick skin is good to have, too).

ICE is an outgrowth of this early 21st century trend of the musician as entrepreneur, the artist as the producer. Although it might be too early to make this prediction, it is my hope that this spirit of entrepreneurship in the arts will be one of the defining characteristics and contributions of my generation of artists.[2]

And here is a third example and another ensemble demonstrating an alternative career path: the Providence String Quartet developed its innovative urban residency, Community MusicWorks (http:// www.communitymusic works.org), over ten years ago in Providence, Rhode Island. Violinist/violist Sebastian Ruth founded Community MusicWorks on the conviction that musicians have an important public role to play in creating and transforming communities. Lauded by Alex Ross in the *New Yorker* as a "revolutionary organization," the quartet lives, rehearses, and teaches in an underserved urban neighborhood. Ruth, a Brown University graduate, started the project with a $10,000 grant from the university's Swearer Center for Public Service. Community MusicWorks is now funded through grants and private donations. By 2009, their budget had grown to $630,000. The organization provides 100 neighborhood children with lessons, the use of instruments, and transportation to performances throughout the region. A substantial waiting list of students is evidence of the program's popularity with young people and their families.

In terms of having an impact beyond their immediate community, in 2006, the organization started a two-year fellowship program that trains young professional musicians in the methodology of community-based performance and teaching careers. Fellows teach, perform, and design programs alongside the members of the Providence String Quartet. The idea is that with this training, the fellows can go out and start their own community-based programs in other parts of the United States and the world.

A common mission runs through the stories of this new generation of musicians: they are finding new ways to connect music with audiences. Musicians are no longer content to perform only in traditional, formal venues, disconnected from audiences and from communities. Musicians today explore ways to find a sense of immediacy, connection, and relevance.

What Does It Take? Part 1 ♦

Keep in mind that careers are developed over years, not hatched overnight. The overnight success story is a media myth: when musicians are interviewed in depth, the overnight success invariably turns out to have been ten or twenty years in the making. There are substantial data that show that it takes 10,000 hours, or roughly ten years of study, work, and experience, to become an expert in *any* field. As detailed in the recommended *Musical Excellence: Strategies and Techniques to Enhance Performance,* "The ten year minimum has been documented in every field of human endeavor that has been examined . . . This rule holds for musicians, novelists, poets, mathematicians, chess players, tennis players, swimmers, long distance runners, livestock judges, radiologists, and doctors . . ."[3]

Though this should come as no surprise to musicians, it is comforting to realize that everyone—genius or not—needs the ten years or 10,000 hours of hard work. Malcolm Gladwell, in his excellent book *Outliers: The Story of Success,* offers examples of Bill Gates and others, detailing how their early years provided them the crucial 10,000 hours of exposure and training necessary to their later success. Mozart, though a prodigy and a genius, had been composing for ten years before he wrote his first "important" work. The point is that genius and talent are not enough. Hard work is essential; there are no shortcuts.

Gladwell also details the experience of the Beatles. As teenagers, when they were just getting started as a band in Liverpool, they hooked up with a local promoter, a fellow with connections in Hamburg, Germany, where they could get ongoing work. In Hamburg back then, Gladwell explains, strip clubs hired rock bands to play exceptionally long sets: *five or more hours each night, seven days a week, for continuous shows.* The Beatles ended up traveling to Hamburg five times between 1960 and 1962, Gladwell explains, "performing for 270 nights in just over a year and a half. By the time they had their first burst of success in 1964, in fact, they had performed live an estimated twelve hundred times. Do you know how extraordinary that is? Most bands today don't perform twelve hundred times in their entire careers."[4]

They had to hone their performance skills, learn a huge number of songs, and figure out how to capture and maintain an audience's attention (not easy when you're a competing with strippers). Gladwell quotes Philip Norman, who wrote the Beatles' biography, *Shout!:*

"They learned not only stamina. They had to learn an enormous amount of numbers—cover versions of everything you can think of, not just rock and roll, a bit of jazz too. They weren't disciplined onstage at all before that. But when they came back, they sounded like no one else. It was the making of them."[5]

Success is a process. As a music career counselor, my job is to help people articulate their dreams, clarify their goals, and determine their next steps. Long-term career goals are realized through everyday choices about the use of time, energy, and money. Whether you're just starting out or are in midstream, these everyday choices are critical. Confucius had it right: the journey of a thousand steps *really does* begin with just one.

Defining the Profession: What's a Musician's "Job"?

In thinking about your dream, it may be useful to reflect on what it actually means to be a musician. The job of "musician" involves far more than performing. Musicians' careers are multidimensional. Working musicians typically "wear different hats" over the course of their workweek and over the course of their working lives. In talking with most active professional musicians, you will find they have multiple ongoing projects that involve performing, composing, recording, teaching, or other arts-related activities. What's more, musicians are often involved in handling performance contracts, publicity, and fundraising for their projects. Most musicians spend a portion of their work lives teaching—not just for the income but because they find it challenging and satisfying. Musicians advocate for arts education and public funding for the arts, and serve their communities on advisory boards and as consultants. So my first tip is this: ask professional musicians about their work lives. You will find there are very few who make a living solely from performing. Musicians' "jobs" encompass a wide variety of fascinating and rewarding work.

Debunking the Myth of Music Career Success

The myth that fuels many young musicians' dreams goes like this: "If I practice really, really, REALLY hard, do everything my teacher tells me, go to the best school, and win competitions, then with luck (and maybe the connections my teacher has), I will '*make it.*'" For many, *making it* means becoming an international "star," making a living as a soloist, and performing with orchestras and in recitals worldwide.

This is a very narrow view of success. In the protective bubble of a music degree program, students can be oblivious to the difficult realities of the "real world." Unfortunately, the bubble also keeps musicians uninformed about the many other nontraditional and entrepreneurial music career success paths.

Only a fraction of the total number of musicians actually makes their living strictly as performers. And only a handful of those musicians are soloists. So, although there's nothing wrong with "going for gold," it can be a problem if a musician views anything short of this as failure. With a narrow view of success, musicians unconsciously limit their careers, their satisfaction, and their professional fulfillment.

"When musicians have a narrow view of the profession, they limit themselves in finding their own best career path," says bassoonist Ben Kamins, faculty at Rice University, former principal with the Houston Symphony, and active freelance chamber player. "There is a misconception amongst music students that you get a job in an orchestra and you live happily ever after. It's incredible to get and keep that job, but it doesn't guarantee artistic satisfaction."

If these are myths, then what can musicians actually do to be successful? When they don't find ready-made work opportunities, or when they simply want something other than what's available, they create their own opportunities. The history of the arts, after all, is a testament to the human drive to create. Musicians compose new works, invent new instruments, and develop music software. They launch new ensembles and performance series, and, in the process, they build audiences and transform communities.

The essential challenge for today's musician is to create a meaningful life's work and a livable income in a highly competitive, evolving marketplace.

The Big Picture ◆

The Higher Education Arts Data Service tracks information for the National Association of Schools of Music (NASM). Of the 606 institutions reporting, the findings for 2007–2008 included these: more than 110,000 students were enrolled in NASM-member college-level music programs in the United States. And in that year over 20,000 people graduated with music degrees.[6] Therefore, competition for "traditional" jobs, such as full-time orchestra positions and college-level music teaching, is exceedingly high. Unfortunately, most graduating musicians have their sights set on these types of traditional opportunities.

To put supply and demand in context, though there are over 1,800 orchestras in the United States, the majority of these are volunteer and educational ensembles. The 52 largest budgeted professional American orchestras have roughly 4,200 total positions for players. In 2003, there were just 159 openings in these orchestras.[7] And the number of applicants requesting an audition for any one of these positions is typically 100 to 200.

As for college-level music teaching jobs, the majority of full-time positions require doctorates and prior college teaching experience. Here, too, the market is flooded with qualified applicants. A single full-time opening can attract more than 100 candidates. In 2008, the Career Services Center at New England Conservatory tracked the numbers of U.S. college music teaching opportunities for specific instruments and found the total number of full-time openings for cello faculty was thirteen; for clarinet, eleven. According to the Higher Education Arts Data Service, the total number of cellists enrolled in doctoral programs for 2008 was 155, and the total number of clarinetists was 138.[8]

However, these highly competitive traditional jobs are only a fraction of the work actually available to musicians. The U.S. music industry is vast and includes a huge variety of work opportunities. And because musicians are generally multi-talented, they often have marketable skills in more than one area. The majority of today's professional musicians create satisfying "portfolio" careers, braiding together part-time work and entrepreneurial ventures to capitalize on their talents, interests, and experience.

▼

"Realize there are many different ways to make a living in music," says Boston-based freelance clarinetist Michael Norsworthy. "Remain flexible, look for opportunities at every turn, and be ready to adjust your viewpoint. There's no ONE way, there are MANY ways."

▲

The U.S. music industry employs roughly 295,000 people in the *core* music industries, which include performers, ensembles, those working for publishers and record labels, and those doing studio and radio work, music instrument manufacturing, and retail. Another 899,000 people are employed in the *peripheral* music industries: those at music schools and recording reproduction companies, and those working as agents, promoters, and venue managers. The total annual revenue for the music industry includes $3.1 billion from the core industries, and another $23.5 billion from the peripheral ones.[9]

What do all these numbers mean for individual musicians? However you slice it, there's a huge range of opportunities for people with music skills and a passion to share music with others. Musicians generally have market-able skills in more than one area, leading to multifaceted careers. If you are creative and open-minded, there are dozens of ways to put your music training and talent to work.

What Does It Take? Part 2 ◆

Winning and keeping an orchestra job demands skills and talents different from those needed to lead a jazz ensemble, write film scores, launch a music software company, or teach at a conservatory. Though there's no formula, there are six important qualities that are critical to all music careers. Do a little self-assessment: do you have some or many of these?

Talent *plus* **hard work** are necessary but *are not sufficient by themselves*. You need more:

Winning attitude: You are motivated, focused, and resilient; you can handle rejection.

Sales skills: You communicate and present yourself well; your enthusiasm is contagious. You can articulate your strengths to prospective collaborators, clients, and employers.

Support system: You have emotional support and encouragement from a group of friends and mentors. And your goals and plans do not cause conflict in your close relationships.

Strategy: You have plans for how to reach both your short- and long-term goals; you have the skills and experience necessary to implement your plan.

If some areas need work, consider yourself in good company. No one has the "perfect package." But knowing what needs improving is the first step to making positive change. The following chapters detail practical ways to enhance and develop these qualities.

Musicians who do well professionally and have the least trouble with the realities of the music profession are those who have most of these six qualities or who have an overabundance in one area that may compensate for a lack in another.

▼
_____

Case Study

Helen O., a talented pianist, has built a good local reputation as a chamber musician/accompanist and has received a number of favorable reviews. However, she is passive in her approach to her career: she does not seek out opportunities but relies on her reputation to generate them. Helen shies away from dealing directly with the business side of her career. She does not actively seek advice from colleagues or networking contacts. She is frustrated that she's not getting more concert dates, doesn't have a manager, and is not commanding the fees she thinks she deserves.

Helen blames the unfair music industry, the competitive market, and the dwindling audience for classical music. *She does not see how her own behavior and attitude may actually be holding her back.*

▲

Musicians, like most people, are fond of complaining. It is easier to gripe about a lack of opportunities than to take control of your life. What could Helen O. do differently? Like most of us, Helen could make better use of her existing support system, cultivate new collaborators, and improve her self-management (until she can attract a manager). Identifying our shortcomings is essential to making improvements. Talking to others can be a great way to gain perspective. You may recognize a bit of Helen in you because there is probably a bit of her in all of us.

To help Helen and others, here are ten basic principles for advancing music careers. I call these the "Success Principles." See how many of these you use now, and consider adopting the others. They do not necessarily demand a lot of time or effort, but they do require adjusting your attitude, modifying habits, and venturing beyond your comfort zone.

Ten Success Principles   ◆

There are many practical steps you can take to advance toward your career goals. But over the years, by observing musicians make their way in the world, I've noticed certain kinds of thinking and behavior that works well. I've distilled these habits into the principles below. These are lifestyle recommendations, ways to think about and deal with the world. Many of these principles are developed further in subsequent chapters.

1. Know yourself. Know both your strengths and weaknesses. Know what you have to offer the professional world. Get feedback from colleagues, teachers, and mentors. Their suggestions and advice can help you chart the path that's best for you.

2. Get to know your industry. Get savvy. Your research should include both talking to colleagues and mentors as well as reading about the arts and the music profession. Stay current by reading relevant music trade journals, blogs, and websites specific to your particular areas of interest. Reading this book is a great start!

3. *Schmooze.* Network; get out and exchange information and ideas with others. When you share career and job information with colleagues, they reciprocate. Networking happens everywhere: at rehearsals, backstage at concerts, in supermarkets, at gas stations, and at most social gatherings. Even if you are shy, you can find a style of networking to suit your personality. Chapter 2 examines networking in depth.

4. *Research your options.* Information leads to opportunities. Read other musicians' bios for ideas about grants, competitions, festivals, and performance possibilities. You can find bios on musicians' websites, blogs, CD liner notes, and in concert programs. Check online for local arts calendar listings to find out what other musicians at your career stage are doing. Make research a habit: schedule time each week to catch up on what's going on in the profession.

▼ ───

As graduate students, two composers—Koji Nakano from Japan and Lior Navok from Israel—both made time to regularly research and follow up on opportunities.

Koji researched competitions open to international students. Applying and winning a few of these led to commissions, summer seminars, and premiers of his works. His pieces have since been performed at the Tanglewood, Aspen, and Bowdoin music festivals, and at Carnegie and Merkin Halls in New York City. And he has had residencies at the MacDowell, Yaddo, Millay, Djerassi, and Ragdale artist colonies.

While still in school, Lior Navok produced a CD of his own works. He then researched where to send it (which radio stations and reviewers). The CD got radio airplay and was reviewed favorably in several publications, and this led to commissions for new works and plans for the next CD. Lior has gone on to receive commissions from the Koussevitzky Music Foundation, the Fromm Music Foundation, the National Endowment for the Arts, and the Jerome Foundation.

It's never possible in life to know how any one project, contact, or opportunity will lead to the next. But in hindsight, we can see how these two musicians' efforts as students served them well in their unfolding careers.

─── ▲

5. *Cultivate an attitude.* Be positive, resilient, flexible, and professional. Keep your ego in check; you need to be able to deal well with both rejection and acceptance. People want to work with those who are pleasant, optimistic, and inspiring. Remember that your attitude is a big part of your professional image.

6. *Assess your interpersonal skills.* Clean up your act. We've all suffered disappointments and difficulties in life. Get whatever kind of help you need,

but make sure you are not inflicting your personal difficulties on others. Because the music industry is a very small, relationship-driven world, we need to be good colleagues to each other (because the person you snub today may be the person who *doesn't* hire you tomorrow).

Musicians spend an inordinate amount of time alone in practice rooms. The solitary and demanding work can contribute to a lack of interpersonal skills and overall self-centeredness. This is how some musicians end up being considered "high maintenance" or "divas." So, be considerate. People will remember your thoughtfulness and optimism, and they will respond in kind. The more you can be at ease with yourself and with others, the more you can benefit from and appreciate the world you inhabit. Do your best to contribute positive energy to all of your life and work situations because what goes around comes around.

▼
Tips on Tuning Up Your Interpersonal Skills

- Before going to sleep each night, think back over the day. Review your behavior and interactions with others. Ask yourself what you would choose to do differently. Be honest. Envisioning new patterns of behavior is the first step to making positive change.
- Ask for feedback from trusted colleagues and friends. If you are unsure of how you are coming across or about how you handled a particular situation, ask a colleague for objective feedback

▲

7. Think like an entrepreneur. This means thinking creatively about what you have to offer and how you can put your musical skills and experience to work, creating opportunities for yourself. Spend time brainstorming with friends and colleagues.

Conductor and vocal coach John Greer, when asked what career advice he had for musicians, described the three keys to success he gleaned from the Canadian entrepreneur Edward Mirvish. These were to "fulfill a need; go against the trend; and keep it simple." John Greer translates these tips for musician entrepreneurs: fulfilling a need means offering something that others want and will value enough to pay you for. Your music needs an audience; think about what you have to offer and who might want this in your community. Think creatively about where in your community you can perform, use your musical skills, and be paid for it. As for Ed Mirvish's second tip, "going against the trend," John reminds musicians to offer something distinctive. Think about specific repertoire and projects that especially suit your abilities and interests. Do you have other special skills? And finally, as for keeping it simple, John says, make sure you keep in mind why you are in music. "Don't be distracted from the big idea—keep your artistic goals front and center. And make sure nothing extraneous or unessential distracts your audience from your mission." Make sure the projects and work you take on reflect your values.

▼

Many musicians create their own performance opportunities and develop their own audiences. Wordless Music Series (WMS) in New York City is a great example. The brainchild of Ronen Givoney, the series presents innovative postrock and electronica acts with classical musicians at a number of venues, notably Le Poisson Rouge, an intimate flexible-seat venue multimedia art cabaret.

A rocker who got turned on to classical, Givoney created a series to "demonstrate that the various boundaries and genre distinctions segregating music today—popular and classical; uptown and downtown; high art and low—are artificial constructions in need of dismantling."[10]

The series' first concert brought two musicians from the group Wilco together with the pianist Jenny Lin, who played works by Ligeti, Shostakovich, and Elliott Sharp. Lauded in the press, the series has garnered a strong following, introducing listeners from both rock and the classical worlds to composers that they might not otherwise encounter. In 2008, the series presented the first American performance of Radiohead-fame Jonny Greenwood's "Popcorn Superhet Receiver," for string orchestra, on a program with music by John Adams and Gavin Bryars.

▲

8. *Communicate what makes you distinctive.* In order to get bookings, media attention, and an audience, you will need to be able to communicate what is special about you and your music making. What is your singular viewpoint? Do you perform any specialized or unusual repertoire? Have you given concerts in unusual settings? This topic is covered in depth in chapter 3.

▼

Cellist Reinmar Seidler had given a few concerts in South America and wanted to follow up on these opportunities. In order to increase his marketability and expand the scope of his touring, he put together a promotional kit to send to prospective concert presenters and music schools. The kit included detailed descriptions of lecture demonstrations and clinics he could offer on early music performance practices for string players and healthy physical approaches to performing (example shown in chapter 3). He offered a distinctive package and it resulted in more bookings as well as more college-level teaching experience for his résumé.

▲

9. *Have both short-term and long-term goals.* Articulating your goals is important. You can't get somewhere if you don't know where you're going. Having realistic short-term goals, for each month or each week, will help keep you focused and motivated. Meeting short-term goals is the best way to work toward your long-term dream. At the end of each chapter there are practical prompts to help you determine your next short-term goals and action steps.

10. *Feed your soul.* How do you recharge and renew your creativity? What inspires you? Pay attention to what helps recharge your imagination and what helps keep your spirit alive. Whether you rebalance by attending to your spirituality, your family life, favorite hobbies, or by communing with nature, make sure that you are taking good care of your spirit.

Remind yourself of why you got involved in music in the first place. Your most basic reasons for being in music are crucial factors to keep you moving forward in your career. Keeping tabs on your motivation—on the essence of what music means to you—should help sustain you throughout your career.

On Inspiration

Israeli composer Lior Navok gave a presentation at New England Conservatory several years ago and spoke about creativity and motivation. In his talk, Lior described the drive that musicians have—the creative internal fire—and he likened it to a small gold box. It's something absolutely personal and irreplaceable in each of us, a precious gift that we need to safeguard. Lior's image of the gold box is powerful—it can serve as a reminder of our mission. His metaphor itself is a gift: when you conjure it, you may also find it has a centering and motivating effect.

Advancing in your career involves fine-tuning your goals, assessing your strengths, and discovering and exploring new opportunities. The kind of musician who puts these success principles into action can be described as an entrepreneur. Cultivate your entrepreneurial skills, and you cultivate your career.

The Entrepreneurial You   ◆

Musicians do not usually view themselves as entrepreneurs, even though they are the quintessential "multi-preneurs." Musicians regularly launch new ensembles, start their own teaching studios, create record labels, and publish their own works. A satisfying work life for a successful musician often includes concurrent start-up ventures. This is just one benefit to being a musician: the diversity of ways you can contribute to society.

Musicians create their own start-up projects for a variety of reasons. They may catch the entrepreneurial bug because of frustration with limited traditional opportunities or because they seek the satisfaction of being in charge of their own project. They may want additional income or the opportunity to perform certain repertoire with particular colleagues. Sometimes entrepreneurship begins with identifying a specific community need and seeing how a musician's skills would meet that need.

Boston-based pianist and entrepreneur Sarah Bob had always been interested in the connections between contemporary visual art and music. In 2000, she founded the New Gallery Concert Series to present the two arts in dialogue. Each concert is presented in collaboration with a corresponding visual art exhibition at the Community Music Center of Boston, where Sarah is on faculty. She selects the visual artwork and commissions composers to write musical responses to it. As of 2008, the series had hosted 26 concerts with over 123 musical compositions, 30 premieres, and hundreds of works by over two dozen visual artists from around the world. The series includes works that span the spectrum from classical-contemporary, improvisation, electronic, jazz, and avant-garde music, paired with sculpture, painting, indoor installations, photography, and film. (See http://www.newgalleryconcertseries.org.)

According to the U.S. Census Bureau, in 2005, on average, 2,356 people each day launched their own businesses. Individual proprietorships or businesses without employees, also known as "lone wolves," had receipts of $951 billion and made up approximately 78% of the nation's 26 million-plus firms.[11] Whether you are starting your own ensemble, establishing a private teaching studio, contracting other musicians for gigs, or marketing and selling your own CD, you too are being entrepreneurial.

In addition to their musical ability, successful musicians tend to possess certain entrepreneurial characteristics, personality traits, and other skills. Not every successful musician has them all, but they often have a high percentage. See how many you possess now; subsequent chapters detail how to develop these skills and cultivate these traits.

Entrepreneurial Checklist

Skills to Manage Your Music Career
- ❏ Interpersonal
- ❏ Writing
- ❏ Public speaking/presentation
- ❏ Negotiation

Personal Qualities for Success
- ❏ Determination
- ❏ Ability to handle rejection
- ❏ Imagination, creativity
- ❏ Flexibility, openness to new ideas

❏ Budget/finance
❏ Teaching
❏ Research

❏ Publicity

❏ Computer

❏ Grant writing

❏ Fundraising

❏ Personal integrity
❏ Intellectual curiosity
❏ Ability to learn from one's
  mistakes
❏ Conscientiousness,
  reliability
❏ Good follow-through,
  detail-oriented
❏ Interest in others,
  willingness to contribute
❏ Optimism

▼

Oboist Jennifer Montbach started Radius Ensemble—a mixed chamber group with its own concert series—so that she could program the music she wanted and experiment with reaching a broader audience.

While she was a grad student, Jennifer gained valuable arts administration experience helping in the start-up of the Boston Modern Orchestra Project, and later took on a job working in the publicity department for the Boston Symphony Orchestra. Through this work, she acquired the necessary skills and professional contacts to launch Radius.

Within its first two seasons, Radius had already received great reviews, created an impressive website and fan list, and was playing to full houses. In addition to all the practice and rehearsals, the work involved forming a nonprofit organization, fundraising, and writing program notes and press releases. The payoff for Jennifer was seeing her vision realized. (See http://www.radiusensemble.org.)

▲

Toni Sikes is the founder of "the Guild," a company that markets and sells online original artwork by thousands of artists. For an Arts Enterprise talk at the University of Wisconsin–Madison, Toni explained that being an entrepreneur is "not a job title: it's a state of mind." And in terms of what's necessary to move forward as an entrepreneur, she said people need to be adept at the following:

1. *Dreaming.* Do you have a vision? In business schools budding entrepreneurs are asked, "What's your 'BHAG'? The acronym stands for your Big, Hairy, Audacious Goal.
2. *Bootstrapping.* Can you take your vision and break it down into manageable pieces, starting small and working long and hard to bring your idea to life?

3. *Networking.* You need to get out and meet people, to gather ideas and suggestions for your work. Toni says, "Schmoozing is a contact sport: you need to rub up against others." (Networking is covered in chapter 2.)
4. *The art of pitching.* You must be able to communicate an engaging and concise "pitch" of what you have to offer others.
5. *The art of doing.* Entrepreneurs have a bias toward action; it's no good having great ideas if you don't act on them. Toni says, "The hardest thing about starting is starting."

Project-Based Career Advancement ◆

Through advising over the years, I have found that musicians often have an idea in the back of their minds for a special project, something they've always wanted to do, create, or help make happen. What I mean by *project* here is a music career-related venture that is concrete and specific. (This is *not a project:* "to become the best jazz ukulele player in the Southwest"! That may be a goal, but it's not a project.) Projects are focused on *doing* as opposed to being: they have timelines and are task-oriented. Projects can be anything from researching and applying for grants to study abroad, to starting a reed-making business, writing a teaching methods book, launching a concert series, or raising money to buy an instrument. Music career projects demand a range of musical and non-musical skills, and they can be tremendously satisfying to work on and complete.

Unfortunately, musicians often keep their project ideas to themselves. Worse, they often talk themselves out of pursuing these projects, thinking they're too ambitious or too time-consuming. The usual reasons given are a lack of time, collaborators, and/or funding. This is a shame, because it is usually these creative project ideas that lead musicians to rewarding and satisfying career paths.

In fact, most music careers are *project-driven.* A musician's contacts and interests generally lead to a series of short- or longer term projects (such as commissions, recordings, tours, teaching studios, and ensembles). These projects, in turn, make up the fabric of most musicians' artistic careers, much more than any particular "job." So learning to manage a project is a great way to learn to manage your career.

To get started, think about what you've been dreaming about doing. Seek out advice and feedback on the projects you have imagined. If you don't at least talk about your project, ask questions, and explore, you'll never have the satisfaction of knowing whether it was actually possible. Ask current or former teachers, alumni, or your music school's career development staff. Ask friends and family if they know anyone who has done something similar. People realize their dreams by talking about them with others and sharing their enthusiasm—which often leads to more ideas, collaborators, plans, and action. Do not underestimate the importance of other people; projects require collaboration, they take a team, if not a village.

Self-Assessment: Where Are You Now? ◆

In order to map your future, you will need to first orient yourself. Career advancement involves two kinds of work: the internal and the external. The internal work involves self-reflection and assessment. The external work involves research and networking. To help with the internal work, here are two essential questions and some help with finding answers:

What Are Your Strengths?

It can help to write all this down as a list. In what areas do you excel? Be specific. Think about all aspects of your musicianship in relation to the career you desire. Performers need to consider their technical performance abilities and levels, interpretive skills, range and repertoire, and performance experience. What is your reputation? How would your colleagues and mentors describe your abilities now? If you teach, what are your specific strengths as an educator? If you are interested in arts administration and music industry jobs, what relevant skills and experience do you have at this point? Everybody should consider their professionalism. Are you known as someone who is easy to work with, who shows up on time and is well prepared?

What Needs Improving?

We *all* have weaknesses. Write them down: be specific and honest. If you are serious about moving ahead in your career, you need to be willing to confront what needs changing and then work on making improvements.

Because we are not usually our own best judges, it's important to get objective feedback. Make individual appointments with three or four trusted mentors who know your work well. Ask people whose professional opinions you value, such as coaches or former teachers. Do *not* ask loved ones or close friends—they are biased, and for this you need objectivity. When you make these appointments, be clear that you are asking for unvarnished feedback on both your strengths and your weaknesses.

Be prepared for honesty. I recommend writing down everything you hear in these consultations—both the good and the bad—so you can sort it all out later. Listen calmly, do not get defensive, and do not make excuses. In meeting with different people, you may get contradicting input. Take time to think it all over carefully. It takes maturity to ask for and to process this kind of critical feedback. Be humble and astute enough to ask for input, and then use it to improve your work—these are the hallmarks of a committed professional.

Clarifying Your Intent: What Is It You Want?

So, what exactly is your dream? What is your desired future? I like to ask the question this way: *"If a fairy godmother were to appear suddenly and bonk you on the head with her magic wand, what would you ask for?"* Write down your answers. What is the life you hope to be living ten years from now? Where and with whom would you like to be living? Do you see a house, pets, and/or children in the picture? Detail what you plan to be doing professionally. Consider how you want to be involved musically in your immediate community. Be specific and concrete about your future goals because you will need to think strategically about how to reach them.

Achieving Goals: Getting from Point A to Point B   ◆

Career concerns and questions are essentially about choices: how to spend time and how to focus one's energy. Many musicians have difficulty figuring out the action steps to take to advance their careers. It can be difficult to see a clear path toward that long-term dream. In order to succeed, musicians need to break down big goals into manageable smaller pieces.

Backward planning is the secret weapon of wedding planners, corporate executives, and savvy musicians. The idea is to work in reverse from your desired outcome, making sure you have a manageable timeline with benchmarking goals along the way to help keep you on track. By breaking down a big list of responsibilities into manageable weekly tasks, the work is doable and the stress is minimized. The trick in managing any project is to think strategically and realistically about what needs to be done and when. It's great to have the satisfaction of crossing off tasks on your to-do list at the end of each week, knowing that you're that much closer to reaching your goal.

▼

Case Study: Determining Short-Term Goals

Suppose that your long-term career goal is to lead your own jazz quartet ten years from now, playing international tours and releasing your own recordings. You have started your own band and have played a few local jazz clubs, thanks to contacts through friends.

The question now is, what would help you move forward, toward your long-term goal? You realize you need to gain more performance experience. So what is an appropriate goal to set for the next six months? And what specific action steps should you take this next week?

A reasonable six-month goal might be to arrange a small regional tour to gain performance, promotion, and booking experience. How should you get started?

Week 1: First things first. You will need to find where your band could play, right? This is basic research. You need to find performance venues in nearby cities that will be appropriate for your music. You can look on the web and talk to other musicians. You'll need to keep track of the information you gather—the names, locations, and contacts of the performance venues. Depending on how busy you are, this research might be a reasonable task for your first week, because it will involve both detailed web searching and connecting with colleagues and mentors.

Week 2: Once you have a list of target performance venues, you need to have promotional materials and a practiced telephone *pitch* before making calls or sending e-mails.

If the band needs to update its bio, sound clips, or website, this may be another week's to-do list. These kinds of action steps are described in detail in later chapters. But for now, we are focusing on how to break down a large goal into manageable pieces. And the most important piece of any plan is choosing the tasks you will complete *this week:* it's all about getting the work done.

▲

Devising Your Career Plan

Goals are dreams with deadlines. Planning ahead drives you toward your goal. Without long-term goals and the concrete plans to achieve these, we are at the mercy of all the distractions and immediate concerns of life around us. The only one who can prioritize your time and energy to meet your needs is you.

▼

"Ever hear about the Harvard study of business school grads? The study monitored graduates of an MBA program from 1979 to 1989. Researchers found that ten years after graduation the three percent who had written goals were making 10 times as much money as the other 97 percent combined."

—Annette Richmond, "How to Develop More Effective Short-Term Goals," on http://www.career-intelligence.com

Even if financial success is not your top priority, writing down your goals is important. It serves to help you consciously commit to your goals. It is a powerful method that focuses your thoughts and energy.

▲

Start with writing down your long-term and short-term goals. You can revise them as you gain more experience. People change, so their goals and plans need to change with them. You may even find yourself revising your plan as you read this book and discover more about yourself and the music industry. That's fine, because researching and assessing your options is an important part of career exploration. The next chapters are all designed to help you fine-tune your career plan, to make it work for you.

Summary

Ultimately, success is about creating a life path that is meaningful. From a holistic viewpoint, lives and careers are all about process—experimentation and discovery. It's up to each individual to make the journey satisfying and rewarding.

▼

Career Forward

Working through these questions will help you move ahead. Writing out your answers will help with thinking through and committing to your goals.

1. How do *you* define success?
2. What *specifically* do you love about music?
3. What *specifically* do you love about being a musician? (This is not the same as question 2.)
4. What is your long-term goal? Describe in detail the life you'd like to be leading ten years from now. Where do you see yourself living? What kinds of work are you doing? Is there a family or significant other involved? A garden? Pets?
5. What is your short-term goal? To progress toward your long-term goal, what do you realistically want to accomplish one year from now?
6. What do you want to accomplish this month that will advance you toward your short-term goal?
7. What's on your to-do list for this week?

▲

2

Cultivating Your Support Network: Making Connections, Building Community

▼

In this chapter:

▲

What *IS* Networking? ◆

Musicians commonly have the wrong idea about networking. They mistakenly believe that it's all about self-interest: the "What can you do for *me?*" approach, sucking up to important or influential individuals. Unfortunately, many equate networking with being manipulative or ingratiating. When viewed this way, most musicians find the idea of networking distasteful.

But networking is actually about creating and nurturing relationships. It's developing relationships over time with mutual friends, trusted colleagues, fans, and supporters. Some of these relationships are closer than others, but we are still talking about real relationships with real people. Think of your network as your community and your support system.

Most networking happens on a very casual basis. People meet each other at concerts, schools, town meetings, grocery stores, restaurants, and churches. We bump into old friends and colleagues, and often get introduced to new acquaintances. Networking is about being neighborly, interested in others, and open to making new friends. It's about connecting with others: sharing ideas, resources, and experience.

Check Your Attitude and Intent ◆

"The most important rule of a healthy network is reciprocity," writes entrepreneur consultant Pamela Slim, "If you only interact with people in your network when you want something (a job, leads for your business, help getting out of a jam) you will destroy it faster than you can build it. Healthy networks are made up of people who truly like and respect each other and help each other willingly without expecting anything in return. To have great resources at your disposal, be a great resource!" (See http://www .escapefromcubiclenation.com)

Having good networking skills means having good interpersonal skills. We are not born with these; we need to learn them and work at them. Business schools provide courses and seminars for students to practice networking, pitching business ideas to investors and "working a room." Interpersonal skills are necessary in all fields, but especially in music. Improving your "people" skills simply starts with becoming more aware of how you interact with others.

I cannot emphasize this enough: the way you approach someone new—your words and actions, *and the agenda behind these*—will determine the outcome of your networking efforts. Don't be a *taker*—the kind of person who is thinking only of his or her own interests, needs, and ambitions. Be a *giver*—the kind of person attuned to the interests of others and who demonstrates a kindness of spirit and a genuine personal concern for others. Adrian Daly, Dean of the Cleveland Institute of Music, in an e-mail conversation on this topic, wrote about "the psychology of our interactions with people." He recommends "thinking about how our interactions can help us get what we want from people, by working to give them what *they* want." This isn't a manipulative game; it's simply acknowledging the fact that we connect better with others if we focus on their interests and concerns. After all, it's very clear to others when we are being self-serving, ingenuous, or when we have an "agenda." The best agenda or mission to adopt is that of contributing positively to your community and the world. Be a good person: treat everyone with kindness and respect.

Why Do It?

Is getting along with others necessary for success? That depends on how you define success. We all know of well-paid, acclaimed musicians and great artists whose interpersonal skills leave something to be desired and whose personal lives are in shambles. Maybe fame and fortune are enough, but most of us want more: a life that is enriched by good relationships and positive interactions with people. Networking is investing in our own artistic community. If it takes a village to raise a child, it takes a community to build a music career. Nobody does it alone.

On the most practical level, networking is how musicians typically find out about auditions, jobs, and performance opportunities: it's word-of-mouth. In the deceptively small music world, it is especially important to be a good colleague, to have a good reputation, and to have a network of friends and contacts. It really is all about the golden rule: if you share useful information and leads with others, they will likely return the favor.

▼

Guitarist Bob Sullivan has been freelancing since his teens. He estimates that 99 percent of the gigs he is offered come from referrals and networking. Bob has played everything from pit orchestra gigs to new music premieres and weddings. His referrals come from colleagues, contractors, conductors, former students, previous clientele, and personal acquaintances. When Bob gets a call for a gig or teaching opportunity and he's overbooked or not interested, he in turn refers this work to colleagues and qualified students. What goes around comes around.

▲

A further reason to network is the simple fact that you need a fan base, people who will come to your concerts, buy your recordings, contribute to your projects, introduce you to other influential contacts, and either hire you or refer you to those who can. But on a more philosophical level, the best reason for networking is to help build a community of supportive friends and colleagues. Your network should include people who inspire and challenge you, not just artistically, but as a citizen and a member of a community.

"It is virtually impossible to create forward momentum in your career without a supportive network of colleagues and friends," writes Pamela Slim in her *Shortcuts to Rekindle the Fire in Your Career*. She goes on to detail the full value of a network: "The purpose of having a deep and supportive network is to take new, positive steps in your life, broaden your awareness of opportunities, and provide objective and critical feedback for your ideas and goals. It is not the volume of people you know that is important; it is the quality of your relationships."

▼
Networking "No-Nos"

1. "Sucking up"
2. Being pushy
3. Being self-involved
4. Failing to follow up and follow through on leads
5. Having unrealistic expectations

▲

Mapping Your Network ◆

Studies have shown that people "know" between 100 and 1,000 other individuals, with differing degrees of closeness. If you don't keep track of these contacts, or have no organized way to reach these people, you are wasting one of your most valuable assets: your support system.

To help make the most of your existing network, put it on paper. These *levels* of relationship can be represented graphically: draw a set of four concentric circles, like the rings of a tree, with you at the center. Consider your existing relationships, the people in your life. Where would you place them on the chart?

- *Inner circle:* approximately five to ten people. These are your closest mentors, trusted colleagues, and friends, the people you turn to for career advice. This is your "personal advisory board."
- *Intermediate circle:* who else do you know? Include your colleagues, former teachers, classmates, family friends, neighbors, and maybe your doctor, dentist, chiropractor, accountant, mechanic, fellow book club members, or basketball buddies. Be as complete as possible.
- *Outermost circle:* these are more casual acquaintances, people who have "friended" you on a social networking site, those who may have attended your concerts.

Write the names of the people in your inner circle and as many as you can think of that belong to your intermediate ring. Here are some questions to consider:

1. How do you stay in touch with these people?
2. How might you reconnect with those with whom you have lost touch?
3. When was the last time you spoke with the people in your inner circle?
4. What would you like to consult with them about?

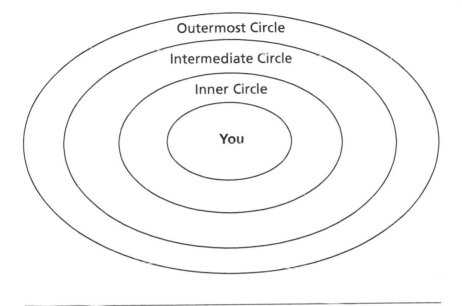

Staying in Touch

To stay connected with their network, the Miró Quartet mails out a colorful holiday newsletter with photos and updates about the group. These include the latest news about recording and commissioning projects, plus personal milestones: weddings, birth announcements, baby pictures. The newsletter is fun to read and helped readers feel personally connected with the group.

Composer Lior Novok is very good at keeping in touch with friends and colleagues. When he is planning a visit or concert in their area, he sends an e-mail inviting them to his concert or suggesting a get together. Though these e-mails are targeted to a geographic group in his e-mail address book, the message conveys a personal invitation. "I'm writing to let you know I'll be back in Boston next month and it would be great to see you!" This is how Lior maintains contacts and friendships with people he met ten years ago, though he now lives 3,000 miles away.

Reconnecting with Former Colleagues: Getting Back in Touch

Have you lost track of some people over the years? Thanks to Google and social media, almost anyone can be found online, and most people like to reconnect with friends from the past. Reconnecting may lead to new collaborations and mutually helpful suggestions and ideas. At the very least, exchanging fond memories with old friends is good for the soul.

Check in regularly with your network contacts; send congratulatory notes, holiday cards, or copies of articles that would interest them. Sarah M. (below) keeps in touch with many people by e-mail, and when a friend has gone out of the way to help, she mails cards and, when appropriate, small gifts or CDs.

▼
_____

Sarah M.'s Story (Part 1)

Sarah M., a vocalist who performs contemporary classical music, made an appointment with me to discuss her wish to find a better teaching position. We discussed places to look for job openings and ways she might collaborate with other musicians at various schools for performances and master classes. When we discussed networking, though, she said she knew no one who could offer her work and did not see how talking to her friends could help.

I asked Sarah whether she had any friends who taught at colleges in other cities, and about the possibilities of them inviting her to give master classes, or lecture-demonstrations at their schools or summer programs. Sarah's current teaching position allows her to do occasional exchange concerts or master classes with other vocalist colleagues at other schools. And these kinds of small-scale initial collaborations may eventually develop into larger opportunities, such as a joint festival or a teacher exchange. These collaborations can help Sarah build her résumé and reputation. By calling her contacts, reconnecting, finding out what old friends are up to, and telling people she's looking for more opportunities, Sarah will not only boost her morale, but also expand her options.

Networking takes time, but it's worth it. Sarah is now planning a summer music institute and collaborating with new colleagues from other schools. This project, and her expanding network, may eventually lead to the new position she seeks. In the meantime, she's energized and fully engaged, making the most of her performing and teaching opportunities.

_____
▲

Mailing Lists ◆

A mailing list is simply your network put to practical use: to send out invitations and notices about upcoming performances, recordings, or any other news worth sharing. You need to have an organized way to reach people in your network and an easy to way to add new contacts. It has never been easier: social media platforms such as Facebook, MySpace, LinkedIn, and many others help people make connections and develop relationships. These sites can be terrific for inviting people to upcoming shows and announcing news about recordings. But using these sites is not enough: musicians need to have their own mailing list system.

Jazz musicians seeking bookings in clubs are often asked about the size of their mailing list. A club manager wants to know how many local people a band can likely draw. A large mailing list is a powerful incentive for a club manager to book a new group. Whatever the genre, the person organizing the performance cannot guarantee you an audience. It is part of the *musician's* job to build a fan base. Posters, calendar listings, and season brochures are not enough. Think about it: you are much more likely to attend a concert if you know the performer and if you have received a personal invitation. And concert presenters are much more inclined to invite you back if you perform well *and* draw a sizable crowd. So, for purposes of invitations to performances, it's important to be able to sort your list by geographic region.

Having a database of contacts makes it easy to print out labels for concert invitations and postcard mailings, and for sending out e-newsletters and fundraising appeals to targeted segments of your network. To build your mailing list, you need a database program, such as FileMaker Pro or Excel, and you may want to use an e-mail management system such as those found on http://www.reverbnation.com, http://mailchimp.com, or http://www.constantcontact.com. Ask your musician friends for recommendations and demonstrations of their programs. For your mailing list database, the searchable fields you want to set up are: first name, last name, e-mail address, street address, city, state, zip code, country, website, and cell phone. With these fields, you can search by geographic location, print out mailing labels, and send e-mail or text invites to either the whole list or any segment as needed. By having a first and last name field, you can send messages that begin with a personalized greeting (such as "Dear Tim" or "Dear Christine"). Go through your current and old address books and your e-mail address lists. You will want to include everyone in the three concentric circles of your network map. Make the list as complete as possible.

Also, make sure to add a field for keyword search. By adding a descriptive keyword *tag* for each entry, you can sort your contacts by who they are and what they do (your keyword categories might include: festival contacts, club managers, concert presenters, media professionals, friends, family, and fans). This allows you to tailor your communications to various segments of your list.

To enlarge your mailing list, provide a guestbook at your performances and offer a small thank you gift for anyone who signs up (perhaps a refrigerator magnet with your ensemble's logo or a free download of your music).

Tell people who give you their e-mail addresses that they will receive your e-newsletter about future performances.

Your mailing list should be *opt-in*—don't ever use anyone else's e-mail list as your own or add people to your newsletter who haven't expressly said they wanted this. Instead, send an invitation to join. Always include an *unsubscribe* option. Don't spam!

▼

Sarah M.'s Story (Part 2)

Vocalist Sarah M. started networking: she called three friends with whom she had previously performed. They were living in three different regions of the country. They were glad to reconnect with her and were interested in what she was up to. They had no job leads to offer, but they were very interested in collaborating on her summer institute project and had ideas for Sarah about finding grant money and commissions for composers to invite to the institute. Sarah's friends also had suggestions for additional people she could contact for more help. So Sarah was off and running.

_____ ▲

Performance Invitations ◆

Once you have a mailing list, you can invite people to your performances. What do you write? We all are bombarded daily with ads, offers, and invitations. Why are some more effective than others? Think about an upcoming performance. Imagine inviting someone who is *not* a musician and who is unfamiliar with your repertoire. Perhaps this is your local barista, hairstylist, your landlord, postal worker, or mechanic. You talk fairly regularly, and they have asked you about your work.

How would you invite this person to the concert? Think about what you would say in person, and then write it down. Make sure you have the important facts about the performance: who, what, when, where, and especially *why!* Why are you excited about this particular concert, and why should this person come to it? Your enthusiasm can be contagious, but you also need to convey specific details of interest to your prospective audience. The challenge is to make your invitations engaging and personable.

When you write an e-mail invitation to a segment or all of your mailing list, write as you would to an individual. Don't send an impersonal-sounding generic performance announcement, such as "Monthly Performance Schedule for the 123 Jazz Trio," with a list of dates. This is not a way to cultivate a relationship! If recipients feel "marketed at" or spammed, then you are doing more harm than good.

Instead, write something more engaging:

Dear Jane: [your segmented mailing list allows you to personalize the mailings]

We'd love to have you join us next Thursday night, May 2, for the 123 Jazz Trio band debut performance at the Spilled Milk Coffee House in Woodstock. We're all fired up to be playing great tunes by Monk and Charlie Parker, plus new originals from our upcoming CD. We'd love to see you there! Below are details about the show and directions to the venue. Let me know if you have any questions.

Your friend,

Tillie Smith

Expanding Your Network: Making New Friends

Networking is about more than cultivating existing relationships—it's important to create new ones as well. In discussing with musicians the idea of making new contacts, I sometimes hear, "I can't do that, I'm too shy," or "I hate making small talk." But networking is not about being extroverted. You simply need to be interested in other people, able to talk one-on-one, and willing to say a bit about yourself and either your project or an upcoming performance.

Most people do this naturally. Notice your conversation when a friend introduces you to someone new. You probably ask the new person about their work, their interests, and where they're from. And you reciprocate by sharing something about yourself. If, in the course of the conversation, you "click," you can ask to exchange e-mail addresses to arrange a follow-up contact. This way, a stranger or acquaintance may become, over time, a trusted colleague, friend, or mentor.

▼ ───

Tool for Success: Your Business Card

Professionals carry business cards because they are a simple, inexpensive tool to make networking easier. Handing someone your business card is a great alternative to handing out your cell phone number on a soggy cocktail napkin. And a business card works much better than trying to memorize an e-mail address that someone tells you in passing. You can exchange business cards with new contacts in order to build your mailing list and network.

What goes on your business card? Your name and what you do (e.g., pianist/ teacher, baritone, jazz trumpeter), plus your phone number, e-mail address, and website. Your postal address is optional. Choose an attractive layout and typeface. Check for online sources for inexpensive business cards such as http://www.vista print.com and http://www.iprint.com.

Make sure that your e-mail, website, and any other contact addresses are appropriately professional. Use internet addresses with your name, and stay away from those that are potentially embarrassing, such as "WorldsBestTenor.com" or "ViolaKing@EgosRUs.com." What you may think of as fun and full of personality may come across as immature or worse. Ultimately, people need e-mail addresses that are easy to find and remember, so your first and last name is best.

▲

Tip: Ask for Advice

If you are working on a particular project and are looking for contacts with a particular expertise, don't overlook the obvious: start with your friends and colleagues. Ask members of your inner circle for suggestions of people to contact about your project. Some musicians feel embarrassed at being direct with others about their goals. But if no one knows what you want, or what you are working toward, how can they help you?

Emerging artists often think that people in positions of power are not interested in speaking with them. Not true. If they have the time, established professionals often enjoy sharing their insights and advice with emerging artists. And, on the other hand, don't overlook the people around you who may have great leads and advice to offer. Also, the alumni office at your university or conservatory may be a great source for networking contacts.

Your approach needs to fit the situation. If you've just met someone of influence or who has substantial experience and perspective in the profession, it is *not* appropriate to ask right away for an audition, lesson, performance opportunity, or job. It's like asking someone to marry you on a first date: it's not advisable. Networking is about developing relationships over time, not about quickie, one-time transactions.

Informational Interviewing

The method to use for cultivating contacts with people in influential positions is called *informational interviewing*. These are appointments you can set up for the purpose of gaining information and perspective from an individual. This is a structured form of networking as a way to make an initial contact, *not* to ask for an audition, performance opportunity, or job. However, this personal contact may eventually *lead* to a job, audition, or performance. So it can be very worthwhile to invest your time in doing informational interviews.

For those just leaving school, making a career transition, or moving to a new city, informational interviews can be especially helpful. They are a tool to expand your professional network, to help you connect with people who can refer you to resources, ideas, and other contacts.

Start your informational interviewing with the people you already know: current or former teachers and experienced colleagues. Although you may see these people often, if you have not had a conversation about advancing your music career, now's a great time to start. Make an appointment to meet and tell your contact in advance that you'd like to get his or her perspective and advice on your career. The meeting can be done over coffee or lunch (you pick up the tab). Prepare beforehand the particular questions you want to ask, tailoring your questions to each individual's expertise. Think of this as practice for future meetings with people you do not already know.

At the very least, the meeting should yield two or three new contacts. Ask if you can use your colleague's name when calling or e-mailing these people. Request a brief appointment (20–30 minutes) in order to ask questions and gather information about a specific area of interest. I would recommend making the initial contact (to someone you've never met) by e-mail.

Take care in writing any professional correspondence, even when it is a quick e-mail. Nothing says "unprofessional" louder than spelling or grammatical errors. Proofread carefully. Take the same care with those details as you do with your music, because your correspondence represents you and your music. The subject line is important. If you are writing to someone new who won't recognize your e-mail address, what you write in the subject line will often determine whether or not the e-mail is read. Try "Request for appointment with you to discuss . . . ," or better yet, use the referring contact's name "Larry Scripp at NEC suggested I contact you."

Below is a sample e-mail request for an informational interview. Jane Smith is an oboist interested in performing with her quintet at local elementary schools. She is contacting the Massachusetts chapter of the national organization Young Audiences because they hire musicians for in-school performances and they have an excellent reputation. Note that Jane is *not* asking to be hired (although, eventually, that may be what she wants). She knows that for now, she needs more experience and wants to develop her presentation skills. She is requesting an informational interview with the program officer, Ms. Borg, in order to gain perspective and advice on how to proceed. Note that each paragraph has a specific purpose, as explained in the bracketed italics at the start of each paragraph.

Subject line: Request for meeting; Larry Scripp referred me to you!

Dear Ms. Borg:

[The first paragraph should establish a connection to the reader by naming your mutual contact or referral, if you have one, and should establish why you are writing—to set up a brief meeting in order to gain information:] Larry Scripp at New England Conservatory suggested I contact you for advice and information regarding arts education performance opportunities in K–12 schools. I would like to arrange a brief informational interview meeting at your convenience to gain from your knowledge and experience in the field. I read with interest the information on the Young Audiences website and am impressed with the range of programs and the artists you make available to schools.

[The second paragraph should establish your credentials: highlight your most impressive, relevant experience and skills so that the reader will think it worthwhile to spend time speaking with you.] I am an oboist, and I teach at the Brookline Music School. My quintet has performed for after-school programs in Jamaica Plain and West Roxbury, as well as at two community music schools. I would welcome the opportunity to find out what you feel makes a great K–12 program and how you'd recommend we work on designing and improving our school presentations.

[The third paragraph should reassure the reader that you are not looking for work, just feedback, that you will call next week, and that you appreciate the help—be enthusiastic.] I would like to see if we can arrange a brief meeting at your convenience. Again, I would appreciate any advice you have to offer, and I look forward to speaking with you.

Sincerely,

Jane Smith

Although this may seem very formal, especially for an e-mail, the idea is that if you are approaching a busy professional and asking for some of their time and expertise, you need to come across as interested, respectful, and professional.

Once you have your informational interview scheduled, a little preparation will help you get the most out of your appointment. For any professional occasion, you should dress cleanly and neatly. You need not wear a suit, but you need to be taken seriously as a professional, so look the part (jeans and a T-shirt is probably inappropriate). The next section describes how you might handle the appointment itself.

How should Jane handle her meeting with Liz? She knows she needs to be conscious of time because Liz is busy. So Jane writes out her key questions in advance:

> What makes a great K–12 performance presentation?
>
> Are there any Young Audiences artists I could meet with or observe?
>
> Do you have any suggestions of resources or organizations that would help my quintet improve its K–12 presentations?
>
> Everyone in our quintet has private teaching experience, but we have no classroom experience. Can you suggest any reading materials on gearing our presentations toward specific curricula and age groups?

The result was Jane had the meeting with Liz and it went great. At the end of it, Jane made sure she thanked Liz for her time and information. And when Jane got home, she wrote and mailed a handwritten thank you card. This is a crucial piece of networking—people need to hear and receive thank yous. And handwritten ones are especially rare and welcome these days.

Elevator Speech   ◆

When meeting new people more casually, outside of any appointment, it's very helpful to have a concise way to introduce yourself and convey what you do and what you are interested in. Just as Jane did in written form above, you need to be able to introduce yourself in person. The handy introductory statement is sometimes referred to as an "elevator speech."

Imagine this: you walk through an office building lobby and step onto an elevator. You look over and find you are standing next to a musician or arts administrator, someone you recognize but have never had the chance to meet. Now is your chance. As you watch the elevator floor numbers tick by, you need to figure out what to say!

Instead of panicking and saying nothing, or saying something you later regret, it's best to have something you have thought about and practiced. An elevator speech is not something formal or memorized. Instead, it should be a set of phrases and content you can use flexibly and comfortably to introduce yourself to others. If you have an elevator speech at the ready, it makes it much easier to meet people. It should be short: about 30 seconds and no more than four sentences. It should be conversational and personal, not a sales pitch. And it should give your conversation partner something to talk with you about—it should have conversation "openings."

To break it down, here is what you need to include:

1. Your name and what you do (instrument/voice type, genre).
2. A credential to establish your most relevant background. This might be a recent performance credit, an ensemble with which you perform, the recent degree you received, or your teaching or arts administration position.
3. Next, briefly state your current project or topic area you are exploring. The person you meet must have a reason to connect with you. You want them to be able to give you an idea or a contact, so you create a conversational "volley" to which your partner can respond. You, in turn, need to be finding out from your companion what *she or he* is interested in and what points of interest you may share.

   If the conversation is going well and your companion seems interested, you can carry on with:
4. A specific request, such as to contact this person in the future to set up a meeting.

Here's an example of an elevator speech I've used: "Hi, I'm Angela Beeching; I run the Career Services Center at New England Conservatory of Music [1 and 2 above]. I just wanted to introduce myself because I heard your performance last month at the X club and I'm a big admirer of your work!"

[The other person responds favorably, so I go on with:]

"I write on musicians' career issues and am working on an article about music entrepreneurs for ABC publication. I'd love to do a short phone interview with you about your XYZ project. Do you think I could e-mail you and set up a time to talk? [3–4]."

Look again at Jane's letter above. Her second paragraph was a concise "elevator speech" in written form that she could easily adapt for an elevator meeting with Liz:

> Hi—I'm Jane Smith, an oboist, and I teach at the Brookline Music School. I wanted to introduce myself to you, Ms. Borg. I recognize you from the Young Audiences website—I'm so glad for this chance to meet you! I have a woodwind quintet and we've performed for after-school programs in Jamaica Plain and West Roxbury, and we love this kind of work. We're interested in learning how to improve our educational programs. Do you think I could arrange to meet with you in the coming weeks to hear your thoughts and advice?

To put the elevator speech into everyday context, in networking conversations, when you're asked, "So what are *you* up to these days?" you should be ready to concisely describe either a project you're working on or an upcoming performance.

Good Phone   ◆

For musicians, a surprising amount of work is taken care of by phone: booking calls, negotiating fees, arranging rehearsals, and screening prospective students. In many cases, musicians make initial contacts with contractors, conductors, and presenters by phone. Your phone manner and habits are a critical part of your professional image. Here are some tips for phone success.

Your own voicemail message should sound professional. Some performance contractors won't leave messages offering work unless the recorded greeting appropriately identifies the musician.

▼

Craig T.—a young musician—had a recorded voicemail greeting with loud, unidentifiable and distorted music that went on far too long before you heard Craig's recorded shouting, "WASSUP, WASSUP!?" Although his friends enjoyed the message, anyone calling Craig with a possible gig or teaching opportunity would probably hang up, assuming his performing and teaching would be as unprofessional as his voicemail message.

▲

When leaving outgoing messages, identify yourself, speak slowly and clearly, state your purpose for calling, and be concise. Leave your number twice to make sure the listener can get it; it's a common courtesy and a big help to those you call. If you tend to ramble, jot down a few notes before making the call. "Hello, this is Jane Smith, and I e-mailed you last week to request an appointment. I will try you again but here's my number: 617–555–1212. Again, it's Jane Smith and I look forward to speaking with you! 617–555–1212." Even if you're the one returning a call, leave your phone number (and don't rattle it off quickly). Make it easy for people to return your call.

Courtesy and respect go a long way. Especially if you are calling someone at home, ask, "Is this a convenient time to talk?" Offer to call back at another time if they sound harried or under pressure. And always thank people for returning your calls, answering your questions, or giving you contacts. When playing "phone tag" becomes frustrating, do not leave a testy-sounding message.

Check your phone voice—call into your own voicemail and leave a message for yourself. Listen back for volume, pitch, and articulation. You may have a habit of speaking too loudly or of mumbling. Ask a colleague for honest feedback and modulate your speaking voice as needed.

Mind Your Manners

When placing a call, first greet the person, then immediately identify yourself: "Hello [or Good afternoon], this is [your name]. I'm trying to reach Ms. Smith." Telemarketers often use the enthusiastic, "Hi Jane! How are you today?" *before* identifying themselves. It is a ploy to get the unsuspecting engaged in the conversation with a stranger, and it puts people on guard, so don't do it.

Here are some more common sense phone reminders:

- Do not chew gum, eat, or drink while on the phone.
- Turn off your radio, stereo, and television.
- Do not use slang or "colorful" language in business conversations.
- Do not work on the computer while you talk to someone.
- Do not talk on the phone while in a restroom.
- Never check messages, text, or take a call while in a face-to-face meeting with another person.
- Turn your cell phone off during all meetings, rehearsals, concerts, and social gatherings.

Backstage Dos and Don'ts   ◆

It's unavoidable: at post-concert receptions, *all* musicians deal with networking. Unfortunately, this is when musicians' behavior can be less than stellar. Some artists hate to go to their own concert receptions because they feel uncomfortable talking with strangers and with non-musicians.

A cultural gap often divides casual concertgoers from performers, especially classical musicians. Perhaps because of all the hours spent alone in practice rooms, musicians may be unaccustomed to the social graces. And socializing exclusively with other performers can exacerbate the awkwardness of conversing with non-musicians.

Attitude is important. At one extreme, I've overheard musicians, while talking among themselves, refer to their audiences with condescension and even contempt. Musicians sometimes speak as though these appreciative yet musically unsophisticated people are unworthy of the performance and of meeting the performers afterward. These kinds of sentiments contribute to the elitist perception of classical and jazz music. Even though no musician would openly behave this way toward well wishers, many musicians may think as such—and their attitudes are damaging.

In contrast, singer/songwriters and contemporary folk artists typically often have excellent rapport with audiences and fans. At concerts, during breaks between sets, performers invite audiences to meet with them and mention that they'll be available to sign CDs after the concert. I have attended showcases and performances in which musicians say, with obvious sincerity to their audience, "I'd love to talk with you afterward" and then tell them where the reception will be.

So check your attitude. At the most basic level, music is about communication and sharing. Not every audience is knowledgeable about your art, so some well-wishers may not use the right musical terminology when they converse with you after the concert. Who cares? These people have made a positive connection with your music and with you. If you want people to connect to your music, connecting with you is part of this. People who attend concerts and like what they hear are naturally curious about the musicians: what they are like as people, what makes them tick. People go backstage and to receptions to learn more about the performers and to show their appreciation for the concert.

Non-musicians are often fascinated by instruments, your training, your rehearsal technique, and your typical workday. They are intrigued by musicians' discipline, memorization, improvisation, and onstage communication among members of an ensemble. It's an exotic world to non-musicians. Be prepared to entertain a wide range of questions.

After your own concerts, you need to accept compliments graciously *no matter what you may think privately.* You may be obsessing over a messed up passage or how your intonation, tempo, or articulation was really #%&* in that movement. Keep your private assessment of your performance to yourself. Avoid quashing anyone else's appreciation of your performance. Accept their congratulations: you have earned it.

Your backstage behavior is part of your professional image. If the performance was booked as part of a concert series, the presenter may understandably consider the reception an important part of the artist's engagement. Artists who interact well with the audience members, donors, and board members help build audiences for themselves, for the particular concert series, and for the art form in general.

When attending other people's concerts you enjoy, you too should go backstage and offer your congratulations. Musicians love to hear colleagues say what they *specifically* enjoyed about their performance. Rather than hearing "Great job," emerging artists in particular may prefer to hear specifics, such as, "I especially loved the range of tone colors you used in the second movement" or "I was so impressed by the effect of that incredibly quiet section in the third piece." Tell the performer or composer which moments stood out for you and why. They will definitely appreciate it.

If you go to a concert given by someone with whom you would like to have a subsequent, in-depth conversation, then go backstage and offer your congratulations. Say what you found particularly compelling and what you especially admired about their performance. Should you get a receptive response, continue with, "If you have some time in the next few weeks [or before you leave town], I would really like to speak with you briefly about . . . [be realistic, specific, and appropriate]." The worst thing that can happen is they will say they are too busy. Depending on what you seek, they may refer you to another person or resource, but they may also say, "Sure, send me an e-mail; here's my card." Note: don't hand them your card expecting them to contact you. This is a matter of respect and deference; since you're the one asking, you should do the contacting. Ask the other person if you may call or e-mail them and if you may have their card.

How to Work a Room ◆

Imagine you are attending a large post-concert reception or a professional conference (such as Chamber Music America, the Classical Singer Convention, or South by Southwest conference). Whatever the specifics, you are faced with a room full of strangers. You may think, "There may be some people here who would have useful career information or contacts for me." But then you may wonder, "How can I talk to strangers when my mother always told me not to?" Read on; here are a dozen tips for "working a room."

1. *Observe.* Look around. Are there people you know? Where is the food and drink? Are there other people who are by themselves? (You might want to strike up a conversation with one of them later.) Also look for conversation groups of three or more that you might join later. Do not worry about whom to talk with yet: just get your bearings.

2. *Use positive self-talk.* We each make our own reality—what we tell ourselves determines what we perceive and how we feel. If you are nervous, you may have these kinds of thoughts playing in your head: "This looks awful," "I wore the wrong thing," "No one looks friendly," or "I can't wait to get out of here." Replace these negative messages with positive and realistic statements. You can choose to think, "These are people I have something in common with; they are musicians and music lovers," "Other people here feel just as awkward as I do," "I may feel a little nervous but it doesn't show," or "This is an opportunity to make a new acquaintance and have an inter-

esting conversation." Do yourself a favor and keep your self-talk positive. This goes for networking as well as for performing!

▼

The former Santa Barbara–based ensemble Anacapa String Quartet ended up with a sponsor for their first CD through good post-concert "schmoozing." It started with a woman who approached them at one of their concert receptions and asked if she could buy their CD. The quartet told her they didn't have one—that they didn't yet have the funds to make a recording. The woman liked the group so much she ended up helping them finance the CD!

▲

4. *Be approachable.* Be open and friendly; stand up straight, smile, and make eye contact. You need to circulate: people will not approach you if you are sitting. To avoid the soggy handshake syndrome, hold your drink in your left hand so you can shake with a dry right.

5. *Strike up conversations* with people waiting in line for drinks or name tags. If you're waiting in line to check in, it's easy to ask the person in front or behind you where they are from and how they heard about the event. Most people welcome a bit of friendly ice-breaking conversation. A pleasant or wry comment about the weather, the food, your surroundings, or about the event you are attending may lead to an interesting conversation. For topics, play it safe: avoid politics, religion, and sex (until you know your conversation partner very well).

6. *Use conversation openers.* Ask open-ended questions, such as "What do you think about the. . . . [performance, speech, workshop]?" as opposed to yes or no questions. Ask questions that show your interest in the other person's perspective.

7. *Approach groups* of three or more. Do not interrupt a twosome—it may be a very personal conversation. But a group of people smiling and displaying easygoing body language are good to approach. As you approach a group, stand a little off to the side, smile, and try making eye contact with one person. If they smile in return, then when there's a pause in the conversation, ask, "May I join you?" and introduce yourself. If you do not get the eye contact at the edge of a group, just move on and try elsewhere. The only way to get good at this is by doing it.

8. *Reintroduce yourself* to people you have met before. Start with a familiar face. If you cannot remember a name, simply say, "Hi, I know we've met before, I'm Jane Smith, [shake their hand] and you are . . . ?"

9. *Get unstuck.* Sometimes you find yourself talking to someone who latches on to you and you need to escape. There are tactful exit lines to use: "Sorry, I need to find . . . [the event organizer, ladies room, or the person my friend mentioned would be here]. It's been so nice meeting you. Have a good evening!"

10. *Exchange business cards* when you have reason to. Write yourself a note on the back of the card reminding you where you met the person and what your intended follow-up action will be. Did you offer to send someone information? Did someone say it was fine to e-mail them to arrange an appointment or referral? Writing a note on the back of the person's card will help you remember to do the right thing.

11. *Be realistic* about networking. An initial chance meeting will not yield a job offer or a performance opportunity. But it may lead to setting up an informational interview or an e-mail exchange of referrals to other contacts, organizations, or resources. At a two-hour networking event, you should probably expect to talk to five to seven people and maybe have one or two substantive conversations. Networking is not about instant gratification.

12. *Follow through.* If you say you will call, send an article, or leave a message for someone, do so. Your promise and your word need to be good. It's the mark of a professional.

Hosting a Brainstorming Party ◆

One other great way to get more out of your network is to harness the brain power of your closest group of supporters. Popular author and career counselor Barbara Sher, who wrote *Wishcraft: How to Get What You Really Want,* and *Live the Life You Love,* originated the success team approach. This involves forming a career support group that meets regularly, once or twice a month. Members give support, contacts, advice, and hold each other accountable for work they promise to do before the next meeting.

I recommend a variation on this approach: hosting your own brainstorming party. The object is to use the collective brainpower of a group of your colleagues and friends to generate ideas and possible action steps toward a specific goal. Here are guidelines:

1. You will first need a **clear directive**: a specific project for which you want feedback. It might be launching your own performance series or festival. Perhaps you want to book a mini-tour of performances in

your region. You need to have a specific project in mind, clear enough so that your team can generate useful ideas.

2. **Invite five to seven people** who know you well, are supportive, and whose opinions and perspective you value. This group may include people from your inner and intermediate network circles. Include non-musicians—they will offer a wider perspective and diverse ideas. It is best *not* to include your spouse or partner because he or she may inadvertently inhibit the brainstorming. It can be hard for those closest to you to entertain a range of new ideas, because they are personally invested. Most likely, you already discuss your career goals, and the point of the brainstorming party is to gather *new* ideas.

3. Invite your team to your home for a **good meal**, and make it clear in advance that after you eat, your guests will be put to work. A weekend brunch can work well for this. After clearing the dishes, have everyone sit in a circle and get a volunteer to take notes.

4. Remember: there is no such thing as a bad or crazy idea; *all* **suggestions get written down**. The trick is not to censor or inhibit ideas; let them fly. Suggestions that at first seem impossible or ridiculous often lead to some of the most creative solutions. Don't worry about funding or other practical issues that may stifle creative brainstorming; the important thing is to fire up people's imaginations. Don't interrupt with "Yeah, but . . ." or "I already tried that" or "That would never work." Be quiet and let the ideas flow, even if you have to bite your own tongue. Remain positive and open-minded.

5. At the end of the party, you will have pages of ideas to consider—far more than you can implement. But the discussion should provide you with energy, a fresh outlook, and unexpected leads. Afterward, **send thank you notes** to every member of your team.

6. You will need to comb through your options and think how to proceed. And you may want to enlist the support of your team to **make preliminary project plans**. This can be a great way to launch a new venture.

Bonus Section: Interpersonal Skills for Ensembles   ♦

Because musicians so often play in ensembles, here are some specific recommendations. Whether you are putting together a jazz trio, new music collective, or a string quartet, there are some essential points to consider. In order to launch and manage your group successfully, you need to consider your choice of collaborators, individual and collective goals, and work styles.

The Right Person for the Job

Choose your partners carefully. In his excellent article for *Musician's Atlas,* "How Bands Die," psychologist/musician Mike Jolkovski writes, "Joining a band with someone is a combination of marrying them, fighting alongside them in a war, and being trapped in an elevator with them. Soon you will have heard every joke they know at least six times, and you will be (over) exposed to the way they talk, drive, eat, and smell."[1]

Your criteria for selecting ensemble members must include more than simply how well they play. You need to find people who can learn new repertoire quickly, who are open to new ideas, and who can both give and receive constructive feedback. Furthermore, members need to have one or more of the non-musical skills necessary to run the group. These include administrative, computer, financial, and networking skills. And of course, groups need members with enthusiasm, patience, and humor.

Jolkovski offers this: "A good rule of thumb is that if you would pick someone to go camping with in bad weather with inadequate gear and not enough food, they might be a good person for your band."[2] Prima donnas spell disaster for ensembles. The most successful groups have members that are sensitive to the feelings of others and who are able to set aside their own egos to direct their energies toward the efforts of the group. For stability and growth, groups need members with personalities that complement and balance those of their colleagues.

Taking Care of Business

Unless your group is totally leader-driven, ensembles typically divide up the administrative and management duties. If one member of the group ends up handling all administrative and logistical tasks, this person will, inevitably, become resentful. In the long run, the groups that survive are those that have effectively divided the workload among the members.

Make the most of each member's strengths. The most charming and extroverted person should probably be the one to make phone calls and act as liaison with concert series presenters and club managers. Think about who is good with computers, with writing, and with finances. To stay on track, members need clearly defined roles and projects. Groups also need to have regularly scheduled business meetings—always held *separately* from rehearsals. Weekly meetings keep people updated and accountable to each other. Shared responsibilities build a shared commitment.

"Decide who has the 'vision' of how the group will develop," advises jazz bandleader Lucinda Ellert. "Is it a democracy, or is this *your* own baby?" Whether you choose a leadership/authority style management or a more democratic nonhierarchical one, each has its advantages and challenges.

Most classical groups adopt a shared responsibility model, meaning that each member, at times, will be in a leadership role. The group may rely on a particular member for leadership in specific matters, but each member of the group has a voice and a vote in the group decisions. In contrast, most jazz ensembles are leader-driven, with the leader/composer writing or composing the majority of the works, and with the other players most often deferring to the vision of the leader but contributing their artistry and ideas to that vision. Unlike string quartets, most jazz ensembles are not full-time commitments, so players are often, at any given time, members of multiple bands or projects and working on a range of their own and others' projects.

Whatever the model, unless all the members of a group share in the vision, there will be difficulties. For some members, the ensemble may be top priority; for others, it may be just another casual gig. In order to adhere to a rehearsal and performance schedule, each group member needs to make a commitment to the ensemble. So, it's crucial that groups discuss goals and expectations. For groups just getting started, a good tactic is to arrange for an upcoming performance or to enter a competition. This can be an essential motivating force, giving the group something to work toward and something to solidify the group identity and work habits.

Working Well Together

Your ensemble needs to develop effective rehearsal habits. In the excellent Chamber Music America brochure, *Can This Marriage Be Saved? Interpersonal and Organizational Guidelines for Ensembles,* authors Janice Papolos and Howard Herring conducted in-depth interviews with ten professional chamber groups (including the Tokyo and Emerson Quartets). From these interviews, the authors extrapolated some "best practices" and recommendations: "Everyone interviewed voiced an important rehearsal rule: Try out everyone's ideas—with absolute conviction—no matter how off the wall they may sound at first. Don't talk it to death beforehand. Play it and *then* have the discussion."[3] Inevitably, some ensemble members lean toward more nitpicky rehearsing, whereas others prefer playing through whole sections to get the sense of line and cohesion. Ensembles ultimately need a balance of both approaches.

As far as rehearsals, the classical groups interviewed in the CMA study generally rehearsed four to five hours a day, four or five days each week. Other kinds of groups have varying commitments and work patterns. Some groups come together only several times a year for intensive rehearsals in preparation for touring or recording projects. What's important is that all the members of the group are in agreement about their commitment and responsibilities.

No matter what the working structure, group dynamics are always fascinating. If a difficulty arises between you and another ensemble member, the CMA guide advises "discussing it with that person and NO ONE ELSE!" If you are unable to resolve the issue, then the two of you should air it openly with the rest of the group.

People have unconscious habits and sensitivities and have differing tolerances for tension within groups. The roles that people tended to play growing up in their own families (such as the "dutiful child," "court jester," "peacekeeper," or "black sheep") are the same ones members typically replicate in adult work group situations. This can be helpful in some cases but not in others. The challenge for all ensemble musicians is to be able to "get over ourselves," our habitual thinking and behavioral patterns, so that we can see things from our *colleagues'* perspectives. That gets at the fundamental challenge and reward in making music with others: we are given the opportunity to be inspired by and to learn from our peers, and we need to be able "to give as good as we get."

▼
___

Career Forward

Writing out your responses to these questions and following the prompts will help you cultivate your network and enhance your interpersonal skills.

1. Who is in your inner networking circle? (Include five to seven of your closest supporters, mentors, and colleagues.) When was the last time you spoke with the people in your inner circle? What would you like to consult with them about?
2. Choose a trusted mentor from your inner circle to contact this week. Arrange an appointment with your mentor to ask questions about your career plans. Which person in your list is best suited for this?
3. List the names of other people with whom you have lost track and would like to reconnect.
4. Start (or update) your mailing list database. Include the names, phone numbers, websites, e-mail, postal addresses, and keywords (for segmenting the types of contacts).
5. What particular area of the music industry or specific skill do you wish to explore through networking? Which person or organization would be a good resource? With whom would you like to arrange an informational interview?
6. If you were to host a career brainstorming party, whom would you invite? What objective would you ask the group to brainstorm about?

▲

3

Developing Your Image: Creating Promotional Materials that Work

In this chapter:

Who Are You?	Bio Basics
Why Promote Yourself?	Photos
Brand YOU	Promo Kits
What's Your *Type?*	

Who Are You? ◆

The image that you project consists of everything that contributes to your reputation. It includes not only the way in which you perform and what your colleagues think of you but also your professional habits: the way you dress, return calls, and follow through with plans. The focus of this chapter is on the components of a promotional toolbox—the pieces necessary for building a musician's professional image.

Why Promote Yourself? ◆

Promotional materials tell the story of who you are and what your music is about. They are necessary for booking performances, attracting audiences, and selling CDs. They are crucial components to telling your story well.

The most basic promotional materials musicians need are bios, photos, and demo recordings. Subsequent chapters will cover recordings and online promotion; here the focus is on the content of written and visual materials.

The good news is that you can create most of these yourself. Musicians often ask, "Can't I just pay someone to do all this for me?" The truth is, whether you hire professionals or do it yourself, you are still ultimately in charge of the content and presentation. Whether you work with an artist manager, publicist, or record label, you need to be an informed and savvy partner in all the decisions about your promotional materials. After all, it's *your* career.

Many musicians have negative associations with any form of self-promotion. I have heard musicians describe it as repugnant, as a "necessary evil." And I often encounter musicians who ask, "Why can't the music speak for itself?"

To put this in perspective, many young performers believe their "job" as musicians is to practice and perform. Period. Some mistakenly may believe that once they become accomplished professionals, they will be protected from the crass world of commerce and the everyday details of handling finances, logistics, and publicity. They may imagine that the details of managing their career will be handled by their agent—or, perhaps, by a fairy godmother!

Here's the reality: handling publicity is part of a musician's job. *You* are the best person to tell your story. The challenge lies in creating promotional materials that effectively communicate who you are and what is distinctive about you and your music.

Brand YOU ◆

Branding is a marketing concept from the business world that many arts organizations and individual musicians have also found useful. Branding is about clarifying your identity, mission, and reputation. It's *not* about having slick promotional materials or creating a glamorous image. Branding, and the promotional effort that stems from it, is about articulating your true self, not putting up a false front. Branding involves communicating with a targeted audience using effective and consistent messages. It's about creating a specific, accurate, and memorable positive impression. In other words, branding is about identifying your core mission and values, then working outward to tell others your story.

We each have stories that help define us as individuals, and we can to choose which of these stories to use in our marketing materials and in our networking. Think through your past, both musical and non-musical. Sort through remembered anecdotes, old photos, and concert programs to help get a sense of what you'd like to communicate about yourself. Think about what you have done as a musician, what you intend to do, what you value, and what you have to offer.

On the most basic level, you need to have a distinct *brand* because otherwise, you are simply just another talented and well-trained performer, one of thousands. Why should anyone take notice? There are simply far too many good musicians. Without something to distinguish you from all the others, you are anonymous. So the message here is to think carefully about yourself, your projects, and your intentions. What is your *mission?* Do you perform unusual or noteworthy repertoire? Have you been involved in interesting multimedia or experimental music projects? Have you performed for interesting charity causes? Your promotional materials should convey what is distinctive and special about you.

What makes all this worthwhile is that working on your brand and promotional materials should help you clarify your goals and your commitment, and should help you take a good look at where you are now so you can plan the next appropriate action steps. Ultimately, your music is a form of communication, a way to contribute positively to the world. Your image and brand should be an extension of this positive energy.

What's Your *Type*? ◆

The first thing you need in terms of your brand and promotional materials is a recognizable and *consistent* typographic "I.D." The equivalent of a logo, or what might be called your "letterhead design," this needs to include your basic information. That is your name, or your ensemble's name, instrument/voice type, genre (if applicable, to clarify), and all your contact details: e-mail, phone, and social media addresses). To promote yourself effectively, choose a typeface (the design style of the letters) and a layout that will efficiently and attractively convey a real sense of both you and your music. This should appear in a consistent format on all your promotional materials: your website, flyer, postcard, CD cover, and all your correspondence.

Large corporations pay hundreds of thousands of dollars to advertising firms to design their businesses logos. Think "Coca-Cola" or "Dunkin' Donuts," and your mind's eye will probably conjure up the distinctive typeface designs of these companies' logos. You may not have the big bucks to hire a top-of-the-line graphic designer, but you can create a letterhead design that looks professional and helps promote your career and your music.

The idea is the same as a logo: by using it consistently, you help readers remember your name and what you do. Letterhead designs convey a certain "image" through the choice of typeface. Typeface can communicate all kinds of personalities and energies. If a picture is worth a thousand words, a typeface is worth at least 700.

For example, here are alternate designs using different typefaces and page layouts. The same name, in four different typefaces, reads like four very different musicians. Each look is professional, yet each communicates a somewhat different impression of the singer and her music.

What image is being conveyed in each version? Instead of simply noting your aesthetic preference, notice the nuance of the typeface and the kind of statement each design communicates. What adjectives would you use to describe each one? Every typeface has a distinct personality. Typefaces can be conservative, elegant, traditional, modern, quirky, fun, or stiff. For insight on typeface, check out the DVD of the film *Helvetica,* the fascinating and surprisingly entertaining documentary about the typeface of the same name and its wide use in design and advertising.

You might be thinking, "But I'm a musician, not a graphic designer! How am I supposed to create a letterhead design?" Don't panic: below is a creative exercise that can make this easy and fun. Simply type your text (name, instrument or voice type, and contact info) into a new document on your computer. Then copy and paste this text seven or eight times down the same page, leaving an inch or so of blank space between each. Next, try out a different typeface and layout with each so that you have seven or eight draft designs. Computers come loaded with dozens of typefaces, and you can buy additional software if needed. Challenge yourself to choose con-

Christine Taylor, jazz vocalist

PO Box 411 Your Favorite City, State 02222 (999) 555–1212
christine@christinetaylor.com • www.christinetaylor.com

(typeface is Britannic Bold)

Christine Taylor, jazz vocalist

PO Box 411 • Your Favorite City, State 02222 • (999) 555-1212
christine@christinetaylor.com • www.christinetaylor.com

(typeface is Century Gothic)

Christine Taylor, jazz vocalist

PO Box 411 Your Favorite City, State 02222 (999) 555–1212
christine@christinetaylor.com • www.christinetaylor.com

(typeface is Kudasai)

Christine Taylor, jazz vocalist

PO Box 411 Your Favorite City, State 02222 (999) 555–1212
christine@christinetaylor.com | www.christinetaylor.com

(typeface is Pristina)

Sample letterhead designs

trasting typefaces and formats: see how different you can make each version look. When you are done, print the page; you may have a different reaction to your designs on paper than on screen.

Choosing the right letterhead design is not simply a matter of which is the most eye-catching. Rather, you want the one that best communicates the image and personality you want to convey. A typeface that you would use for a party invitation or poster design may not be the best choice for your professional transactions. Get feedback from mentors and colleagues. Once you have chosen your design, use it on all professional correspondence: your bio, résumé, business cards, website, CD liner notes, and any other career-related materials requiring your name and contact information. For establishing and maintaining a consistent image and brand, letterhead design is key.

▼

Customize Your Signature

For your e-mail correspondence, you may want to consider using a signature: an automatic text message that appears at the bottom of each e-mail message you send. Your signature can be a version of your letterhead design. Use color if you like; it will help distinguish your signature from the message, but be sure to stick to the darker, most visible colors.

People sometimes use an inspirational quote at the end of their e-mail signatures. If you decide to do this, choose your quote carefully because it will accompany your name on every e-mail. The quote then becomes part of your image. It works like an advertising tag line, as in the Bissell vacuum cleaner company's "Life is messy; clean it up" and Apple's "Think different." My friend and colleague in career services at Berklee College of Music, Peter Spellman, uses this quote from Benjamin Disraeli, "As a general rule, the most successful people in life are those who have the best information." This is a great quote for Peter because he is dedicated to connecting musicians with career information.

▲

Bio Basics ◆

The next essential promotional piece in a musician's professional toolkit is the bio. Despite the name, a bio is *not* a biography: it is not a chronicle of your life history. Rather, a musician's bio is a marketing piece consisting of background information written in paragraph form, conveying what is distinctive and compelling about you and your music.

Bios are used on websites, in concert programs, and for grant and competition applications. They are also used for booking performances and to attract media attention and audiences to these performances. Bios in programs give the audience a chance to find out about—and be impressed with—the performer before she appears on stage. When a bio is part of an application, it helps selection committees develop a three-dimensional view of the musician and his work.

Veteran music career advisor John Blanchard, director of alumni affairs at Manhattan School of Music, recommends thinking of a bio as a "call to action—inspiring audiences to become loyal fans and ticket-buyers, inspiring concert presenters to book you for their series, inspiring ensemble leaders to engage you as a soloist, inspiring club owners to hire you for their establishment." By thinking of bios this way, it becomes clear that they need to be much more than dry listings of performances, degrees, and teachers.

For people who book artists, a bio is often the initial introduction. Your bio needs to be compelling enough to motivate the concert presenter reading it on your website to actually click on and listen to your sound sample. Offline, printed bios used for booking purposes are typically short: one page (a few paragraphs) in length, printed on letterhead paper. These may be sent along with a CD to help pique the reader's interest enough to put the CD in to listen to it.

Most musicians have several versions of their bio, each tailored for a different situation. What an audience member wants in a concert program bio is different from what a grant selection committee wants or what might interest a music journalist. What's more, publications often have strict space limitations, so it can be helpful to have both short and long versions of your bio. The secret of writing an effective bio is to approach writing it from your intended readers' perspective. Put yourself in their shoes: what would they find interesting?

Most musicians use bios that are, unfortunately, just plain boring. They tend to read like laundry lists of awards, performance credentials, and degrees. Many bios give no indication that the musician is an actual person with interests, passions, and projects. The challenge in writing a bio is to convey what makes you individual and distinctive.

On the following page is a now outdated version of the cellist Joshua Roman's bio, found on his website and on that of his artist management, Opus 3 Artists, back in March, 2009. Read it to see whether you get a sense of what his viewpoint on music is and what is distinctive about him. Do you get a clear message about his mission as an artist? And you may want to compare it to his current version at http://www.joshuaroman.com.

Let's analyze this bio. Yes, of course he's got impressive credits, but take a look at *how* the bio is organized. The first paragraph tells us three things about Joshua. It first gives Joshua a label "Classical Rock Star," setting up the reader's expectation that this will be accounted for in the bio. Then there are two sweeping statements: that he has a wide-ranging repertoire, and that he has "an absolute commitment to communicating the essence of the music at its most organic level."

Dubbed a "Classical Rock Star" by the press, cellist Joshua Roman has earned a reputation for performing a wide range of repertoire with an absolute commitment to communicating the essence of the music at its most organic level.

Since winning the Principal chair in the cello section of the Seattle Symphony at the age of 22, he has become a favorite of Seattle music lovers, with sold out solo and chamber performances throughout the city.

When not performing in or in front of a Symphony Orchestra, Joshua is likely to be found on the stage of a club, performing music as varied as jazz or rock, as well as chamber music or a solo sonata by Kodaly or Bach. His fearless pursuit of new challenges has led him to expand his horizons and embark full-time on his growing solo classical career.

His interest in and exploration of new music have led Joshua to work with many composers in performance of concerti, chamber music, and solo works, including works of his own. Among the composers with whom Joshua has collaborated are Samuel Adler, Gabriela Lena Frank, Syd Hodkinson, Aaron Jay Kernis, Paul Schoenfeld, and David Stock.

As a concerto soloist, he has performed with the Seattle Symphony, Spokane Symphony, Oklahoma City Philharmonic, Cleveland Institute of Music Orchestra, and the Wyoming Symphony. The 2008/09 season will include, among others, performances with the Edmonton Symphony, Quad City Symphony, Stamford Symphony, and a return to the Seattle Symphony for the premiere of the David Stock Cello Concerto.

In addition to his solo work, Joshua is an avid chamber music performer and has enjoyed participating in the Seattle Chamber Music Society.

In the spring of 2007 Joshua was named Artistic Director of TownMusic, an experimental chamber music series at Town Hall in Seattle, which allows him to create programming that reflects the many influences on his music making. He also has enjoyed collaborations with musicians such as Sergei Babayan, Earl Carlyss, Franklin Cohen, Desmond Hoebig, William Preucil, Ann Schein, Joaquin Valdepenas, and Christian Zacharias.

Joshua's desire to communicate takes him beyond diverse concert venues. In the summer of 2006 in response to his own growing awareness of the atrocities in Africa—specifically Rwanda—he traveled with his violin-playing siblings to Uganda, where they played chamber music in schools, HIV/AIDS centers and displacement camps, bringing a message of hope through music.

Joshua began playing at the age of three. He studied with Lacy McLarry, concertmaster of the Oklahoma City Philharmonic, beginning his cello studies on a 1/4 size cello. He played his first public recital at the age of ten. Homeschooled until the age of 16, when he left to pursue his musical studies at the Cleveland Institute of Music, Joshua received his Bachelor's Degree in Cello Performance in 2004, studying with Richard Aaron. In 2005 he also received his Master's Degree from the CIM, studying with Desmond Hoebig, Principal Cellist of the Cleveland Orchestra. Joshua is grateful for the loan of an 1899 cello by Giulio Degani of Venice.[1]

This is a tall order for a bio to come through with the details to back all this up, particularly the final point on communicating the essence of music. But Joshua Roman's bio does all this by detailing his interest in performing in nontraditional spaces, and by describing his repertoire of new works, commissions, and collaborations. He also has started his own experimental music concert series. His more traditional repertoire credentials are established with the details of his orchestral and concerto soloist experience. As for his commitment to communicating what music is really about, the paragraph on Joshua's humanitarian work in Africa is compelling testimony of his mission of "bringing a message of hope through music."

Note the order of the information and the topics covered in each paragraph, and how that order affects your impression of this musician. Think about how different your impression of him would be if the bio had begun with the actual fifth paragraph—the one listing his concerto soloist experience. Paying attention to these organizational details will help you write a bio that conveys what is special about you.

Your Bio in Six Easy Steps

This is the quickest method I know for writing an effective bio. Instead of plunging in and writing a draft or trying to rewrite your existing bio, I recommend this step-wise approach. In the end, it saves time and yields better results. Ending up with an engaging bio is worth the effort.

1. *Start by making a list of potential items for your bio.* This is your raw material, a compost heap of the ideas and details you might include. List the following:

- The venues where you have performed: the names of the performance hall, series, club, or festival, and its city and state (or country if abroad). Do not list only the venues you feel are important: list them *all*.
- Detail your community and education work: performances at senior centers, preschools, hospitals, or other nontraditional venues; these listings are good to show that you are comfortable with all kinds of audiences.
- Any awards, grants, scholarships, or competitions you have won.
- Recording projects (with repertoire, collaborators, and labels if applicable).
- Range of your repertoire: list five to eight composers whose works you perform. Emphasize the less standard composers to showcase the widest range in your repertoire. List any premieres of new works and interesting repertoire of upcoming performances.

- Names of the ensembles with which you have performed and the artists with whom you have collaborated (those with some name recognition are best to include).
- Quotes from reviews or from letters of recommendation (as long as you have permission from the letter's author).
- Interesting musical projects, what you're especially interested in or focusing on lately; include upcoming plans.
- Interesting non-musical hobbies and interests, such as causes or community efforts with which you've been involved.
- Unusual biographical anecdotes, such as how or why you chose your instrument, or any dramatic or unusual story about your training and decision to become a musician.
- Education information: schools you attended, degrees received, your well-known teachers, coaches, master classes, and conductors.

At this "composting" stage, do not self-censor; don't edit out things you think are not good enough for a bio. Now is the time to just get everything down; edit later. Forget about the order, or about making sentences and paragraphs—just make the list. It should be more comprehensive and wide-ranging than your résumé. Be as inclusive and thorough as possible, because this is the construction material from which you can build a better bio.

Bio Hazard

Bio writing can be a challenge. In writing bios, musicians usually have one of two problems. Either the writing is overblown and hyperbolic—far too grandiose—or else it suffers from low self-esteem.

For those that are overblown, the best treatment is to get rid of sweeping generalizations and unsubstantiated descriptors. Steer clear of comparisons and clichés. Stick to concrete details and facts: where, with whom, and what you have performed. Delete extravagant adjectives and adverbs.

As for bios afflicted with low self-esteem, the recommended treatment is similar: stick with concrete, specific details of what you've done. Emerging musicians often feel inadequate: that they are lacking the "right" kinds of credentials. But paradoxically, these same musicians often leave out some of their best bio material. They either have forgotten or don't include the performances, projects, and awards that they assume are not impressive enough. Do not discount your accomplishments. What may not seem impressive to you is often perceived very differently by others. The concrete details of your actual experience will help build a comprehensive and positive impression of you as an artist at this point in your career.

It is good to keep track of all your career-related credentials, and if you have not yet done so, this will give you a reason to start. If you can't remember where a particular performance occurred, or the name of an award you won, look it up on the web or ask family and colleagues. Enlist your colleagues and friends to help: they can remind you about your accomplishments and give you perspective on how an outsider might view them. This is also a great excuse to reconnect with former teachers and coaches who may have the information you seek and would like to hear from you. Keep your list saved on computer so it can be easily updated.

List any noteworthy personal information, such as how and why you became an early music enthusiast, or why you specialize in traditional music of the African Diaspora; write down a description of any unusual hobbies you have. Can you describe what drives you personally? What is your mission? What are the projects you have been most invested in?

We each have stories we tell about ourselves (and others tell about us) that reveal different aspects of our personalities. It is these stories that eventually reveal who we are, what we want, and where we are headed. What are your stories?

▼
_____

Word to the Wise

Warning: List only what you have actually done. Do not embellish, exaggerate, or fabricate, because lies inevitably come back to haunt you. Be accurate and honest in how you present yourself. It is too small a world to risk your reputation.

Don't worry about what you have or have not done at this point in your career. Don't waste time or energy comparing your accomplishments to those of others. Being envious and competitive is pointless. You are where you are right now: *this* is the starting point from which you build your future.

Focus on presenting the credentials and experience you *do* have. Tell whatever is most compelling in your story: the goal is to get the reader interested in you and your music.

_____
▲

2. *Choose an opener for your bio.* Read over your list as though you were an objective outsider. Circle the top three most impressive or interesting-sounding items on the list. Bios should grab the reader's attention immediately. Your lead may be a quote, a single item, a group of impressive-sounding awards, or a group of performances at interesting venues. It may be an unusual multimedia project you participated in, premieres of new works, or a research project that led to performances. Whatever you choose, your opener should not be about your earliest musical experiences, because your bio

should *not* be in chronological order. Here are sample bio openers, chosen as leads because they were the most compelling items for these particular ensembles and individuals:

"Boston Baked Brass first drew national media attention during the running of the 100th Boston Marathon, when the group performed for the mid-race wedding of two of the runners."

"Clarinetist John Q. Public has premiered over 30 works by composers such as Elliot Carter, Hans Werner Henze, Marc Anthony Turnage, Ralph Shapey, Michael Finnissy, Sydney Hodkinson and Eric Mandat. With a repertoire ranging from Mozart, Beethoven, and Brahms to Corigliano, Boulez, and Ferneyhough, Mr. Public's eclectic and innovative programming is redefining the clarinet concert experience."

"Violinist Jennifer Liu made her solo debut at age 12 with the Chi-shien Symphony Orchestra in Kaohsiung, Taiwan, performing Bruch's Violin Concerto in G minor. Four years later she became the youngest soloist ever to appear with the Kaohsiung City Symphony Orchestra, performing the Mendelssohn concerto."

3. *Group similar items together by topic.* Depending on your list, you might group ensemble performances together, or awards and scholarships, or community-based performances for children or seniors. But don't group items by either year or location, because you do not want to write a chronological bio. Once you have your groupings, they are easy to turn into topic paragraphs.

4. *Write a draft.* The easiest way to do this is to concentrate on one paragraph at a time, one topic per paragraph. For instance, if your list contains a grouping of contemporary music performances and premieres, draft a paragraph focused on the topic of your commitment to new music. With a set of draft paragraphs, you can then choose an order for these, linking them logically by using transitions to signal a new topic. For instance, if the previous paragraph highlighted solo performance experience and the next one is focused on ensemble work, the new paragraph might start with, "Active as a collaborative artist as well, Ms. So-and-So has performed with the ABC Quartet at the 123 Festival in Quebec." As you write sentences and then paragraphs, alternate how you refer to yourself (e.g., as Tina Appleton, Ms. Appleton, and "She").

5. *Back up all general statements with specific examples.* If you use a phrase like "is playing to rave reviews across the United States," then the

reader understandably expects your bio to include numerous press quotes from well-known music critics throughout the country. Without these details, you lose credibility. If you write "has performed recitals in New England and in the Midwest," then you must back this up with specifics, such as "on the ABC concert series in Boston and the XYZ series in Chicago." If your bio claims you have a "wide repertoire," give examples like "repertoire ranging from Monteverdi to Haydn, and Schumann to Harbison." Without the details to back up your generalizations, you will not be convincing. Readers are very much attuned to advertising messages and "hype." Concrete details and examples assure them that you are indeed every bit as accomplished as your bio indicates. Resist all temptations to write sweeping, grandiose statements.

6. *Proofread:* Find and fix the typos, run-on sentences, and grammatical errors *before* you send out anything. *Read it out loud.* Your ear will pick up many things that your eye will miss. Show your bio to three people, and have them proofread and edit. It's not at all unusual for musicians to write five to seven drafts before finalizing a bio.

▼ ──

Bio "Dos"

- Do highlight your most impressive credentials.
- Do write your bio in the third person: use she/he, and Ms./Mr. (not "I").
- Do be careful how you handle dates. There is no need to include the date of every award, performance, scholarship, or degree. *When* things happen is nowhere near as important as *what* happened.
- Do include all your contact info in your letterhead design at the top of your printed bio or PDF version, and double-space the bio text for easier reading.

Bio "Don'ts"

- Don't write in chronological order! Don't start with "Jane Doe began her studies at age three . . ." Unless you are already world-famous, your earliest musical experiences won't be all that interesting to your readers.
- Don't start with your educational credentials—save this for the end of the bio.
- Don't use unattributed comparisons: it is presumptuous. Don't write, "The best of his generation" or "The most promising and accomplished jazz guitarist of the decade" unless you are quoting a review or a statement from a respected and well-known mentor.
- Don't use clichés such as "unique." Besides being a cliché, it's redundant: each of us is, by definition, an individual, so don't state the obvious. Avoid hackneyed phrases such as "critically acclaimed," "rising star," and "quickly establishing herself as one of . . ." and "has had the privilege of studying

under . . ." These are all clichés: they sound trite and mechanical. Don't try to "dress up" or "puff up" your bio with fancy words and flowery language. In the end, it's the concrete facts of the story itself that make an impression, *not* the adjectives.

▲

What Makes You Special?

An effective bio contains something memorable that helps fix the artist in the reader's mind. It may be your particular (or unusual) repertoire, the nontraditional performance spaces where you have presented concerts, a cause you support, a degree outside of music, or a research project. For the reader, these features help make you distinct from others, memorable and three-dimensional.

John Blanchard, at Manhattan School of Music, advises that adding information about your hobbies and interests may be a plus. It can generate readers' interest as well as media attention, depending on what you have and how you present it. Here are some of John's guidelines:

Boring/Vague	*Specific/Interesting*
"Avid outdoorsman"	"200m Gold medal winner in the 2006 Mazda Swim Meet in Denver, Colorado"
"Likes to read"	"Has published an article exploring the influences of American 'beat' poets on 1960s jazz"
"Collects antiques"	"Is the proud owner of several vintage guitars from the Big Band era, including a 1939 Gibson L-5 . . ."
"Is married with three children"	" . . . as a volunteer soccer coach, has led her son's junior high school team to two district titles"

The left column has vague, generic statements. The right column has specific, memorable details. Such details in a bio can bring a musician to life as a multifaceted human being, not just someone with a series of degrees and performances.

▼

Bios for Ensembles

If you are writing a bio for a band or ensemble, don't assume that your readers are familiar with the instrumentation or sound of the group. Not everyone knows what instruments comprise a brass or woodwind quintet or a piano trio. Describe the repertoire and the range of sounds your ensemble can deliver in a way that is engaging and informative.

For example, a brass quartet's bio includes "delights audiences with their rich, finely blended sound, and interpretations that range from warm and lyrical to festive and rousing. Their repertoire includes Renaissance and Baroque music of Gabrieli, Bach, and Handel, as well as ragtime, Stephen Foster favorites, and gospel arrangements. From its core quartet of two trumpets and two trombones, XYZ Brass can expand to perform as a quintet or larger ensemble."

Make clear what your ensemble offers. At the bottom of their bio is: "XYZ Brass is available for concert presentations, master classes, lecture-demonstrations for K–12 audiences, as well as for weddings, holiday parties, special events, and business functions. See www.xyzbrass.com."

▲

As you read musicians' bios, instead of comparing your credentials to theirs, read analytically to learn tips on bio construction. Ask yourself, what stands out in this bio? For individual bios, do you get a real sense of the musician as a person—her specific musical interests and passions? For ensembles, do you get a real sense of the group—its mission and distinctiveness? Notice how the bio is structured—is the lead compelling? How is the material organized? How does it flow? Is your interest maintained throughout? Reading analytically to evaluate the effectiveness of other musicians' promotional pieces will absolutely help you improve your own.

Bio examples are shown on the following pages. The names and contact information for some of these artists have been changed "to protect the innocent." However, Kevin Harris's bio is real (as of 2009), as is that of Second Wind, although it's from a few years ago. And those of Rhiannon Banerdt and Daniel Rios are actual bios as of 2009 during their undergraduate years (thus their contact information has been "anonymized"). To read more bios of emerging classical artists, you may want to check the websites for the Chamber Music Society of Lincoln Center Two Artists or any other major competition or festival that lists bios of young artists. For jazz, you may want to check out http://www.allaboutjazz.com and http://www.jazzcorner.com.

Vivianne Vocalist, soprano

123 My Street #6 Our Fair City, MA 02115 (617) 555-1212
vvocalist@hotmail.com

In the Boston area, soprano Viviane Vocalist has appeared as a soloist with the New England Conservatory Chorus, the Boston University Women's Chorus, and the Boston University Collegium Musicum, performing repertoire ranging from Orff's *Carmina Burana* to the Bach *St. Matthew Passion*. Ms. Vocalist has also been featured on WCRB broadcasts as soloist and section leader with St. Paul's Cathedral Choir. Her recital performances have included John Harbison's *Mirabai Songs*, the Bach *Coffee Cantata*, and the *Bachianas Brasileiras No. 5* by Villa-Lobos.

As a chorister, Viviane Vocalist has performed with the Choir of Trinity Church, the Boston University Chamber Singers, and the New England Conservatory Chamber Singers. Her choral repertoire includes Libby Larsen's *Billy the Kid* and Daniel Pinkham's *The White Raven*. She has performed in Symphony Hall, Jordan Hall, the Tsai Performing Arts Center, and Marsh Chapel.

Pursuing a strong interest in early music, Ms. Vocalist has studied and performed at the Austro-American Institute in Vienna. Based on her own manuscript research of composer Marianna Martines, a contemporary of Mozart, Viviane Vocalist produced a modern printed edition of a Martines cantata. Ms. Vocalist performed this cantata at Boston University the following year.

A native of Long Island, Viviane Vocalist is currently pursuing a master's degree at New England Conservatory in Boston, studying voice with Carole Haber. Ms. Vocalist received her bachelor's degree in music from Boston University, graduating *summa cum laude* and with departmental honors in Voice.

Ms. Vocalist's upcoming projects include a solo recital at New England Conservatory, solo appearances with the New England Conservatory Extension Division Youth Chorale, and a tour of England with St. Paul's Cathedral Choir. The cathedral choir, with Viviane Vocalist as a soloist, will be releasing a CD later this year.

[Note on this Bio's organization: the 1st paragraph topic is solo and recital work; 2nd is choral work; 3rd is special interests and projects; 4th is home and study; last is upcoming projects.]

Kevin Harris, jazz pianist

www.kevinharrisproject.com kevin@kevinharrisproject.com Cell (617) 738-0116

Jazz pianist Kevin Harris plays a distinctive combination of traditional and contemporary music. The native Kentuckian's compositions and arrangements vary from explosive polyrhythmic pieces to introspective ballads. Harris has performed at the Wang Theatre, Columbia University, Jordan Hall, Berklee Performance Center, Les Zygomates, Blue Note New York and Milan, Italy, Wally's Jazz Café, Scullers, and the Regatta Bar. His music contains the varied influences of Chopin, Marcus Roberts, Keith Jarrett, Danilo Perez, and Thelonious Monk.

Harris' Boston-based trio includes drummer Steve Langone and bassist Kendall Eddy. Kevin's first CD, *Patient Harvest*, was released in 2002; in March of 2007, Harris released his second CD, entitled *The Butterfly Chronicles*, and, in 2008 his new CD, *Freedom Doxology*, was released at his performances at the Regatta Bar in Cambridge, MA and at the Blue Note in Milan, Italy.

Kevin holds a Master's degree in jazz performance from the New England Conservatory and an undergraduate degree in music education from Morehead State University, KY. At NEC, he studied with Fred Hersch, Mike Cain, Cecil McBee, George Garzone, and Danilo Perez, and performed with George Russell, Benny Golson, and Bob Brookmeyer.

After graduating from New England Conservatory in 2000, Harris worked as an accompanist for jazz and pop vocal ensembles at Berklee College of Music. That same year, Harris started five separate band programs with help from "Arts In Progress," a Boston-based arts organization. In the summer of 2007, Harris served as jazz piano instructor for students from Brazil, India, and South Africa during the Northeastern University Fusion Arts Program. Currently, Harris teaches trumpet, piano, and jazz band at the Cambridge Friends School and the Charles River School. Harris also teaches privately at his studio in Boston.

In earlier years, Harris was invited by the mayor of New Orleans to perform for the Alpha Phi Alpha Forum at the Mahalia Jackson Theater for the Performing Arts in New Orleans. During high school, he was selected to appear on the nationally broadcast Black Entertainment Television program *Teen Summit*, a showcase for U.S. talent.

Committed to community and to getting kids involved in music, Kevin has also conducted instrumental improvisation clinics (K-12) in public and private schools throughout the nation and in St. Thomas, Virgin Islands. A typical educational performance of Harris' involves interacting with the audience; he thrives on communication. "Participation," he says, "is what keeps our souls alive."

[2009]

Rhiannon Banerdt, *violinist*

1 String Street, Boston, MA 12345 (617) 555-1212
rhiannonbanderdt@NotHerRealEmail.com

Violinist Rhiannon Banerdt has performed a wide range of solo and chamber music on five continents. At age 14, she made her solo debut with the New England Youth Ensemble in Pietermaritzburg, South Africa, performing Bruch's Violin Concerto in G minor. The next year, Ms. Banerdt performed Bach's Double Violin Concerto with John Banerdt of the Philadelphia Orchestra in Philadelphia's Verizon Hall as a winner of Strings International Music Festival Kimmel Center Competition. She has presented solo and chamber performances at the Taos School of Music in Taos, New Mexico, and at the Quartet Program in Fredonia, Boulder, and Bucknell. Her numerous solo recitals, at venues such as New England Conservatory and Walnut Hill School for the Arts, have included works by Bach, Fauré, Stravinsky, and Szymanowski.

A former member of the Amethyst Piano Trio, Rhiannon Banerdt was selected for the semifinals of the 2006 Fischoff National Chamber Music Competition, and the same year was awarded first prize in the International Chamber Music Ensemble Competition. As first prize winners, the trio was invited to play at Weill Hall in New York, where their performance was hailed by Edith Eisler, correspondent for Strings Magazine, as "real music-making—concentrated and deeply felt."

Ms. Banerdt strives constantly to expand her artistic boundaries by exploring new music, blurring genre boundaries, and going beyond the conventions of classical performance to connect with audiences. Dedicated to the performance of new music as well as old, Ms. Banerdt has collaborated with a number of composers to present premieres of new music at New England Conservatory's Jordan Hall, as well as other venues in the Boston area. She has performed new works by Malcolm Peyton, Osnat Netzer, Niall Conor-Garcia, and Chia-Hui Hung. She has also collaborated with such non-classical artists as fiddler Mark O'Connor and accordionist Cory Pesaturo. In addition, Ms. Banerdt is passionate about the development of innovative music education and community programs. She is a member of the newly formed Discovery Ensemble, a chamber orchestra which, in partnership with the City of Boston, will present a series of linked workshops and performances in Dorchester, an underserved community in the Boston area, throughout the 2008-2009 season. In an effort to reach a wider audience, she has performed in numerous non-traditional venues, from libraries, community centers, and schools to street corners and outdoor movie theaters, and particularly enjoys working with children.

Ms. Banerdt is currently completing an undergraduate degree at the New England Conservatory, where she studies with Lucy Chapman. Her former teachers have included Marylou Speaker Churchill and Lyndon Johnston Taylor. She has also coached with Lydia Artymiw, Edward Dusinberre, Martha Katz, and the Borromeo, Brentano, and Shanghai string quartets.

[2009]

Daniel Rios, oboist

100 Reed Street, Boston, MA 12345 (123) 456-7890 daniel.rios@NotHisRealEmail.com

A native of San Antonio, oboist Daniel Rios has performed with many of the area's premier musical groups, including the San Antonio Symphony, San Antonio Opera, and the Olmos Ensemble. It was with the Olmos Ensemble, made up of the principal musicians of the San Antonio Symphony, that Daniel made his professional chamber music debut at the age of 14. With the Olmos Ensemble's founder, oboist Mark Ackerman, Daniel has presented recitals in San Antonio, with programs ranging from the standard oboe repertoire, to an early music program, a concert of music for oboe/English horn and organ, and a concert of works by Latin and Texan composers.

In the summer of 2008, Daniel attended the Music Academy of the West in Santa Barbara, where he performed as principal oboist of the Academy Festival Orchestra. While in Santa Barbara, he played numerous chamber music concerts, giving performances of the Mozart Oboe Quartet, Poulenc Sextet, and the Poulenc Trio. Mr. Rios also gave a critically acclaimed performance of the *Ballade for Oboe and Piano* by Hendrik Andreissen, which was hailed in the Santa Barbara News Press as "romantic, sensitive and handsomely played."

Daniel Rios has had the opportunity to perform with such acclaimed artists as Warren Jones, John Gibbons, and the Parker Quartet. He has also served as principal oboist of all the New England Conservatory orchestras, including the conductor-less Chamber Orchestra. He currently serves as principal oboist of the Discovery Ensemble, an orchestra whose mission is to provide music and education to citizens of the Boston area. Upcoming projects with the ensemble this season include community concerts and educational programs. Daniel will also perform a solo recital at New England Conservatory, featuring Joseph Schwantner's *Black Anemones*, Francis Poulenc's *Trio for Oboe, Bassoon and Piano*, and Richard Strauss' *Oboe Concerto in D*.

Currently residing in Boston, Daniel attends the New England Conservatory, where he studies with John Ferrillo and Robert Sheena of the Boston Symphony Orchestra.

[2009]

Second Wind Recorder Duo

Players Roxanne Layton and Roy Sansom
26 Flett Rd., Belmont, MA 02178
tel (617) 489-3906
dellalsansom@earthlink.net

The Second Wind Recorder Duo is noted for its virtuosity, musical insight, and wit. *American Recorder* praised Roxanne Layton's and Roy Sansom's performance as "... evocative, emotional, intense ... the applause went off the gauge." Lloyd Schwartz of the *Boston Phoenix* described them as "stellar."

The Second Wind Recorder Duo explores repertoire from the Middle Ages to contemporary music, offering imaginative and inventive programming. Their concerts often include works by Chopin, Telemann, Poulenc, Machaut, Bartok, and C.P.E. Bach, as well as the players' original compositions and arrangements.

Since its inception, Second Wind has performed at the early music festivals in Berkeley and in Boston, and on the Society for Historically Informed Performance summer concert series. The duo has toured the Southeast, performing in Atlanta, Jacksonville, Augusta, and Durham, and has traveled to Australia to teach and perform for the Recorder Society of Western Australia and the Recorder Society of Tasmania. As a team, Roy and Roxanne have also appeared with the New World Symphony, the Utah Opera, and the Boston Lyric Opera, among others, to critical acclaim. Both Roxanne and Roy are long-term members of the acclaimed Emmanuel Music, performing in their weekly Bach cantata series, and they have both recorded for American Gramophone and Koch International.

Beyond Second Wind engagements, Roxanne Layton has appeared as soloist with the New Orleans Philharmonic and the Handel & Haydn Society Orchestra in Boston. With the *Mannheim Steamroller*, she has toured extensively, with appearances including the *Today* show and the *Tonight* show on NBC, and at two White House Christmas performances. Roy Sansom has performed with the Boston Pops Orchestra and the New York City Opera. His recordings include the Bach Brandenburg Concerto No. 4 and the Monteverdi 1610 Vespers, with Boston Baroque on Telarc Records. He has taught and coached for many workshops and seminars including Mountain Collegium, Pinewoods, and for the Institute for Historical Dance in Salzburg.

The Second Wind Recorder Duo is available for concert bookings, lecture-demonstrations, master classes, and ensemble coachings. For further information and a demo recording, call or write to address above.

[2005]

Dan Alias, Jazz Guitarist/Composer

1 Main #2 Boston, MA 02115 (617) 555-1212 dalias@email.com www.hiswebsite.com

A multifaceted musician, Boston-based guitarist and composer Dan Alias has appeared in a wide range of venues, from New York's CBGB's to Washington DC's Kennedy Center and Boston's Jordan Hall. Other performances include appearances at the Banff Jazz Festival in Alberta, Canada, and the South by Southwest Independent Music Conference in Austin, TX. In recent years, Mr. Alias performed as a member of the New England Conservatory Honors Jazz Ensemble, a select group chosen to represent the Conservatory to the public through a series of concerts in the Boston area.

Mr. Alias is also active as a performer and interpreter of contemporary classical music. He worked under the direction of composer Lukas Foss on a performance of Foss's *Paradigm for Five Instruments* at the New England Conservatory. Upcoming projects include an orchestral performance of John Cage's *Cheap Imitation,* under the direction of Stephen Drury, to be premiered locally at Boston's Jordan Hall. A recording of the work is to be released on Mode Records CD series, *The Music of John Cage.*

Dan Alias is currently completing an undergraduate degree in Jazz Studies at New England Conservatory in Boston. He has studied privately with artists such as Mick Goodrick, Danilo Pérez, Jerry Bergonzi, and Charlie Banacos, and has been coached in ensembles with George Russell, Cecil McBee, and Allan Chase. Mr. Alias has performed in master classes with guitarist John Abercrombie and bassist William Parker. Dan Alias graduated with a bachelor's degree in sociology from the University of Miami, Coral Gables, FL.

Bios for Composers and Improvisers: The Challenge of Describing Your Music

Bios are a challenge for all musicians to write, but especially for composers and those who improvise. These musicians have the added work of describing their own music. Elvis Costello famously compared writing about music to dancing about architecture. Nevertheless, a written description is often necessary for introducing a composer's work. A bio should help build a bridge between a composer and her audience.

Composers and improvisers need descriptions of their music for grant proposals and applications for festivals, grad schools, and artist residencies. This description should serve as a compelling and distinctive "preview" to help motivate readers to listen to sound clips, read scores, or come hear the performance. In networking situations, when people inevitably ask, "What kind of music do you write?" answering that you write or play "free jazz" or "contemporary classical" is not specific enough. People want to get a real sense of what your music is like, *especially* if they are considering hiring you or commissioning you.

It can help to take a few tips from visual artists: they typically have to write *artist statements* that accompany their work at exhibitions, on websites, and for portfolio reviews. At its best, an artist's statement reads easily, is informative, and adds to the reader's understanding of the artist, his intentions, and his work. At its worst, an artist's statement is difficult to understand, is pretentious, and irritates rather than informs. Some composers' descriptions of their work have similar shortcomings.

▼

Writing Prompts

To generate material for your description, try answering these questions:

- How would you describe your music to a new acquaintance, someone you wish to invite to an upcoming performance?
- How have your mentors or colleagues described any of your particular works, or your work overall?
- What you are reaching for in your compositions? What is it you seek to realize in your work?
- Instead of writing a description of *all* your music, try writing a description of a particular work or project. For example, describing its instrumentation, form, particular features, techniques used, or the occasion for its composition.
- What are your sources of inspiration—ideas, writers, visual artists, other musical or non-musical influences?
- Do you have a specific approach or philosophy toward music?

▲

Excerpts from Composer/Improviser Bios

"The instrumental and electroacoustic music of composer Alexandra Gardner combines explorations into the rich details of acoustic sound with a visceral percussive energy to create dynamic sonic landscapes. Drawing inspiration from sources ranging from mythology and contemporary poetry to her training as a percussionist and collaborations with cutting-edge musicians and artists, Gardner is building new audiences for contemporary music with an expressive sound and a flair for the imaginative and unexpected." (http://www.alexandragardner.net)

"Meredith Monk is a composer, singer, director/choreographer and creator of new opera, music theater works, films and installations. A pioneer in what is now called 'extended vocal technique' and 'interdisciplinary performance,' Monk creates works that thrive at the intersection of music and movement, image and object, light and sound in an effort to discover and weave together new modes of perception. Her groundbreaking exploration of the voice as an instrument, as an eloquent language in and of itself, expands the boundaries of musical composition, creating landscapes of sound that unearth feelings, energies, and memories for which we have no words. She has alternately been proclaimed as a 'magician of the voice' and 'one of America's coolest composers.' During a career that spans more than 35 years she has been acclaimed by audiences and critics as a major creative force in the performing arts." (http://www.meredithmonk.org)

"Dead Cat Bounce invokes Charles Mingus and the World Saxophone Quartet with their 'tightly arranged, swirling contrapuntal reeds and multipart, blues n' roots-infused tricky compositions' (Jon Garelik, *The Boston Phoenix*). Their eclectic approach to rhythm is informed by traditions from the Caribbean, Deep South, Brazil, Eastern Europe and Detroit. In Dead Cat Bounce, solo and collective improvisations energetically complement the poise of its ever-expanding compositional repertoire. According to Dave Leibman, Dead Cat Bounce 'does it all with exquisite writing, the subtle use of a bass-drum rhythm section and above all a definite sense of communication between the members that I am sure will be apparent to even the casual listener. These young Boston-based musicians are not just playing music on the page, but listening and communicating together.'" (http://www.deadcatbounce.org)

From singer-songwriter Jonathan Coulton's sonicbids bio:
"His songs about vengeful nerds, ennui-afflicted clowns, self-loathing giant squids, and devotees of a certain Swedish prefab furniture store are in-

sanely clever without being too clever for their own good. They repeatedly lure you into laughing before suddenly breaking your heart. And the sick part is, you keep coming back. Coulton's is the voice of every spooky elementary school kid who could never quite keep his shirt tucked in or shoes tied; every lovelorn mason and mad scientist; every one of us who has ever sat despairingly on the floor, surrounded by parts of an Ikea endtable, weeping over our Allen wrenches." (http://www.jonathancoulton.com)

Photos ◆

We live in a visually oriented culture, so publicity photos are a must for professional musicians. Also referred to as "promo "or "head" shots—or, in the "old days" of the twentieth century, "8 × 10 glossies"—publicity photos are used for websites, posters, brochures, CDs, and in seeking media attention. For singers, headshots are required on résumés at most auditions and competitions.

Photos are powerful communication tools. We all make snap judgments based on first impressions. People who see your headshot make assumptions about you and your music before they ever hear you perform a note. An effective photo is one that makes a memorable, positive impression and helps convey your intended image and brand.

▼

Tip: Newspaper, magazine, and online arts calendar editors often highlight selected performances for their "pick of the week" sections. They have limited space, so from the many performing arts events offered, they can choose only a few. How do they decide? In part, they select based on the photos, choosing the most unusual, dynamic, or engaging shots. Do they use conservative, traditional, head shots? No. An editor wants photos that will cause readers to stop, look, and read; often, these are images that seem to suggest a story or have some extra dynamic element to them. Artists should have an assortment of such photos suitable for a range of uses. If possible, have both verticals and horizontals (called *landscape* shots) available, because editors often select a photo based on the size and shape space they have left on a page.

▲

What Does a Photo Communicate?

Photos create immediate and lasting impressions. They impart a sense of the individual's musicianship and personality. Effective photos convey distinct aspects of a musician's persona, such as imagination, intelligence, confidence, and sensitivity. Unfortunately, photos can also communicate a negative image. We've all seen shots that unfortunately suggest that an artist is immature, inexperienced, arrogant, stiff, or vacuous.

What should you aim for in a publicity photo? Your photo image should look like you (on a good day) and should communicate a real sense of your personality—the version of yourself revealed through your music. This is not about glamour or sex appeal, or trying to look like a fashion model. It's about your artistry, your musical personality. What you want is the real *you* captured in a photo that is interesting and memorable, and that helps convey what is distinctive about your music.

The Adjective Exercise

Browse the websites of any performance series or arts calendar. Look at pictures of musicians you have not yet heard perform. Choose a shot and ask yourself, based on this photo alone, what do you imagine this musician's performance will be like? What adjectives come to mind? Do this exercise with a few friends—it can be interesting to see how other people view the same photos. This exercise is a warmup for helping you determine what you want your next photo to communicate.

On the next pages are samples of musicians' publicity photos, taken by Boston photographer Susan Wilson (http://www.susanwilsonphoto.com), Atlanta-based photographer Angela Morris (http://www.angelaphotography.com), and the New York City–based photographer Jeff Fasano (http://www.jefffasano.com). Play the adjective game with them: what words would you use to describe the sense you get of these musical personalities? What image is being communicated?

Choosing a Photographer

In order get an effective promo shot, you need to do your homework. Check out websites of interesting performing arts series, clubs, or festivals to get a sense of what's current for musicians and bands playing music similar to yours. Browse through local arts events calendars online and in print to see which promo shots get media attention. You should go through thirty or more shots to get a sense of the good, the bad, and the unusual.

Choose a photographer whose work you admire. Find professionals who specialize in musicians' photos, as opposed to those who shoot yearbooks, weddings, or babies. Your photographer needs to know the business—what's current and what's getting used in the media. Ask colleagues for referrals, and when you see a musician's publicity shot you like, look for the photo credit to get the name of the photographer.

Baritone Aaron Engebreth (http://www.florestanproject.org/artists/engebreth
.html); photo credit Susan Wilson, http://www.susanwilsonphoto.com

Once you have the referrals, look at the photographers' work online. Make sure you find examples you like. Call and talk with the photographers to see whether you feel at ease with them. A good photo reveals your genuine personality, so you need to feel at home with your photographer in order for a head shot to reflect the real you.

Jennifer Stumm, violist
(http://www
.jenniferstumm.com);
photo credit:
Angela Morris
http://www
.angelaphotography.com

Imani Winds (http://www.imaniwinds.com); photo credit Jeff Fasano,
http://www.jefffasano.com

Is Hiring a Pro Necessary?

Musicians often ask if they really need to hire a professional photographer.
They want to save money by having a talented relative, friend, or colleague take
their photo. Susan Wilson, one of Boston's top musician's photographers, addresses
this question on her website (http://www.susanwilsonphoto.com). "When you hire
a pro, you're not just hiring a person with a more expensive camera than your Uncle
Fred. You're hiring someone who knows how to make you (or whatever the subject
is) look awesome, using an artistic eye, an ability to put the subject at ease, and the
technical skill to give you a riveting image that everyone will notice. You're hiring
someone who can take your vision of yourself (or of the subject you want shot),
and mold it into something eye-catching, truthful, and new. If those things don't
matter to you, phone Uncle Fred immediately."

Good professional publicity photos have a specific look, most often the result of years of the photographer's training and experience. Can people tell the difference between a professional-quality shot and something less than? Absolutely. Moreover, when you hire a professional, you are paying for the expertise that will produce more good shots per appointment time. Overall, it's a smart investment.

▲

Costs

For a professional photo shoot in Boston, as of 2010, you can expect to spend between $350 and $700 (more if you are a duo or a larger ensemble) although "photographers of the stars" will charge over $1,000. Make sure you know what your session fee covers, because hidden costs can add up. Discuss all fees in detail in advance to avoid any confusion or misunderstanding about the bill. Your photographer should take a minimum of 100 shots (preferably more for an ensemble in diverse poses and at different angles. The more pictures your photographer takes, the more options you will have. Check on how many shots are included in the fee. Ask about retouching and the cost of a finished master shot. With most photographers, you are paying for the creation of the photos (skill and expertise), an agreed amount of time for the shoot and delivery of the final product, a print or scan of select images, the reproduction rights for use of the images, plus all expenses involved, such as postproduction digital work and processing. According to U.S. copyright law, it's the photographer—not you—who owns the negatives. So make sure you know exactly what you are paying for and what you should get in return.

Before Your Shoot

Come to your shoot prepared. Determine which types of photos you want: formal or informal; a head shot, full body, or partial; indoor or outdoor; on location or using a backdrop; with or without instruments or cases. You'll need to make decisions about clothes, hair, makeup, and jewelry. Bring ideas about lighting, mood, and style. Remember that each of these "minor" details will be reflected, good or bad, in your final photos. Plan for getting two types of shots: one formal and one less so, with changes of clothing, lighting, and mood.

▼

Tip: Photographer Susan Wilson recommends bringing along "reference shots." These are photos of yourself that you either love or hate. Be ready to explain why. This is so your photographer will know that, for instance, you cannot stand how your nose looks from a certain angle or that you are self-conscious about your chins. If your photographer knows what you want, you will have a much better chance of being satisfied with the results. Show samples of other musicians' promo shots you like for their mood, composition, or lighting.

Before the shoot, Susan also suggests making a list of adjectives describing what traits you want to your photo to convey (serious, self-assured, creative, introspective, etc.). Be specific about how you want to come across. Your photographer cannot read your mind, so you need to make sure to effectively communicate the image you want your photo to convey.

▲

What to Wear

In terms of attire, we are not always the best judge of which colors, cuts, and designs are most flattering for our body type. Get advice from someone with professional experience. The "personal shopper" staff, available by appointment at most upscale department stores, can be very helpful for advising.

Bring several changes of clothes to your shoot—two formal (one all black) and one semi-casual. Make sure your outfit projects your intended image. Include clothes that you would actually wear in performance and also clothes that appropriately reflect "you." Stick to solid colors; black is flattering to most people. Wear minimal jewelry (take off watches) so that your face remains the primarily focus. Keep it simple: your publicity photo is not a fashion ad.

For print and online purposes, it can be helpful to have both black-and-white and color options. With digital photography, you can get photos shot in color and then processed into black-and-white as needed. Note that flattering, bright colors show up as grays when translated into black-and-white photos.

The "you" in your photos should be consistent with how you appear when you perform. If you always wear glasses in concerts, wear them in your photos. (Your photographer will have a much easier time if your glasses are non-glare or if you can pop the lenses out for the shoot.)

Regarding makeup: many women opt to have a professional do their makeup before a photo shoot. You can get made up at a department store counter for free (or for the cost of a lipstick). But do ask your makeup artist to tread lightly; you want a light, natural look so that you are still easily recognizable *without* makeup.

▼

Tips for Your Shoot
- Get a good night's sleep the night before; it makes a *big* difference.
- Get everything ready the day before (clothes chosen, cleaned, and pressed) so that the day of your shoot is easy.

- Arrange for a stress-free morning and an easy commute so that you can be relaxed and focused at the shoot. The camera reads whatever is on your mind—really!

Bring the following with you:

- Comb and brush
- Lip balm (helps to keep your lips from sticking to your teeth while you smile)
- Powder from a compact; this is handy to cover the shine on your nose that will come from being under the lights.
- A friend and/or recordings to play during the shoot to help you relax.

▲

During the Photo Shoot

A good photographer will begin the session by asking questions to help you get the results you desire. Tell your photographer how you plan to use the photos (for a CD cover, online, for print media). By talking with you before the shoot, the photographer will also get a sense of you as a photo subject; this is important in determining how best to photograph you. Describe again the professional image you want your photos to communicate (and make sure you have thought all this through in advance so that you can articulate it clearly).

In photos, your thoughts (or lack thereof) are readable on your face. During the shoot, in order to have a compelling expression, you need to have something going on behind your eyes. As a musician, you have vibrant stories to tell through your music: your story-telling skills are part of what you want your photo to convey. Janice Papolos, author of *The Performing Artist's Handbook*, recommends that during the shoot you think of loved ones, favorite memories, or a juicy secret. These thoughts evoke real feelings—enthusiasm, warmth, and wit—that will show in your expression.

After the Photo Shoot

Depending on how busy your photographer is, it may take a week or so until you receive your photos. Ask your photographer to recommend particular shots (in many cases, the photographer will ask that you make the first cut, then they will help you decide among your favorite images). It can be difficult to be objective, so make the most of having expert advice.

Once you have chosen the best of your shots, your photographer will make a "master" final version, with any touch-ups as needed. For the digital version, you should ask for both a high-resolution file (8 × 10 inch, 300 dpi TIF), suitable for printing and high-quality publications, as well as a well as a low-resolution file (8 × 10 inch, 72–150 dpi JPEG), suitable for websites and e-mailing (these won't overload someone's e-mail or crash their server). If you want hard copies, your photographer can print an 8 × 10 master. It's generally not necessary to send a print anymore, however, because most of the mass reproduction labs are happy to work from your high-res digital file, which you can mail on a CD or upload on their FTP site. These photo reproduction shops specialize in quantity photos for discounted rates. Look for package deals for less than two dollars per 8 × 10. Ask your photographer for referrals. A second option—which is great if you have an active website—is to have your new publicity photos downloadable for clients in both high- and low-resolution formats. The photos you send out or make available for promotional purposes (hard copy or electronic) should be labeled appropriately. You should also, whenever possible, make sure to include the photo credit (such as "Photo by Patricia Smith").

Promo Kits ◆

With a letterhead design, bio, and photo, you now have the beginnings of a promo kit. Musicians put their electronic promo kits (EPKs) on their websites to make it easy for others to download photos and information for booking purposes. Components of your kit may also be useful in applying for grants and teaching jobs. It is particularly helpful to have PDF files of your text-based documents, such as your bio, so that the formatting and typefaces appear as you intend. For an easy way to have your EPK immediately available online and accessible to all, check out http://reverbnation.com and http://www.sonicbids.com, which you can use in conjunction with your existing website, social networking sites, or as a stand-alone.

The Extras

On the following pages are descriptions and examples of additional promotional pieces useful to musicians. When choosing which additional promo kit items to create, think of your intended recipients. In assembling materials for a competition, grant, or for booking performances, tailor your materials appropriately for the intended recipients.

- *Letters of recommendation:* These can be extremely helpful for emerging artists. Ask mentors if they would consider writing you letters of recommendation. One way to go about this is to request feedback on your demo recording. If the response is enthusiastic, ask your listeners if they might offer testimonial quotes or letters for your kit. If you have performed for a concert series, club, or festival and the organizer's response was positive, ask for a letter. A strong recommendation from a fellow presenter can be a powerful incentive for someone else to consider booking you. Just make sure you get permission before using anyone's letter or quote in your promo materials.

- *Quote sheet:* Once you have acquired several letters of recommendation from presenters and mentors, consolidate the best excerpts into a single document. Musicians often have difficulty choosing the best sound bites. Get advice and suggestions from experienced PR professionals. If you do not have PR contacts, this is a great opportunity to find them through networking. And when you have reviews, include the best quotes along with the names of the publications (and the reviewers' names if they are well known).

- *Rep list:* Anyone considering booking you will want to know what music you have to offer. Applications for competitions, festivals, grants, and teaching jobs often require repertoire lists. Classical performers use *repertoire lists,* what nonclassical performers usually call *play lists*—these are simply listings of the works you have performed and have available. Works are presented alphabetically by the composer's last name on the left and the titles on the right. Composers promoting their own music use "work lists," with titles, instrumentation, dates completed, and timings. Bands that play multiple genres should organize the play lists by genre category. Ensembles also often list originals in one category and covers or jazz standards in another.

  For classical instrumentalists, it can be helpful to organize works into "Solo Repertoire," "Chamber Music," and "Concerto Repertoire." Singers typically divide their repertoire into categories such as opera roles, musical theater roles, and recital rep. Art song repertoire can be segmented by languages.

  A variation of a standard repertoire list is a version that lists the selected repertoire and projects available for the coming season. Such lists can be titled (with the appropriate date) "Repertoire Available: 2014–2015."

  Creating or updating your rep list can give you a boost of confidence as you survey all that you have performed and have to offer. Working on your list is also helpful for future planning, as you can identify the works you would like to add next.

- *Available programs* showcase one or more full concert program you can offer, listing the work titles, movements, composers, and their dates. Interesting or unusual programming can be one of the best ways for emerging artists to win the attention of presenters, audiences, and the media. You may have an interesting idea for combining works not traditionally heard, or you might offer a program with an innovative theme, multimedia work, or premiere.

- *Recent engagements* detail where you or your ensemble has performed. List performance venues without dates, in order of most prestigious to least. Include the name of venue (the hall, festival, or club), with city and state (and country, if international). A variation on this is an "Upcoming Engagements" list, detailing venues already booked for the upcoming season (with dates included). For those just getting started, these lists may be ideas to consider for the future as you gain more experience and credentials.
- *Media:* highlight any reviews or articles that have been written about you or your ensemble. If you have had any media attention, include it in your kit (JPEGs or photocopies as applicable)—people who book concerts want to know if you have drawn media attention. Reviews can be hard to come by, but there are other types of media coverage you can include: previews of performances, calendar listings, blog postings by influential writers, and award notices. Include human interest pieces that feature you, whether for your music or for other community work, an unusual hobby, or anything else interesting and positive.

  To present these pieces well, cut out the original article along with the publication's *banner* (its name and location) and the date the piece ran. Resize the banner and article separately on an 8–1/2 × 11 sheet of paper to create a balanced presentation. This will become your master copy. You can then scan the document to create a JPEG and add it to your electronic press kit. When hard copies are needed, you can make photocopies and direct the reader's attention to the juiciest portions by using a highlighter on the copies (not on the original). Another option is to identify the best quotes, enlarge them on a photocopier, and paste these on top of the article, so that both the publication's name and a portion of the article are still visible, but the *pullout quote* is most prominent. This can also be scanned and converted into a JPEG for use online.
- *Workshops:* In addition to mainstage performances, you may wish to offer additional programming. These days, presenters are particularly interested in artists who can offer audience engagement activities such as clinics, master classes, workshops, and pre- or post-concert talks. Create a page describing your presentations.

▼ ──

Kitchen Table Test

This is adapted from the excellent presentations of arts consultant Deborah Obalil. She recommends that before you put together your own kit, you first gather examples of other professional musicians' promo materials. Visit your local performing arts centers and other venues; pick up flyers, postcards, and brochures advertising upcoming performances. These typically have photos, a few quotes, and a short bio. Shuffle them in among your own existing materials and spread everything out on your kitchen table. Pick up one item at a time and examine it. Do a mini-analysis on each for the following:

Ability to speak to the heart
Consistency of image (in use of language and tone, typeface, other visuals)
Focus toward a specific audience
Magnetism—how and why does it attract your attention?

Deborah says, "The real value of the kitchen table test is to learn how to stand out from the crowd. By looking at all the materials in one place, you can quickly see what cuts through the clutter and what doesn't. Then, looking more in depth at those pieces that stand out, you can discover how to make your own materials more effective." (See http://www.obalil.com.)

- *Flyers, one-sheets, or postcards:* Single-sheet flyers or postcards can be useful to provide a quick overview or introduction to an ensemble, band, or soloist. Flyer fronts generally have an interesting and inviting photo of the artist or ensemble, their name, and a few media quotes. On the reverse, flyers often include a brief bio, additional quotes, and possibly another photo—often more casual than the one on the front. You can create flyers using desktop publishing programs, scanning in your photos, and using a color copier. Engaging a graphic artist friend or a design student from a local art school can also save you money.

    However, postcards can be an affordable and versatile alternative to flyers. Postcards can be used for mailings, invitations, and inserts for both performances and recording releases. Postcards typically have an image of the musician(s) on the front announcing the upcoming performance or album release, and on the back, details and contact info. Cards can also include a press quote or bio excerpt. There are many inexpensive printers online; see http://www.jakprints.com, http://www.1800postcards.com, and http://www.modernpostcard.com.

    Cyber publicist and author Ariel Hyatt recommends 3 × 5 or 4 × 6 double-sided printed color postcards. In "How to Be Your Own Publicist," Ms. Hyatt writes, "They're more versatile, and a better investment than the old fashioned 8 × 10 prints. They look great and professional, and extra postcards not used in press kits can be sent to people on your mailing list, or you can give them away at gigs." (See http://www.arielpublicity.com.)

▼

Beyond the Kit

Consider offering promo items for giveaways or sales at performances and on your web site. Bands regularly sell "merch" emblazoned with their logos. The terrific ensemble eighth blackbird offers a wide variety of fan merchandise bearing their distinctive "8bb" logo. Fans can buy 8bb boxer shorts, thongs, beer steins, wall clocks, fridge magnets, messenger bags, as well as T-shirts for toddlers or the entire family. Offering these items is a way to help build and strengthen a fan base. On their website, enthusiasts can click on the group's "store" which is linked to its cafepress pages (http://www.cafepress.com manufactures the items and handles the purchase transactions). Groups can also sell these items alongside their CDs and DVDs at performances. Audiences regularly want to take home a souvenir of a live concert experience. They want to connect with the artists, and purchasing albums and memorabilia, visiting the group's website, and subscribing to its e-newsletter are all good ways to do just that. (See http://www.eighthblackbird.com.)

▲

Putting It All Together

After creating individual promotional pieces, you can present them online as your electronic press kit. There are still occasions, though, when hard copies of your materials are useful or preferable: at auditions, at booking conferences, with the media, and in networking situations. Make sure that your name and contact information—in your chosen letterhead design layout—is on *every* promo piece. For hard copies, your materials can be organized into a folder or stapled together as a packet.

For folders, you can use the two-pocket, solid-color folders available at most office supply stores. On the front, you can design a label with your name and instrument or voice type, using your consistent letterhead design. If the inner pocket has slots for this, you can insert your business card. Because folders are bulky, you may want to, instead, simply create an inexpensive color-copy flyer with your photo and name. Using this as your cover sheet, you can then slip it into a clear plastic folder or just staple it to your supplemental materials. Attach your bio, quote sheet, available programs, or any other appropriate materials. Quantity is unimportant—do not "pad" your kit. Instead, send only what is relevant to that reader (for example, a recital series presenter will not be interested in concerto repertoire).

The following pages show sample promo kit items: rep lists, recent engagements, quote sheets, available programs, and workshop lists. They are included for perusing and analyzing. You may not have or need all these items. Remember, your promo kit should be tailored to your intended recipient's interests. Do not worry if you are lacking particular materials; you can always add them in the future. The point is to make the most of what you have now and to present it well.

Summary

Your promotional pieces serve as your calling card—they introduce you to others—so remember that first impressions are lasting ones. Invest the necessary time and effort to create promotional materials that illuminate who you are and what your music is about. Your materials should reflect your high standards of professionalism and artistry.

▼

Career Forward

Working through these practical suggestions will help you in creating and improving promotional materials.

1. Design six or seven draft versions of your letterhead design using different typefaces and layouts. Print them out on a single sheet. To help you choose a final design, get feedback from colleagues and mentors with publicity or graphic design experience.
2. Write a draft bio using the recommended six-step method outlined in this chapter. Gear it toward a specific purpose (such as a grant application, performance program, recital booking, or teaching application).
3. Compare and contrast photos of musicians you have not yet heard perform. Find them online at a performing arts center website, and choose 6 or 7 to analyze. What does each photo communicate? Imagine each musician performing. What adjectives come to mind? Which photos are most effective? Why?
4. For your next photo shoot, what would you like your headshot to convey? Use four adjectives.
5. Make a draft of your rep list; include the entire repertoire you have performed and/or composed. Make sure you carefully check the spelling of all titles and composer names. Choose the most appropriate categories to highlight the range of music you have to offer.
6. Do you have letters of recommendation from mentors, coaches, or people who have booked your concerts? If not, ask the three most appropriate people. If they have not heard you perform in a while, invite them to an upcoming concert or send them your latest demo recording and ask for feedback. This is a great excuse to reconnect with people in your network. If they respond enthusiastically, request a letter or quote from them.

▲

Carl Troubadour, Trumpeter

1 Main St. • Boston, MA 02116 • (617) 555-1212 • carl@alias.com

Trumpet & Piano Repertoire

Damase, J.M.	Hymne
Enesco	Legend
Hindemith	Sonata
Honegger	Intrada
Kennan, K.	Sonata
Peeters, F.	Sonata

Trumpet & Organ Repertoire

Damase, J.M.	Trois Pières Sans Paroles
De La Lande, M.R.	Suite
Hovhaness	Prayer of Saint Gregory
Pinkham	Psalms
Sampson, D.	The Mysteries Remain

Trumpet & Soprano Repertoire

Aldrovandini	De Torrente
Bach	Cantata 51
Bassani, G.B.	Quel Che Dice
Conrad, L.	The Chariot
	The Path
Handel	Eternal Source of Light Divine
	Let the Bright Seraphim (Samson)
	Revenge
	The Trumpet's Loud Clangor
Melani, A.	"All'Armi, Pensieri"
Plog, A.	Two Scenes
Purcell	Thus the Gloomy World
	Trumpet Song, from Massaniello
Scarlatti	Seven Arias
	Su Le Sponde Del Tebro
	Vaga Cintia

Example: Repertoire list

Sarah Songster, singer/songwriter

Recent Engagements, New England

Clubs (Massachusetts)
Club Passim, Cambridge
Colonial Inn, Concord
Kendall Café, Cambridge
Kevin's Café, Pepperall
Old Vienna Kaffeehaus, Westborough
Plantation Club, Worcester

Bars / Restaurants / Coffeehouses
Café Pierrot, Milford, NH
The Courtyard, Manchester, NH
Coyote's, Framingham, MA
Dolphin Striker, Portsmouth, NH
Hermanos, Concord, ME
Jerky's Café, Providence, RI
The Pickle Barrel, Killington, VT
The Rock, Newport, RI
Sugarloaf Lodge, Sugarloaf, ME
Wellesley Inn, Wellesley, MA

Theaters
The State Theater, Portland, ME
The Ioaka Theater, Exeter, NH
The Strand Theater, Providence, RI
The Music Hall, Portsmouth, NH

ABC Artist Management, 1 Main St. Boston, MA 02116
contact John Doe: tel/fax (617) 555-1212
john@JohnDoeArtists.com
www. JohnDoeArtists.com

Example: Recent engagements list

Second Wind Recorder Duo

Players Roxanne Layton and Roy Sansom
26 Flett Rd., Belmont, MA 02178
tel (617) 489-3906
dellalsansom@earthlink.net

"The applause meter went off the gauge . . . their personalities also helped set
in relief the lines of a duo by Telemann and shaped the evocative, emotional,
intense Xylophobia . . ."

—*American Recorder*

"Roy Sansom and Roxanne Layton, recorders, made the piece [Bach
Brandenburg Concerto #4] sound much easier than it is and negotiated the
high tessitura without a hint of shrillness."

—*The Boston Globe*

"The recorder players [in the Boston Early Music Festival Orchestra] were
particularly fine."

—*The Wall Street Journal*

" . . . stellar . . . sexy recorders (yes, recorders, especially in their undulating
introduction to the duet of the two sirens . . .)"

—Lloyd Schwartz, *The Boston Phoenix*

"What Second Wind has, in fact, is a rich blend of exquisite technique and
diverse repertoire stretching from 14th century dances to Sansom's own
compositions and arrangements."

—*Middlesex News*

Example: Review quotes

Reinmar Seidler, cellist

P.O. Box 548, Boston, MA 02130 • (617) 524–2736 • reinmar.seidler@umb.edu

Available Programs 2011–2012 Season

Program 1

Solo Cello Spanning 3 Centuries

2 Ricercari, for cello solo (1689)	D. Gabrielli
Ricercar in C Major	
Ricercar in d minor	
Suite No. 5 in c minor, for cello solo (ca. 1720)	J.S. Bach

Intermission

Suite No. 1 for Solo Cello (1964)	Britten

Program 2

Fables and Fantasies for Cello and Piano

Fantasiestücke	Schumann
5 Stücke im Volkston	
A Fairy Tale	Janacek
Capriccio	Foss

Intermission

Variations on *"Frog He Went a'Courting"*	Hindemith
Serenade	Henze
Tango, Boogie, and Grand Tarantella	S. Hodkinson
Sonata	Britten

Example: Sample programs

Reinmar Seidler, cellist
P.O. Box 548, Boston, MA 02130 • (617) 524–2736 • reinmar.seidler@umb.edu

Selected Workshop Topics

Baroque Performance Practices for the Modern String Instrumentalist
An introduction to the various musical tastes and styles of the Baroque era, designed specifically for players of "modern" instruments. Includes the art of Rhetoric—music as "text"—the functions of music in Baroque society, Baroque musical architecture, contrasting national styles, ideals of sonority, and an introduction to 18th-century ornamentation.

The Healthy, Happy Cellist—Techniques for Healthier Playing
Discover how physical tension differs from energetic expression. Explore ways of integrating rhythm more deeply into the whole body, and learn how to let musical shapes guide physical response patterns. Clarifies the false dichotomy of "technique" versus "musicality." Specific practice methods are shared for changing those habits that can make players uncomfortable.

The Compleat "Basso Continuist"—Baroque ensemble playing for cellists
Explore the musical architecture of 17th- and 18th-century repertoire and its special demands on the continuo player. Develop a sensitivity to harmonic progression and tonal function in order to shape bass lines powerfully and expressively. Examine both ensemble and solo repertoires.

Music, Politics and the Visual Arts in Post-Revolutionary Mexico
Multimedia presentation relates the "social-realist" painting, architecture, and mural work of Diego Rivera, Jose Clement Orozco, and David Alfaro Siqueiros to the symphonic and chamber music of Silvestre Revueltas and Carlos Chavez, as together they forged a vivid and politically-charged artistic identity for the new Republic in the 1920s and '30s, using folk elements and consciously non-European techniques.

Example: Workshop offerings

4

Expanding
Your Impact:
Making Recordings

Jenny, a talented pianist and master's degree candidate, stops by to ask a question. She is recording a few pieces to submit with her application for a major competition. She also has a degree recital this spring that she will have professionally recorded. Jenny asks, "How can I get more use out of these recordings?"

Jenny's housemate is Amy, a terrific jazz vocalist with her own band. Amy has been gigging steadily throughout her student years. She uses her demo and promo materials when contacting club managers and festival organizers. She wants to do a full-length album and "shop it around" to labels. Amy asks, "How can I get a record contract?"

Bob stops by and proudly hands me a copy of his new CD, asking me to listen to it when I have a chance. With his brass quintet last year he played twenty concerts plus lots of in-school and library educational performances. "Now that the album is done," Bob says, "I want to know how to promote it online, get it reviewed, and use it to get more gigs. Any ideas?"

These are composites of many conversations I've had with musicians over the years. This chapter is about unpacking answers to questions about recordings.

Emerging musicians often lack information and perspective on the recording industry. Consequently, the path to a successful recording project can be strewn with unforeseen roadblocks. Many musicians rush in to recording projects without considering key questions. They may spend thousands of dollars making a recording that ends up in boxes, collecting dust in a closet. Don't let this happen to you.

Consider realistically what a CD can and cannot do for your career at this point. Like any endeavor, a recording is an investment of time, energy, and money. As a rule of thumb, it's best to ask questions and do research *before* you invest. Why do you want to record now? What should you record? Who is your audience? What do you plan to do with the recording? What will you need to spend? This chapter is designed to help you evaluate your options by exploring the *why, what, how,* and *how much* of recordings.

Essential to promo kits, recordings are used in booking performances, for prescreening in auditions, and in applications for competitions, music schools, and festivals. They are also typically required for grant applications and college teaching jobs. Musicians make their CDs and DVDs available for purchase at their performances, on their websites, via online retail sites, and in a few remaining retail stores. For most musicians, though, recordings are far more effective and valuable as promotional tools than as a significant source of income.

Why Record? ◆

For most musicians, the real reason to record is to express oneself—to create something new. But before launching into a recording project, think *specifically* what you want to achieve. Be clear about your purpose and your expectations. Ask yourself, do you want to:

- Use your recording for applications and auditions?
- Use it as a demo for booking performances?
- Use it in contacting the media, for possible reviews or articles?

- Document your original compositions?
- Sell the recording at performances?
- Sell it online?
- Sell the recording on consignment at local shops?

Clarifying your purpose and goals is an important first step in any large project. But no matter what your reasons are, you'll make better decisions with a basic understanding of the recording industry.

The Recording Industry and You ◆

Forty years ago, well-established artists and major orchestras had long-standing recording contracts with major labels. These labels would also regularly scout for younger talent. In those days, there was a larger audience for both classical and jazz, and consequently, major labels invested in more artists and released more recordings.

Back then, careers were built and balanced on a "three-legged stool" of recordings, radio, and touring. Each leg was necessary to support the whole career. The record labels invested money in promoting their new releases on radio, in stores, and through their artists' touring. In the 1950s and '60s, there were enough radio stations, concert series, and music critics to support this system. Ultimately, it made good business sense because there was a ready audience interested in this music. The *New York Times* reports that in the early 1960s, classical music still accounted for 33 percent of all record sales in the United States. Today, according to the Recording Industry Association of America, classical and jazz record sales each account for about 3 percent of all sales.

Today, file sharing and technology have made it easier than ever to record and distribute music. Because everyone can and does record, the market is flooded with recordings. The challenge lies in cutting through the noise to gain media attention and develop a fan base. Changes in radio technology and licensing have resulted in fewer opportunities for terrestrial radio play to reach broad audiences for classical and jazz music. And there is no longer a clear connection between record label support and touring. It is no longer a streamlined system; the three-legged stool has become quite wobbly.

The Lowdown on Record Labels

Major Labels

The three biggest labels, as of this writing, are Warner Music Group, Sony BMG, and Universal Music Group. These are huge, multinational media conglomerates, and recordings make up just a portion of their business dealings. These companies put significant amounts of money into marketing a small set of superstar musicians of all genres, but generally ones with immediate name recognition. These are people like Yo-Yo Ma and Renée Fleming in the classical arena and Wynton Marsalis and Diana Krall in jazz. A recording project for one of these celebrity artists can cost hundreds of thousands of dollars. The blockbuster-style promotion campaigns for these artists' albums can include full-page newspaper and magazine ads, as well as billboards, television, and radio ads.

Indie Labels

For the majority of other musicians, working with a record label means working with one of several thousand indie (independent) labels. Unlike the majors, most indie labels specialize in one or more specific genre (such as classical, folk, jazz, or world). Indie labels vary in size from one-person operations to large, competitive companies. Some well-known, large classical indie labels are Naxos, Harmonia Mundi, Hyperion, and Chandos. Well-known jazz indie labels include Thirsty Ear, Concord Jazz, the Hat, and Palmetto. And there are thousands of smaller indie labels as well. Though promotional budgets for indie releases are often quite modest in comparison to those of the major labels, indie releases are also typically marketed more strategically to niche audiences.

How a Label Evaluates a Project

If you're hoping to release an album with an independent label, you need to do your research. Find out which labels record emerging artists. Check the websites for these labels, and read about their releases and the artists. Are you at a similar career stage? Indie labels often have information on their site about how to contact them with possible recording projects. Get advice and recommendations from mentors with experience in the recording industry. If you don't have such contacts, check with your school's alumni association and start networking!

If a label decides that you have a *marketable* product and project, you might be offered a contract. You may not be used to thinking of your artistry—or your music—as a product. But a record contract is a business deal. The label has to determine if there's an audience for your album—if it has a chance at making decent sales. Signing a musician to a contract is a business investment; the record label is a business and, as such, needs to make a profit in order to *stay* in business.

Picture this: an emerging, talented classical artist—with no name recognition and not much performing experience—has a project to record standard repertoire (Bach, Beethoven, Brahms). There are already six well-known recordings available of the same repertoire by very established artists, past and present. So why should any label be interested in this young artist's project?

Now picture this alternate scenario: an emerging artist has a recording project of new works by a composer who has captured media attention, or perhaps a project to record undiscovered gems by an historic composer. In this case, the project may be of interest to a particular niche audience and niche indie label. Different labels have different priorities. Do your homework, and find out what kinds of projects various labels are interested in.

For example, the Naxos label is well known for its extensive catalog of composer series recordings. Started as a budget line of high quality CDs, Naxos now has a huge catalog with many series, including ones dedicated specifically to guitar, organ, opera, historic performances, contemporary classical, and jazz. Naxos has frequently signed emerging artists to record the works of specific composers.

Another label, New World Records is a nonprofit label dedicated to the proliferation of both new and neglected treasures of American music: classical, jazz, traditional, and folk. The label's web site, http://www.newworldrecords .org, has proposal guidelines for submitting potential recording projects.

In general, labels look for projects with a compelling *hook* or *concept*. The project needs to be of interest to a niche audience, and it needs to have the potential to attract media attention. Recording project concepts can range from "New American Works for Solo Clarinet," to "The Mozart Effect: Smart Baby Lullabies," or "Guillaume de Machaut: Motets." The potential market for the smart baby album is much larger than the other two, but there probably is a niche audience for each of the other project ideas, depending on the fan base of the performers and their promotion plan.

Do You Really Want a Recording Contract?

Caution: "getting signed" is not all it's cracked up to be. With the majority of record label contracts, it is the *musician* who pays for the recording and manufacturing of the album and who hires a publicist to promote it. The label handles the manufacturing, some of the promotion, and the distribution. In working with a label, musicians relinquish control over most of their project, including the budget, choice of recording engineer and producer, promotional campaign, and the bulk of any profits. What do musicians get in return? They get whatever cachet comes from releasing an album under the label's name and whatever assistance the label can offer in terms of distribution and marketing.

Here's how the money works: until *all* of the costs of the manufacturing and production of the album is made back in sales (recouped), you, the musician, won't make a dime. And when you do finally make a profit, it's a small percentage of each album's purchase price. If sales are good, you may recoup the money you originally invested, and break even—otherwise you will take a loss.

The effort and money a label puts into marketing your album depends on the contract, the project, and the label. In some cases, if a tour was part of the signing deal, then the money made from performing also goes to the label. And there are cases of musicians recording an album for a label and the label deciding not to release it. So before signing *any* contract, have it thoroughly checked out by an experienced entertainment lawyer. For help finding such a person, consult the Volunteer Lawyers for the Arts; the VLA has local chapters nationwide (http://www.vlany.org).

The Entrepreneurial Solution ◆

The recording industry has undergone massive changes in the past ten years. Technological advances have upended the old business model. Widespread downloading and sharing of music files has left record labels with dwindling profits and musicians with a fraction of their earnings. Labels have merged or gone out of business. Record stores have become obsolete. And as audiences have gravitated to other niche genres, classical and jazz radio programming has become scarce.

On the positive side, technology has also made it easy and inexpensive for musicians to record, promote, and distribute their own music. The model of an independent, entrepreneurial, and successful musician is quickly becoming the norm. Today, musicians are taking matters into their own hands and going the do-it-yourself route. Musicians who release their own recordings have some specific advantages: they control the project, artistically and financially, and keep more of the profits, eliminating the need for the middleman.

There are now companies to help with the production, marketing, and distribution of your music. Digital retailers, through which you can sell your tracks and albums, include CDBaby, iTunes, Nimbit, Amazon, and Magnatune. These services offer far more favorable rates than the old-school models.

Many musicians have started their own labels or formed cooperatives with other musicians to start a label. Violinist Gil Shaham's contract with Deutsche Grammophon was cancelled after ten years and more than fifteen albums, so he started his own label, Canary. Cellist David Finckel, of the Emerson Quartet, and his wife, pianist Wu Han, started their own label, ArtistLed, in 1997. Since then they have recorded and produced thirteen albums, which they market online at http://www.artistled.com. Flautist Ransom Wilson's label, Image Recordings, has released CDs by violinist Joseph Silverstein and pianist Christopher O'Riley. GM Recordings, founded by composer Gunther Schuller, focuses on jazz, classical, and multigenre works. Other artist-run labels include composer John Zorn's Tzadik label, Bang on a Can's Cantaloupe Music, violinist Paul Zukofsky's CP2, pianist Santiago Rodriguez's Elan Records, and cellist Matt Haimovitz's Oxingale records. Since 2003, the Borromeo String Quartet has made recordings of their live performances available through their Living Archive Project (http://www.livingarchive.org).

Legally Yours: Copyright Issues ◆

Whether you start your own label or simply record a demo, you need to consider some essential legal issues. You want to avoid recording anything you might not legally be able to release.

Copyright is essentially about authorship of original work. Copyright law provides that the creator of a work owns the rights to it. Technically, copyright is established automatically when a musical work is created and established in a *tangible* form, such as in a recording, score, or lead sheet format. Therefore, melodies and improvisations (as well as ideas) that are not in a fixed or tangible form (written down or recorded) are *not* copyrightable.

Every musical recording inherently contains two separate and distinct copyrights. There is the copyright for the musical composition (the piece itself, no matter who performs or records it), and then there is the copyright for the sound recording (a particular performance fixed in tangible form). This means that if you write a song, you own the copyright for the musical composition. If you are the performer who records someone else's song, you own the copyright for the sound recording (as distinct from the composition). And if you perform and record your own song, you own *both* copyrights.

Copyright is designed to help protect your work from unauthorized use by others. To illustrate, think about how you might feel if you found your recording being used—without your permission and without your being compensated—to sell a product on television. Copyright law is set up to help ensure that creators of original work receive proper credit and due compensation.

Copyright is actually a bundle of rights. As the owner of a copyright, you have the exclusive rights to do any of the following:

Make copies of your work (to publish, photocopy, or create multiple recordings)

Distribute copies of the work (such as selling sheet music or recordings)

Perform the work (the specifics on performance licensing is detailed in chapter 6)

Display the work publicly (applies to visual displays of scores)
Make derivative works (such as arrangements and transcriptions)

Each of these rights is distinct and may be administered separately. This means that as the copyright owner, you can *license* another person or entity to use one or more of these rights, such as the right to create an arrangement of your composition or to use your recording in a TV commercial.

Although copyright is established automatically with the creation of a work, *proof* of copyright is established by registering with the Library of Congress Copyright Office. The process to secure your copyright registration is simple. Go to the U.S. Copyright Office website (http://www.copyright.gov) and download Form CO with its instructions. Note: the Copyright Office has done away with the method of offering different forms, like "SR" for sound recordings; Form CO is the form for all types of works, and you note which type of work predominates. As of this writing, you can pay $35 online or $50 by mail to register the copyright.

Along with payment, you need to send the properly completed application form and two copies of your recording or score. There are helpful FAQs and downloadable circulars on the copyright office website. Circulars include updates on both Copyright Office procedure and the law; if you haven't registered a work in more than a few months, it is good to reread the relevant circular to make sure nothing significant has changed.

You may have heard of the "poor man's" copyright protection method. This involves sending yourself a copy of your album or your original score by registered mail through the U.S. Postal Service and keeping the sealed postmarked envelope as dated proof of authorship. This method is *not* recommended. Should the copyright be contested and legal action be pursued, an officially registered copyright is authoritative evidence. More significantly, registration is a prerequisite for gaining access to the court system to enforce your copyright; it also entitles a victor to statutory damages and attorneys' fees.

Licensing Issues ◆

Think of the Golden Rule. Just as you would want others to respect your copyright and refrain from unlawful use of your recording, so should you take pains to respect composers' copyrights. To record a copyrighted work, you need to obtain a *mechanical license* from the copyright holder, usually the publisher or composer. A mechanical license allows for the manufacture and distribution of a recording of a work. You need a license to record copyrighted works whether or not you intend to sell the recording.

However, you do *not* need a mechanical license if the copyright on the work has expired. In most cases, works published in the United States before

1923 are considered "in the public domain" and may be freely recorded, adapted, sampled, or arranged. In most cases, works published after 1922 but before 1978 are protected for ninety-five years from the date of publication. As of this writing, copyright protection for works composed on or after January 1, 1978, generally lasts the life of the composer plus seventy years. This is just the bare outline of very complicated legislation, so you need to check the copyright status of any particular work you plan to record (or to arrange, sample, or perform).

If you plan to record a work that has as yet never been recorded, then you negotiate the license directly with the copyright holder (the composer or the publisher) and confirm your agreement with a written contract that both parties sign. This is usually not a big hurdle. Many composers are enthusiastic to have their compositions recorded and will gladly grant you their permission. If you are not already in contact with the composers whose works you wish to record, find their contact info online, through their publisher, or through one of the performing rights organizations (PROs). In the United States, these are BMI (Broadcast Music, Inc.), ASCAP (American Society of Composers, Authors, and Publishers), and SESAC (Society of European Stage Authors and Composers). The vast majority of U.S. composers are registered with either BMI or ASCAP (you can register with only one). Classical composers seem to gravitate more toward ASCAP, whereas the majority of jazz composers are with BMI. The staff members at these organizations are very helpful. They're advocates for new music and they want you to perform it, so don't hesitate to call or e-mail with questions, but note that there are also very helpful FAQs on their websites.

If a work has already been recorded, the process to license subsequent recordings is more straightforward. For these, you obtain a *compulsory mechanical license*. The cost for the license is set by Congress, and the fees are dependent on the length of the work, the number of copies of the recording planned, and the intended online use. The administrating organization for mechanical licenses is the Harry Fox Agency (HFA). For current rates, see http://www.harryfox.com. If you would like to make fewer than 2,500 copies of your recording as either physical products (CDs, cassettes, or vinyl) or permanent digital downloads, you can request licenses at the HFA site under "Songfile." Keep in mind that CD manufacturers require proof of mechanical licenses before they will begin work on a client's recording, so it's essential that you obtain the licenses *before* you record. For more details, see the FAQ page on the HFA website.

Creative Commons

In recent years, digital technology has made copyright law tremendously complicated. Many composers and musicians these days are experimenting with sampling and mashups, using excerpts of other musicians' recordings to create sound collages, new works, and parodies. Traditional copyright does not allow for this creative experimental use of work to be done without permissions and licensing. Many musicians find the standard copyright laws too restrictive. The organization Creative Commons provides musicians a range of alternatives.

Creative Commons (CC) licensing enables works to freely circulate on a legal basis while still preserving the owner's copyright. CC licensing allows for legal downloading and file sharing for creative use of original work. Many pop and rock musicians give their music away online for free or on a "pay what you will" basis. The idea is to cultivate a sense of community, build fan loyalty, and allow for co-creative efforts. (See http://www.creativecommons.org.)

Creative Partnering with Your Fans

Brooklyn-based singer-songwriter Jonathan Coulton (http://www.jonathan coulton.com) is an enthusiastic supporter of Creative Commons. He has built a large fan base for his live shows and recordings. His successful independent online music business model was profiled in a 2007 *New York Times* piece, "Sex, Drugs and Updating Your Blog."[1] Coulton's example is indicative of the new generation and its relationship with technology, fans, and the industry. He sells his recordings on his own websites but also through CDBaby, which places the recordings on the sites of many online retailers (iTunes, Rhapsody, Amazon, Napster, and more).

Coulton also posts free podcasts and downloads of his music on his website. He explains why on his site's FAQ page: "I give away music because I want to make music, and I can't make music unless I make money, and I won't make money unless I get heard, and I won't get heard unless I give away music." He releases all his music under an Attribution/Non-Commercial Creative Commons license, which allows fans to use his music for any nonprofit purpose provided they credit him and his website. His fans have made videos using his songs and Flickr slide shows using Creative Commons photographs to accompany Coulton's music. With Creative Commons licensing, Jonathan allows and encourages fans to co-create and collaborate. This helps him build and cultivate his fan base for his live shows and tours.

Whether you use standard copyright or Creative Commons licensing, make sure you include the appropriate notice on your album cover and disc label. There are two standard copyright notices to include with recordings. One covers the sound performances on the recording, indicated by a Ⓟ (for phonorecord), followed by the year the copyright was established and the name of the copyright owner (usually the label). The other copyright notice covers the text and artwork on your album, indicated by ©, followed by the year the copyright was established. More flexible legal language may follow, such as "All rights reserved. Unauthorized duplication is a violation of applicable laws" or "All rights reserved. Unauthorized copying, reproduction, hiring, lending, public performance and broadcasting prohibited." See the albums in your collection for examples of this language. Also be sure to credit the composer and any other copyright holders whose work is incorporated into the album.

Creative Commons licensing is represented with ⓒⓒ. Make sure that if using this you include the appropriate language for the version of the Creative Commons license you have chosen.

Now, with a basic overview of copyright and licensing, the next question is, what repertoire will you choose to record?

What to Record ◆

Musicians need recordings for different reasons at various career stages, but the most basic recording a musician needs is a demo. A brief ten- to twenty-minute demonstration, or *demo*, recording showcases a musician's abilities and repertoire. You can select three or four contrasting short works or movements to highlight your strengths and the range of your repertoire and skills. The order of your selections should make an interesting contrast of mood, tempo, and texture.

The first work on your demo should be your best. Competition judges and concert presenters simply do not have time to listen to everything they receive. You really have only the first twenty seconds of a recording to create a great impression and grab your listeners' attention so that they want to hear more.

▼

Chicago-based clarinetist and composer James Falzone made his first full-length CD using the edited recording of his master's degree recital, a program of his original compositions. James's music combines elements of jazz, world, and classical; his works include both scored and improvised material. Although James sells recordings at his performances, his goal in making the CD was not to make money. It was an investment in his future career.

Cost-wise, for a professional-quality recording, James got off easy; there was no studio time involved, because it was an edited recording of a live performance. He did not pay his collaborating musicians (as friends, they played his recital as a favor, and he gave them gifts and a great dinner). James paid $80 per hour for the editing. The bulk of his budget went to professional artwork and printing, manufacturing, and packaging.

James's budget was about $3,500. If this seems high, keep in mind that for a professional-quality album, independent musicians often spend $6,000–$10,000. Can recordings be made for much less? Yes, but if you want *professional quality*— sound, artwork, liner notes, packaging, promotion, and marketing—you should expect to invest real money.

For James's investment of $3,500, what did he gain? James initially sent out about 100 CDs as promos, and after that, 1 or 2 every month. He sells between 5 and 20 albums at each of his performances. But the real payoff has been in opportunities and connections. James says, "So many people have heard my music—people who would not otherwise. The CD got radio play in Massachusetts, Vermont, and Illinois, and this led to more gigs. I also sent the CD when I applied for several teaching jobs [and he landed them] and it gave me a degree of prestige at gigs because I had a product to sell."

Choosing Repertoire: Four Essential Questions

1. What repertoire do you have ready to record that is polished and at a professional level? Talk with colleagues and mentors: get honest feedback.
2. Does this repertoire demonstrate your own individual "voice"? You should *not* sound like an imitation of any teacher or favorite recording.
3. Is the repertoire appropriate for your demo needs? If intended for a competition, does your repertoire meet the requirements? If your demo is to be used for booking concerts, is the repertoire representative of what you plan to perform in coming seasons?
4. Is the work you plan to record under copyright protection? If so, you'll need to obtain a mechanical license in order to legally record it.

Recordings of live performances can be used effectively as demos. Concert series presenters prefer live recordings, and these are often required for competitions and grant applications. Live recordings have an adrenaline edge, an electricity that is absent from studio recordings. When using live performances as demos, edit out all tuning and adjusting of chairs. The applause should be edited to fade in and out briefly between works, and the breaks between movements can be shortened as needed.

Learn the Lingo: Glossary of Basic Recording Terms

DAT: Digital audiotape. DAT recorders work by translating sound digitally into the binary language of numbers: zeros and ones.

Distributor: Company that distributes recordings to retail outlets. Major labels have their own distribution companies. There are independent distributors as well, some large national ones and other smaller regional companies.

Engineer: The skilled professional who transfers your live performance to tape. Recording engineers choose the appropriate equipment, place mics, check levels and balance, and may do mixing and editing.

Manufacturer: Company that produces CDs from a master recording; it may also print and assemble the graphics, and package, shrink-wrap, and ship CDs to you (or a distributor). Of course you can burn your own CDs, but if you need them in quantity, use a manufacturer such as Disc Makers.

Master: The first generation of your recording, the *original* from which duplicates are made. Note: send out only copies, never your master!

Mastering: The final process after editing to complete a professional-quality recording. Mastering should be done only by an experienced professional, usually someone hired specifically just for this step. The mastering engineer runs the tape through multiple processors to adjust the dynamic range, equalize or add reverberation, and create consistency from one cut to the next, conforming to the standards for radio broadcasting and professional labels.

Mixing: The blending of recorded tracks to perfect balance and volume; used for multitrack recording sessions (in which more than two stereo mics are being used).

Producer: Person who helps oversee the recording session, listening carefully to catch whatever the performers may miss. Producers mark scores, help decide what *takes* to use and what needs to be rerecorded. A producer can save you precious and expensive studio time. Your producer should be a trusted colleague or mentor, someone who knows your playing or singing well.

Retailers: Companies that sell recordings. The top-selling music retailers (as of 2008, according to Businessweek.com) were iTunes, Wal-Mart, Best Buy, Amazon, and Target. Note that CDBaby partnerships allow for a musician's albums to also be available on iTunes, Rhapsody, Amazon, and many other partner services. And in your immediate vicinity, there may be independent stores interested in selling local artists' CDs on consignment.

▲

Choosing an Engineer

If you want a professional-quality recording, hire an experienced professional engineer. Get recommendations from colleagues and mentors. Music schools have recording engineers on staff who may freelance or give you referrals. You want someone experienced and knowledgeable about the type of music you plan to record. Ask to hear samples of your prospective engineer's work. Find out exactly what is included in the engineer's hourly rate: setup, editing, and any extra charges for equipment rental. Make sure you discuss with your engineer the type of sound you want *before* you get to the recording session. You might even provide your engineer with one or two examples of CDs with the recorded sound you want (the amount of "room" sound, reverberation, and sense of immediacy).

How and *Where* to Record ◆

Once you have determined what to record and why, next comes *how*. Whether you plan to record a twenty-minute demo or a full-length album, you have three options:

1. Record in a professional studio.
2. Hire an engineer to record "on location."
3. Rent or borrow the equipment and do it yourself.

These are all good options. What matters is which one best fits your budget, timeline, and project.

Recording in a Studio

If you choose to record in a studio, keep in mind that rates vary depending on the studio's equipment, location, and its local competition. Most studios do not provide concert-quality grand pianos; if you need one, you will face fewer choices and higher fees. In the Boston area, the hourly rates, as of this writing, range from $50 to $200 per hour. When choosing a studio, get references from trusted colleagues. Ask to hear samples of demos or any commercial releases. You may also want to visit or tour a prospective studio to make sure you'll be comfortable recording there. Studios typically offer various package deals with a certain number of recording hours, an engineer, and editing. Compare studio offerings carefully.

Recording on Location

The second option to consider is recording on location, most often in a performance venue. This is generally how classical recordings are done, to take advantage of the acoustics of a particular hall or to use a specific piano. In Boston, New England Conservatory's Jordan Hall is used extensively for solo and chamber music recordings (Yo-Yo Ma records there).

Do some research to find where musicians in your area record. If you have a church job or a teaching gig, you may be able to use a great space for free or at a discounted price. Be careful about the reverberation in the location. Look for an ambient (or room) sound that's not too "boomy," but warm and cushioned. When scouting potential sites, bring along a personal recorder, and try the space out, recording several phrases to get a sense of the acoustics.

Keep in mind that an inexpensive venue with great acoustics may not be a bargain if there is outside traffic or indoor noise (such as heating or ventilation) that interferes with the recording. For these reasons, some churches with superb acoustics can host recording sessions only in the spring and summer months between the hours of midnight and 4:00 A.M.

Do It Yourself

The third recording option is the DIY route. You can do it all yourself or enlist a friend with recording experience and equipment to help. If you have access to a space with good acoustics, you might be able to record with rented or borrowed equipment at minimal cost. As a graduate student, I recorded demos at SUNY Stony Brook in the school's concert hall and hired a fellow student as engineer. If you have the right equipment and know how to use it, almost any good acoustic space will work. If you need a piano, your choices are limited; if not, you have far more options. And yes, good demo recordings have been made in stairways and even in bathrooms.

At the start of your session, be sure to check levels and balance to avoid distortion. During playback, if you sound distant and you hear too much room sound or reverb, then place the microphones closer. Conversely, if the sound is too immediate and dry, the microphone is too close.

▼

How to Avoid "Studio Shock"

Musicians new to recording sessions may be surprised or thrown off guard when they first hear their sound played back. There is often a difference between what we hear while we perform and what the recording equipment picks up. To avoid this shock, record yourself regularly. My advice is to purchase a portable mini recorder and use it every day in the practice room.

Professional percussionist Mark Worgaftik says that it was when he started recording himself regularly, as a grad student at Juilliard, that he really started to make substantial improvements in his playing. Mark thinks music students should be required to record practice sessions and rehearsals. Recording yourself helps you educate your ear.

▲

Preparation for the Recording Session

Come to your recording session absolutely prepared. Don't waste expensive recording time with rehearsing. Many people find it helps to memorize the repertoire they plan to record. This allows them to concentrate better and listen more carefully. If you plan to read from music, rearrange any page turns so that they can be done as silently as possible. Or you may need to bring a friend to turn pages.

Before your session, record run-throughs of entire movements using your own recording equipment. Listen to the playbacks for technical or interpretive points and for extraneous noise. If you have a habit of tapping your foot or making other sounds as you perform, now is the time to quit. Notwithstanding Glenn Gould, Keith Jarrett, and Pablo Casals, no one wants to hear musicians hum and groan. Be careful of your breathing and any noisy body movements before and after each take—clean beginnings and endings are important.

If you plan to record in a studio, your practice recording sessions are best done in a dry or "dead" space, such as a carpeted room with a low ceiling. Get accustomed to how you sound in a nonreverberant space.

If you go the do-it-yourself route, practice using the equipment in advance of your session. Try recording selections off the radio or a CD to make sure you can properly set the recording volume level.

What to Bring to Your Recording Session

- ❏ Two extra copies of the sheet music (scores for ensemble works). These are for your producer and engineer to make notes in; the scores you bring should be marked with measure numbers to save expensive recording time when you need to refer to specific phrases.
- ❏ Tuning fork or tuner.
- ❏ Metronome—to check the tempi of any repeated takes.
- ❏ Extra strings, reeds, valve oil, and any basic instrument repair equipment: expect the unexpected.
- ❏ Folding wire stand(s)—these do not block sound the way the solid metal ones do.
- ❏ Music stand lights: depending on the space, extra lighting may be necessary.
- ❏ Quick snack food in case your energy sags (bananas and power bars are good for this).
- ❏ Water: keep yourself hydrated.
- ❏ Layers: light weight shirts or sweaters so that you can adjust your comfort to the recording location temperature
- ❏ Your patience and sense of humor: you will need both!

Tips for Making the Session Run Smoothly

Warm up before your session, but not too much. Discuss (again) with your engineer the type of sound you want in the recording. At the start of your session, record a few passages to check for balance and level. Listen to these brief playbacks and then re-check periodically during the recording session.

Plan the order of what you want to record, with an estimated time allotment for each piece or movement, and keep to your schedule. Some musicians find it best to record the most difficult works first, when they are fresh and have the most energy. Others find that starting with an easier movement or work is best because it establishes a level of comfort and confidence.

In general, if you have not "nailed" a passage, section, or movement after three takes, you most likely will not get it in that session. If you have recorded a passage twice without getting it, take a short break or record something else and come back to it later. Don't force it.

How much recording time do you need? Setup time to check equipment, arrange the mic placements, and establishing levels can take—depending on the group—up to an hour. The ratio of recording time to finished product is generally 4 to 1. To make a fifteen-minute demo can easily take over two hours. Be realistic: schedule enough time.

During the session, *slate* all the takes, announcing into the mic at the beginning of each recorded selection the name of the specific work or movement and the take number. For example, "Schubert E^b Trio, first movement, take two." This makes for easier editing afterward. Your producer can help by writing comments, noting which takes and segments are the most promising, but you can do the same, so keep a notepad nearby.

Once the recording session is completed, the next step is editing. Wait a day or two before listening to all the takes. Give yourself (and your inner critic) a rest so that you can listen more objectively. You will need to decide which takes to use whole and which need edits. Depending on the equipment and expertise of your engineer, some performance glitches can be fixed with editing. It can be relatively simple to splice together portions of two takes, depending on a number of factors, so ask your engineer. Come prepared to your editing session with a list of which takes and sections you want to use so that you don't waste expensive time during the session.

If you plan to use the recording for more than demo purposes, the final editing step is mastering. This is necessary for a polished, professional-quality sound, as for commercial releases and necessary for radio broadcast use. Mastering is a separate step done by a specialist with particular equipment and expertise. Ask for recommendations.

Whether you make a quick demo for a competition or a full-length album to sell at performances, there is more to it than simply recording the repertoire. There's a range of issues to consider if you want to make your recording available in physical form.

The reason physical CDs persist is that fans still want to purchase something tangible, a souvenir of sorts, when they attend live concerts. The format may change, but having something physical that includes graphics and written information about the music, the performers, and composers is still compelling for audiences worldwide.

Artwork and Graphics ◆

The first impression a recording makes is often *visual*. You *see* the cover design of an album online first, before you hear it, and what you see may affect whether or not you decide to click through, listen, or buy. The same is true at concerts: we peruse albums prior to buying them. If someone hands you a demo recording, you look before you listen. Graphics have an immediate impact and make a statement about the value of your music and your professionalism.

Your cover design should attract attention and draw viewers' interest to the album. If no one feels compelled to look closely at your CD, why would they listen to it? Your cover art should pique the viewer's interest and communicate a real sense of your music: its energy, mood, period, or genre. Whether you use a simple jacket envelope or a plastic jewel case with liner notes, you need to consider the impact of the visuals.

▼
_____

How Graphic-Savvy Are You?

Examine your own albums. You probably have a wide range of music of varying genres. Most likely you have releases from both major and indie labels, along with self-produced albums. Similar to the "kitchen table test" in the previous chapter, here you can use the floor. Choose a random sampling of your physical albums, about thirty, and spread them out flat on the floor so you can sit back and take a look at the covers as a group. Imagine that you are browsing a display table. Which covers most attract your attention? Which are you most drawn to? Why? Is it the colors, the artwork, an interesting photo, the typeface, or graphics? Noticing what attracts your attention and why is great preparation for making smart choices about your own artwork.
_____ ▲

If you're making a recording purely for your own satisfaction, then by all means choose your favorite colors, artwork, and typography. You have no one to please but yourself. However, if you plan to use your recording to build an audience and advance your career, then you need to consider more than your own personal preferences. The choices of album graphics contribute to your image. More than just packaging, CD graphics make a statement about you, your professionalism, and your music.

Use a professional graphic designer with album cover experience. Why hire a pro? Professional designers have years of computer skills and experience using specific design programs. They use these to create the proper composites, formats, and specifications necessary for printing album covers. An experienced graphic designer will save you headaches and dollars when dealing with printers and your manufacturing company.

However, you may be able to save money by hiring a design student. For graphic designer referrals, ask everyone in your network. Ask at any recording studios or smaller indie labels in your area. Make sure you see examples of several artists' previous album covers before hiring anyone.

"Have a concept idea for your artwork and be able to articulate this to your graphic designer," says Israeli jazz pianist Eyran Katsenelenbogen. "But also let them give their input and be open to their ideas. After all, you are a musician, while your designer has the necessary visual skills and training." Your designer can also help you find a range of choices for the artwork to fit your concept, as well as take care of any necessary licensing for use of the artwork for the cover.

CD manufacturing companies offer various packages that often include design, layout, jewel boxes, bar code, assembly, and shrink-wrapping. Be a savvy consumer: get recommendations and compare package deals at several companies. The graphic design services included in these package deals are usually a limited set of formulaic design templates. My advice is to get input from a pro: the finished result should be an album cover you'll still be proud to look at five or ten years from now.

What Info Should Be Included with a Recording?

Provide the following recording information in both physical liner notes and as a download on your website:

- ❏ Composer names and publishing information for each work. To research these details, use Harry Fox, ASCAP, or BMI. Look at major label recordings for examples of how to present this, and be consistent.
- ❏ Titles and movements (include year of composition if a work is new or obscure).
- ❏ Timings of each track in minutes and seconds, plus the total timing of the album.
- ❏ Names of all performers and their instruments or voice types.
- ❏ Bios of performers.
- ❏ Program notes about the works and composers.
- ❏ Texts and translations, if applicable.
- ❏ Name of label (if you have signed with a label or if you create your own).

❏ Contact information: your website URL, your label's, and/or your manager's. For booking performances and building an audience, this is essential.
❏ Copyright notices.
❏ Credits for the recording engineer, recording location or studio, photographer, graphic designer, and any reproduced artwork (including title, artist, and permission notice).
❏ Thank-yous and acknowledgements of contributors, funders, family, and so forth.

Program notes and bios should be well written: engaging and informative. They should be appropriate for a non-musician reader; leave out technical terms and jargon. Once you have written your draft text, have a professional writer edit it. A music publicist or journalist may be your best bet. Ask any public relations staff at local arts organizations for referrals. For ideas on how to engage a non-musician audience, see chapter 6; for ideas on bios, chapter 3.

▼ ──────────────────────────────────────

Pianist Catherine P. made her first CD using an edited version of one of her degree recitals. She wrote about this fact in her liner notes and later regretted it. She found that some people, when they read the liner notes, prejudged the performance as "student" level, and viewed the album as less than professional quality. Catherine's advice: "If you use a degree recital recording to make a CD, keep the circumstances of the performance to yourself! Simply state the performance occurred at XYZ University or Conservatory and never mind the why."

────────────────────────────────────── ▲

On the Disc Itself

Because discs and cases or envelopes inevitably become separated, you need to repeat the most crucial identifying information on the disc itself, including the following:

❏ Title of album
❏ Name of ensemble or soloist
❏ Contact info (website URL is sufficient)
❏ Titles of works and movements and their track numbers
❏ Copyright notices
❏ Name of label (including your own)

Bar Codes

If you want to sell your album through any retailer (online or otherwise), you must obtain a universal product code (UPC), otherwise known as a bar code. A series of vertical lines representing a unique twelve-digit number, a bar code identifies the company offering the product (a label or a CD manufacturer) and the particular product. Assigned by the Uniform Code Council, Inc. (http://www.uc-council.org), bar codes allow retailers to track sales and merchandise. They make it possible to scan the CD, digitally recording the sales transaction. As of this writing, it costs $750 to obtain a bar code. However, through CDBaby and some CD manufacturers, you can arrange for a barcode that will cost only about $20. Be sure to check exactly what any package deal includes. The bar code should be printed on the back cover jewel case insert (make sure your graphic designer knows how to handle this). It is also possible to affix bar code stickers (available through CD manufacturers) on top of the recording's polywrap after the CD is completed, but it's far easier to incorporate it into the original design and printing.

With these basic recording issues mapped out, the next big topic to tackle is money. How will you fund your recording project?

How Much? Financing Your Recording ◆

What does it cost to make a recording? It may be next to nothing if you record using your own equipment and simply upload your recording to your website or social networking platform. At the other extreme, recording budgets can run to hundreds of thousands of dollars (what major labels spend on recordings with full orchestras). To produce a *professional-quality* CD, independent musicians often spend $6,000–$10,000 to record, edit, master, manufacture, and promote an album. Your costs will depend on where and how you do the recording, your collaborators, and your choices about manufacturing, packaging, and promotion.

If you know that you need to raise part or all of the money for your recording, the first step is to find out how much the project will actually cost. You need to write a budget. A project budget is simply a plan for handling finances. It has two parts: *expenses* are the itemized costs; and *resources* are the itemized assets, the existing available resources. Budgets help people think through complex projects so they can make informed decisions.

First, write a list of *all* your anticipated expenses. Leave nothing out; nobody likes encountering unforeseen costs. You may need referrals and price quotes for specific items, such as recording engineers, mastering, disc manufacturing, photographers, or graphic designers. Ask friends and colleagues; call local recording studios for prices, and call your local music school's audio department for recommended freelance engineers. Be a savvy consumer: get *several* price quotes from recommended professionals for each item in your budget.

Use the budget outline below as a template, writing in all your possible expenses and all the resources you plan to commit to the project. With expenses itemized in the left-hand column and resources in the right, the goal is to get the two sides to balance each other. This is where the term bottom line comes from: the bottom line totals should be equal, so that your expenses do not exceed your resources. However, if your resources do not cover your anticipated expenses, then read on. The next section focuses on creative ways to finance your recording project.

▼

Write Your Budget

Expenses	Resources
Collaborating musicians:	Savings:
Studio costs:	Loans:
Hall rental:	Grants:
Recording engineer:	Gifts:
Producer:	Other:
Editing:	
Mastering:	
Piano tuning:	
Graphic design:	
Photography:	
Liner notes editor:	
Copyright registration:	
Licensing fees:	
Bar code registration:	
Artwork printing:	

Promotional Expenses
Press materials/mailings:
Promo material printing/assembly:
Mailing to radio/media:
Follow-up phone costs:
Booking fee(s) associated with release concerts:
CD release flyers/invitations:
Online retail distribution fees:

Total:	Total:

▲

Focusing now on just the expense side of a recording budget, here is an example of what a musician's budget actually looks like. This is a composite based on several recent jazz ensemble recordings done in Boston.

▼

Recording Project Budget
Expenses

Musicians' pay:	$0 (good friends)
Recording session food:	$300 (thank-you party for musicians)
Licensing fees:	$0 (no fees for original works or for public domain works)
BMI:	$150 (initial charge for solely owned publishing companies)
Studio time (record, mix, edit):	$1,100 ($55 × 20 hours)
Mastering:	$500 (4 hours studio time, 2 masters and a reference copy)
CD production:	$1,500 (1,000 CDs, four-panel booklet, full color)
Copyright registration:	$35
Graphic design:	$300
Photos:	$300
Promotional mailings:	$650 (for bookings and for reviews)
Publicist:	$1,500
Postcard:	$225 (design and printing)
Postage:	$160
Poster:	$150 (design and printing)
CD release concert hall rental:	$500
CDBaby distribution:	$35
	Total: $7,405

▲

Your costs may be quite different from these, based on your specific situation, resources, and plans. The important thing is to do your research and get accurate numbers for all the expenses your project entails. No one wants to complete a recording session only to find there's no funding left for manufacturing or promoting the album.

Options for Financing: Fundraising Projects and Personal Loans

Some musicians borrow money to make recordings, whereas others raise funds with contributions from their extended family, friends, and supporters. Many musicians use a combination of fundraising and loans. Your best asset for either raising or borrowing money for a record project is your own network. These are the people already invested in your career advancement, who know you well and are interested in seeing you succeed.

To make her first CD, jazz vocalist Linda B. needed to raise $5,000. Among her network of contacts, she identified five fairly wealthy people who were already supporters of her musical work. These five were people who came to her concerts regularly and knew her well. Linda asked each for a personal loan of $1,000, knowing that this amount of money was fairly small change for them. All five said yes, and Linda made out loan agreements for each, including repayment schedules. With the $5,000, Linda made her debut album and then paid back every penny. She has since gone on to make several more albums. Linda realized later, after she'd gotten to know these five supporters even better—that they would have been happy to simply *give* her the money, because they wanted to contribute to Linda's success and her career advancement. The moral of the story is this: you too may be able to raise the money for your recording with the help of your circle of supporters. You may even be able to do it without going into debt.

So make a list of potential contributors to your recording project. List people who know you or your family well and who have shown interest in your career. Use your network list from chapter 2. I guarantee that you know people now who would contribute to your project. It's a matter of how you ask them, how much you ask them for, and how much discretionary money they have to give. Chapter 11 covers fundraising in detail and provides the outline for organizing a small-scale fundraising campaign. So don't rule out the possibility of raising the money to make your recording.

As for loans, be careful. Don't attempt to finance your recording project by juggling credit card payments or by taking out a high-interest loan. Personal loans, like the ones Linda B. arranged, can be made for a mutually agreeable interest rate (or better yet, no interest) with a manageable repayment schedule. However, you should base a repayment schedule on income *other* than album sales. This is because, for most musicians, a recording—especially a first one— is primarily a promotional tool and *not* a substantive source of income.

Grants for Recordings

Finding grant money for recordings can be a long shot, because the majority of funders focus their giving on causes and projects that serve a broader community need. However, you may have affiliations with local community organizations that make various professional development grants and scholarships available. Sometimes church groups, community clubs, and local businesses have small-scale grant programs or will make one-time special contributions to specific projects. In smaller cities and towns, it may be easier to apply for and be awarded such funding. So if you are currently living in Manhattan, but your hometown is a small close-knit community in the Midwest, then do your grant research when you visit the folks back home.

Contact the reference librarians at the local library and inquire at the chamber of commerce, social service agencies, and religious organizations. Your best connections to accessing local funding will be through the people who know you well and who are interested in your career.

▼

Made in America

The Aaron Copland Fund offers a grant program for recording contemporary American music. Applications are accepted from nonprofit professional performing ensembles, presenting organizations, and either nonprofit or commercial recording companies. So, for example, an ensemble with an idea for a recording project of new American music might shop their project idea to an indie label, and if interested, the label might apply to the Copland Fund for support for the project. Grants range from $2,000 to $20,000 to support the release and dissemination of previously unreleased contemporary American music as well as reissues of recordings no longer available. See http://www.coplandfund.org/recording.html.

▲

For a full discussion of fundraising and grants, see chapter 11. Note: there are also some competitions that offer prizes of CD production (see the companion website http://www.oup.com/us/beyondtalent).

Selling Advance Copies

You may be able to finance at least a part of your recording project by selling advance copies of the album to your network of supporters. This can be done at performances, by mail order, and online. For this to work, you need to have a healthy-sized network. For instance, if you have raised a portion of your budget and need to come up with the last $2,000, you could raise this by selling 100 advance copies of your album for $20 a piece. Your friends, family, and network contacts are the people most willing to pay $20 for an album that has yet to be made. As an added incentive for advance purchasers, consider inviting them to an album release party, performance, or reception.

Excellent planning is essential. You would want the album release to be no more than a few months from the time of the mailing. People will not want to wait six months for the recording, and they will feel cheated unless you deliver on time.

▼

Jazz accordionist and composer Evan Harlan has financed several CDs by selling advance copies. An active performer, Evan has a good-sized mailing list of enthusiasts. He financed his recordings by mailing flyers out to his network, announcing the forthcoming album. The flyers were simple yet well designed, done on 8–1/2 × 11 paper, folded in thirds. On the flyer was an engaging description of the music for the new album, the expected release date, testimonials and quotes about his live performances and previous recordings, and an order form to purchase the new CD by mail. The selling point to the reader was, "Be the first on your block to get the new Evan Harlan album."

▲

Crowdfunding

The concept of harnessing the power of your fan base to help support artistic ventures is a very old concept, but these days it's called crowdfunding, and there are a number of services to help with this, including http://www.slicethepie.com and http://www.sellaband.com.

Here's an example from Kickstarter (http://www.kickstarter.com), a popular online service for managing fundraising projects. The cellist Ovidiu Marinescu needed to raise $7840 to make his full budget for recording the complete Bach Cello Suites. On the site, Marinescu posted a description of the project, and a quick video to introduce the project to propsective donors. Donors who pledge at specific levels receive thank-you gifts in return. Ovidiu offered tracks or whole autographed previous albums and some of his "package" deals at higher levels included a cello lesson, an oil painting, and a private recital. He raised $8,337.

Each Kickstarter project is given a deadline; if the dollar goal is met in pledges by that date, the donors' credit cards are charged and Kickstarter turns the total over to the group leader (in this example, Ovidiu). If the goal is not met by the deadline, Fundable deletes the ledgers and no credit cards are charged anything. This all-or-nothing model ensures that funding goals are met, so projects can be completed.

On a grander scale is ArtistShare, launched in 2002 by musician and computer programmer Brian Camilio. ArtistShare enables fans to invest directly in musicians' recording projects. In return for investing at specific levels, fans get access to the artist's creative process as "thank you" benefits.

Jazz artist Maria Schneider, fed up with the unfavorable contract terms she'd experienced with traditional labels, chose the ArtistShare route. In 2004, she became the first musician to win a Grammy with an album distributed exclusively on the Internet, and in 2008 Maria Schneider won another Grammy. Both albums were funded and distributed through ArtistShare.

With her album *Sky Blue*, Schneider's fans who contributed at the lowest funding level ($9.99) got in return the downloadable version. At higher levels, fans also got transcriptions of the solos, artwork from the CD, and downloadable interviews with the artists. The highest level of participation

Schneider offered was $18,000—and for this, the fan was listed as executive producer on the album. According to a Feb. 7, 2008, article in the *Wall Street Journal*, "Schneider said she came to ArtistShare because she wasn't seeing any royalty income even when she sold 20,000 CDs. Under a standard record-company deal, an artist receives a few cents per CD but usually only after the company has recouped its production and marketing costs."[2]

In *Taking Note: A Study of Composers and New Music Activity in the United States*, the contrast of Schneider's experience with traditional labels and with ArtistShare is detailed:

> A studio recording normally cost her approximately $30,000. A contracting record company would pay her a $10,000 guarantee followed by royalty income. Even after months of royalty payments, Schneider's out-of-pocket deficit was still $13,000. In contrast, her agreement with ArtistShare for her latest album, *Sky Blue,* gave her 85% of total earnings, which for her totaled nearly $170,000, which more than covered her initial investment.[3]

Keep in mind that in order to work, this type of funding model—crowd-funding—depends on having a crowd, a fan base. Most musicians finance their recordings with a combination of savings, assistance from family and friends, plus loans, grants, or advance copy sales. Musicians are creative and resourceful people, and these qualities are necessary in handling the business and budget issues of recordings.

Sales: How to Turn a Profit ◆

How well a musician does selling recordings depends on a number of factors, not the least of which is the quality of the album, in terms of the performance and the sound quality of the recorded material. Other considerations include the musician's performance activity, the effectiveness of promotional efforts, and whether the album is favorably reviewed. Yet the most critical factor determining album sales is the size of the musician's fan base.

To illustrate a range of album sales results, let's imagine that an emerging artist, Fran, has just completed a recording project. As planned, Fran spent $6,000 total and had 1,000 CDs pressed. Of these, she will use 300 for promotional purposes, mailing albums to radio stations, critics, and performance presenters for potential bookings. This leaves 700 for Fran to sell, in hopes of recouping some or all of her investment. She plans to sell albums at her performances, by mail order to her network, by consignment at local specialty shops, from her website, and through online retailers via CDBaby.

If Fran performs 20 concerts the year the album is released, selling an average of 10 CDs at each performance, that yields $3,000. By selling 190 more through her network and online through CDBaby, that's an additional $2,850. If she sells a final 20 albums on consignment at local shops, that's another $150. Altogether, that amounts to 410 albums sold, for a total of $6K, and she recoups her initial investment. If she increased these sales to 660, through additional performances, an enlarged network of contacts, and a more aggressive sales campaign, Fran could make a profit of over $3,000.

So why is it that the majority of musicians fail to recoup the money they invest, let alone make a profit? There are two reasons: first, musicians tend to overestimate the number of albums they can realistically sell, and second, they underestimate the work involved in sales. Think carefully about the appropriate number of albums to press for promotional and other purposes, and how many of these you will likely sell. If you're not performing regularly and don't yet have a substantial mailing list, then do *not* expect to recoup your investment. Instead, think of the money spent on the album as the necessary entry fee to your professional career.

Some recording projects are more profitable than others. Projects with more commercial value include ones with a hook, or an immediate or timely appeal, such as albums that tie into an idea of current popular interest. For instance, recordings focused on a particular composer and released in an important anniversary year of the composer may have an easier time gaining media attention. Or if a current popular film or book focuses on music of a particular period and your release corresponds to this period, again, this may be good for attracting media attention.

Some musicians use more commercially successful recording projects to finance their other niche projects. The recording industry itself does this each year, releasing and rereleasing Christmas album classics in time for the annual holiday shopping bonanza. Holiday album profits then finance other projects. You might consider this model. There is a guitar duo, a couple, who financed their children's college expenses on the proceeds from their Christmas album. Holiday music is an "evergreen" project, as it is renewed every year. Holiday albums are not for every musician, but the basic idea is worth considering. Look for ways to connect your music to some larger cultural interest area, because this may result in an album that attracts media attention, concert presenters, and audiences.

Selling Your Music Online ◆

There are a number of online retail services that make it easy for musicians to distribute their music electronically. When your fans can hear a sample of your music and then immediately purchase a single track or an entire album, that's terrific. Services and prices, of course, change over time, but here some basic online service options, compiled from information supplied by the Future of Music Coalition (http://www.futureofmusic.org):

CDBaby sells digital and physical albums, and the artist sets the price. For digital releases, CDBaby keeps 9 percent of the purchase price and $4 for each physical album sold; the rest goes directly to the artist, who is paid every week. CDBaby services also offers artists' placement of their recordings on iTunes, Rhapsody, Amazon, and others. Mechanical license rates are paid to composers, although this is the artist's or their label's responsibility (not CDBaby's).

iTunes is a digital retail store through which consumers buy individual tracks or albums at set prices. Single tracks are $.99, and albums are $9.99; artists typically get $6.50–$7.00 per album. iTunes is used by unsigned artists as well as indie and major label artists. The compensation rate for signed artists is based on their contracts. Mechanical license rates are paid to composers, and again, this is the responsibility of the artists or their label.

Amazon Music Store is a digital retailer for selling MP3 tracks. Users purchase single tracks for $.98 and albums usually for $8.99, although some tracks have steeply discounted prices. Similar to iTunes, artists get $6.50–$7.00 per album. Mechanical license rates paid to composers are again the label/artists' responsibility.

Nimbit.com is a sales, promotion, and distribution company offering independent musicians a range of services to sell music, tickets, and merchandise directly to their fans from their own websites. Nimbit offers their musician clients a widget, which is an online tool to embed in their website, blog, or e-mail. The monthly service rates depend on the range of service the musician wants. Mechanical license rates paid to composers are again the label/artists' responsibility.

Rhapsody is an online subscription streaming service that also features download options. For the streaming subscription, users pay $12 a month to have access to a huge library of albums and tracks. Paid downloads are separate charges. For the streaming, labels get a negotiated direct licensing fee; and artists are paid the digital performance royalty fee as tracked by SoundExchange. Though these digital performance fees to artists are quite small (pennies per play), over time they can become a good supplement to an artist's income. Rhapsody has licenses with ASCAP, BMI, and SESAC for songwriter/publisher performance compensation.

Magnatune is a label that sells digital and physical CDs, with variable pricing and online licensing. Consumers download albums or tracks and can choose their own price between $5 and $18. Acting as a label, Magnatune keeps 50 percent of sales and licensing, and the artist gets the other half. Mechanical license rates paid to composers are the artists' responsibility.

ArtistShare is a label whose releases are underwritten by the artists' fans. Fans buy physical and digital releases at varying rates, and for higher fees, they can purchase access to the artist's creative process—for example, attending rehearsals, recording sessions, and gaining credit on the album liner notes. Artists reap the majority of the revenue raised, with ArtistShare keeping a small percentage. Mechanical license rates paid to composers are the artists' responsibility.

Pandora is a webcast station format built around music recommendation engines. There is the free, ad-supported model, or else users can pay $36 a year for the ad-free version. Users can search for the music that they like, and the service then makes recommendations based on the user's preferences. Pandora helps expand the consumer's musical knowledge and exposure to music and performers they are likely to enjoy. Pandora also links to Amazon and iTunes for digital sales. Digital performance royalty fees are paid to the label and artist via SoundExchange. Pandora has licenses with ASCAP, BMI, and SESAC for songwriter/publisher performance compensation.

Sirius XM Satellite Radio is available to those who pay for equipment plus a monthly subscription fee, about $13 a month. Sirius pays the SoundExchange digital performance royalties to labels and artists. Sirius has licenses with ASCAP, BMI, and SESAC for songwriter/publisher performance compensation.

Podcasts are online audio files, analogous to an online indie radio station. Users can either subscribe to a podcast or simply listen online. There is not usually a compensation model in place, unless something has been specifically negotiated in a contract. The idea is to freely share music, lectures, and any other audio files, primarily for promotional and educational purposes.

Selling CDs at Performances

For most musicians, the best way to sell recordings is at their live shows. After a performance or at intermission, fans are more likely to make an impulse purchase. On a good night, your audience bonds with you and your music. Consequently, they want to take home a bit of the evening's "magic" as a souvenir and as an extension of their connection with you.

For many musicians, the albums they sell at performances substantially augment their performance fees. As a clarinetist friend says, the sales of recordings at her performances often turn a not-so-well-paying gig into a very good one. Chapter 6 covers booking performances in detail, but in the meantime, here are ways to promote your CD at performances. You need to make appropriate choices among these options according to your audiences, programming, and performance venues.

Tips for Good Sales at Gigs

- Consider programming your performances with at least some of the selections from your recording. While on stage, be sure to introduce the repertoire and explain that you recently recorded it on your latest album.
- At some point during the concert, announce—or have someone do it for you—that your album is available, and explain where to find the sales table. And tell the audience that you will be happy to meet them and sign CDs at the reception after the performance; this will boost sales.
- Arrange to have a friend handle the sales table. "Dress" the table in an attractive nonwrinkling fabric covering so that the sales table area is noticeable and welcoming. Make it easy on your customers; you need to be able to accept credit cards and issue receipts. CDBaby sells credit card swipe machines very reasonably priced. And it's good to offer your recording at a special discount "live performance price" (but this should still include the sales tax).

▼

Note: for tax and financial management purposes, you need to keep accurate records of your sales. Tracking how many albums you sell, at what price and where, is necessary for tax purposes—as well as for evaluating and refining your CD marketing plan. Find a qualified accountant (perhaps a friend of the family) to help you organize a basic bookkeeping method, and make sure your friends at the sales table follow through as instructed. See chapter 10 for detailed finance and tax issues.

▲

- Use a guest book at the sales table to get people signed up for your newsletter and performance invitations. And then make sure customer info gets added to your network database.
- Consider having giveaways at the sales table: inexpensive promotional items printed with your group's name, logo, and website. Postcards, refrigerator magnets, and memo pads are all fine, along with anything else that is both cost-effective and creative. Check out Zazzle, Cafe-Press, and Vistaprint for custom promotional items.

▼

Mail Order Sales Tips

- Add a shipping and handling fee to the price of the album.
- Provide a choice of shipping methods (first-class mail, UPS, FedEx).
- Include a business reply card or a self-addressed stamped envelope to get more contact info and get people on your mailing list.
- People like a menu of choices. Include extra items to order, like your ensemble's T-shirt or mug.
- Consider doing a cooperative mailing with your colleagues' CDs. Using a combined mailing list, you can pool your resources and increase your profits.

▲

Consignment Sales at Stores

Check to see if your local bookstores might carry your album. They may have a special interest in local artists. Depending on a store's space and layout, there may be opportunities for local musicians to present live in-store performances. Check out the possibilities in your area.

There may also be local specialty shops or restaurants interested in your music. Think specialty boutiques, high end wine stores, art galleries—go to these stores, introduce yourself to the manager, bring a portable CD player with your album, so others can listen. He or she may agree to play your album in the shop and keep a small display for sales at the register. You can purchase small display stands through many CD manufacturers.

If a store agrees to sell your recording, you need to provide the manager with a consignment agreement, stipulating the terms of your arrangement. You provide the CDs (with bar codes) and the store only pays you for what they sell, minus their commission. A simple consignment agreement between you and the store can serve as the receipt for the CDs you provide. Below is an example of such an agreement. The amount the album sells for and the amount of the store's commission is something you negotiate with the store manager.

Promoting Your Recording ◆

The way to kick off all these sales efforts is by celebrating your album release with a well-promoted concert and party. To make the most of your album release, make it an event. Plan a performance party, and invite everyone on your mailing list. Get friends to invite their friends. Create a "buzz" in the local media. The goal is to have people reading and talking about you, your music, and your recording. And use a guest book sign-in to get the contact info of everyone who comes to add to your database and expand your network.

Where should you hold the event? To keep costs down, consider venues where you have connections, such as a local temple, school, community center, supporter's home, or any workable setting with the acoustics you need.

Consignment Agreement

Date _____

Consigned to _____
                                    (name of store)

Address _____   Phone _____   e-mail: _____

copies of the recording titled _ _____,

_____
        (label name)   *(catalog number)*

Suggested Retail Price: $_____
Price to Consignee: $_____

Payment is due when additional recordings are consigned or _____ days after the receipt of an invoice for records sold. Full returns accepted.

Recordings are the property of _____ and
                                            (you or your label)
may be removed at their discretion.
Thank you,

_____
                (signature of consignor, you)

_____
                (signature of consignee, the store,)

For further savings, you may have friends or family who can sponsor or cater the reception.

How do you announce the event? Below is the text from an invitation I received years ago for a chamber ensemble's CD release event. Analyze the invitation; look for the specific *selling points* to give you ideas on how to plan and promote your own event.

This is an effective marketing piece for this type of ensemble and event. The selling points include the following:

- Special occasion value (not just a CD release, concert and party, but the group's tenth anniversary)
- Quality of the venue (a historic inn)
- Specific repertoire (the CD selections plus rarely heard works on rare instruments)
- "Fancy extras" (champagne and dessert reception in a ballroom) plus guest artists
- Exclusivity ("Seating is limited; subscribe early!")
- Easy directions included

CD RELEASE CONCERT & PARTY

The Tenth Anniversary Season will mark the release
of Musicians of the Old Post Road's second CD
Trios and Scottish Song Settings of J.N. Hummel.
For this special event at the historic Wayside Inn, the ensemble will
perform selections from the new CD and will offer rare period
instrument performances of chamber music and songs by Felix and
Fanny Mendelssohn. The Inn's ballroom will provide an intimate
setting for this lively evening, which will conclude with a
champagne and dessert reception.

Suzanne Stumpf, flute; Julia McKenzie, violin; Daniel Ryan, cello;
Michael Bahmann, fortepiano;
with guest artist Pamela Dellal, mezzo-soprano

Saturday, March 20, 8:00 p.m. • Wayside Inn, Sudbury

Seating is limited! Subscribe early!

For reservations, please call the office at (781) 466–6694, or
send e-mail to musicians@oldpostroad.org, or check our website at
www.oldpostroad.org

Wayside Inn • Sudbury: Located just off of Route 20 in Sudbury.
From Route 128 take exit 26 west; from Route 495 take exit 24 east.

"[The performers] bring grace and elegance to their
period instruments"

—*The Strad, London*

- An impressive endorsement of the quality of the group (the quote from *The Strad*)

Your e-mail invite should be short and friendly yet provide all the critical selling points and details. Make sure your message includes hyperlinks to all relevant websites. And for life beyond your CD release event, send newsletter updates at regular intervals with invitations to your performances.

Fiddler and singer Lissa Schneckenburger performs an array of traditional and contemporary folk repertoire, from Down East New England to Irish, Scottish, French Canadian, and contemporary folk music. To promote the release of one of her early albums, *Different Game,* Lissa planned three release concerts. She had done quite a bit of performing in three New England cities and had sufficient support and contacts to organize a small CD release tour. Lissa researched the media contacts for each city and sent out press releases as well as invitations to her mailing list. She also sent announcements to the appropriate folk-oriented music organizations and businesses in her three target cities. Her work paid off; the turnout at each performance was terrific, and she was able to make a "buzz" in not one but three communities. (See http://www.lissafiddle.com.)

Publicizing Your CD Release

To create media attention for your album, you could spend a small fortune on paid advertising, or you could get a range of media attention for *free*. Free is better. The way people get their stories and events into the news is by sending out press releases to bloggers and other media contacts at newspapers, magazines, and radio stations.

You'll need to put together a list of local and regional media outlets to which you can send notices about your album release. There are also online arts calendars (sponsored by newspapers, radio stations, and tourism offices) where you can post your information. In addition, many service organizations are devoted to specific areas of the music profession. Examples include Chamber Music America, American Guild of Organists, as well as all other specialty organizations for particular instruments. To find these, do an online search for "music organizations" and "music associations." Many of these groups publish newsletters with relevant news from the field, so they might publish a notice about your CD release, an interview with you, or even a CD review. Finally, if your music or your ensemble itself has a particular ethnic or national orientation, you may find relevant cultural associations and media outlets to help you reach a target audience. See chapter 7 for writing releases and contacting the media.

A word of caution: in and of itself, releasing a CD is not particularly newsworthy, as thousands of CDs are released each month. However, if the album includes a premiere of a new or seldom-heard work, or if the recording project was funded in an unusual way, then these specifics might be the *hooks* needed to interest a journalist or editor. To write an effective press release, consider what is interesting about your music, your ensemble, and you. Think of human-interest angles—does your group have an improbable story about how you first got together, or do you have interests beyond music that a general reader might find engaging? Look for angles that help the media turn a simple CD release into a compelling profile piece that would engage a broad readership.

For example. A few years ago I received a CD release notice for the Jacques Thibaud String Trio's "Berlin Music at War's End 1944–46," released on Sophia Classics. It features works by Schoenberg, Gideon Klein, and Villa

Lobos, who each, in the same period but under very different circumstances, wrote their only string trios. Who is the audience for this album? First of all, the trio is excellent, so there are their existing fans and audiences from their touring. Then there are other potential album buyers: people interested in World War II history, those interested in Berlin itself, and those interested in one or more of the three composers. A targeted marketing plan for this album might include sending posters, flyers, or press releases to libraries and museums, as well as reaching out to memberships of historical societies and musicological associations.

To find journalists who might consider writing about you or your group, cyber-publicist Ariel Hyatt suggests working backward. Start with bands or other musicians doing work similar to yours and musicians who are at a similar career stage. Google these artists to find articles written about them and get the names of the journalists who wrote the articles. Look for appropriate media outlets and the specific journalists who would consider reviewing your album. In her excellent article, "How to Be Your Own Publicist," Ariel Hyatt recommends, "Call or e-mail the reviewers, politely introduce yourself and ask if you can send them your CD for consideration. This is a much better technique than the old school method of getting a 'media list' and blindly mailing precious materials out in bulk." (See http://www.arielpublicity.com.)

Getting Reviewed ◆

To get your album reviewed, compile a media list of people who review recordings of your genre in newspapers, magazines, and on the Web. A listing of print and Internet publications with album reviews can be found on the companion website http://www.oup.com/us/beyondtalent.

To get your CD reviewed, send it out to music journalists at appropriate publications with a personalized letter, not a generic "To whom it may concern." The letter should describe the repertoire on the album and include engaging and relevant information on the background of the performers. The purpose of the letter is to personalize an introduction to the album so that the journalist will consider reviewing it. It can work well to send the letter and CD along with a *one-sheet*—a single sheet that has your bio, photo, website and other relevant URLs, plus a compelling description of the album.

In sum, with recording projects, planning can help minimize frustrations and maximize success. Use some type of project management system to keep organized. This can be as simple as a detailed list on your computer, with tasks and deadlines to keep track of what needs to be done when. You can program an online calendar system to send you reminders of the deadlines. This can make any large project manageable and help reduce the stress involved. It is possible to scale recording projects to fit almost any budget but not every aspiration. So clarify your purpose, plan your work, and work your plan.

Radio Play

In order to get airplay for your album, you need to compile a media list of appropriate radio stations and the program directors (for your genre of music) at these stations. The process is to send each radio program director a personalized "pitch" letter along with your CD and bio. To search terrestrial radio stations by location, see http://www.musicalamerica.com (classical) and http://www.allaboutjazz.com (jazz). For online radio stations, see http://www.live365.com. An added incentive for investigating online radio is that through SoundExchange, artists can receive royalty payments for airplay.

Radio stations are particularly interested in playing albums of groups or soloists with upcoming *local* performances, so timing is critical. Indicate in your letter that you are available for and interested in a radio interview before an upcoming local performance and specify that date. Check if your local public or college station broadcasts studio performances. In order for a radio station to consider playing your CD, it must be mastered professionally and be available for purchase online. Include information in your pitch letter about how the CD can be purchased.

Career Forward

Answering these questions and following these prompts will help you advance your recording project.

1. Who is the prospective audience for your recording? Describe, and be specific. How many people do you have in your network? What niche audiences might be particularly interested in your album?
2. Once your recording is completed, what do you plan to do with it? What is your marketing and promotion plan? Go for detail.
3. If you need to raise funds for your recording, how are you planning to do this?
4. How many recordings do you plan to send out for promotional purposes? To whom do you plan to send these?
5. How much are you expecting to make in sales? Where and how are you planning to make these sales?
6. What individuals and organizations can you contact to get referrals and suggestions about your recording project?

Recording Project Planning Worksheet

Complete the following worksheet to think through your next recording project:

- ✓ *Why* do you want to make this recording?
- ✓ *What* repertoire would you like to record? What is the copyright status of each of these works?
- ✓ *How* do you plan to do the recording—on location? In a studio? Do-it-yourself?
- ✓ *How much* money will you need? Detail all your anticipated expenses and your financial resources for the project:

Expenses	*Resources*
Collaborating musicians:	Savings:
Studio costs:	Loans:
Hall rental:	Grants:
Recording engineer:	Gifts:
Producer:	Other:
Editing:	
Mastering:	
Piano tuning:	
Graphic design:	
Photography:	
Liner notes editor:	
Copyright registration:	
Licensing fees:	
Bar code registration:	
Artwork printing:	

Promotional Expenses
Press materials/mailings:
Promo material printing/assembly:
Mailing to radio/media:
Follow-up phone costs:
Booking fee(s) associated with release concerts:
CD release flyers/invitations:
Online retail distribution fees:

Total:	Total:

5

Building Your Online Community: Social Networking, the Web, and You

For musicians today, an online presence is a necessity: giving fans access to your music, information on upcoming performances, and insight into your personality and creative process. These days, it seems that in order to exist, you need an online presence. Google yourself. Can people find you? If not, they may assume you're not a working musician and not a professional. And if your only online presence is for social purposes, then anyone wanting to find out about (or hire) you as a musician will move on to consider the next person.

Savvy musicians have their professional profiles on multiple social media sites such as Facebook, MySpace, LinkedIn, Twitter, and YouTube. And on each of their profiles, they include links back to their own websites, where fans can find the most complete information and ways to connect. With the rise of social media platforms, an individual's web*site* has come to be considered just one facet of a more comprehensive web *presence*.

The good news is that it's never been easier or less expensive to create an online presence that represents you and your music well. But busy musicians understandably have difficulty finding the time and energy to spend on this. What's worse, it's an ongoing struggle, as there will always be new software, gadgets, and gizmos on the horizon. No matter what the latest innovation may be, some core issues remain constant. Whether we use the postal system and a typewriter or the latest social media platform, it's all about connecting with audiences. Keeping this overarching purpose in mind will help you make decisions on how best to allocate your time and resources. Communicating does take time, but there are ways to keep things streamlined and to keep your music-making your top priority.

Ultimately, whatever online tools you choose to adopt should be the ones that best fit your particular situation, mission, and goals. Your online presence should reflect your goals, your values, and what you want to convey to audiences about yourself and your music.

▼

Being in the Know

To stay on top of developments and new ideas in the profession, read what professional artist managers, concert presenters, and publicists read: http://www.artsjournal.com. Available as a free e-mail subscription, ArtsJournal is a daily digest of some of the best arts and cultural journalism in the English-speaking world. It's a good way to quickly browse headlines and to find the article gems that you want to forward and discuss with colleagues and fans.

And there are many terrific music writers with blogs, offering perspective on the changing music world. Below are a few to check out, but see the companion website for more musician blogs listed by instrument and interest areas, http://www.oup.com/us/beyondtalent.

Alex Ross's *The Rest Is Noise,* http://www.therestisnoise.com
Andrew Dubber's *New Music Strategies,* http://newmusicstrategies.com
Amanda Ameer's *Life's a Pitch,* http://www.artsjournal.com/lifesapitch
Greg Sandow *The Future of Classical Music?*
    http://www.artsjournal.com/greg
Andrew Taylor's *The Artful Manager,*
    http://www.artsjournal.com/artfulmanager
Jazz bloggers: check out Larry Blumenthal, David Adler, Doug Ramsey, and
    Howard Mandel

▲

Social Media and You ◆

Social media is all about connecting. It's about cultivating active relationships and forming online communities of shared interests. Examples of social media platforms include Facebook, MySpace, LinkedIn, Flickr, YouTube, Twitter, and Wikipedia. These platforms allow users to create, upload, and share content, participate in conversations, and form virtual communities. The important and lasting concept here is that what people want and expect online is to engage *actively*.

As detailed in the previous chapter, singer-songwriter Jonathan Coulton encourages fans to create new works based on his music, under a Creative Commons license. Coulton's fans have made videos using his songs and Flickr photo slide shows to accompany his songs (see the menu item "user-generated content" on his site, http://www.jonathancoulton.com).

Another example of this trend is Yo-Yo Ma's collaborative music project with IndabaMusic. Ma recorded the melody of Dona Nobis Pacem (Give Us Peace) and offered this to his fans as material for virtual collaborations with him. Fans could add their own countermelody or anything else to create something new. Go to the site to hear the results: http://www.indabamusic.com/contests/show/yo-yomacontest.

Social media platforms can serve as a powerful reminder of the function of music in society. Social media is evidence of the essential human need to connect with others and form communities. As musicians, our fundamental work *is* community building. The arts bring people together. We create community when we perform, teach, and advocate for the arts. And with online tools, we now have more ways to help fans connect with us and with each other.

Second Life Music

Second Life (SL) is all about user-generated content. SL is an online platform for a three-dimensional virtual world in which participants are represented by avatars. These avatars interact with one another through socializing, dancing, fundraising, taking classes, and attending concerts. As reported by ABS-CBN News in March 2009, "The number of people that have joined the virtual world since it was created in 1999 eclipsed 15 million last year. The average number of people logged on to Second Life at any given time is about 70,000."[1]

As for SL music, there are many events held that combine live and virtual performances. Here are a few examples. Composer Pauline Oliveros has been active in SL with mixed media performances including electronics, spoken word, and SL avatar dancers. And as part of the National Black Arts Festival, jazz trumpeter Russell Gunn played live online in Acropolis Gardens, one of SL's virtual venues. For another example, BBC Radio organized a two-day SL music festival on a rented virtual island. The SL festival was organized to sync with a real-world festival in Dundee, Scotland. The virtual festival site had a huge screen showing a simulcast live performance from the festival in Dundee.

Second Life offers musicians opportunities for performing before new audiences, and building a fan base through online community building.

▼

Text Messaging

At the Kennedy Center's outdoor performances, audiences were asked to send a text message in order to "opt in" and receive announcements about upcoming performances. Similarly, U2 front man Bono has used text messaging to have audiences participate in fundraising causes and consciousness awareness campaigns. Asking audiences to text you or your band at intermission, with questions they would like answered at your post-concert reception, might be a way to start a dialogue with a new fan who just may become a supporter or future donor.

▲

Social Media Basics: Making Friends

Social networking sites can connect you with hundreds, even thousands of fans, friends, and supporters. You can easily invite "friends" to upcoming shows, send bulletins with updates, and swap ideas and feedback about each others' profiles, music, and projects. For musicians without a website, setting up a profile on Facebook, MySpace, or any other social media site is a good starting point for establishing a more substantial online presence.

The big idea behind all of the social networking platforms is that people want to make real connections with real people. It's about dialogue, not about spamming people with marketing messages. The way to build a network and fan base on any site is by adding friends. This takes time and effort. Responding to the messages that your friends send you and sending out invites to your performances is time consuming, especially if you are doing this on multiple sites. All this can certainly be overwhelming. The time you spend is a necessary investment, though, if you want audiences at your performances and people to purchase your recordings. Make sure you add links for all your profiles on your business cards and on your promotional pieces. Make it easy to be found.

The good news is that there are services designed for one-stop updating that will sync all your accounts. In other words, you can add your latest performance dates or project news on one site and it will automatically make the necessary changes in all the others on which you have accounts. See Posterous, Atomkeep, and Ping.fm for starters, but again, explore the latest options.

As for choosing which social media platforms you should be on, check out where successful colleagues are found online. If your crowd of musicians and fans are not on a particular social media platform, then you do not need to be there.

Cyber Safety

Your website, as well as all your social networking profile pages, should be appropriately professional. In the world we live in, there's no way to keep one social media site strictly for your personal life and another for your professional personae. It's up to each of us to decide what is too personal or private to put online. Employers now routinely Google prospective job candidates before choosing interviewees. Be circumspect about the information and photos you include on any site, because inappropriate language, comments, or photos are not the way to build a reputation as a professional.

And, just as in the rest of life, there are some unsavory folks online, so be careful about what personal information you post. Do *not* post your phone number, birth date, home address, or any other information about your personal habits and schedule because this might jeopardize your privacy and security. Be professional *and* safe.

▼

Check These Out

Below are suggested sites (as of this writing) for musicians to explore. Check the companion website for additions and updates http://oup.com/us/beyondtalent. And ask friend and colleagues for recommendations; search for the most current social networking platforms to fit your particular situation. Find a custom solution to fit your career goals.

Blogging: Posterous, Wordpress, Blogger, Typepad, Movabletype

Bookmarking and news: Delicious, Stumbleupon, Digg

Microblogging: Twitter

Music: Bandcamp, Instantencore, Soundcloud, Divshare

Performance date info/calendars: Upcoming, Eventful, Jambase

Photo/video sharing: Flickr, Picasa, Photobucket, YouTube, Vimeo, SlideShare, Divshare

Playlists, listening recommendations: Pandora, iLike

Other social networking platforms (for posting profiles and making connections): *Facebook, MySpace, Bebo, Xanga, Plaxo, LinkedIn (LinkedIn is used primarily for business contacts and professional colleagues' networking: can be great for finding out about the people who run concert series, teach, work in arts organizations)*

DIY social network: Ning (allows you to create your *own* social network on your site, to manage your contacts)

Shared work online (great for ensembles): Google Docs

▲

Website Overview ◆

There are several reasons to have your own website, as opposed to simply using social networking profiles. With your own website, you have complete control over how it looks and how it's customized, it can be more easily found on search engines, and it can appear as more "serious" or professional than a Facebook fan page or MySpace musician profile. A website can be your home base, a hub to which all your social networking sites connect. And it can be the place for interested fans and colleagues to find the most complete information on you and your music.

Musician websites used to be static online brochures. The emphasis has shifted from what people can *find* on a website to what people can *do* on it. Think of a website as a catalyst. The idea is to get visitors listening to your music, reading your blog and posting comments, signing up for your mailing list, volunteering for your street team, donating to a project, purchasing merchandise, or participating in a quiz, raffle, or contest. Above all else, your site should allow listeners to hear and download your music.

Websites can produce powerful three-dimensional impressions of musicians, both as artists and as individuals. Your website should be an extension of you and your artistic vision. It should effectively convey your personality. Everything on your site should be carefully chosen to represent you and your music: from the choice of typeface, colors, and graphics to the text, sound clips, photos, and video. Because concert presenters check online for information about artists they are considering booking, it is important that the impression you convey is neither amateurish nor generic. Presenters, like fans, often judge books by their covers.

▼
___

When asked about musician websites, baritone Tom Meglioranza (http://www.meglioranza.com) offers this: "Now that musician websites aren't novelties anymore, I don't want a website to be eye-catching. I just want information. I want it to load quickly (without animated introductions). I don't want to be forced to listen to music. I want its information laid out in a clear, non-eye-straining, and easy-to-navigate way. The musician websites I visit most often are the ones with interesting blogs: Nico Muhly, Jeremy Denk, Jonathan Biss, Rinat Shaham, Sid Chen, Anne-Carolyn Bird, David Byrne, Helen Radice, to name only a few of the blogs I regularly check."

___
▲

Planning is important. Think about what you want from a website and what you're hoping to accomplish with your site. Think about your potential website visitors and their interests. Clear goals, planning, and research will help you achieve a more cohesive and ultimately more effective website.

Site Analysis ◆

The best way to educate yourself about websites and to prepare for designing
your own is by viewing lots of musicians' sites with an analytical eye. As you
view other musicians' websites, ask yourself the following questions:

What image of the artist (or ensemble) is being conveyed?

What adjectives would you use to describe the image created by the
site?

Is the site easy to navigate?

Does the front page open quickly? Or do Flash animation and other
features slow it down?

Does the site offer opportunities to contact and interact with the
musician(s)? And is there incentive to do so?

Are there interesting links? Does the site link to other musicians and
relevant organizations?

Is there anything fun or unusual on the site? Any surprises?

How does the site help the musician build an audience (or does it)?

If you were considering hiring this musician for a performance, would
you find the information on the site relevant? Interesting?

Would you visit this site again? Why or why not?

What ideas does this site give you for your own?

▼
Sites to Peruse

To gather design and content ideas, make sure you look at a *broad* range of
musicians' websites. This means looking at more than those of your friends and
colleagues or of those musicians who immediately come to mind. For example, for
those working on promoting a string quartet, do *not* simply look at other quartet
sites. Here are some that you may not have seen:

- Singer/songwriter Jonathan Coulton, http://www.jonathancoulton.com
  (simple, stripped down but extremely effective: fan-oriented, distinct
  personality, and funny)
- Violinist Rachel Barton Pine, http://www.rachelbartonpine.com (audience-
  oriented with an e-zine, podcasts, video, blog, free downloads)
- eighth blackbird, http://www.eighthblackbird.com (great blog—reveals the
  "inner" eighth blackbird)
- Ethel, http://www.ethelcentral.com (great photos, description of projects,
  conveys sense of the ensemble)
- Imani Winds, http://www.imaniwinds.com (check out their comprehensive
  education programming)

- Conductor Edwin Outwater, http://www.edwinoutwater.com (creative and fun blog)
- So Percussion, http://www.sopercussion.com (inviting, distinctive)
- Bassist/composer, Ben Allison http://www.benallison.com (good graphics, distinct image)
- Singer/songwriter, Jill Sobule http://www.jillsobule.com (terrific example of fan-funded recording projects)
- Pianist Jonathan Biss, http://www.jonathanbiss.com (interesting, thought-provoking blog)
- Bang on a Can, http://www.bangonacan.org (inventive)
- Providence String Quartet's Community MusicWorks, http://www.communitymusicworks.org (clear mission)

Website Building Basics ◆

To get started creating a website, the first thing you need to do is obtain your domain name (the URL address that you type into your web browser). All domain names are completely unique and are registered with the Internet Corporation for Assigned Names and Numbers (ICANN). For a modest fee per year, you can own the exclusive rights to http://www.*yourname*.com, unless, of course, someone else already has it. Popular sites to register your domain name (as of this writing) include Doteasy, Godaddy, and Register.com.

Make sure you compare a range of services carefully; check out all the features with any package offer. It can be confusing because many companies offer domain name registration along with web hosting. But it can be important to register your own domain with a separate company from your web host, so that in the event that you want to change web hosts, there is no delay or difficulty using your own domain name.

Further, it is becoming equally important to secure your social media names as well (i.e., "myspace.com/yourname" and "twitter.com/yourname"), even if you don't plan to use these platforms anytime soon.

Web Hosting

A website is in essence a small piece of real estate disk space on a hard drive called a server. Each server connected to the Internet has a unique number, called an IP address. A domain name points web users to a specific IP address. In order to "lease" space on a server, you need to set up a web hosting account. This is different from your Internet service provider (ISP) such as Comcast or Verizon. Basic web hosting accounts start at $5 per month, although they have varying contract lengths and features: bandwidth, data transfer, and storage. For starters, here are two to consider: Dreamhost and Media Temple. But ask around: you want to get recommendations and go with a reliable company with a history of great customer service.

Site Construction

One of the easiest ways to build a site (and one of the best deals) is to use a free blogging platform. This is easy and you don't need to know html to make a great site, although knowing a little is helpful to customize your site. As of this writing, popular blogging platforms are Wordpress, Blogger, Typepad, and Movabletype.

Alternatively, for Mac users who want to build their own site from scratch and aren't afraid of diving in to the technical, there's iWeb and the more advanced Rapidweaver.

There are also many "templated" website design/hosting services, in which users can create a site using a choice of pre-packaged design templates. As of this writing, one that is low cost and popular with musicians is dynamod. There are also some services that offer free web hosting with basic templated designs. With these, note that the website URL you get may include the web host company's name (making it harder to remember and perhaps appear less "serious") and often some advertising. But using one of these can be a great way to get started.

Free templated sites and hosting:
http://weebly.com   http://wix.com
http://www.yola.com   http://www.terapad.com
http://www.webs.com   http://webnode.com

Costs

Creating a website can cost anywhere from virtually nothing to thousands of dollars. To find an affordable web designer in your area, Chokdee Rutirisari, a Boston-based designer, recommends Craigslist. He says, "Lots of designers who have day jobs seek freelancing gigs through Craigslist. Just make sure you see their portfolio before agreeing to work with them. Also, I would recommend signing some sort of contract or agreement before any money changes hands. Going rates for a good designer can be $35–$50 per hr." Depending on whom you hire and what is done, the cost for an entire site can range from $300 to $1,000.

Savvy do-it-yourselfers can instead purchase web design software, such as iWeb or Rapidweaver, and Dreamweaver (for $100–$400) and become their own designers. You can often download free trial versions of software to test and learn the program. For those still in school, there are often educational discounts available. Some musicians find they like website design and develop sideline freelance work creating sites for colleagues.

You can also hire a design student to collaborate with you and to teach you enough basic html code so you can make changes to the completed site as needed (again, you could find such a consultant on Craigslist). A great resource for budding web designers and those going the DIY route is webmonkey, which has tutorials, style sheets, tips, and articles. But, no matter who builds it, your site should be completely search-engine friendly and accessible. This means it should be Web Standards compliant (and an experienced web designer/consultant will know how to do this).

There are some lower-priced alternatives that you may want to consider until you have the time, money, and energy to invest in a website. Consider purchasing your domain name and directing it to your MySpace or Facebook profile until your own website is up and running. There are the free templated sites listed above, And again, there's the recommended free blogging platform option: Wordpress, Blogger, Typepad , and Movabletype.

Selling Your Stuff

Selling anything directly off of your website can be costly and complicated because of the software needed to provide secure credit card transactions. However, third-party sites will list your merchandise and manage the transactions and sales for you in return for a percentage of the profits. Examples are CDBaby and Bandcamp (free!) for your music, and Zazzle and CafePress for merchandise such as T-shirts, mugs, and just about anything else. With Nimbit, you can do it all: sell recordings, tickets, and merchandise directly to your fans. You place a convenient link or widget on your website to direct your fans to where they can make purchases. These services take major credit cards and are licensed vendors.

Traffic

In the end, what you need is not just a great-looking site, but traffic *to* the site. What your site links to and who links to your site is crucial. Cultivate a network of connections. Make sure you're listed on the alumni pages of your alma mater with your website link. Do likewise with any of your ensembles and any institutions where you teach: get your bio and a hyperlink to your site included. If you are a member of a service organization (such as Chamber Music America or the American Music Center) or on a teaching artist roster, see if your name and link can be listed on their website.

To make sure your website can be easily found on search engines, consider how your website pages are tagged. This has to do with how the pages are described, titled, or tagged in html code. Think about how people might try to find you online, with your instrument or voice type, genre, ensemble, where you teach, or other projects. These items can be included in how your website is tagged to help people find you. Each page of your site should have specific title tags based on the content of that page. This is one more reason to work with a knowledgeable consultant.

Once your site is up and running, you can use Google Analytics (http:// www.google.com/analytics) to get free site traffic analysis. These reports can tell you geographically where your visitors are coming from and which pages on your site they are opening. This can be very helpful both in fine-tuning your site and your promotion efforts.

Cultivating Your Fan Base   ◆

The whole point of attracting visitors to your website is to build a fan base so that you can attract audiences to your performances. So your website needs a mailing list sign-up. This should be an easy opt-in method to get e-mail addresses of interested folk. But it's great if you have a way to includenames and zipcodes, so you can segment your list to alert fans when you will next be performing in their area. Provide incentives, such as a free download of a track with every sign-up. As detailed in chapter 2, many musicians use Reverbnation, Mailchimp, or Constantcontact.

You also want to find out who among your fans is willing to volunteer to help promote your performances. On your site and at your shows you can solicit for "street team" members: enthusiastic fans willing to help promote performances and more. Your site can also have a volunteer sign-up (ReverbNation makes this easy). Members of your team may be willing to cater the reception or help design, print, or distribute flyers and posters. A fan may want to help out updating your website or contacting media. You may be able to attract a "fifth Beatle"—a fan assistant to you or your ensemble who can handle specific tasks and responsibilities to help you succeed.

Newsletters   ◆

E-newsletters are the most effective way to alert your fans about upcoming performances and to cultivate their support. Newsletters are most successful when they incorporate great photos along with interesting and personal news and viewpoints. Remember that your newsletter is about cultivating a community. It should *not* be just a list of upcoming gigs (everyone is sick of online advertising). With a good a mailing list management system, you can send tailored newsletter announcements to segmented contacts of your mailing lists.

Music publicist Ariel Hyatt says newsletters need three essentials: the *personal* (your thoughts, ideas on . . .); the *news* (your latest career-related highlights); and *one call to action* (this can be to get people to "friend" you on MySpace or Facebook, to offer you suggestions on where to tour next summer, or to give you feedback on a proposed concert program idea).

To make it personal, take the reader inside your creative process—what was the recording session like? Do you have photos from your last performance or tour? What is your "latest find" or inspiration? This might be a recording, restaurant, recipe, book, or article. Something you can provide a link to. Aim for content that is engaging for your colleagues as well as for non-musicians.

Website Design Tips ◆

These tips are adapted from Bob Baker, author of many music career guides:

- Fit the most important information onto your home page on one screen. Don't overload your visitors. Keep it simple! Beware; flash and animation can take too long to load, may be unreadable on certain platforms, and can make specific pages and information hard to find on search engines
- Use "white space," and avoid clutter—make your site pages easy on the eyes.
- Put the most important info or image in the upper left of each page. Studies show that this is where visitors start, so put your name, instrument, or essential image there.
- Place "eye anchors" carefully on the page. Because people scan web pages, use concise text, short paragraphs, bullet points, and eye-catching graphics judiciously.
- Think of having a "call to action" on each page, a goal for something you want the visitor to *do.* This might be to sign up for your newsletter, listen to a sound clip, or purchase a track, a ticket, or some merchandise.
- Ask friends to surf your site, and watch them to learn what they are attracted to and what they actually read and do on your site.
- Provide distinctive resource information on your site: a reason for visitors to stay and read and return. This might be links to your favorite benefit causes, local restaurants, YouTube clips, or tips and recommendations for students.

What's on the Menu ◆

Below is information on some of the most common items on musicians' websites. You may not need or want all of these, but they are worth considering.

Blogs: are easy and free to create, and can be used as a website or as a feature of a website. They are very customizable, and blogging platforms provide design "themes" and it's simple to add handy widgets for adding audio and video clips. See Wordpress, Blogger, Typepad, Movabletype.

Blogs are for story telling: when effective, they draw the reader in to the writer's world and perspective. Blogs are enlivened with photos, videos, quotes, and, of course, the writer's commentary on these. Of course you want to promote your upcoming performances and recordings, but a blog should really be about cultivating a relationship with your fans. There needs to be more than marketing messages in your blog posts. Postings should be concise, newsworthy, and entertaining because most people have limited time and patience for online reading. Find good tips on writing blog posts at http://www.copyblogger.com.

On the eighthblackbird ensemble's blog, I read one of the group's "favorite posts." The topic was flutist Tim Munro's comedic backstage accident titled "Anatomy of a Head Injury." And another posting transcribed the after-concert "twitterings," as the six members tried to decide who was going out for beer. These postings give the reader a real sense of the humor and personalities of the group. Readers feel invited to and included in the party.

When I first visited conductor Edwin Outwater's website and blog, he had up a YouTube clip of a great vintage comedy skit with Sid Ceasar and Nanette Fabray "doing" the first movement of Beethoven's 5th as a couple's argument. Below that he had posted a description of his most recent performance, an orchestra/electronica concert with Mason Bates. Outwater had a link to an article about his orchestra's education program and then two YouTube clips from the latest political campaign, and his commentary on these was simply the question, "Isn't it about time artists got MORE political?" This all creates a strong positive impression of the conductor's humor, his music, and the way he thinks. I was won over and interested to hear his recordings and performances *because* of his blog posts. (See http://www.edwinoutwater.com.)

If you're not yet performing enough to keep a tour diary, then consider using your blog for opinion pieces and commentary on topics about which you are passionate. The idea is to enable a communal online discussion, and to start an interesting dialogue thread. You need to have a topic that you care about and know enough about to jumpstart a series of conversations. One musician writes about food and bread baking, another friend writes on the topic and idea of community. Greg Sandow writes on the future of classical music (http://www.artsjournal.com/greg). Your topics may include politics, religion, and other incendiary topics. Just remember, once you post anything, you have published it for anyone and everyone to read: all your friends, family, and colleagues, as well as current and potential employers. Be clear about what to keep personal and private.

Many musicians start blogs and then find it difficult to keep up with ideas for new postings every week or so. Therefore, it can be helpful to invite guests to post on your blog, perhaps an interesting collaborator, mentor, or student of yours. You can also keep an idea file for future postings in case you run out of ideas. Interesting blog posts can focus on your favorite historical sites, recipes, pop culture, favorite books, and movies.

Bio: The version of your bio for your website should be brief and engaging, fit easily on one screen with plenty of margin, and have room for a photo. But it can be great to provide options, a concise one-paragraph opener bio and a link to the rest, or else menu buttons for the short and long bio versions. If the website is for an ensemble, have both a group bio and links to individual member bios.

Performance Calendar: listings should include when, where, and what you'll be performing, ticket info, a hyperlink to the venue's website, and travel directions with a link to mapquest or another mapping website. Depending on the music you perform, you may want to include brief, well-written program notes on the composers and the pieces (written for a non-specialist audience). You may find a skilled friend or fan willing to help write these.

Sounds: Having examples of your music is essential! You can include downloadable sound files or MP3 clips that showcase your music. A popular platform, as of this writing, is SoundCloud, on which you can upload your music with no file size limit and then embed the link on your site. There's also Bandcamp and Divshare. The sound clips you provide free can be "teasers" to prompt listeners to purchase tracks or entire albums, and come to your live shows. Your music page should include links to the:

Purchase page: Provides links to the online retail sites where your albums and tracks are available, such as CDBaby, iTunes, Bandcamp, Amie

Street, Magnatune, TuneCore, Nimbit, and Amazon's CreateSpace. In general, these companies take a portion of the profit in exchange for handling the digital distribution and sales. For manufacturing and selling other merchandise (T-shirts and such), many musicians use CafePress, Zazzle, as well as Nimbit.

Photos/Videos: Embedding YouTube clips from your performances can be a terrific way to engage your readers. Years ago I stumbled onto a flutist's website with an embedded YouTube video clip. It was a video of a community education performance he had presented for a museum audience. In the video the flutist performed a solo work standing in a gallery near a painting, with his listeners standing and gathered around him to hear the music and view the artwork. The video was especially effective because of the camera position: the video was shot from behind the performer's right shoulder, so that the viewer saw his audience's response, his movement, and the great location. The clip was very effective because the emphasis was on the *audience's* positive response.

Make sure you use a variety of photos throughout your site. And still shots can be "animated" as slide shows (with Flickr, Photobucket, and others). It is great to have less formal shots on pages that focus on teaching, education concerts, and audience engagement. If your site is for an ensemble, use group shots on most pages, but have individual shots to accompany the individual bios.

Press or testimonial page: If you quote your reviews, make sure you include the newspaper name, city, and state. If the critic is well known, include his or her name. If you do not yet have reviews, you can use quotes from mentors, concert presenters, or club managers, as long as you have obtained their permission. In other words, if someone has written something positive about you and your music in an e-mail or recommendation, simply ask, "Would it be OK to use your quote on my website?"

Electronic Press Kit (EPK): This can be a specialized portion of your website offering versions of your promo materials geared towards booking and media purposes. Here you can provide several lengths of your formal full bio as well as programming materials in ready-to-print downloadable PDFs. Include a series of high-resolution JPEGS for downloading use by presenters and the media. And many musicians use the site Sonicbids to post their EPK, giving club managers and presenters one more place to easily find them and access sound samples.

Links page: You want to have fun, interesting, and relevant links to other websites. Think what your visitors might be interested in, such as links to other ensembles you collaborate with, resource sites for musicians and music enthusiasts, plus non-music sites you find interesting. You may want to list links in topic categories, keeping the number of links per category to seven or fewer. You can update or rotate these links as you find new ones.

FAQ page: Many websites have a Frequently Asked Questions page. For musicians and ensembles, this can be a fun page with quirky personal information interspersed with factual, interesting tidbits about your group, repertoire, and upcoming projects.

Contact info: Make it easy for people to connect with you.

Mailing List Sign-up: stay in touch with your fans. Offer them an incentive for signing up, such as a free download of your music. When you ask people to sign up for your mailing list, consider asking for their zip code. There are performing groups who plan their tours based on where their fans are. You can offer a free download of a performance in exchange for signing up and leaving a zip code. It's very easy to set up a mailing list signup. Popular services include Constant Contact and MailChimp.

Interactive elements: The most successful and popular web pages are those that are interactive. Include a music trivia quiz, questionnaire, or a raffle for free CDs or tickets. To connect even more with your visitors and supporters, think of ways to involve them in your music. Radius Ensemble reserves the last concert of their home season as an audience choice program. People vote on the group's website for the repertoire for the final concert, choosing encore performances from the pieces performed at the earlier concerts that season. There are a number of sites that provide free interactive tools you can use on your site:

http://www.bravenet.com
http://www.misterpoll.com
http://www.widgetbox.com
http://www.sparklit.com
http://www.surveymonkey.com

Educational pages: If you teach, you may want to have a portion of your website devoted to your teaching. And if you play a somewhat unusual instrument, consider including a page on the history, construction, or me-

chanics of the instrument. Marimbist Nancy Zeltsman's site (http://www
.nancyzeltsman.com) is terrific and includes a basic technical introduction
to the marimba and a memo to composers on writing for the instrument.
Nancy has premiered many new works and has had many commissions; this
information is not only helpful for her future composer collaborators, but
for the future of the art form.

Trombonist Mark K. has a brass quintet and a teaching studio. On the
front page of his website, visitors click on the area of first interest, the quintet or the teaching. This simplifies what might have been a confusing menu
if the two areas were combined. The quintet does lots of gigs, weddings, and
corporate events. Its pages include an ensemble bio and separate bios for
each performer, a repertoire list, sample programs, descriptions of workshops and booking information.

More remarkable is the teaching studio portion of the site. Its menu has
separate areas for kids, for advanced students, and for parents. Mark includes (for parents) his teaching philosophy statement, his teaching credentials, a short bio about his teaching experience, and his studio policy. There
are resource and method books listed, as well as advice on how to encourage
children to practice. For students, there are recommended CDs, an "expectations" section, audio files, fingering charts, and music theory worksheets.
In addition, there's a student news section, featuring the accomplishments
and photos of his students and a special set of links just for kids. The teaching portion of the site is thorough, engaging, and impressive. It's helpful for
both students and parents.

The Internet has made this the age of the entrepreneurial musician. Technology has made it easy and inexpensive for musicians to enter the professional market place, build their fan base, promote performances, and sell
recordings. Just keep in mind that the particulars on your site should be tailored to your career, projects, and goals. Take time to think carefully about
who you are, what story you want to tell, and whom you want to reach. Then
just get started: it can be as easy as uploading a version of your one-sheet with
a few clips of your music, a calendar, bio, your email, and some photos!

▼

Career Forward

Writing down your responses to these questions will help you create an effective online presence.

1. What is it you want from having an online presence? What is it you want your
   website and social networking to do for you?

2. Which musician websites do you visit regularly? *Why?* Which musician blogs do you read? *Why?*

3. What is it you want your site to convey about you as a musician, person, and citizen? What image do you want to communicate?

4. What could make your website distinctive? What projects could you feature on your site? What hobbies and interests would you want to include?

5. What do you want visitors to *do* on your site?

6. What incentives could you provide to encourage visitors to sign up for your mailing list?

7. How will you drive traffic to your website?

8. If you do not have a website, or have one that needs improving, what is preventing you from moving forward with the project?

▲

Interlude:
Five Fundamental
Questions

Clearing the Runway: Removing Obstacles to Your Success

Before venturing further with the practicalities of your music career, there are some larger conceptual issues that need attention. The five questions below speak to the essentials that determine your satisfaction in your career and life. These core issues often go unexamined by musicians. Unfortunately, when not dealt with, these issues can be stumbling blocks on your career path. Thinking over these questions can help you clear the path to your future.

1. Why Are You in Music? ◆

It's easy to get bogged down in everyday life and lose sight of why you first got into music and what you value most in your musical activities. There are many ways to be involved in music, so knowing what you want out of your involvement is essential to making good choices. Understanding your motivation will help you decide which projects to pursue and how to spend your time and energy toward creating a satisfying life in music.

Musicians rarely grapple with this crucial question of their motivation. If you take the time to reflect, you will most likely identify a range of reasons for your involvement in music. What's more, goals and ambitions often change over the years. So periodically reexamining your fundamental drive will help you assess whether or not the journey is worthwhile. Bear in mind that we are all "works in progress."

The Motivation Quiz

There are no right or wrong answers here. There is only the value of examining your motives. Check off all the reasons why you are in music. Add more as needed.

- ❏ Love of music itself, both as a listener and as a performer
- ❏ Passion for *making* music—the physical, intellectual, and emotional experience
- ❏ Love of performing, being in front of an audience, the adrenaline rush, the excitement, the applause
- ❏ Connecting with the audience, sharing a sense of community and communication
- ❏ Desire for acceptance, encouragement, approval (from parents, teachers, peers, and audience)
- ❏ Attraction to the "musician lifestyle," the idealism, ambition, and the daily rhythms of practice, preparation, and performance
- ❏ Sense of accomplishment
- ❏ Sense of identity, mission in life
- ❏ Sense of belonging to a community of the arts, something larger and more essential than a mere job or profession
- ❏ Challenge to surpass one's limitations, to constantly improve
- ❏ Communication: music as a means of expression that is more fulfilling than either words or any other arts discipline
- ❏ Other reasons? Add yours here:

2. How Do You Define Success? ◆

Musicians can be so focused on improving their abilities as performers that they avoid defining the version of success they actually seek. How do you picture success? What does creating a satisfying life in music mean to you?

When advising musicians, I generally run into two extreme camps. On the one hand are the complete idealists, interested only in *artistic* success, not financial success. They don't care what they have to do to make a living as long as they have time and freedom. These people proudly wear the "starving artist" badge, and dealing with any aspect of the business of music is viewed as "selling out." Unfortunately, this extreme position is difficult to maintain without a trust fund or second income.

On the other hand are those musicians who define success as having a major international career, worldwide acclaim, and the imagined appropriate financial reward for such stature. For these people, success means fame and the rarefied atmosphere of superstardom.

But outside the arts, other highly skilled, accomplished professionals are considered successful even if they are *not* famous. The idea is illustrated in this riddle:

What do you call a person who graduates from an Ivy League medical school at the bottom of his class?

A doctor.

How does this apply to musicians? There are highly skilled and accomplished musicians who do not consider themselves successful because they have not attained national or international recognition. They may perform locally and regionally, and have created wonderful lives for themselves and their families. They may combine performing and teaching with recording, freelancing, and other work. Viewed from the outside, their lives seem interesting, varied, and satisfying. But they may not consider themselves successful because they have not achieved "superstar" status. It's not unusual to hear gifted and experienced older musicians lament the fact that they never got that lucky break or the major label contract of their dreams. And they may express some version of "I could have made it big if only . . ."

To me, the problem in all this is how narrowly musicians define success and how they discount their own value and achievements. How you define success for yourself determines how you will measure your life's work. Your estimation of your accomplishments can either contribute to your happiness or make you bitter and resentful.

So when you take the measure of your life, what kind of yardstick will you use? As you advance in your career, you need to notice and appreciate the everyday triumphs, the series of small successes along the way. It's important to be both practical and patient; long-term career development is about process. It requires separating the fantasy of media-hyped stardom from your own values and goals.

Goals and priorities can change over the years. Your goals at age 20 are different from what they will be at age 30, 40, or 50. Look at how the priorities of Astrid Schween, the cellist of the Lark Quartet, have shifted more than once over the years. Early in the quartet's history, the Larks had a grueling tour schedule, playing 100 concerts per season. Later on, as several members were starting families, they focused more on New York City–based community engagement and education work and asked their manager to limit their touring schedule. These days, Astrid is excited to be adding concerto and recital work to her schedule, something she had no room for earlier on.

Besides your own goals changing, available opportunities will change as well. Technology has fundamentally changed the way music is heard and taught, distributed and purchased. As audience demographics change, so does the arts economy. Orchestras, opera companies, jazz clubs, and festivals are all undergoing rapid change. As you develop your career, you will need to be open to exploring new opportunities and expanding your skill set.

Many musicians find that as they develop their careers, they want to make a larger impact, to help improve their own local communities and beyond. This is one of the reasons we find that the leaders of major arts institutions are typically either practicing artists or former artists. Whether it is the head of the National Endowment for the Arts, the managers of performing arts centers, symphony orchestras, or conservatories, these leaders typically started out as artists and then found they also had the interest and the ambition to improve organizations and communities.

It's also important to acknowledge that career success and happiness do not necessarily go hand in hand. Life is just more complex than that. Talk to people you consider successful, people in any profession. Ask them about their definition of happiness. Most often, people speak of seeking a balance in life, of having meaningful and challenging work balanced with a rich personal life. In this balance is where many find satisfaction, contentment, and joy.

3. Is Your Thinking Getting in Your Way? ◆

The phrase "he's his own worst enemy" encapsulates the idea that individuals can sabotage their own chances of success. The problem lies typically in how these people view their circumstances—it's about their thinking. The way we think about ourselves and the world determines how we experience it.

For musicians, there's a particularly common syndrome, a type of problematic thinking. It's a black-and-white "music versus business" dichotomy, and this results in an unfortunate "us versus them" attitude. The two columns below illustrate some of the contrasting thought associations—the way musicians think (and talk) about the artistic and the business sides of the profession. These are slightly exaggerated, but all based on my experience of advising musicians.

▼ ——————————————————————————————

Thought Associations

How do you think about music itself and about the business side of the music profession?

Music as Art *versus*	*The Business of Music*
Good (clean, pure)	Bad (dirty, commercial)
Us (musicians, people who "get it")	Them (everyone else)
True calling	"Selling out"
Realm of imagination, creative	Tedious, dull

Focus on practicing, performing	Focus on money, paperwork, and "administrivia"
Feeling "at home"	Feelings of discomfort, distrust
Being idealistic (perhaps unrealistic)	Being pragmatic (perhaps limited in imagination)
Art for its own sake	Music as a profession (way to earn money)
Self-satisfaction	Music for others (an audience)
Expect/wait for that "lucky break"	Do-it-yourself, artist in charge: an entrepreneurial attitude

As you read down the columns, consider your own associations with art and business. And consider this: nothing in life is ever really 100 percent good or bad. There are positive and negative aspects on both sides. The real problem here is that for musicians, this good versus bad thinking prevents them from dealing effectively with both sides of their careers. And both sides are necessary for success. This polarized thinking can prevent musicians from taking charge and from moving forward in their careers. It can keep them isolated and disconnected from others, even from potential supporters and collaborators. Careers don't happen in a vacuum. The best alternative to the "us versus them" dichotomy is to think in terms of partnerships.

4. What Kind of Partnerships Are You Creating Through Your Music? ◆

Consider the live performance experience itself. Arranging a concert involves plenty of work: securing a venue, handling the publicity, writing and printing program notes and invitations, organizing a reception, and more. To be successful, performances usually need a team of people, all working together for one goal: a successful musical experience for both the performer and the audience. Who is on your "team"? How are you treating them?

The "us versus them" thinking separates musicians from the people who are actually their partners in this artistic process. To get beyond the us/them trap, remember that performers work in partnership with others to create the live concert experience. The diagram below shows the process and the collaborators. With this illustration, notice that the performer is not in the center, and is not a lone figure, but is, in fact, part of a team. The performer—with or without a manager—works with the presenter to arrange the performance date and negotiate details. Then, in order to attract an audience to help create the live musical experience, a performer needs to connect with media outlets.

Everyone in the circle is a partner in the process. They are all contributing to the desired outcome, which is a successful live musical experience.

It may seem strange to see the audience in the circle of collaborators. What is the audience's role? What does an audience contribute? For musicians, a successful performance may mean a high level of technical accuracy and a close approximation to their ideal interpretation. For the concert presenter, the successful performance may mean a full house, a good postconcert reception with the artists and donors, lots of media attention, and names and addresses of potential new season subscribers. But what does the audience want?

Several years ago I heard the Borromeo String Quartet perform the Schoenberg String Quartet Op. 7, a dense, difficult, forty-five-minute work that I had never heard before. The performance was spectacular. But what I found most memorable was my experience during the performance. For once, I was not analyzing the work or the performance (the curse of a trained musician as audience member). Instead, I noticed my own experience, my pleasure in watching expressive, passionate performers, and in the collective audience response. The audience's intent listening made a kind of palpable electricity in the hall. At times my thoughts were racing, trying to keep abreast of my own sensory overload, thought connections, and trying to take in the total experience of the performance. Because the piece is one long movement, a sustained experience, I was even more conscious of my continuous thought process. At some point after the quartet finished, during the applause and cheers, it dawned on me that each person in the audience had experienced something individual, perhaps nothing at all like what I had felt. But as a communal experience, it was clear we had all shared in something powerful.

I used to think of performances as fairly one-way transactions. The musician gives the performance, and an anonymous audience receives it. At the end, the audience signals its pleasure or displeasure. But now I think of the performance not as the sounds the musician produces but as the *experience* created by the audience and the performer in partnership. What I mean is that the real performance occurs in each listener's mind, the nonverbal dance of ideas, emotions, reminiscences, and associations. The performance experience is creative, associative, individual, and communal. In the best situations, a performance creates a sense of community between musicians and audience.

What do you imagine your audience getting from your live performance? What do you imagine runs through their minds as they listen? It can be difficult for trained musicians to imagine what nonmusicians experience, because they may not listen critically. The audience may be there for entertainment or as an escape, a break from their hectic lives. People come

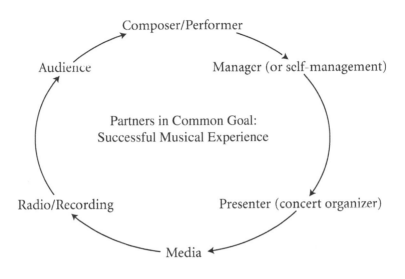

Process and collaborators in live performance

to concerts to mark special social occasions for family and friends, or because they seek a source of inspiration, solace or comfort, an emotional and intellectual challenge, or a spiritual release.

As for the question of partnerships, it's worth considering: who *are* your partners? If you feel a sense of being part of a larger effort, and that others are pulling with you, it can improve your experience as a performer, and can improve the quality of your interactions with others.

"I believe that musical talent is a gift given and that it is inextricably bound to social responsibility . . . I believe that musicians are agents for positive change in the world."

—Pianist Kwang-Wu Kim, former administrative director of El Paso Pro-Musica, an innovative community music program in El Paso, Texas, at his inaugural address as president of the Longy School of Music in Cambridge, Massachusetts.

---

5. How Meaningful Is Your Work? ◆

In a culture obsessed with materialism, celebrity, and status, it can be easy for musicians to feel marginalized. Musicians often feel disconnected from their community and people working outside the arts. But stepping back from everyday concerns allows musicians to take in the bigger picture of how music functions in our culture. It is important to at least occasionally consider the larger purpose of music.

After the terrorist attacks of September 11, 2001, the sheer number of memorial concerts showed how important music is in helping people express and process powerful emotions. For the first anniversary of the attacks, the "Rolling Requiem" project presented worldwide, continuous performances of the Mozart Requiem. Each performance began at 8:47 A.M. (the time of the first plane crash), so that the performances in each time zone circled the globe in sequence. I attended a Boston-area performance of the Requiem, held at one of the churches in my neighborhood. The building was packed beyond capacity, with people listening outside on the front lawn. It was so crowded that speakers were used to broadcast the performance into the basement, where organizers had set up chairs for another 100 people to sit and listen. They'd had only a few rehearsals, and because the orchestra and chorus were made up of community volunteers, it was not a very polished performance. I sat there in that crowded basement, listening to a spotty, heartfelt reading of a masterwork, surrounded by neighbors and strangers, all members of a community grieving together. I have rarely been so moved by any performance. For me, this was a powerful reminder of how music serves humanity: by creating ritual and meaning. In these ways, music *creates* community.

Each of us has moments when the importance of music is illuminated and the value of our work is made apparent. Which moments in your life have crystallized, for you, the value of music? If it's not about becoming rich and famous, then for you, what *is* it about? For anyone planning to devote his or her life to music, it's important to clarify its value and purpose in society.

Self-Assessment Inventory

The internal process for career growth involves coming to terms with your motivation, getting an accurate reading on your current abilities, and gaining the perspective needed to make appropriate positive change. To help your process, ask yourself the following questions:

- When do you feel most whole?
- Who is the person you want to become?
- What has been working well for you so far? *Why?*
- What has not been working so well? *Why?*
- How can you connect your music with your community?
- How can you help build audiences for your music?

These essential questions are worthy of revisiting throughout your career. Your perspective on these core issues resonates throughout your work and your life. Responding to these questions should help clarify your values and help you make career and life decisions based on these values.

Below is a terrific article with still more questions to consider concerning the creative process, performance, and practice. This article is by trombonist Abbie Conant and her husband, composer William Osborne, reprinted by permission. This piece is one of several interesting articles found on their website: http://www.osborne-conant.org.

Abbie Conant was formerly solo trombonist of the Munich Philharmonic. The *International Trombone Association Journal* has featured Ms. Conant in a cover article and described her as "in the first rank of world class trombonists." She performs as a soloist and performance artist internationally and is a professor of trombone at the Staatliche Hochschule für Musik in Trossingen.

Composer William Osborne has received two ASCAP awards, a doctoral fellowship to Columbia University, alternate to the American Rome Prize, and a major prize from the Theater Commission of the City of Munich for his Beckett productions. He founded the Wasteland Company in 1984, along with his wife Abbie as the main performer, to explore women's roles in music theater. In recent years they have performed his compositions in over 115 cities in America and Europe to great critical acclaim.

21 Questions for Young Performers ◆

By Abbie Conant and William Osborne

Many of these questions for musicians stem from our work in music theater, and suggest how interdisciplinary endeavors might enhance one's understanding as a performer.

1. Are you practicing and performing with a sense of authenticity and commitment, or working as if you had a musical factory job?
2. Some stage directors are interested in the "performer's personality and process." Are you working with such people, or simply preparing to be a cultural institution's "personnel"?
3. Do you try to discover the musicality of a piece for yourself?
4. A performance is a sort of response to the public. The ability to respond begins with silence, stillness and neutrality. Receptivity. Can you respond when performing, or are you too buried in routine or fear?

5. Are you trying to discover your own identity as an artist? Find it, feed it, fatten it. Think of the stage personality of Maurice Andre, Jean-Pierre Rampal, Maria Callas, or Louis Armstrong. Every person has the potential to express his or her own identity. Who are you? How will you find your artistic identity?

6. A stage director uses responsiveness, receptivity, and intuition. Do you direct the music when you play?

7. Have you thought of working together with a composer or performer to develop a music that fully expresses your identity? Is there a music that is really yours? If not, why not? What would such a music be?

8. To explore yourself without performing (just practicing) leads to excessive introspection and inaudible music. With a little practice and encouragement you can evolve as a performer who projects his or her ideas. Are you learning by doing? How often do you perform?

9. Do you practice to be aware of and remove habits and clichés? Do you practice mechanically?

10. There are three steps to "recreating" a composition. The first is the existential, which is considering what the piece means to you. The second step is the psychological, which is considering the composer's motives for writing it. The third is the semiological, which is determining how you will perform the work so that others can perceive its meaning. Have you considered these steps? How will your performance make vivid the composer's motives, and your inner relation to the composition?

11. We communicate when we perform. Have you considered that everything has a meaning, including your presence on the stage?

12. Do you realize that humans think with their whole bodies, and not just the brain? Do you realize that performing is essentially an act of the body? Do you consider it presumptuous to consider performance as poetry in space made possible by intense physical preparation?

13. Art is the creation of symbolic forms. How do you highlight and detail your performance to create an iconic vividness?

14. The antics do not make the clown, it is when he or she reveals some truth about him or herself. Authenticity. Is it the technique or acrobatic perfection that makes the musician? Do you reveal the truth about your inner identity when you perform? How can you learn to?

15. Have you noticed how instantly and unthinkingly you catch yourself when you slip on the ice? It's not instinct. When you were born you couldn't even walk. When you play do you make active the knowledge that resides in the body? When you practice are you adding the right knowledge to it?

16. Music and theater were given birth by the same muse. Do you realize that every concept, idea, or method in theater has its corollary in music, and vice-versa? Do you realize how this understanding can enrich your music?

17. Have you considered your internal repertoire of physical, imaginative, and emotional skills? Are you trying to increase them? What are you calling upon when you perform? What do you have to offer as a human being?

18. When you practice and perform do you confront yourself in a state of perpetual discovery?

19. Do you practice with the goal of making things so natural and spontaneous that you no longer feel your body? You must divest your body, it must in effect cease to exist. Ironically, only then does it really begin to exist. Do you "subdue the flesh" by removing its blockages?

20. What are you doing to learn to come before a public and not be afraid?

21. Perhaps music isn't sound. Perhaps it doesn't exist outside of our heads, because nothing in the world is a perfect realization or performance of our abstract ideals. Are you learning to operate with your mistakes? Every performer must. It is part of the human condition to constantly proceed from failure. Is there not a certain frailty and miraculousness to creation?

6

Booking Performances: Artist Management and Self-Management

The Big Question ◆

Jenny is a talented and ambitious pianist in her mid-twenties who's won several regional competitions. She makes a career advising appointment to discuss her career. Since getting her master's degree two years ago, she's been teaching at a local community music school. She also teaches a few students privately, is the accompanist for a voice teacher's studio, and has performed with several local new music ensembles.

At the appointment, I ask how things are going. Jenny says, "The teaching is OK, I like working with kids, but this isn't what I had in mind for life after graduation. I really want to be making a living as a performer, playing solo recitals. I was hoping you could give me the names of a few artist managers so that I can get representation."

I'm asked a version of the question "How can I get management?" about once a week. And similar to the question "How do I get a record contract?" the answer takes some deconstructing.

Myths about Artist Management   ◆

Unfortunately, there are many common misconceptions about artist management. Here are a few of the most pervasive:

> Myth #1: Careers happen like this: if you are talented, practice hard, and win big competitions, you will be rewarded with a manager who will make you a success. Your manager will provide enough well-paying performances so that you will not need to have a "day" job.

This is NOT the way it works.

> Myth #2: Finding a manager is a straightforward process. You simply send in your publicity materials with a letter requesting management, someone signs you on, and then you become a success.

Also, not true.

> Myth #3: Once you have a manager, your career will take off. Your manager will handle all of the business aspects of your career—the details of publicity, contracts, and finances—leaving you free to practice and perform.

Again, this is not the way things actually work.

> Myth #4: In order to get bookings and have a successful career, you need a manager.

Absolutely not true.

Reality: What Managers Actually Do

The main work of artist managers is booking concerts for their artists, and negotiating the fees and contracts for these performances. An experienced, successful manager is someone who has built solid relationships with presenters—the people who organize concert series, festivals, and residencies.

Managers use their connections and skills to promote and "sell" their artists to presenters. Managers do this "sales" work by phone, fax, e-mail, and in-person meetings at regional and national booking conferences.

There are some differences in artist management among genres. Beyond getting bookings, artist managers also create or oversee the development of their artists' promotional materials. Classical artist managers may also arrange for commissions, for their artists to audition for conductors, and may help secure full-time residencies or make connections with record labels. Generally, artists work in *partnership* with their managers.

Unfortunately, there are many more talented and deserving artists than there are ready-made performance opportunities. It can take an enormous amount of time and energy for artist managers to get bookings for their artists, especially on the higher-profile concert series. There are also many more musicians seeking artist management than the industry can support.

Who's Who?

Today, people are working in expanded capacities, as the industry is transformed by changes in funding, audience interest, and technology. The roles of managers, producers, and presenters (and sometimes artists) are becoming somewhat blurred. It's not always a straightforward buy-and-sell transaction. Musicians are becoming presenters of their own series, and some start their own festivals. Artist managers are sometimes working as producers and partnering with presenters. Though the job descriptions are becoming blurred, here are the basics:

Artist managers book performances for the artists they have agreed to represent; they may also advise on artists' career projects and promotional materials. Managers must develop and maintain good relationships with presenters. Managers face stiff competition in trying to book artists for a shrinking number of prestigious concert series opportunities.

Booking agents book artists to perform at a variety of concert and commercial venues (such as cruise ships and hotels). They generally do not get involved in promoting their artists' long-term careers, or in recording or commissioning projects. Booking agents typically work with pop, rock, and jazz artists.

Personal representatives are hired to work on behalf of an artist, booking concerts and managing specific aspects of the artist's career.

Presenters are in charge of engaging artists to perform for their audiences. Presenters curate performance series, festivals, and residencies. They may work for many different types of venues, such as universities, libraries, and arts councils. Presenters oversee the bookings and contracts for the artists, as well as the publicity and finances for the series. Because ticket sales cover only a fraction of the costs of presenting a series, fundraising and budget concerns are a big part of the job. Presenters must also consider the balance of the entire concert series they book, so that they provide a variety of offerings appropriate for—and of interest to—their community.

Producers organize performances; this may include renting the performance space, choosing and editing the program, hiring the performers and backstage crew, renting sound and recording equipment, managing the publicity, and scheduling rehearsal times and sound checks.

Publicists work to get media coverage for an individual or organization. They write and send press releases and PSAs (public service announcements) to newspapers, radio, television, and online media outlets. They may work for an organization, such as a label or a festival, or on a freelance contract basis for particular artists, handling a performance project, tour, or CD release. Their goal is to gain media attention for their clients.

▲

How Artist Management Works ◆

There are many factors that go into a manager's decision about which artists to represent. Of course, a manager must believe in the musician's artistry and ability to communicate with audiences. This is somewhat subjective, a matter of taste and interest on the manager's part, but it is also a matter of the artist's track record of success, reputation, career readiness, and personality. A manager needs to know that the artist has "booking potential," that the manager will be able to interest presenters in booking this artist. And of course, managers must consider the balance of their roster. If a manager already represents a solo harpist (not an easy act to book), it is unlikely that she would consider adding another. And if a manager is stretched thin with the number of artists he is representing, it may be impossible to add any more.

Here is the bottom line: managers need to sign artists who can earn them a profit, who already have a track record of excellent performances and reviews, or who have just won a major international competition and are attracting significant media attention. No matter how much artist managers love music and love working with musicians, they are still in a *business*. In order to stay in the business, they must be able to earn an income.

Classical managers' standard commission is 20 percent of the artist's gross concert fee paid by the presenting organization. For jazz and other genres, the commission is 10–15 percent. In addition, artists are billed for their share of the necessary expenses, which include artist roster advertising, brochures, long-distance telephone for sales calls, postage, travel to booking conferences, and the artist's promotional materials. The expenses are typically invoiced to the artist as monthly or quarterly bills. In most cases, managers have their artists sign initial contracts of 2–3 years, with an automatic yearly renewal. The contract agreement details the artist/manager working relationship: the financial arrangement, the exclusivity, and geographic reach. Some contracts are for North American representation only; artists may have other management in other parts of the world. Classical musicians' artist contracts are typically exclusive: they cover all performances the soloist or ensemble is involved in, no matter how the performance opportunity comes about. Jazz artists often do not have exclusive contracts because they typically work concurrently with multiple ensembles and consequently end up working with multiple booking agents for various projects.

The three major classical New York artist management companies are Columbia Artists (CAMI), Opus 3 Artists (formerly ICM), and IMG Artists. These firms have the largest artist rosters, and often the most well known artists. And these firms have the most clout in negotiating contracts with festivals, record labels, and orchestras.

There are also mid-level management firms, with somewhat smaller rosters, such as Barrett Vantage Artists, Thea Dispeker, Alliance Artist Management, Melvin Kaplan, and Colbert Artists Management. Finally, there are many small firms, generally one- or two-person offices, including MCM Artists, BesenArts, Sciolino Artist Management, and many more. The advantage of mid-size and smaller firms may lie in the often greater amount of personal attention the artists receive.

To find listings of artist managers, see *Musical America,* the annual international music industry directory. You can browse *Musical America* (hard copy or online version) at your local music school's library and read about the various artist management firms and see which artists are on their rosters.

To find out more about how artist management works, visit the National Association of Performing Arts Managers of America website (http://www.napama.org). Read the ethical guidelines for the profession to get a good idea of what to expect from a manager and what questions to ask if you are considering working with a particular manager.

Before signing any contract or investing in management representation, be sure to do your homework: ask for the names and phone numbers of past and current artists the manager has represented. Check these references carefully. Before an artist signs with a manager, there is usually a courting period when both parties are checking each other out. A manager without appropriate skills, contacts, and experience is a bad investment. Overall, the chemistry between artist and manager has to be right, because the working relationship is a partnership.

After signing with a management firm, it may take a whole year before an artist gets any work. This is because most presenters of mid-size and larger series book several seasons in advance, so it can take that time for word to get around about an interesting new talent. And, once an artist or ensemble has secured management, he or she still needs to cultivate and maintain an excellent working relationship with their manager.

In his article "The Quest for Management" (published in Chamber Music America's *CMA Matters* in October 2007), artist manager Robert Besen (http://www.besenarts.com) writes that he counts on his artists "to work *with* me, not simply depend on me." His roster includes the Daedalus Quartet, the Orlando Consort, and guitarist William Kanengiser (of the Los Angeles Guitar Quartet). Besen explains that he is most effective as a manager when his artists not only deal professionally with booking and performance details, but also take a proactive approach, feeding him "creative ideas about repertory and other projects" and leads on new venues. "I like to work with artists who are effective at pressing the flesh," adds Besen, "those who get to know presenters, board members of presenting organizations, important members of the presenters' communities."[1]

Robert Besen also addresses the key questions artists should ask themselves when considering management: "Are you working? Are you getting re-engagements? Are you earning decent fees? Do you have a following? Do you have a recognizable and compelling artistic personality? Do you have something compelling for a manager to sell and for presenters and their audiences to buy?"[2]

> *Take the artist management quiz:*
> How many concerts did you play last season?
> What was the total amount you earned from last year's performances?
> Next, take 20 percent of last season's concert fees and ask yourself, would a manager be interested in signing you? In other words, have you generated enough work and media attention to interest a manager?

Professional managers are not in the business of growing anyone's career from scratch (unless you are a world-class child prodigy). Managers simply cannot afford to invest time and energy in this process. *However, there are effective ways for emerging artists to manage themselves.*

How *Not* to Get Artist Management ◆

Musicians often prepare elaborate, expensive promotional kits and send them to all the managements listed in *Musical America*. Every week these management companies receive stacks of unsolicited promo kits with letters from artists requesting representation. These letters and kits, by and large, go unread. The management companies have their hands full trying to book the artists already on their rosters. So, without a personal contact to an artist manager or the specific knowledge that the artist manager is looking for an up-and-coming wind quintet or solo harpist (if that's what you do), then you're simply wasting time and money sending materials that will only be discarded.

However, management companies may be interested in hearing a new or emerging artist if an esteemed performer, teacher, or presenter recommends the artist. If you have a mentor with management contacts who feels you are ready for professional representation, he or she can invite these people to your next concert or write a letter of introduction for you.

Without these contacts, you might wonder, what's an aspiring artist to do?

The Truth about Competitions ◆

Yes, there are some competitions that offer preprofessional artist management to the winners. Such competitions include those sponsored by Astral Artistic Services, Concert Artists Guild, Young Concert Artists, and Pro Musicis International. These competitions offer winners artist representation and concert bookings for several years, after which some artists are successful in moving on to full professional artist management rosters.

There are also other competitions (Van Cliburn and the Honens competition for pianists, and the Sphinx Competition for Black and Latino string players) that offer the winners a number of concerts, solo engagements with orchestras, and/or a recording. These prizes and the media attention may be helpful in gaining the interest of potential artist managers. See the companion website for additional information on competitions.

But the truth is that no competition guarantees a career, and there are many musicians who win prestigious competitions these days and do not get artist management. So, putting all your hopes on winning a competition is like gambling with the odds stacked against you. Competitions are fine but not as one's primary strategy for creating a career.

The real challenge for emerging artists is not how to get a manager; it's how to get an audience, how to build a fan base, a reputation, and media attention. The new music group Bang on a Can makes for a good case in point. It started with three young composers, fresh out of Yale, who were interested in music "from between the cracks," between minimalism and rock, between written and improvised music, between music and noise, between live performance and electonica. In 1987 they put on their first concert, a twelve-hour extravaganza of new music, and called it the "first annual" Bang on a Can Marathon, without knowing whether they could attract a following. They thought the actual audience for their music was likely to be those interested in contemporary visual art and film, not the traditional classical music crowd. So they concentrated their efforts on spreading the word to people who visited galleries and art events. Their hunch paid off. Since then, the group has established a touring ensemble, the Bang on a Can All-Stars, part rock band, part amplified chamber group. In 2000, Bang on a Can started the People's Commissioning Fund, which invited audience members to give, as little or as much as they could, to a fund for commissioning new works. In addition, Bang on a Can now has a summer educational festival for young composers and performers located in the Berkshires at the Massachusetts Museum of Contemporary Arts. All this came from three composers with an idea. This is the entrepreneurial approach. You can create your own performance opportunities and attract new audiences without a manager.

Self-Management: Your Best Bet   ◆

Here is the good news: you do not need to win a major competition in order to get your career going. Nor do you need a manager to get concert bookings. It *is* possible to successfully self-manage your career. The basic idea of self-management is that *you* are in the driver's seat.

The truth is that nobody is going to be a stronger advocate for your music than you. No one will get as excited about it or have as much at stake in it as you. So, instead of hoping to win the right competition or wait for someone else to give you opportunities, why not take charge of your own career? Mozart and Phillip Glass both wrote and performed their own works, rented halls for performances, organized their own ensembles, and produced their own concerts. Yes, all of this takes considerable work, but take heart: there is a long history of musicians as creative and successful entrepreneurs.

Booking your own concerts is not rocket science, but it helps to acquire certain skills. In coaching musicians in this process, I've found that when the work is broken down into bite-size pieces, most musicians can book their own concerts. After all, musicians routinely analyze and understand complex musical works. They break these down into manageable sections to practice and to master. Self-management simply means putting some of these same critical thinking and organizational skills to work in another direction, toward career projects.

It helps to keep in mind that all careers start locally. So, first arrange performances in your immediate community. The goal is to gain experience and to start building an audience, adding names to your mailing list, and perhaps gaining media attention. All of this can lead to bookings at larger and more prestigious venues.

Whether you have a manager or are doing it yourself, there are some absolute essentials with which everyone must come to terms. Freddie Hart, artist manager for Triple Helix, describes the necessary discussions artists need to have with either their managers or with themselves: "Have open and honest communication about goals but also about where you are now. It's important to have realistic expectations." At the beginning, it may be far more important to gain performance experience than it is to be earning fees. Hart recommends to "Be clear about how important the money is (or isn't) in terms of validating your self worth." Tying one's self-esteem to the fees paid for performances is a losing battle. Hart advises musicians to "remember why you want to be performing in the first place."

Alternatives to Traditional Management ◆

When a musician has built a solid local and regional reputation and fan base, he or she is in a good position either to attract professional management or to hire and train an administrative assistant to handle portions of the self-management work. Assistants may be skilled (or trained) in managing press material updates and mailings, making "cold calls" to presenters, writing contracts, managing the musician's mailing lists and website, and writing program notes.

▼

Mike J., a Boston-area clarinetist, has specialized in contemporary music, premiering and commissioning many new works for solo clarinet. He had self-managed his career while in school and also pursued finding professional management for a few years, but to no avail. Finally, he found a friend with a background in orchestral management who agreed to work as his personal representative on a 20 percent commission basis. The first season, Mike's friend booked him fifteen solo engagements with regional orchestras in the Midwest. This made a great addition to the New England area bookings that Mike had arranged on his own.

▲

There are many examples of ensembles that started as self-managed groups and went on to hire their own artist representatives (the Cavani and Cypress String Quartets, Synergy Brass Quintet, and the ensemble Asteria are just a few). These groups were self-managing until they reached a threshold where they needed—and were able—to hire outside help. The artist representative may be paid on a per-project basis, on a monthly retainer, or on an hourly or weekly rate basis.) Early on, the Kronos Quartet brought on board Janet Cowperthwaite as their artist representative and the "fifth member" of the quartet: an integrated member sharing equally in the financial risk and rewards of the group. The Kronos quartet is structured as a nonprofit (this is a legal and tax status that helps with the fundraising and grants necessary for most arts organizations to operate). Today, Janet is managing director, with a staff of eight administrators, all working for the Kronos Quartet/Kronos Performing Arts Association, and they handle all of Kronos's booking, travel, promotion, production, and fundraising.

Another alternative to traditional management is described in *Making Music in Looking Glass Land,* a terrific music career guide by Ellen Highstein (published by Concert Artists Guild). In the book, Highstein outlines the idea of creating a cooperative management. A group of musicians or ensembles may collectively hire a personal representative to work on their behalf, either on a commission or retainer basis. Alternatively, the musicians themselves may divide up the work, delegating the telephone and e-mail contact, graphic design work, and the administrative and bookkeeping duties. The work can be assigned according to the members' abilities and preferences. Highstein writes that these alternatives to traditional management can have "several advantages over individual or self-management: they can enable group members to pool information and contacts, to spread the work and cost of self-management among the members or allocate it to a salaried person, allow the member musicians to control the kinds of musicians on the roster and allow the members to say, 'Call my manager,' with honesty and confidence."[3]

Where to Perform ◆

Ultimately, you need to find places to perform. Because all careers start local, look for venues in your community. To get ideas, ask your mentors, teachers, and colleagues for suggestions of places to perform. Read your local arts calendar listings online to find who is performing where in your area. Familiarize yourself with the various concert series and venues, and check their websites. Beyond your network, your sleuthing should include checking websites for the itineraries of other emerging musicians. Where are they performing?

Barbara Raney, who managed Epic Brass for many years, recommends that emerging artists "approach smaller series with smaller budgets and make them an offer they can't refuse! Practice six degrees of separation: if you want to get to a series, plot a course through the people you know and the people your people know. Your message is more compelling when you can say, 'Jim Barker suggested I call . . . ' "

You may have more than one geographic area for possible performances, such as where you live now, where you attended school, and where you grew up. You can get presenter lists from your state and regional arts agencies (see the companion website). With contacts and performance opportunities in multiple locations, musicians can arrange "micro-tours," performing the same program in several different communities to gain exposure and experience. And the good news is that in smaller cities and towns, emerging artists often have an easier time getting media coverage and reviews.

The Elegua duo, cellist Ginevra Ventre and pianist Claire Black, organized a concert in New York's Adirondack region where Black grew up. The two had attended Baldwin-Wallace College as undergraduates and enjoyed rehearsing and performing together. Though they were then, in 2008, at different grad schools, Ventre and Black wanted to continue performing together. The duo made a list of possible places to play and got help from Claire's family friends in the area.

At their initial concert in the region, they had a guest book for audience members to sign and leave e-mail addresses. After the concert, the duo sent thank-you notes to everyone, and some people wrote back, offering ideas and contacts for future performances and assistance with getting press coverage. "Claire and I were surprised at the extent to which audience members were willing to help," Ventre said.

Their initial performance in the spring grew into a summer tour of eight concerts; the range of venues included a local hospital, elementary school, a community art center, church, art gallery, and a nursing home. Ventre explained their process: "To negotiate the fees, we investigated the venues' websites (if they had one), and Googled them to research all that we could. When we talked to the presenters we asked what their budget was and what other kinds of entertainment they hosted, all to get an idea of what would be an appropriate fee to ask for. We also bartered, in some cases exchanging a lower fee for help with publicizing the performance and the tour." The following summer, the duo presented a local composer's piece on one concert and another concert was recorded for broadcast on the regional NPR radio station.

Alternative Performance Sites

Think beyond established concert series and festivals. Think of places that are already attracting audiences or attendees but do not currently present concerts. Visit your public library; ask the reference librarian for help researching potential venues. Your local chamber of commerce and arts council also are good resources. You may find non-traditional sites with surprisingly good acoustics where people are enthusiastic to have your music. Check out your local sources:

Museums	Hospitals	High-end condominiums
Parks and recreation	Resort hotels	Boys and girls clubs
Historical houses	Prisons	Rehab centers
Churches/temples	Libraries	Colleges/universities
Community centers	Hospice centers	Chamber of commerce
Senior centers	Public schools	Adult education centers
Shelters	Alumni associations	Community music schools
Veterans' associations	Private schools	Civic clubs (Elks, Rotary, Lions)

Another great way to cultivate a fan base and supporters is to arrange "house concerts." These can be held in apartments, country homes, or city lofts. They can be organized as specific fundraising events for a special list of invited guests, or they can be a great way to try out a new program in advance of a more formal concert date. Fortepianist and harpsichordist Andrew Appel is the founder of Four Nations (http://www.fournations.org), a Baroque ensemble based in New York's Hudson River Valley. Since the mid-1990s, Appel has been organizing a fall series called the Hudson River Harvest Concerts. Each concert takes place in a privately owned site of historic interest or in a particularly important home in the region. To organize your own house concerts, start with the people in your network. Find out who has the larger living spaces, a piano (if needed), and who might be interested in hosting or sponsoring a house concert.

▼

Finding Your Niche

Here's a tip from self-managing jazz pianist Bradley Sowash. In "Self-Marketing for Artists," Sowash advises musicians to "find a niche for which you alone are suited. Find where people gather around your niche concept, and you have a new outlet for performing that can be in addition to your concert career. I know a guy who wrote and self-produced an instrumental recording of songs about flowers and herbs mentioned in Shakespeare. He could have named them Song #1 or Opus 43 but he hooked his notes to flowers through his titles. Do you know where he gigs and sells merchandise? Flower shows. Since jazz worship services are a part of my offerings, I go to church events to promote them . . . How many other touring performers do you think set up booths at flower shows and church conventions? With zero competition, it's easy to stand out among bud vase wholesalers and angel jewelry vendors."[4]

▲

Effective Programming: Engaging Presenters and Audiences ◆

Before contacting a presenter or venue manager, you need to make sure that the program you offer is compelling. Think about it from a presenter's point of view. A relatively unknown artist, whose name alone will not attract an audience, playing a recital of standard repertoire—does that sound like a box office draw? If an artist offers only traditional repertoire, why should an audience attend? They can stay home and listen to recordings of these same works by any of their favorite legendary artists. Presenters need to consider whether or not an artist can attract an audience. So, for emerging artists without name recognition, innovative programming is the answer.

In effect, a presenter "curates" a concert series the way a museum curator plans an art exhibition. Museum curators carefully select and arrange the artwork, with the idea that each single work is experienced in relation to the whole exhibition. Likewise, a presenter books individual performances with the balance of the entire series in mind. Curators write and print descriptions of the individual works and of the exhibition itself. Presenters do the same. And they both work to publicize their shows to attract, engage, and enlighten a community audience. There are many factors that go into presenters' decisions about which artists to book. So being rejected may simply mean that your program does not fit a presenter's plans for that particular season.

One of the best ways to interest presenters—as well as critics and audiences—is by programming unusual pieces, or pairing well-known works with non-traditional ones, or by using thematic programming (building a program around a particular thematic idea).

To gather creative ideas for programs, ask other musicians, collaborators, faculty, and music librarians. In terms of programming for non-traditional venues, consider how a concert might fit with the organization. You might offer a museum a program of music related to its collection of twentieth-century Expressionists, or a program built around a particular type of artwork such as miniatures, portraits, or landscapes. If the venue is a school, considering developing programs for specific age groups. Does the organization have a special fundraising event coming up that could use a performance after the gala dinner? In preparing for your booking calls, it's important to have at least one program organized and to be able to describe it engagingly.

Radius Ensemble is a flexible, mixed chamber group with a set of core players, headed by director/oboist Jennifer Montbach. The ensemble produces its own concert series. Jennifer approaches programming individual concerts by first choosing a piece she loves and wants to program. Then she asks herself which potential themes or ideas suggested by this piece could be explored in the rest of the concert. She also asks herself what pieces might make for interesting contrasts. The idea is to think creatively to develop imaginative programs that will help draw media interest and audiences. (See http://www.radiusensemble.org.)

Creative Programming Tips

To generate more ideas, consider building programs around the following:

- The premiere of a new work (especially by local composers)
- Unusual pairings (e.g., Baroque ornamentation and contemporary improvisations—a program exploring the parallels between the two, with classical and jazz works)
- Works that explore a thematic idea, such as war, passion, faith, time, redemption, or healing
- Works inspired by myths or legends
- Works inspired by dance forms, the visual arts, or theater
- Music from a particular country
- Celebration of a local event, person, holiday, organization, or anniversary
- Collaboration with a guest artist from the local community: a musician, dancer, or a video artist
- Music inspired by literature
- Pairing of music with live poetry or short fiction readings

Assuming you have developed one or more potential program to offer and you have a list of possible performance venues to pursue, the next step involves a little more sleuthing.

Booking Your Own Concerts ◆

Next, do some research about your potential presenting organizations and venues. Much of this research can be accomplished online, by reading carefully the venues' websites, and the rest by making exploratory phone calls. Keep a notebook or spreadsheet to organize the information you find for each venue.

Find out the following:

- What is the range of the organization's existing programming?
- Are the acoustics appropriate for your music? (Check what types of groups perform there now.)
- What is the seating capacity of the hall or space? (Emerging artists should look for a smaller venue that your friends and fans could fill.)
- Does the venue host any family or educational programming, partnerships with local schools?

- If they do present music, what is the career "level" of the artists? Find out if emerging local musicians perform there. Check who is performing there this season; find these artists' bios on their websites, and check their backgrounds and credentials. Some larger-budget series book only well-known artists with professional management. So target the venues appropriate for your current level of experience.
- Examine the series' staff and board of trustees' lists posted on their website. Ask friends and colleagues to find a personal connection with the series so you can convert a "cold call" into a warm one with something like "Beatrice Fortner suggested I contact you."

After you have researched your list of local venues and have a compelling program organized, you can make initial exploratory calls to fine-tune your information. Smaller-budget series are often booked by volunteers, part-time staff, or people who have various other duties at their institutions. Whomever you reach, be gracious. Always make a note of the name of the person you are speaking with, so that when you call you can greet the person by name.

Booking Calls: Five Elements of a Pitch

To be effective in booking your own performances, you'll need a succinct, well-crafted *pitch,* a 20–30 second statement about you or your ensemble. The purpose of the pitch is to interest presenters in you and your music, so that they will want to listen to your demo and read your promo kit. You basically have the first 20–30 seconds in a call (or on a voice-mail message) to pique a presenter's interest. In that brief time, you need to cover the five points below, otherwise you will lose the presenter's attention and she or he will end the conversation quickly.

A pitch is not a blurb you memorize and recite verbatim when making booking calls. It should be, instead, the equivalent of elevator speech material (see chapter 2) that you can use flexibly as part of your conversation. It is important to have this material thought out and to feel comfortable using it before you make any calls.

Remember: the call should be a dialogue—back and forth, a real conversation. The five points outlined below are the major areas you need to cover, but of course, you will need to be responsive to whatever reactions and questions you get from the presenter.

1. *Identify your name and what you do* (genre/ensemble, etc.). "Hi, my name is Jane Doe with the ABC Brass Quintet"; "Hello, my name is Ron Tompkins calling on behalf of the XYZ Jazz Trio"; or "Hi, I'm a violinist here in Tucson; my name is Marla Thompson."
2. *Establish a connection with the organization, the presenter, the series, or the community.* If you have a personal contact in common, use it:

"Betty Kim suggested I contact you." Or "Tim Porter, the baritone who performed for your series last year, suggested I call you," or "Wendy Jones, on your board of trustees, suggested I get in touch with you," or "I grew up here in Northfield, and have attended many exhibitions at your gallery space."

3. *Give a third-party endorsement.* Include one or two of your best credentials. This will give the presenter evidence of your abilities and experience as a performer:

"I recently won the ABC competition."
"I recently performed on the DEF and GHI concert series."
"I recently received the KLM grant."
"I graduated with honors from the 123 music school and have performed with the 456 ensemble."
"My ensemble recently released a CD that got a good write-up in XYZ journal."
"My ensemble has presented well-received family concerts at the Whoville Library and Whatsit Community Center."

4. *Program idea: explain what specifically you are offering.*

Pitch for a club: "We've just completed our debut recording and are looking to book album release concerts this fall. We'd like to include a date in your area."

Pitch for historical society or architectural college: "I noticed on your website that you offer family programs, and I wanted to let you know about our educational programming. We've got two programs pairing architecture and music that we thought would work well at your site. The programs are fun and interactive: emphasizing how a piece of music is constructed. We work with the children in 'building' a new piece of music, relating architectural concepts to musical ones."

Pitch for a women's college: "I've got a program of works by women composers—including new works by two regional composers—that might be of interest to your college students and local alumni."

Pitch for a bookstore, library, or college lecture series: "I've got a new program that pairs spoken word and music inspired by literature, that I perform together with local actor Tom Beakman reading."

5. *Propose next steps:*

"May I send you some information?" . . ."What specifically would be most helpful? . . . Should I send you this electronically or in hard copy?"

> (*Note: your full hard copy promo kit is expensive to produce. Don't send the full kit unless it's requested. Give presenters just what they ask for, but include a note telling them what else you have, in case they want more.*)
> "And, I'll call to follow up in 2 weeks. When are the best times to reach you?"

Once you've developed your pitch statement, practice it with colleagues and friends. Do a "pretend" booking call, having a colleague or mentor play the role of the presenter at the other end of the line. This will help you feel more confident when you do these calls for real.

If No One Answers

If you call and get only voice-mail, leave a brief message introducing yourself and concisely explain why you are calling. Leave your phone number but promise to call again. Wait four or five workdays and then try again, leaving another message if no one picks up. After that, try a few more times, experimenting with different days of the week and different times of the day, but don't leave any more messages. If after five or six attempts you still cannot reach the person, move on.

Follow Through

Keep scrupulous notes about all your presenter contacts. Keep a log of all presenter interactions so that you can track when you called, what you sent, and when to make the follow-up contacts. If you promise to send a presenter something, make sure you do it right away and personalize what you send. This can be an e-mail note with a link to your website and your EPK. Or, if sending hard copy materials, it can be either a typewritten or handwritten note, something like this:

> Dear So-and-so:
>
> I enjoyed speaking with you today about your series! Here are the materials you suggested I send you: bio, fact sheet, and CD for my jazz ensemble, Four Minus One. I am very interested in the Sunday afternoon jazz programming you mentioned and the diverse audience you are drawing. I believe we have a program that might be a good fit and will call in two weeks to follow up.
>
> Best Wishes,
>
> Eric Platz

If you say you'll call to follow up, do it. When you call, remind the presenter who you are and what you sent. Be personable and positive.

Possible Outcomes to Presenter Calls

1. *Rejection.* Remember that when presenters say no, they're not rejecting you or judging your music. They are simply saying that what you're offering does not fit with their series—now. It may in the future, or it may not. You will need to determine whether this presenter is appropriate for you at this career stage. Be cordial, and ask the presenter for suggestions of appropriate other series where you might be a better fit. And thank them for their time.

2. *"Don't call us, we'll call you."* A presenter may say they will call you if they're interested, as a way to let you down gently. If so, keep this presenter on your mailing list and periodically send career updates and invitations to your performances.

3. *The presenter is interested!* She or he may ask you detailed questions about your performance history, ideas for programming, the number of people on your mailing list. Talk in terms of the fit your performance might make with their series. Be personable. You are building a relationship with this presenter. Sometimes a presenter is interested for a future season, not the immediate one. If this is the case, ask when it would be best to follow up and then make sure you do so.

▼

In "Self Marketing for Artists," Jazz pianist Bradley Sowash writes, "Offering many different booking options is my first secret to filling up a performance schedule. For example in the last 12 months, my engagements have included solo piano concerts, educational appearances, guest speaker appearances, jazz worship services, benefit concerts, retail CD signings, concert CD signings, arts organization panelist, teacher training, master classes, private lessons, and conference workshop leader . . . A lengthy list to be sure but united under one consistent artistic and personal vision. If your schedule is scant, you might ask yourself, 'What else can I do with these skills?' "[5]

▲

Negotiating Fees ◆

If the conversation is going well, the presenter may bring up the question of your fee, either suggesting a fee or asking what your fee is. Do your homework in advance. If you know people who have performed on this series, ask them what range of fees this presenter has paid.

Because some presenters receive public funding, your state and local arts agencies may be able to give you information about their fee range.

Many smaller community series have limited budgets. Libraries and community centers may pay $300–$1,000, with little or nothing extra for transportation or lodging. But these series can be the best kind to get started with, to build a fan base and gain local or regional media attention. Presenters of larger concert series may pay emerging solo artists $1,000–$3,000 and ensembles $2,000–$5,000.

Know your bottom line. To determine whether or not a fee is acceptable, calculate the total expenses you anticipate for this performance (your accompanist fees, travel, any lodging costs.) If you have any technical requirements (drum kits, amplification, or video equipment), find out what the presenter can provide and what you would need to bring or rent. This will affect either your expenses or the presenter's. The details of technical requirements should be clarified in your negotiations and then confirmed in your written confirmation or contract. Typically, these are inserted into a contract as the *technical rider*. Once you know the costs involved, you are in a better position to accept or decline the performance date.

In negotiating your fee, it's always best if you can get the presenter to name a possible fee or indicate their budget range first, but if you are asked what your fee is, be prepared to say something like:

> "My (or our) usual fee is _____" and then PAUSE! . . . (Don't fill the silence!) Wait a beat or two for the presenter to react. She or he may say, "That's fine" or "Oh, we can't pay that much" or "That's a little steep for our budget."

After they react, then you can say (if you are willing to negotiate), "I'm willing to work with you on this" or "I can be somewhat flexible."

Former artist manager Barbara Raney suggests, "If you can't get the fee you want, ask the presenter if he or she can make it up in in-kind services, such as meals, or transportation." Presenters may be able to offer discount lodging or accommodations at the home of a board member or contributor. In the end, you'll need to weigh the benefits of doing the performance (the exposure and experience) against the costs to determine your acceptable fee.

The idea to convey is that you are reasonable, that you want to work as a team with the presenters to help make this series successful. Show that you're easy to work with. Think long term. Remember, it is not about booking one particular gig; it's about building a professional relationship with a presenter who can potentially book you again and recommend you to others.

These three issues will affect how reasonable the offered fee is:

1. Whether or not you can sell your recordings at the performance. It is not unusual for presenters to ask for a percentage of the CD sales,

especially if they provide equipment or staff to assist with the sales. Ask and then confirm your arrangement in writing as part of the contract.

2. Any special equipment or lighting needed for the performance. Discuss who provides what (tuned piano, amplification, percussion, screen and video projector), and specify these arrangements in the contract as your "technical rider."

3. Transportation and lodging arrangements. Generally, when it comes to these considerations, artists are on their own. So unless the presenter has offered or agreed to provide accommodations or travel, you will need to consider these costs as you negotiate your fee.

Presenters often have a board of trustees or a programming committee to satisfy. So a presenter may need to get approval before making a firm offer for a booking. This can take several weeks, especially with colleges and university presenters. Musicians need to be patient through the process.

Confirmations/Contracts ◆

Once you and the presenter have a verbal agreement on a performance date, fee, and related details, you need to confirm all this in writing. Signed contracts help insure against surprises and misunderstandings that can mar a performance experience. Many presenters send their own contracts to performers. Read these carefully, and, if needed, add an attachment to clarify specific details. If the presenter does not mention a contract in the conversation, then you should send your own contract or letter of agreement. It should include these items:

1. Date, time, location of the performance.
2. Fee and specifically how and when it is to be paid (by check, made out to the artist, received at the performance).
3. Any special equipment or arrangements you've agreed upon can be specified in the technical rider (such as Steinway grand piano tuned to A440, page turner, particular lighting, amplification, or permission to record).
4. Arranged times for sound check and rehearsal in hall; name and contact information for the facility's manager or on-site person to get into the hall.
5. Any special parking, transportation, and lodging arrangements.
6. Whether or not you may sell your CDs at the performance, and any specified cut of the CD sales for the presenter.
7. The box office phone number.
8. Cancellation policy.

Make sure that you get detailed directions well before the performance, along with parking and lodging recommendations as needed.

Note that a contract becomes valid only when both parties—the presenter and you—sign it. When using your own contract, send two unsigned copies to the presenter, who signs both and sends both back to you. Then you sign both copies, keep one, and send the other to the presenter for her or his records. This procedure ensures that you do not first sign something that gets amended later. Below is a sample contract.

Booking a Regional Tour ◆

Organizing a tour usually starts with an initial booking of an "anchor" date. Next, the artist looks for other possible venues in the region that will make the expense of travel, food, and lodging for this date worthwhile. There may be nearby schools interested in master classes, residencies, or lecture demonstrations to "tag on" to the anchor date. And there may be other venues in the region to help develop a single performance into a tour. The anchor date presenter can often suggest other presenters in their region. Keep in mind, though, that presenters do not want your other regional tour performances to compete for the same audiences and media attention. In other words, make sure the next gig is not in the next nearby town.

Veteran artist manager Barbara Raney offers this advice: "Be geographically strategic: target places that are easy to get to and won't consume your travel budget. Also try locations with a good concentration of presenters so you can offer 'en-route' fees and invite other potential presenters to preview your performance." You can identify venues within driving distance where you might be able to do a series of performances, a mini-tour of "run-out" concerts. Once you have a great program to offer presenters and an initial "anchor" date booked, it can be easier to interest other presenters.

Below is a sample e-mail pitch for possible tour dates:

Dear Ms. Smith:

Ms. Jones at the ABC Concert Series in Portsmouth suggested I contact you. She's booked our string trio, Trifecta, for her series this spring. We have a terrific program that we're taking on tour in your region— it's an evening of tangos, rags, waltzes, and other dance tunes. She told us great things about your series in Portland, especially about the innovative community programs you do with the parks department.

I hope you'll check out our website; it has recordings from our live concerts, http://www.Trifecta.com. We have dates open for the first two weeks of April. I would love to find out more about your program

Music Performance Contract

From: Jane Doe   To: Ann Smith, Executive Director
           16 Chilcott Place #1   Smithtown Concert Association
           Jamaica Plain, MA 02130   1 Main St.
           617/555-1111   Smithtown, MA 02111
           jdoe@aol.com   978/555-2222
           asmith@SCA.org

This contract is intended to confirm the following agreements.

- Soprano Jane Doe, herein after referred to as "the Artist," agrees to perform a concert for the Smithtown Concert Association, herein after referred to as "the Presenter," at the First Congregational Church in Smithtown on Wednesday, November 10, 2012, at 8 pm. The concert will consist of the attached programmed repertoire, subject to change by the artist. The concert will last approximately 90 minutes with one 15 minute intermission included.
- The Presenter agrees to pay the Artist $ _____for the concert, payable in U.S. dollars by Certified Check or Money Order, to be given to the Artist on site prior to the start of the concert.
- If an invoice is required before payment, please state: Yes   No
- The Presenter agrees to furnish one Concert Grand Piano, preferably a Steinway or best Concert Grand in the area, properly tuned and in top playing condition, for the use at the performance.
- Rehearsal and sound check will be 2-4 pm the day of the performance.

Person to notify upon arrival:

_____

Name

_____

email   Phone

- The Presenter agrees to provide the Artist with four comp tickets to be held at the box office.
- The Presenter agrees to allow the Artist to sell her CDs at intermission and immediately following the concert. The Presenter will provide a table and chair in the lobby for this purpose. The CD sales will be managed by the artist with no assistance from the Presenter.
- No recording of this engagement shall be made, reproduced or transmitted from the place of performance, in any manner or by any means whatsoever, in the absence of a specific written agreement with the Artist relating to and permitting such recording, reproduction or transmission. The Signatory Artist may enforce this prohibition in any court of competent jurisdiction.
- The Artist shall be under no liability for failure to appear or perform in the event such failure is caused by or due to the physical disability of the Artist, or acts or regulations of public authorities, labor difficulties, civil tumult, strike, epidemic, interruption or delay of transportation service, or any other cause beyond the control of the Artist.

Signed _____ Date _____
            (Presenter's signature)

Signed _____ Date _____
            (Artist's signature)

Artist's social security number or Federal ID number for payment and tax purposes:

_____

Example: Performance contract

and discuss the possibility of our working together. I'll follow up in a few days with a phone call.

Looking forward to speaking with you,

Jane Doe

Creating a Concert Series

Some musicians create their own performance opportunities by starting their own series. Cellist Eric Edberg, on the faculty at DePauw University, started a summer concert series in 2005 in Greencastle, Indiana. On his blog (http://ericedberg.blogspot.com), Eric writes, "There's a warm and appreciative audience for classical music in Greencastle, and the culture of our small town is such that 'classical' is a selling point, not something to call by another name, not something that needs to be transformed into a post-classical something else."

Eric explains that it started

> with six bi-weekly concerts as a way to keep me playing and practicing during the summer, and I played on most of the concerts. Now it's grown to fourteen concerts, from the week after DePauw's Commencement until the week before classes start, and while I play "support cello" on a number of them, only two or three really feature me in a significant way. When I started it, I didn't want it to be too much of an "Eric Edberg and friends" sort of thing. There's an aspect of that to it, of course, but hey, I am the one putting it on! This summer, so many colleagues and friends wanted to play it was hard to fit everyone in.

The performers include doctoral students from nearby Indiana University, members of the Indiana Symphony, and others. Asked what he finds most satisfying about his festival work, Eric explains it's been "gratifying to see the difference the festival has made in the life of the community. And both the audiences and the performers have been happy."

▼

Cellist Eric Edberg offers these tips for anyone contemplating starting a series or festival:

1. Find a community space you can use low-cost or free.
2. Think carefully about scheduling to avoid competing with other community events.
3. Don't do it alone—get help! Build your support through your community relationships.

▲

Performance Licensing

If you plan to perform a composer's work that is under copyright protection, you need a performance license. Most concert halls, university auditoriums, and festivals have "blanket licenses" and pay dues regularly, so that composers can be compensated the royalties they are due.

However, if you plan to perform in any non-traditional performance spaces that do not generally hold performances, you'll need to obtain a license. To do so, you can contact one of the performing rights organizations (PROs) that grant licenses. Don't be worried: this is not a huge difficulty or a large expense, but it is important to take care of.

In the United States, there are three PROs: BMI (Broadcast Music, Inc.), ASCAP (American Society of Composers, Authors, and Publishers), and SESAC (Society of European Stage Authors and Composers). These three organizations were formed, in part, to track performances for composers and publishers. The staff members at these organizations are very helpful, so don't hesitate to call or e-mail with questions, and there are also very helpful FAQs on their websites.

Conclusion

Are you waiting for a prince (or princess) charming of an artist manager to grace your career? Until you find the manager of your dreams, you will most likely need to *self*-manage, booking your own performances. To enhance your reputation and build your track record, start local and small. There are places in your community where you could be performing in the coming months, and *you* are the one who can to make this happen.

Make sure you plan carefully, offer engaging programs, research performance sites, prepare a script for booking calls, practice negotiating fees, and close the deal with a written contract.

▼
_____

Career Forward

Write down your responses to the following prompts in order get started booking your own performances.

1. List three people you know and could call to ask about possible performance opportunities. Think about the people in your hometown, family friends, and former teachers. Think beyond the typical concert series. Consider museums, historical homes, libraries, and other community gathering sites.
2. Describe one or two programs you could offer these venues. List the proposed repertoire, with the timings of works. Consider any points of connection

between the program and a possible venue (such as a program of literary-inspired works offered to a library or bookstore series).

3. To prepare for making booking contacts, write your pitch statement, including the five essential elements.

4. Practice your calls with a colleague or mentor, and then go for it!

▲

7

Telling Your Story: Attracting Media Attention and Building Audiences

In order to win media attention—and an audience—you need to have something to promote, something interesting and informative, and worth the audience's time. You need to communicate what is distinctive about you and your music. What is your *mission?* Do you perform unusual or noteworthy repertoire? Are you involved in interesting community-based, or experimental music projects? This chapter focuses on the how-to of media relations, but all of this work is based on the essentials of knowing who you are and what you have to offer.

What Is Newsworthy? ◆

Regarding coverage of music-related events, journalists and news editors are expected to first report on the major happenings in their readers' areas. This means that daily and weekly papers focus primarily on major performing arts groups (the symphony, opera, or major presenting series). After that, it may be up to the journalist or critic to determine what readers want. So what actually gets media coverage next? What can an emerging artist offer that will attract media attention?

Unusual, innovative programming

The premiere of a new work: is there a story around the inspiration for the work, its dedication, commission, or about who is performing and why?

Collaboration with a well-known artist

Collaboration with an artist from another discipline—a dancer, graphic artist, or novelist

Performance in an unusual setting (e.g., the 100th anniversary of the Boston Marathon)

A local "celebrity" narrating a work on the program

Benefit concert for a worthy cause

A performance to celebrate a national holiday, anniversary, or season

Repertoire chosen to reflect and focus on local history, a particular ethnicity or culture, the opening of a new community building

A personal connection to work(s) on the program: the performer studied with the composer, or the performer is related to the composer, or the performer is returning to this work after a hiatus of ten years

Interesting tie-ins to the performance: a CD release, location, or anniversary

Beyond Performances, What Else Is Newsworthy?

Not all press releases are written about performances. Here are some of the other good reasons to contact the media:

Winning a grant, award, or competition

Commissioning a new work

Launching a tour

Releasing an album

Starting a concert series or festival

Announcing the new season of performances at your series or festival

Launching a competition for a new work for your ensemble

Participating in a summer festival

Accepting a teaching position

Launching a private teaching studio or after-school music program

Human interest: quirky personal stories about you or your ensemble,
such as how your group first got together, how you creatively
financed your CD, how you booked your own cross-country tour,
stories about buying instruments, or unusual "day jobs"

Broader Arts Coverage: Issues in the News

The media are also interested in arts stories about broad trends and issues.
Can you offer information, experience, and interesting examples of a trend
or issue in the arts? Journalists and editors might be interested in writing an
article that would briefly profile and quote a number of musicians and ensembles to tell a larger story. You can *pitch* such a story idea by contacting
journalists by phone or e-mail and offering a brief and concise description
of your story idea. Emphasize what is current and new with this topic, and
why it would be of compelling to their readers. Broader topics of interest to
arts journalists and editors include the following:

Funding issues (private and public, at national, state, and local levels).
Recording industry issues (copyright, artist-run labels, creative online
promotion, recording technology).
Arts education issues (K–12 music education, teaching artists, residency programs).
Economic issues such as the impact of the arts on the local economy.
Interesting stories about how concerts spur other spending (dining,
parking, local shopping). Do your own audience poll at intermission
to get statistics.
Arts events as benefits for a cause. (The cause may be the main news,
and the fundraiser gala dinner may be on the society page, but the
performers can also reap the benefits of the media attention.)

When you start following arts coverage, you will find that it is not just
relegated to the arts pages. Public relation specialists work creatively to find
connections between the arts and other news topics. You can see stories
about musicians as businesspeople and entrepreneurs in the financial news
section, musicians as teachers in the education news, and interview pieces
on local musicians in the city or neighborhood news sections of newspapers
and webzines.

Attracting an Audience   ◆

In order to attract an audience to a performance, you need creativity, planning, and some media savvy. With a timeline and some advance work, you

can help generate media *buzz*. By sending well-written press releases and invitations, you can build your fan base, grow your reputation, and attract media attention. This is the process for taking your performing career to the next level.

Once you have a performance date booked and confirmed, the next step is to draw an audience. If you're producing your own performance, you'll need to handle the publicity yourself. If you're being presented on a series, you still need to be an active partner in the publicity process. You and the presenter both want the performance to be a success—to draw a large and diverse audience and to attract positive media attention. But most arts organizations are understaffed and underfunded. If the presenter can do only a portion of the work, you need to do the rest.

Once the performance date has been confirmed, have an open discussion with the presenter (or venue manager) about what she or he is willing and able to do to promote the show. You want to find out how the organization handles publicity so that you can be helpful in these efforts. Whether you will be performing in a club, an art gallery, a children's museum, or on a traditional concert series, here are good questions to ask the person arranging the event:

> Is there an e-mail list of subscribers (or organization members)?
> Can they do an e-mail blast or postcard mailing for your performance?
> Do they use social media platforms? If yes, how many people do they reach?
> Is there an event booklet or a season brochure?
> If yes, will your performance be included on it? When does the mailing go out?
> Does the venue manager send press releases to local newspapers, magazines, bloggers, online arts calendars, and/or radio stations? If so, which ones?

In order to effectively promote your concert, presenters typically have to meet strict print and mailing deadlines for posters, programs, and brochures, and strict media submission deadlines for calendar listings, webzines, and radio. To meet these deadlines, presenters need your program content, program notes, bio, photos, and CDs for possible radio play. These are the essentials of what is often referred to as a media kit or press kit (a version of your promo kit designed for sending to the media). It's essential to have these items ready and to send them promptly when requested. Have a variety of high-resolution photos (at least 300 dpi). And have a variety of lengths of bios, to fit the presenter's needs. In short, make it easy for the presenter to publicize your concert. Respect the deadlines.

If you're producing the concert yourself, you'll need to meet your own deadlines for all this. Is it possible to do a strictly electronic promotional campaign, sending e-blasts and text messages to your fans and forgetting all the mainstream media? Absolutely, but here again, you still need to plan what to send out, when, and to whom.

Send invitations. If the presenter mails postcards to season subscribers, ask if you may have a stack of these to send to your own mailing list. You can also make your own postcards through various online services such as http://www.modernpostcard.com, http://www.jakprints.com, and http://www.1800postcards.com. On the front of the card, musicians often have their photo; on the back is the invitation, with the date, time, venue, and contact info plus room for the mailing label.

Personalize the postcard invites by writing on the back (in blue, purple, or green ink, so it stands out from the black print), something like, "Hope to see you there!" or something more personal for special guests, friends and family. These personal messages may be the tipping point for getting people to come to your concert. An attractive postcard invitation can be put on the fridge, used as a bookmark, and carried as a reminder.

Still, postcards alone are not enough: you want to have a multifaceted approach, using e-mail, texting, social networking, and in-person invitations. Word-of-mouth is powerful. And timing is critical. When sending both print and e-mail invitations, time your print mailing so that folks receive the postcard about ten days before the performance and then send the e-mail, text messaging, or social network invitations five days before the performance—and a reminder on the day before. Ask a group of your friends who are coming to the concert to be your "digital street team" and spread the word electronically, via e-mail and text messaging. Get them to invite everyone *they* know to the concert.

I've also received very clever and funny video invites to concerts as well—including one in which the performers sang an improv in which the lyrics were the invitation and details about the concert. Whatever methods you use, plan carefully. There can be a fine line between being assertive and being a pest, so tread lightly!

Next, you'll need to expand beyond your network and the presenter's subscriber list to contact the media.

Paid Advertisements versus Media Relations

To clarify, paid advertisements for performances, recordings, and teaching studios can be found in many media: in newspapers, newsletters, and magazines (both on- and offline) on radio and television, and in concert programs. Advertisements for concerts are often presented in newspaper and magazines in text boxes at the sides of the news articles written by journalists and reviewers. Google ads running in the right-hand margin when you do a search are the online equivalent. This kind of promotion is paid for by the musician or by the company representing the musician. Paid advertising in the more prestigious newspapers and magazines is extremely expensive and therefore beyond the means of most emerging artists. Online advertising can be much less expensive, but it has not been proved effective for promoting performances.

However, there *is* another route to getting information about your performances, recordings, or teaching studio into the media. It is more effective than advertising and it's absolutely *free!* Here's how it works: media outlets make their money through paid advertising charges and subscription charges, but the real reason people subscribe to these outlets or visit these websites is to get the local *news.* The media—newspapers, webzines, radio, TV—*all* need content because subscribers want to know what's happening and what is of interest in their communities. Journalists need story ideas, material to turn into articles, interviews, features, reviews, and calendar listings. Consequently, journalists are sent bucket loads of story ideas in the form of press releases every day. From these, journalists choose what is most engaging and relevant for their next issue, radio program, or blog update.

Because it's written and edited by professional journalists, a news article carries far more weight than advertising. It's the equivalent of having a trusted colleague tell you, "Go see this movie, you'll love it! And here's why . . ." as opposed to seeing the print ad or the trailer produced by the studio that's releasing the film.

Later in this chapter you will read how to write press releases and present news story ideas to the media. And rest assured, the majority of published news stories start out as press releases. And these releases are written and sent by either professional publicists or musicians like you.

Do You Need a Publicist? ◆

"A publicist is the professional you hire to be your ambassador to the media," writes Janice Papolos in *The Performing Artist's Handbook.* Publicists work either on a per-project basis (such as publicizing a particular concert or album release) or on an ongoing, retainer basis. A publicist's job is to plant the seeds for news stories in the media to create buzz about the musician. Publicists send out press releases and photos, CDs, and press kits to contacts in the media. They follow these up with phone calls, pitching their story ideas to journalists in hopes of generating interest and potential articles on their musician clients.

When you hire a publicist, you hire the strength of their contacts and reputation with the media, along with their writing ability and experience in promotional campaigns. Publicists' fees depend on the market in which they operate and the scope of the project. To promote a single concert or a CD release, fees can run $500–$1,500 and up, depending on the amount of work done and the clout of the publicist.

When should you hire a publicist? Janice Papolos writes, "There must be a story behind you that the publicist can work with, as well as newsworthy events on the horizon such as a concert or record." So until your career is far enough along to warrant a full promotional campaign, most likely you will handle the basic work of publicity on your own. The good news is that this is very doable.

As an alternative to hiring a publicist, some musicians consult with a skilled media relations professional, to get feedback on strategy and on drafts of press releases. Arts consultant Jeffrey James (http://www.jamesarts.com) recommends that musicians new to media relations talk to more established colleagues. "Find out how successful groups write press releases and handle their public relations . . . find a mentor, or take a publicist or established arts professional to lunch or ask for a consultation. It's well worth it!" In some cases, a few pointers and editing suggestions may be all you need to get your newsworthy items published.

Types of Media Coverage ◆

There is a range of types of media coverage to go after:

1. *Calendar listings* are postings of a community's arts and cultural events. Calendar listings are found on city or community websites, in newspapers, magazines, on- and off-line. Events are also announced on radio and TV as public service announcements (PSAs).
2. The *Arts "Pick of the Week"* or *"Critic's Choice"* section in newspapers (both on- and offline). These are highlighted performances and events, selected by an arts editor or journalist. These may be prominently displayed in a pullout section in a physical newspaper, or for the online version, prominently placed, often with photos and more details than the other listings.
3. *Preview articles* for a particular concert, including program details and information on the musician's (or the ensemble's) background, and often a photo and quotes from the musician interviews. Intended to stir reader interest in community events, preview articles are found mostly in daily and weekly (as opposed to monthly or quarterly) publications.

4. *Feature articles:* in-depth profiles of particular musicians or ensembles. These may be tied to a significant milestone in the musician's life (recently winning a big competition or launching an innovative commissioning project). Or it might be a human interest story about a particularly compelling non-musical event or circumstance (overcoming cancer, maintaining an unusual sideline occupation, or organizing a benefit for a worthy cause).
5. *Reviews of recordings.*
6. *Reviews of live performances.*
7. *Articles on broader trends and issues in the arts,* such as funding, education, copyright issues, and economics. These can often include mini-interviews and profiles of individual musicians and ensembles.

Do It Yourself

"Most musicians operate from a scarcity mindset," says music publicist Ariel Hyatt. In contrast, she says, "Successful people choose to see the abundance and potential in any situation." In other words, fretting over the fact that you do not have a *New York Times* review is simply a waste of energy; there are many other ways to build buzz. In "How to Be Your Own Publicist," Hyatt writes, "Getting that first article written about you can feel daunting. Two great places to start are your local weekly hometown papers (barring you don't live in Manhattan or Los Angeles), and any music website that you like." Hometown weeklies will often take the press release you send about a local musician (yourself) doing well (performing, teaching, winning awards) and print it verbatim, especially if you include a good photo. Other ways to build buzz include being interviewed in a webzine or being featured prominently on a blog oriented toward your musical niche. (See http://www.arielpublicity.com.)

Acquiring Media Savvy

To find where you might be able to get media coverage, do your research in your local area. Part of being a successful musician is being aware of current ideas and opportunities. If you're not reading about who is performing what and where, you're missing out on program ideas you can borrow, potential collaborations with colleagues, possible bookings, and more. Find out where your local arts scene is covered. Check out the local daily and weekly newspapers, radio programs, webzines, online calendars, and the blogs that cover your music genre. Keep current on the arts in your community and learn what gets media coverage.

Press Releases ◆

A press release is an announcement issued to the media, designed to answer the *who, what, when, where,* and *why* about your performance, special event, or other news. Press releases are sent to media outlets and may be used in part or used verbatim—printed or uploaded "as is" to the newspaper, journal, newsletter, or webzine.

A release should effectively demonstrate why your news item merits media attention. It should outline the news story and provide pertinent background information. Arts journalists receive dozens of press releases each day, and part of their job is to select from these the most relevant and engaging news for their audience.

What do the media want? Editors and journalists want *news.* They need content: ideas and information of interest to their particular audience. You are potentially a supplier of that content. If you want a newspaper or website editor to consider your news item for publication, or a radio programmer to announce your listing, you need to submit your information in the proper format: a press release.

There can be an unexpected benefit to working on all of this. Deciding how and what you want to communicate about yourself to the media may cause you to re-examine your choices in programming, performance venues, and more. Former reviewer for the Newark, New Jersey, *Star Ledger,* Paul Somers, notes in his "Getting Ink" article, "You must inevitably come to the question, 'Why are we giving this concert?' This most fundamental question must be answered if you are to have success with both the press and the audience."[1]

How to Write a Press Release in Seven Steps

Press releases should be written in the declarative. State the facts—use the active voice to describe without expressing feeling or judgment. This is *not* advertising, so no hyperbole, please!

1. *Write a headline* for your release that encapsulates the main focus of the story. Make it catchy or engaging for readers. If you're from the area, emphasize your local connections, because editors (especially at smaller media outlets) are looking for news of special interest to local readers. Note: headlines are often written in all capital letters and always in bold.

    ABC STRING TRIO LAUNCHES RESIDENCY PROGRAM AT HOMELESS SHELTERS

    SOPRANO CONQUERS STAGE FRIGHT, WINS INTERNATIONAL COMPETITION

    FIFTH ANNUAL BRASS BASH WELCOMES TUBA-TOTING MAYOR AS GUEST ARTIST

LOCAL VIOLINIST PREMIERES NEW THEATRICAL WORK: VIVALDI WITH VAMPIRES

2. *Cover the essential facts in your opening sentence* (your *lead*). This should be the who, what, where, and when (the four Ws). Your language should be succinct and direct.

> The Quintet of the Americas will present a special program of Polish music for wind quintet on Sunday, April 27, 3 pm at the Kosciuszko Foundation, 15 East 65th Street, between Fifth and Madison, in Manhattan.

3. *Consider the why*—the fifth W. *Why* does this news item matter? What's the real *story* here? Is what you have to say of interest to others in your community? Journalists need to provide readers with thought-provoking information about the cultural happenings in their area. If the item is of only marginal interest to a select group of readers, then you'll have a hard time gaining media attention. Emphasize what would be of interest to the general (nonmusician) public. Make sure your release passes the Who Cares? and the So What? tests.

4. *Stick to concrete facts.* Newspaper editors want news, not advertising. Avoid superlatives or hype. Instead, state your credentials, such as the other impressive places where you've performed or the awards you have won. Include quotes from presenters or teachers (if you've first obtained their permission). You can also quote yourself, as though you'd been interviewed, as long as you have something interesting and fresh to say about the repertoire or some other aspect of the performance. Note that some journalists prefer *not* to get quotes from other journalists, so use these with discretion.

> Ms. Smith is looking forward to returning to Whoville for this performance and says, "Whoville is where I got my start. So I'm thrilled to be performing for both new and old friends to help celebrate the opening of the ABC community center."

5. *Watch your language*—think carefully about your target audience. Consider submitting your release to appropriate specialized newspapers. If the paper is published in a language other than English, it's best to send the press release in that language. And in whatever language you use, avoid music jargon or technical terms that might alienate an average reader. Find engaging ways to describe the program so that nonmusicians can understand it.

Hill's work, "Thoughtful Wanderings," features natural horn and a taped accompaniment of nature sounds and percussion instruments. The piece was inspired by the music of the Native Americans from the Plains.

6. *Use short, well-organized paragraphs*—newspapers prefer them. Keep these to two to three sentences each, in logically organized units of thought. After the lead paragraph, where the essential information is covered, subsequent paragraphs should flesh out the story with background info on the performers and details about the program, composers, and sponsors. Keep in mind that editors assume that the essential info is in the top of the release (inverted-pyramid style), so they generally cut from the bottom.

7. *Double check your details.* Don't forget the all-important information such as the performance day, date, time, venue name and street address, the ticket price, and the necessary contact information. Leaving out crucial details is an all too common mistake and is very often why releases don't make it into print. Have friends proofread your work carefully before sending it out.

There are three examples of press releases on the following pages. The first is for a single concert; the second release announces a chamber ensemble's opening concert of its new season; and the third is an announcement of a teaching appointment and a concert that a trumpeter sent to his hometown newspaper.

There are certain conventions for writing and formatting press releases—the norms that journalists and editors expect from potential news stories. By following these guidelines, your press releases stand a greater chance of being read and published.

Press Release Formatting Tips

- At the top of the release, list your name, telephone number, and e-mail address (or those of the most appropriate contact person in charge of answering any questions the media have pertaining to the release).
- Put the release date underneath the contact info, indicating the desired date for publication ("For Release: April 5, 2014"). Or, if the time is ripe, write "For Immediate Release" and the date you're sending it.
- Start the release with the city and state (in bold), the location from which the news is being generated.
- Use double spacing and wide margins to make it easy for journalists to read and edit.
- Keep it brief: one to three pages. If sending the release as a hard copy and it runs more than one page, write "continued" or "more" at the

Contact: Jeffrey James Arts Consulting
(516) 797-9166 or jamesarts@worldnet.att.net
For Immediate Release
April 18

Quintet of the Americas Presents All-Polish Program in New York on April 27

New York, NY—The Quintet of the Americas will present a special program of Polish music for wind quintet on Sunday, April 27, 3 pm at the Kosciuszko Foundation, 15 East 65th Street, between Fifth and Madison Avenues in Manhattan.

This program will feature Grazyna Bacewicz's "Quintet for Wind Instruments," Maciej Malecki's "Suite for Wind Quintet," Alexandre Tansman's "Suite for Reed Trio," and Robert Muczynski's "Quintet for Winds" (1985).

Tickets for the April 27 concert, which include a reception with the artists following the concert, are $25 ($20 for KF members) and can be reserved by calling the KF office at (212) 734-2130.

The members of the Quintet of the Americas are Sato Moughalian, flute; Matt Sullivan, oboe; Edward Gilmore, clarinet; Barbara Oldham, horn; and Laura Koepke, bassoon.

The Quintet, founded 26 years ago, has toured extensively in over 300 cities in North and South America, Eastern Europe, and the British West Indies. They have twice received the ASCAP/CMA Adventuresome Programming Award, and were recipients of the Chamber Music America Residency Program Award. They are currently the Quintet in Residence at New York University. The group has released several CDs, including woodwind music from North and South America. The Quintet of the Americas has premiered over 50 works, commissioned over 20 new pieces for the woodwind quintet repertoire, and made numerous arrangements of their own. More information about the group can be found on their website at http://www.quintet.org.

This concert is made possible with public funds from the New York State Council on the Arts, a state agency.

For more information about the Quintet of the Americas, contact Jeffrey James Arts Consulting at 516-797-9166 or jamesarts@worldnet.att.net.

END

Example: Press release announcing an individual concert

Contact: Jennifer Montbach
617.792.7234
jmontbach@radiusensemble.org
FOR IMMEDIATE RELEASE
Aug. 20

**RADIUS ENSEMBLE OPENS ITS FIFTH SEASON AT THE
EDWARD M. PICKMAN CONCERT HALL, 27 GARDEN STREET IN CAMBRIDGE
ON SATURDAY, SEPTEMBER 27 AT 8 PM**

"Radius ensemble is first rate . . . The players represent a new generation of chamber musicians, and their youth and informality has attracted a younger, more diverse audience."
    Richard Dyer, *The Boston Globe*

Boston, MA—Radius Ensemble, directed by Jennifer Montbach, opens its fifth season on Saturday, September 27, at 8 pm at the Edward M. Pickman Concert Hall, 27 Garden Street in Cambridge. The concert includes Alberto Ginastera's "Impressions de la Puna" for flute and strings; "Amour Fou," a piano trio by the avant-garde conmposer John Zorn (of "Naked City" renown); Mozart's quintet for piano and winds; and Luciano Berio's brilliant and timely "Opus Number Zoo" for wind quintet.

There will be a free pre-concert talk at 7 pm with Mary Greitzer (Harvard University), and the concert will be followed by a free reception with the artists, with goodies from Carberry's Bakery and Café. Tickets are $10 (cash or check at the door), $5 for children and college students. Subscriptions are available. Call 617.792.7234 or visit http://www.radiusensemble.org for more information.

Performers include director and oboist Jennifer Montbach, pianist Sarah Bob, flutist Orlando Cela, pianist Alison d'Amato, clarinetist Eran Egozy, violinist David Fulmer, horn player Anne Howarth, cellist Mickey Katz, violinist Annegret Klaua, bassoonist Sally Merriman, and violist Julie Thompson.

Radius Ensemble has earned rave reviews and a dedicated following in just four years by reinvigorating classical music for a new generation. A chamber music ensemble of winds, strings, and piano, Radius Ensemble performs music from the classical period to the modern era, from beloved masterpieces to undiscovered gems. Its musicians are outstanding young professionals inspired by tradition, willing to take risks, and committed to connecting with a diverse group of listeners. Founded in 1999 by oboist Jennifer Montbach, Radius Ensemble's season includes a four-concert subscription series at Pickman Hall in Harvard Square, a free Saturday-morning family concert, and a free community ticket program offering tickets to disadvantaged children and their parents or mentors.

Pickman Hall is wheelchair-accessible and convenient to public transportation. Large-print or Braille programs are available by request; please ask about additional accommodations if needed. Radius ensemble, Incorporated, is a 501(c)(3) non-profit organization and a Massachusetts public charity.

###

Jennifer Montbach, Director
Radius Ensemble
45 Pine St. Concord, MA 01742 P: 617.792.7234
W: radiusensemble.org E: jmontbach@radiusensemble.org

Example: Announcement of ensemble's new series

CONTACT: James Knabe
faculty, School of Creative Arts
(617) 641-4493
FOR IMMEDIATE RELEASE
May 1

LOCAL MUSICIAN APPOINTED TO FACULTY POSITION, ANNOUNCES BOSTON DEBUT

BOSTON, MA—Former Iowa City resident, trumpeter James Knabe, son of William and Judith Knabe of Iowa City, has been appointed to the music faculty of the School of Creative Arts in Lexington, MA. The School is affiliated with Grace Chapel, the largest church in the New England area. This school serves numerous communities including Boston. At the school, Mr. Knabe will teach private trumpet lessons, music history courses, and will conduct a brass ensemble.

James Knabe will also make his Boston-area solo debut at Grace Chapel in Lexington at 8:00 pm on Friday, May 26. The program will include familiar and unusual works by Handel, Hovhaness, Copland, Neruda, and Vaughan Williams. Artists joining Knabe for the recital are pianist Elenye German, soprano Kimberly Cone, organist Douglas Marshall, and narrator Nancy Gerber.

A former student of David Greenhoe at the University of Iowa, James Knabe is now pursuing a graduate degree at the New England Conservatory in Boston, where he studies with Peter Chapman and Charles Schlueter of the Boston Symphony. Knabe has performed with the Boston Civic Symphony, Boston Chamber Ensemble, and the Dubuque Symphony Orchestra. He currently plays principal trumpet with the North Shore Philharmonic Orchestra. He returns to Iowa this summer for a series of master classes and recitals. When asked about his latest success, Knabe said, "I consider myself very fortunate to have received a great musical start growing up in Iowa City, and I look forward to returning home this summer to re-connect with my musical roots."

###

Example: Press release, intended for hometown newspapers in Iowa, announcing a teaching appointment and recital in Boston, and appropriately emphasizing local Iowa connections.

bottom of page; then, in the header of the continued pages, write, for example, "Radius press release, Aug. 20, 2010, p. 2 of 3." To indicate the end of the release, finish it with "END" or ###.

- For releases sent via e-mail, don't use an attachment, but send the text in the body of the e-mail message and aligned left to minimize any difficulties in formatting.
- Use quotation marks to indicate titles of compositions (newspapers do not use italics).
- Stylistic conventions for months and numbers are as follows: Aug. through Feb. are abbreviated, whereas March through July are written out; and numbers one through nine are written out, whereas numerals are used for 10 and above.

On the next pages are more examples: a calendar listing, a radio announcement, and a cover letter sent by a publicist requesting a review of a new CD. To read examples of a wide variety of music press releases, see http://www.musicalamerica.com. And note that many larger performing institutions place their recent press release announcements on their websites.

Compiling Your Media List ◆

The most important media contacts to gather first are local listings. Find out who the arts reporters are in your area. You should also add strategic regional and national publications where appropriate. Your list needs these details:

- Name, title of journalist/editor, and the name of their publication or organization (make sure of exact title, as in with or without "The"), plus the section of newspaper he or she covers (calendar, arts pages, special column, or features)
- Mailing address
- Phone number and e-mail address
- Website
- Publication schedule (daily, weekly, monthly, quarterly)
- Deadlines for receiving info

Gather your media contact information and put it into a database format with the rest of your mailing list so that you can customize and send both e-mail and print releases as needed. Media lists need constant updates, because people change jobs and media outlets may change focus. People hate to get mail addressed to their predecessor, or with their name (or their organization's name) misspelled, or with their title wrong. Keep your media list updated and readily accessible.

collage
new music

david hoose *music director*
frank epstein *founder*

po box 230150 boston ma 02123 | **www.collagenewmusic.org**

FOR IMMEDIATE RELEASE

CONTACT:
Danny Lichtenfeld

Phone: (617) 325-5200
info@collagenewmusic.org

**Collage New Music and Janna Baty present *Exotic, Neurotic, Erotic*
Music of Luciano Berio, Ralph Shapey, and Fred Lerdahl**

Boston, MA — Live-wire Janna Baty joins Collage New Music in her prismatic singing of
Luciano Berio's vivid multi-national *Folk Songs* and Fred Lerdahl's *Eros*, an electrified and
electrifying display of Ezra Pound's heated poem, "Coitus." Pianist Christopher Oldfather
and percussionist Frank Epstein convene to tackle the radical-traditionalist voice of
maverick Ralph Shapey in the Boston premiere of his *Gottlieb Duo*. The exotic, the
neurotic, the erotic.

Who	Collage New Music, with soprano Janna Baty
What	Exotic, Neurotic, Erotic: Music of Luciano Berio (*Folk Songs*), Ralph Shapey (*Gottlieb Duo*), and Fred Lerdahl (*Eros*)
When	Sunday, January 12, 2003 at 7:30 p.m.
Where	Suffolk University's C. Walsh Theatre 41 Temple Street, Boston—behind the State House on historic Beacon Hill, between Derne and Cambridge Streets. *Wheelchair Accessible*
Tickets	$20 at the door or by calling (617) 325-5200; $7 students/seniors. *Free* to students from Boston Conservatory, BU, Harvard, Longy, MIT, Milton Academy, NEC, Tufts, Suffolk, and Walnut Hill.
Info	Danny Lichtenfeld, Collage New Music (617) 325-5200, info@yellowbarn.org

Example: Calendar listing, the most basic form of a press release; it contains the essentials
and is mailed to appropriate calendar editors in plenty of time to meet their deadlines.

Contact: Jeffrey James Arts Consulting
(516) 797-9166 or jamesarts@worldnet.att.net
STARTING DATE: Feb. 12
ENDING DATE: Feb. 28

PUBLIC SERVICE ANNOUNCEMENT

"NEW YORK VIRTUOSI (Ver-choo-OH-see) CHAMBER SYMPHONY PRESENTS CONCERT
FEATURING INTERNATIONALLY RENOWNED GUITARIST"

WORDS: 77
TIME: 30

THE NEW YORK VIRTUOSI CHAMBER SYMPHONY PRESENTS A CONCERT ON SUNDAY,
FEBRUARY 28 AT 3 PM AT THE HILLWOOD RECITAL HALL OF CW POST UNIVERSITY IN
GREENVALE. THE VIRTUOSI WILL BE JOINED BY INTERNATIONALLY RENOWNED GUITARIST
VIRGINIA LUQUE (LOO-Kay) FOR A PROGRAM THAT INCLUDES A GUITAR CONCERTO (con-
CHAIR-toe) BY RODRIGO, VIVALDI'S FOUR SEASONS AND MOZART'S EINE KLEINE NACHTMUSIK
(EYE-nuh KLINE-uh NOCKTmoozik). FOR FURTHER INFORMATION, PLEASE CALL THE NEW
YORK VIRTUSOSI AT (516) 626-3378 . . . THAT'S 626-3378 FOR THE NEW YORK VIRTUOSI.

WORDS: 57
TIME: 20

THE NEW YORK VIRTUOSI CHAMBER SYMPHONY CONCERT, ON SUNDAY, FEBRUARY 28 AT 3
PM AT THE HILLWOOD RECIATAL HALL OF CW POST UNIVERSITY IN GREENVALE, WILL
WELCOME GUITARIST VIRGINIA LUQUE (LOO-Kay) FOR A PROGRAM THAT INCLUDES
VIVALDI'S FOUR SEASONS AND MUSIC BY RODRIGO AND MOZART. FOR MORE INFORMATION,
CALL THE NEW YORK VIRTUSOSI AT (516) 626-3378 . . . THAT'S 626-3378.

WORDS: 45
TIME: 15 seconds

THE NEW YORK VIRTUOSI WILL PERFORM MUSIC BY RODRIGO, VIVALDI, AND MOZART ON
SUNDAY, FEBRUARY 28 AT 3 PM AT THE HILLWOOD RECITAL HALL OF CW POST UNIVERSITY
IN GREENVALE. FOR MORE INFORMATION, CALL THE NEW YORK VIRTUSOSI AT (516) 626-3378
. . . THAT'S 626-3378.

WORDS: 31
TIME: 10 seconds

THE NEW YORK VIRTUOSI PRESENTS MUSIC BY RODRIGO, VIVALDI, AND MOZART ON
FEBRUARY 28 AT 3 PM AT THE HILLWOOD RECITAL HALL OF CW POST UNIVERSITY IN
GREENVALE. FOR MORE INFORMATION, CALL (516) 626-3378.

Example: Public Service Announcement (PSA) release intended for radio. Note: Radio
stations are required by law to include a certain number of public service announcements
for nonprofit organizations and free community events. For releases sent to radio stations,
include phonetic pronunciation guides for any words the average reader might be unsure
of how to pronounce, especially names of performers, composers, and titles of works.
Provide the word count and accurate timing it takes to read the announcement. Include
several versions of different lengths, in order to give the radio announcer choices to fit
whatever time is available. Also include the starting and ending dates for when the
announcement should be aired.

Beacon Communications
1753 Beacon St., Number 2
Brookline, MA 02445

Telephone: 617.232.1212
Email: KMYRON@SHORE.NET

April 27, 2002

Steve Greenlee
The Boston Globe
135 Morrissey Boulevard
Boston, MA 02107

Dear Steve,

The Shimon Ben-Shir Group will be celebrating the release of their debut CD *Shades* at Ryles Jazz Club, 212 Hampshire Street, Cambridge, on Wednesday May 29 at 8 pm. Enclosed is a copy of the CD for your consideration for a review in *The Boston Globe*. The band is based in Boston, but the members represent far-ranging regions from around the world. The music reflects the individual journeys the musicians have taken to come to share a musical vision and a common language . . . jazz.

The musicians in the Ben Shirim Group have considerable performance experience, playing in venues around the world with jazz luminaries and, in two cases, playing before a king and a president. I believe your astute readers would enjoy learning about good jazz by local musicians. The CD has been getting airplay on the Jazz Gallery with Al Davis on WGBH radio and is currently available at http://www.yoursound.com, where the band is also featured; and at Flipside Records in Brookline. Enclosed is a list of upcoming performances in the area.

I hope you like the music. Thank you so much for your time and consideration. If you have any questions or would like additional material, please don't hesitate to let me know.

Sincerely,

Kevin C. Myron
Beacon Communications

Example: submission for CD review from publicist Kevin Myron to Boston Globe jazz critic Steve Greenlee.

Your Local Media List

- Local newspapers/magazines (daily, weekly, monthly, quarterly) with specific names and contacts for the arts reporters and community calendar editors
- Appropriate radio station programmers
- Local commercial and community TV station arts reporters
- Website editors for community arts calendar listings
- Your college or university's newspaper and alumni magazine
- Newspapers from your former hometown
- Webzines and blogs

How do you get all this information? To research for your local list, visit your university or public library and ask the reference librarian if there is a compiled directory for local media. And ask about the *Encyclopedia of Associations* (for specialized music organizations with newsletters). For national media contact information, see http://www.musicalamerica.com. And check the companion website for many more links to media listings.

Regional and National Exposure

Online CD reviews (by professionals and fans) can be posted on CD retailers such as CDBaby, iTunes, Amazon, and many others
University newspapers, their radio stations, and alumni magazines (check with your alma mater)
TV (your local community cable access channels)
Instrument-specific journals (for example, *Flute Talk, Brass Player, Classical Singer, Saxophone Journal, Wind Player, Strings, Strad, Keyboard*; to find more, see *Musical America*)
Membership organizations with relevant journals, newsletters, or website listings (Chamber Music America, Percussive Arts Society, Early Music America, Chorus America; to find more, see *Musical America* and the *Encyclopedia of Associations*)
Music education journals (*American Music Teacher, Music Educators Journal, American String Teacher, Journal of Singing*)
Music magazines (such as *DownBeat, Gramophone, Jazziz, Opera News, The Instrumentalist, Jazz Times*)
Large groups of music professionals for posting press releases:
Musical America, http://www.musicalamerica.com
Music Industry News Network, http://www.mi2n.com
Billboard Publicity Wire, http://www.billboardpublicitywire.com/
Databases for posting concert information:
http://eventful.com

http://upcoming.yahoo.com
http://www.jambase.com
Press release directories for posting to the media outside of music:
http://www.24–7pressrelease.com
http://www.pr.com
http://www.prlog.org

Send It Out!

For releases about performances, you may have several types to send: simple calendar listings, full releases, and radio releases. Pay close attention to deadlines; you may need to send releases at least five months in advance for monthly magazines, two weeks in advance for weekly newspapers and radio programs, and ten days in advance for daily papers.

Most news outlets prefer to receive releases by e-mail, but there are still some that prefer hard copies. Check the publication's website for submission directions before sending. For an e-mail press release, use the left-hand text alignment (do not use centering or indents, because your formatting will be lost when the text is transmitted by e-mail). In the text, when you first mention the performers, ensemble, and presenter, include their hyperlinks, and if you are performing new music, include the composers' links as well.

Press releases should be sent as text in the body of the e-mail, not as an attachment. Journalists (like all of us) are wary of computer viruses from attachments. Also, do not send JPEG photos or MP3 sound clips as attachments with your release. These kinds of files are too large, and they quickly clog and disable a journalist's e-mail in-box. Instead, with your e-mail release, include a link to your website, EPK, or your social networking site. On these sites you can have your music clips and downloadable high-resolution (at least 300 dpi) JPEG photos available. Make sure your photos and sound clips are clearly labeled with your name. Having this easy access online can mean the difference between getting media coverage and not. Journalists and editors unable to get the details they need may simply decide to include the next musician's news instead of yours. Make it easy on the media to tell your story!

▼

Inviting Critics to Review a Performance

Newspapers and other print publications are experiencing tough financial times as people rely more and more on websites and blogs to access news. Consequently, there is less coverage of the arts in the mainstream press. Although getting a good review can help a career, a review can neither make nor break a career. The best approach is to do what you can to get listings and preview articles for your performances. Send releases, invitations, and ideas for articles. You may need to build a track record, to be on a critic's radar screen for several seasons before getting reviewed. Be persistent, professional, and patient.

The following will help you to attract a critic to your performance:

- Have a compelling program.
- Schedule your performance so it does not conflict with major performances in your area. Plan ahead. Get the season listings early from presenters and performing groups in your area. Monday and Tuesday nights, in general, are less crowded with competing performances.
- Send a release and invitation two to three months in advance, to give the reviewer plenty of notice.
- With the release, send a letter inviting the critic. Ask the critic to call or e-mail you to have two complimentary tickets left in her/his name at the box office.
- Ask a teacher or other well-regarded mentor who knows the reviewer to extend the invitation.

Note: It can be far easier to get media coverage and possibly a review in smaller communities, so think about the smaller towns and cities where you might organize a performance and invite the local media.

▲

Tips on Being Interviewed ◆

Whether you're asked to do an interview for radio or for a profile article, it will go better with some preparation and perspective. Radio interviews may also include an in-studio performance or the playing of a recording of yours. Print interviews are often conducted by phone. In any case, you'll be more comfortable, articulate, and interesting if you do some homework in advance.

Some people imagine that their music will speak for itself. If that were true, then there would be no reason to have liner notes, bios, printed programs, or artist interviews. People want to get to know at least a little about performers and composers: they want to make a connection. With a well-prepared interview, you can do just that and come across as both interesting and personable.

If you are worried that preparation will make you too self-conscious and you want to come across as spontaneous, never fear! The idea is not to memorize anything to recite by rote. Instead, by thinking in advance about what makes you tick as a musician and what you are particularly enthusiastic about, you can be prepared with stories to tell. You'll be ready to speak with enthusiasm, instead of struggling to come up with anything to say.

1. Find out whatever you can about both the interviewer and the media outlet in advance. Google the interviewer and the radio program or publication for the details. Address the interviewer by name during the interview. If you're being interviewed at a distance from where the performance will take place, include references to the local area where you will be performing. You could mention looking forward to that city's signature food item, its sport team, or art museum, or anything else you're looking forward to experiencing. It should be genuine and reveal your enthusiasm for traveling to this city.

2. Think carefully in advance about what makes you and your upcoming performance distinctive. Think about what *you* would be interested in hearing about if listening to or reading the interview. Write it down. You need two or three specific points: your answers need to be focused, concise, and revealing. Be prepared to give answers that contain your two or three points no matter what questions you're asked. Make sure that you communicate what is most important for listeners or readers to know about the upcoming performance. This is what politicians do, of course, but it's also a useful strategy for musicians!

3. Think about the stories you have, possible anecdotes that illustrate your two or three points. These might include how you first got hooked on music or how you came up with the idea for this concert or ensemble. Having a memorable anecdote or example can make an interview come to life.

In Ellen Highstein's excellent book *Making Music in Looking Glass Land*, published by Concert Artists Guild, Thomas Bartunek, president and general manager at WQXR-FM, offers the following comments about being interviewed:

> Be prepared with an anecdote or two that will create a personal note and create a connection with your listeners. A story about how you choose your repertoire, or what it means to you, is usually more engaging than the history of the works and the dates of the composers. Something that reveals your humanity—how the string broke during the last performance and what you did to deal with the emergency, for example—creates more sympathy and engages the listeners more than a list of your credits. Try to also show that you care that the audiences enjoy what you will present. Listeners need to know why they should

attend your event, and for that they need to know *why you?* and not *why Brahms?* and, above all, *why me—why should I go?*[2]

Timeline for Publicizing Your Next Concert ◆

To help organize your preparations for a performance, have a checklist and timeline. Find out what publicity the presenter will do and when so that you can coordinate your efforts. In publicizing concerts, you need to send releases and invitations out in the right form, to the right people, at the right time.

Beyond your friends and the press, you should also invite other local presenters, influential musicians, conductors, artist managers, and colleagues. Even if they do not come, you will be getting on their radar screens. Remember, building buzz paves the way for future opportunities.

Six Months Before
- ❏ Research and compile your media list.
- ❏ Update your mailing list, including influential local musicians, conductors, artist managers, and presenters.
- ❏ Send press releases to quarterly publications (check deadlines!).

Three to Five Months Before
- ❏ Send releases and make phone calls to any specialized radio shows that do guest interviews and/or live performance broadcasts. (You need the lead time because these shows are booked so far in advance.)
- ❏ Send press releases to monthly publications (check deadlines!).

Two to Three Months Before
- ❏ Invite local critics.

Six Weeks Before
- ❏ Send releases to radio program producers.
- ❏ Send releases to local cable channels and online calendars.

One Month Before
- ❏ Send releases to weekly publications.
- ❏ Send calendar listings to all.

Two to Three Weeks Before
- ❏ Send releases to daily publications.
- ❏ Send Internet releases to online calendars and magazines.

Seven to Ten Days Before
- ❏ Send personalized invitations to your mailing list, perhaps a postcard with a handwritten "Hope to see you there!"

Five Days Before
❏ Send e-mail and/or text message invitations to your mailing list.

One to Two Days Before
❏ Send reminders to your mailing list

After the Concert

The next day, send thank-you notes to everyone who assisted you in the performance—this is a good way to help the presenter and other supporters to think positively of you and to want to work with you again. Andrew Kohji Taylor, a violinist who performs frequently in the U.S. Northeast and in Japan, found that once he started sending handwritten thank-you notes to presenters after his concerts in Japan, his return engagements were much more frequent. Andrew was really getting to know these presenters as people—and they liked working with him and wanted to invite him back.

Send e-mail thank-yous to the fans who signed your guest book, and add these people to your database. Scan copies of any media coverage you received about the performance for adding to your EPK.

How to Grow a Career ◆

The process is cyclical: promoting every concert includes inviting the people in your network and sending information to the media in order to create buzz and grow your fan base. Getting media attention can make it easier to get airplay on local radio stations. It should also result in bigger audiences and increased album sales. Ultimately, all this activity can lead to more bookings at more prestigious venues. The periodic buzz of media attention (from a CD release, concert review, new project, or profile article) helps advance a musician's career to a new level. This is how performance careers advance from the local to the regional and national levels. Each performance needs to be promoted, no matter how established the performer. And musicians need to regularly launch new projects for the sake of their careers as well as their artistry.

▼
_____

Career Forward

Work through the following questions and prompts to help promote your performances with the media.

1. Do you have an updated mailing list? Does it include media contacts? If not, start now. Don't forget your local media and neighborhood papers, and the

specific membership organizations and magazines for your instrument or genre.

2. List five local media outlets where you could send a press release about an upcoming performance.

3. Write out a story idea for a press release that you could send to your hometown weekly newspaper. The focus of the pitch should be on an upcoming performance or a teaching project you're currently involved in, or an award or grant you have recently won.

4. Recall the last concert you gave. Now, as an exercise, think like a publicist and write a dynamic press release for it, one that would attract an audience and a critic. Emphasize the most compelling features of the concert—is it the performers, the occasion, the program, or something else?

8

Connecting
with Audiences:
Reaching Out
and Reaching In

▼
▲

What Is Residency Work? ◆

The focus of this chapter is your audience, on helping them make powerful emotional connections to your music. It's about what you can do to help the audience become actively engaged with music. This is at the heart of what music is actually *for*—it's about communication and connection. It's a two-way street;the rewards are not just for the audience.

Presenters often refer to this essential aspect of musicians' work as *community engagement* or *residency activities*. There are also other terms, such as *outreach,* although this word can have negative connotations. Outreach can imply a one-way elitist transaction, a kind of cultural imperialism, whereas *community engagement* connotes collaboration and participation. For the sake of ease and consistency, we will use the term *residency work,* here, as do many presenters.

What Is a Teaching Artist?   ◆

As for the musicians who do residency work, in the United Kingdom they are called *animateurs,* or, more recently, *music leaders.* And in the United States, in the past few years, musicians (as well as visual artists, dancers, and actors) who do this work are often called *teaching artists.*

Arts consultant and author Eric Booth offers this definition: "A teaching artist is a practicing professional artist with the complementary skills, sensibilities, and commitment of an educator, who engages people in learning experiences in, through, and about the arts." And the Arizona Commission on the Arts defines *teaching artist* simply as "an educator who integrates the creative process into the classroom and the community." Teaching artists work in a wide range of settings, from primary and secondary schools to hospitals, prisons, shelters, community centers, retirement homes, and museums. Residency work is challenging and rewarding. Teaching artist skills are becoming essential for musicians. Due to a lack of music education in the schools, the competing demands for audience leisure time, and the hunger in our cultures for meaningful social connection, teaching artist skills have become essential for today's musicians, and for the future of music.

What's in It for You?   ◆

Doing residency work is personally demanding because it calls into question the artist's relationship to music, to performing, and to the audience. This work often helps musicians re-ignite the fire that originally drew them to music. It can reconnect them to the purpose of their performances and their original musical inspirations. Composer/bassoonist John Steinmetz explains that residency work helps musicians improve their performances, "because through thinking about what to demonstrate to the audience and how to explain it, performers get clearer about the musical message they want to communicate."

As an undergraduate, pianist Kazuha Nakahara designed a residency at a local retirement home. She became the home's intern artist-in-residence for a semester, earning college credit. Her performance space was the living room of a brownstone, with a Steinway in need of repair. Her audience was a group of about twelve retirees. Some were quite knowledgeable about classical music, whereas others were just glad to have a young person come visit. Over the course of a semester, Kazuha presented ten programs of both solo and chamber repertoire. She brought in guest performers and in all the programs talked about the music with the residents, asking questions and getting to know them over the course of the semester. She planned her programs and her discussion points beforehand. For some of these, she brought in art prints and maps to discuss various connections between the music and its context. And she and the residents talked about their own connections to music, history, and geography.

At first, she found it difficult to "switch gears" between talking and playing, because each demands a different kind of focus. And there were all the unforeseen happenings in the presentations, from residents' unexpected reactions to discussions, to health emergencies and fire alarms. But with more experience, Kazuha grew more confident and at ease with the performing, talking, and transitions between the two. Talking and making music are, after all, both forms of communication. And it's probably inevitable that when you perform in arms' reach of people you've gotten to know over time, that the performing becomes more personal, more human, and more about sharing.

Most of all, Kazuha got to know the residents, and they got to know her. She was surprised at how interested the residents were in her personally and by the end of the residency; she was surprised at how much they had come to mean to her. As a result of Kazuha's residency work, she found that *all* of her performing felt more personal and more meaningful.

Residency work entails an inner process of self-reflection as well as an outward focus. Musicians need to "get into the minds" of their audience, to imagine what it is that people actually want. Doing residency work can sharpen your performance and communication skills, inspire you to develop compelling programming, and build your performance experience and reputation.

In addition, residency work can offer an opportunity to explore new collaborations. Musicians can create partnerships to explore a wide range of musical and non-musical interests with composers as well as artists from other disciplines. Today's musicians and audiences are often fascinated with projects that combine music with visual art, dance, literature, technologies, or theater. These kinds of projects can be rich in connection and "entry" points that help both audiences and performers find meaning and relevance.

Finally, on a most practical level, there is good money to be made in doing residency work. Many presenters book only artists who can do both main stage performances and residency activities, and do both of these well.

There is far more demand for effective residency work than there is for formal concerts. This is because there is simply more grant funding available for arts education presentations than for traditional concerts.

Why Bother? ◆

Is residency work necessary? Musicians often think, *But if I perform really well, the audience will "get it." The music should stand on its own. After all, music is the universal language.*

It can be difficult for trained musicians to imagine what going to a live concert is like for the general audience, for people who may be inexperienced with art music, who don't play or read music, and who have never paid close attention to it.

Try to put yourself in their shoes.

Have you ever been to a museum or art gallery and been confronted by a work you simply didn't "get"? And maybe your friends and family were raving about the work, but you were at a loss and felt left out? Well, many people have the same experience with *art music*—the kind that one has to pay attention to, be it Bach, Coltrane, Zwilich, or Shankar.

People often miss out on getting *more* out of music because no one has helped them to engage more fully with it, to *hear* more in the music. Many non musicians experience music as aural wallpaper, the backdrop of their daily life, creating ambiance for commuting, shopping, dining, and at work. The fundamental listening skills musicians take for granted, such as hearing melody distinct from accompaniment, and distinguishing instrumental timbres, changes in tone color, tonalities, tempo, and contrasting themes—these are all skills that people learn. Audiences need to practice listening in a new way in order to catch these distinctions. And it can be quite easy for people to begin hearing more in music—it may only take a minute—but people need help learning how to do it. We often ask audiences to pay attention without giving them any clue as to *how* or for *what* to listen for specifically. In his excellent article "Resuscitating Art Music" (http://www.musicunbound.com/artx2.html), bassoonist/composer John Steinmetz writes, "It's not hard to perceive musical details but often listeners need help learning how to aim their ears."

The whole point of paying attention to art music, of perceiving the details, is that this can lead to making stronger emotional connections to it. Sometimes all a new listener needs is a chance to hear a work several times. Through repeated hearings of a work, live and recorded, a listener starts to get a sense of the shape and features of a work. With repeated hearings, listeners start to have the pleasure of recognizing themes, discovering new details within the familiar, and having the satisfaction of perceiving a work as a complete "narrative" experience, with a beginning, middle, and end, much like a story with an exposition, conflict, and resolution. So, designing residency activities that offer listeners a "preview" of themes or key sections—before the full performance—can work well. And some musicians program concerts in which a new work (not too lengthy) is played twice, with some commentary in between, to give the audience a second crack at what they might have missed.

What Does Residency Work Encompass? ◆

Residency work is often about going *to* the audience, meeting them on *their* turf and performing in nontraditional spaces, such as school gyms, retirement homes, or office complexes. Residency work at its best is engaging, interactive, educational, *and* artistic. This applies to the work whether it's a single presentation for a sixth-grade class, a postconcert audience talk with musicians sitting on the edge of the stage, or a monthlong residency at a community center.

For most presenters, the primary goal of residency work is to bring music to those who would not otherwise attend main stage concerts. But the idea of residency work is to do *more* than simply expose people to great music. In many cases, residency work is focused on education: on helping audiences learn about the instruments, the musicians, the music, and each other.

Exposing people to it and educating them about art music does not necessarily lead to converted fans. People become fans because they get an emotional charge out of an experience. But unless people are "invited in," they may never have the chance to find if they get an emotional charge. Residency work is all about the "inviting in."

For many, the formality of traditional Western classical concerts can be a real turnoff. The audience is asked to sit quietly in rows, at a distance from the performers, without making noise or speaking until intermission, and God forbid anyone should applaud at the wrong time! All of this creates a barrier between audience and artist. So, in recent years, presenters and musicians have been rethinking the *how, where, when,* and *why* they give concerts.

The Fischoff National Chamber Music Association in South Bend, Indiana, presents concerts performed in local homes and businesses. This is chamber music the way it was intended to be heard, in intimate settings. Ann Divine, the executive director for Fischoff, has scheduled concerts in museums, cafés, and furniture stores, incorporating good food and good company. The idea is to make both the music and the players more approachable. (See http://www.fischoff.org.)

And in Texas, Da Camera of Houston presents a main-stage series plus educational programs at schools and other community settings. Their family series includes four weekend afternoon performances at the Houston Zoo, complete with a question-and-answer session and a musical petting zoo, to give children a chance to see, touch, and play musical instruments. (See http://www.dacamera.com.)

Lastly, the Myrna Loy Center in Montana presents visiting musicians in turn-of-the-century landmark buildings in Helena, including performances in the city's cathedral, its capital building, and the former governor's mansion. Great music heard in beautiful and unexpected settings makes for memorable experiences. (See http://www.myrnaloycenter.com.)

What's in a Name?

Traditionally, *residencies* referred to artist-in-residence programs, long-term positions for ensembles or composers (occasionally for soloists) at colleges or universities. These positions are quite difficult to attain because they are generally offered only to well-established groups. It's nice work if you can get it, but these are not the only kinds of residencies available. There are also residency positions for emerging ensembles, in which players study with distinguished faculty members as part of a graduate degree or diploma program.

In recent years, the definition of the term *residency* has been extended to include shorter-term arrangements, from a few days, weeks, or months, sometimes with performance activities at multiple sites. Examples range from a touring musician's three-day stay in a community doing work in the schools, to an ensemble's concert series at a museum, or a quartet's full-time tenured position at a university. These are all considered residencies.

Jazz vibraphonist and composer Stefon Harris participated in a residency several years ago at the University of Iowa Hancher Auditorium (http://www.hancher.uiowa.edu), one of the leading presenting series in the United States. Hancher's former artistic director Judy Hurtig invited Stefon to collaborate in a residency with poets during the university's renowned literary conference, the International Writing Program. Before the residency, Stefon was sent the participants' written poems and recordings of their readings so that he could get a sense of the sounds of the various languages and voices. Then, over two evenings during his residency, Stefon and his band, together with the poets reading, created the music and the order for the performance. Stefon prepared written and improvised works to be performed with each poem as it was read by the author. The works were presented in a continuous poetry cabaret-style performance at the student union. It was a big success. The poets got a chance to present their work in a dramatically new context, and Stefon got an interesting creative challenge and access to a new audience. The presenting series at

Hancher also got great media coverage for the innovative event and the opportunity to collaborate with one of the university's most well known programs, setting the stage for future collaborative projects. It was a win-win situation for all the residency partners as well as for the audience.

▼

Questions for Exploring Residency Work

In planning effective residency work, musicians need to balance various needs and interests: their own, their audience's, and the sponsoring organization's. Ask yourself the following questions:

About you:
Why are you interested in doing this work? What are your goals and
motivations?
What would make this a successful experience from your point of view?
What repertoire would you like to use?

About your audience:
Who is the prospective audience? A high school ninth-grade class, a
retirement home, the local Rotary club?
What needs and interests does this particular audience have?
What would you like the audience to get out of this?
How can you help your audience actively connect with your music?

About the prospective partnering organization:
What is the organization's reason for wanting the residency activities?
What would your partner like the audience to get out of the residency
program?

▲

Talking to Audiences ◆

For many musicians, talking with audiences is where residency work begins. Being able to introduce yourself and your music from the stage is a terrific starting point for more complex residency activities. Most presenters welcome and expect musicians to introduce one or more works on a program, especially any new or unusual pieces. Although speaking to audiences is a welcomed and important part of performances, many musicians do not seek out coaching or feedback on their public speaking skills. This is a shame because many people are nervous about speaking in public and can benefit from basic coaching on these skills. So don't make the mistake of leaving this aspect of your performance unpolished.

What you say and how you say it can help build rapport with your listeners and a sense of cooperation and community within the audience. Your attitude plays a major role in your speaking. Imagine, for any performance you give, that you are in someone else's home, and that a number of other people have been invited to come and meet you there. You can take the approach, no matter what the setting, that this is an intimate house concert, and you are welcoming people to the performance. Your remarks should help everyone (including you) feel comfortable and "invited in." Be gracious, because you are in a sense both a guest and a host for the evening!

The Borromeo Quartet presents a popular early evening concert series, four to five concerts each season, at their home-base institution, the New England Conservatory. The concerts are programmed on weekday evenings for just one hour, 6–7 P.M., during which the quartet presents and talks about a single work. These brief concerts are convenient for students and commuters to fit it in before going home or out to dinner. The Borromeo at first intended these concerts to be a small, in-house series for students, colleagues, and friends, but it proved to be so popular that they had to move it to a larger hall. The quartet's format is to first talk about the piece, pointing out specific musical details in each movement and playing examples. Then they play the entire work through, and, finally, they open the floor to any and all questions from the audience.

The quartet's first violinist, Nicholas Kitchen, does most of the talking for the group. Although he is a gifted communicator and educator, Nick also readily admits he has worked hard on these skills. His approach to the audience is friendly, interested, and enthusiastic. And he's not afraid to talk about tough pieces that can seem forbidding to audiences. Nor does he shy away from describing the emotions of a work or what the experience is like for the quartet members.

In presenting Bartok or a late Beethoven quartet, for instance, the group first plays short examples to demonstrate how a motivic idea is worked out over the course of a movement. The group sometimes deconstructs a section, demonstrating how the composer takes an initial theme, breaks it into pieces, and then uses these fragments to build the movement. Having the quartet play short examples first and show how the work progresses helps the listener to recognize and follow the narrative arc of the work when it's played through. With this kind of introduction, audience members—both classical groupies and novices—can have a satisfying listening experience.

As for the audience that comes to the Borromeo's early evening series, they include music students, retirees, fans of the quartet, and working adults in the area. Because of the mix, the questions afterward are surprising and fun. People ask specific and technical questions about the work, or about the quartet's instruments, the mechanics of playing, and the lives of touring musicians. The audience has a good time getting to know both the music and the players, and consequently this popular series has attracted a loyal following. (See http://www.borromeoquartet.org.)

What to Talk About

Stick to *experiential* issues, how the music is perceived and experienced by listeners. Highlight personal reactions, histories and stories around a work, both your own and/or the composers.'

Remember that this is not a music theory or history class. Your remarks should not be about teaching facts or delivering information; they should be tools to aid in the listening experience. Strike a balance: avoid using musical jargon and technical terms, but beware of sounding patronizing. It's easy to alienate novices simply by using technical terms like *contrapuntal, cadenza, sonata form,* and *dominant seventh chord.* As John Steinmetz writes,

> Many musical phenomena can be described using normal English words. Musical terms are only needed to direct attention to something in the music that has no word in English. (For example, "getting louder" is better than "crescendo," but "cadenza" might be worth using in some pieces, as long as you explain what it means.) Use words to help focus attention on the aspect of music you want the listeners to notice, but the main emphasis should not be not on what you say but on the musical examples, on things that the listeners can hear.

To find a focus for residency presentations with specific repertoire, try brainstorming with a free association exercise. You can do this with members of your ensemble and with friends, both musicians and non-musicians. Listen to a recording or play through a movement of the work you plan to use, and then discuss it. When you hear the piece, what associations come to mind? The composer's spiritual or religious background? The political realities in the world at the time? Chaos theory? The fragility of life? The nuances of dialogue, of musical "conversation"? One or more of these associative thoughts may make a great entry point into the music. This can be a launching pad for a fascinating discussion with your audience. Part of what you can do in residency work is to name these associations, to reveal your own reactions to the music to your audience. In a sense, by your example, you can encourage audience members to explore their own musical associations and reactions. This helps people deepen their connections to music.

Finding the Right Entry Point ◆

In his excellent book, *Reaching Out: A Musician's Guide to Interactive Performances,* David Wallace writes, "Entry points can help people to appreciate musical works in essentially three ways: on a purely musical level, on an intellectual/metaphorical level, or on a personal, emotional level." Here are Wallace's recommended questions to ask yourself, in choosing the right "entry point" for any piece:

> What makes this work great?
>
> What excites me about it?
>
> What do I especially hope my audience notices?
>
> Is there anything unusual, cool, or striking about the work?
>
> Is there any musical element or metaphor that underlines the entire work?
>
> What entry points would make good aural or visual "hooks" for first-time listeners?
>
> What difficulties would a first-time listener encounter in the work?
>
> Is there anything pragmatic or historical about the work that would help a listener?
>
> What aspects of the piece are so strong and immediate that they need no activities to highlight them?[1]

Structuring Programs ◆

To work well, a program needs a specific, clear focus and theme. Otherwise, it may come across as a haphazard collection of pieces interspersed with talking. There needs to be a structure, with a beginning, middle, and end. Build a program around an idea that the audience can explore together with you. David Wallace advises that a good program theme fulfills four basic criteria: that it:

> Is intriguing, challenging, or entertaining for both performers and audience.
>
> Invites musical exploration, not just demonstration
>
> Has an emotional or intellectual "bite."
>
> Is musically strong and original.[2]

▼
_____

Program Theme Examples:

How tension and resolution work in music

Improvisation

How an ensemble works: negotiating, team work, decision making

The element of surprise

Humor in music

Exploring musical form and structure

Compositional choices: having the audience try out changing the tempo, dynamics, articulation, and tonality of a piece.

Exploring a period in history (music connected to history)

Programmatic music: pieces that tell stories

Exploring a particular culture or region

Composer portrait (centered on the work and life of a particular composer)

Exploring connections between a work and another art form (visual art, dance, drama, literature)

▲

Sometimes a program theme emerges from the chosen repertoire, and other times musicians find the repertoire to fit the theme they choose. Brainstorm with friends and colleagues to find entry points, themes, and interactive possibilities for your programs. Though this takes time and effort, creating a satisfying program is worth it. Your program should challenge you, whether it is the first time or fifteenth time you present it. There should be elements of spontaneity and fun in every presentation, and that is fed by your encouraging the audience's response and participation.

▼

Tips for Residency Work

From Nancy Christensen, former education director for Chamber Music America and current managing director of the artist management firm MCM Artists.

1. "Talk to other musicians who are experienced and successful with this kind of work." For referrals and contact info of teaching artists in your region, check with your state arts agency, Young Audiences, Inc., and with Chamber Music America.
2. "Observe successful musicians doing their residency programs." Most people are flattered to have a fellow musician ask to observe their work, and most would be happy to spend time with you afterward discussing residency work opportunities.
3. "Before doing any residency work do your homework. Before the gig, call and talk to your contact at the residency site—the presenter, classroom teacher, or activity director. Find out about your audience, their community, and about the performance space. For school performances, make sure you know what the students are studying now. Find out if the school has a music teacher, any other local arts organizations working with the school, or no music or art instruction at all."
4. "Use humor, be genuine. Your audience wants to respond to you personally."

▲

Designing Programs for Adults, Seniors, and K–12 Audiences ◆

Adult Programs

Adults can be very self-conscious about their musical knowledge. So make sure your approach is not in any way condescending. The goal is to create an atmosphere of fun, open inquisitiveness, and exploration.

Whether your audience is a group of college students or insurance brokers, if you are doing residency work for adults—people without musical training—find links between what your audience is familiar with and the music you present. Look for points of reference and connection between a kind of thinking they are familiar with and successful in, and the new area, the music you are offering. What is great about this approach is that it helps make meaning. We live in a culture in which the media inundates us with disconnected facts and information, so any chance we have to connect ideas across disciplines helps us make sense of our world. Finding meaning is one of life's chief pleasures, so don't underestimate what you actually have to offer.

The String Trio of New York, a violin, guitar, and bass jazz ensemble, offers a series of college-level educational programs called "The Human Residency." These programs were developed to highlight the natural links between music and a variety of subjects including mathematics, philosophy, art, psychology, sociology, business, and more. The trio's program "The Mathematics of Jazz" includes a discussion of the use of numbers in music, from the overtone series and rhythmic subdivisions to intervals and figured bass. Their program "The Business of Collective Initiative," designed for economics and business classes, involves the discussion of how the ensemble is organized and managed as a collective group. The trio has presented these innovative sessions on many campuses, including Dartmouth, Penn State, and Stanford.

The Guild Trio had an eight-year residency with the State University of New York at Stony Brook's Medical Center, a teaching hospital. The trio's residency included an educational *Illness and Inspiration* series and their *Frontiers* colloquium on creativity in science and art. The trio also presented a series of five concerts, each in the teaching hospital's lecture center, and conducted a ten-day annual amateur chamber music seminar. The residency helped to foster a greater sense of community among faculty, students, staff, and patients.

Senior Programs

Performing for seniors can be especially gratifying because elders are often the most appreciative of audiences. If you're just getting started with talking to audiences and designing interactive concerts, you might want to start by offering a program to a local senior center. Retirement and nursing homes, assisted living facilities, senior day centers, and Alzheimer's units are all possible sites for residency work. These facilities offer a range of care and programs to elders with varying health needs. All of these types of facilities have activity directors who organize social and cultural programs for residents. It's good to go meet these activity directors to view the possible performance settings and to find out what kinds of programming their residents especially appreciate.

In doing residency work for seniors, it's important that your audience can hear you well. You need to be able to project your voice well or else use a microphone. And keep in mind that older people may have difficulty sitting through long programs, so introducing each piece and even each movement often works well. Still, it's not unusual to have disruptions during programs. Some people may need medication or particular assistance. A musician's job in the face of such distractions is to be understanding, kind, and flexible.

Some retirement homes book formal concerts of strictly classical music. But more often, homes look for a mix of classical, jazz, and familiar standards from musical theater and the Great American Songbook. If you have (at least as encores) a few standards by composers such as George Gershwin, Cole Porter, or Jerome Kern, and can get your audience to sing along, that's great. Think of programming at least some familiar music that your audience knew when they were growing up.

K–12 School Programs

To work successfully in K–12 school environments, it's important to be aware of school culture. Teachers and school administrators are very busy with many competing demands. Schools are under tremendous pressure these days for accountability, and standardized testing often drives curricular decisions. Funding is tight and time is short, and this means that artists wanting to do residency work need to design programs that enhance, reinforce, or extend the school's core curricular focus. Each state has its mandate and required curriculum. The Arts Education Partnership website lists each state's arts requirements, assessment policies, and teacher certification information (see http://aep-arts.org).

So, whether it's for a single forty-five-minute assembly presentation or a monthlong residency, musicians need to design programs that fit the school's schedule and culture, and that support the work of teachers and their curricula. Effective in-school residency work helps link music with other areas of learning. An example would be connecting math and music through exploring fractions in the context of rhythmic notation, and demonstrating how music is organized in time. Other programs connect science with music by exploring the properties of sound waves, how instruments produce sounds, and how these are perceived and recorded. And there are many possibilities for connecting music and social studies: exploring history, culture, indigenous music, and geography.

Programming for children should be imaginative, creative, and fun. The Music Center of Los Angles County offers a wide variety of programs to schools in the area. On their website, you can read brief descriptions of these programs, such as the following:

> *Musica Angelica's* program entitled *Musical Super Heroes* introduces grades K–6 to the world of ancient Greek and Roman mythology. The ensemble—a soprano, tenor, and lutenist, all highly accomplished professionals based in the Los Angeles area—play intriguing instruments, perform opera scenes, dances and instrumental music of the Baroque period. Colorfully costumed and highly interactive, the program invites audiences to participate as it shows how these marvelous myths are relevant to the family of man. (http://www.musiccenter.org)

Greg Pliska, an arts education specialist at the Lincoln Center Institute, recommends finding links between what the students are learning in a given grade and what you the artist can offer. To find out what will work best in schools, invite a teacher out for coffee or lunch and a consultation. Ask what issues, ideas, and concepts the students are tackling in different grades. Find out what's being explored in the curriculum that you might enhance with an innovative residency program. Pliska also suggests that you ask teachers what kinds of residency work would be most helpful for them and their students. As you develop programming ideas, check these out with teachers and get their feedback and suggestions.

To get acclimated and to understand the culture, ask to spend a day visiting a school. Spend part of the day with a teacher, visiting classrooms. And spend time with the administrators—and with children on the playground—to see how a school really functions.

▼

The Four Nations Ensemble is an early music group with a core ensemble of harpsichord or fortepiano, violin(s), flute, and cello. Four Nations has had long-term residency programs working with inner-city schools in the Bronx and in Brooklyn. The harpsichordist Andrew Appel described some of their residency work several years ago at a Chamber Music America conference: "Our approach is to engage students in a project that involves their skills and imagination and helps us, the musicians who are strangers and unfamiliar with their communities.

We ask a group of 9th or 8th graders to work as a marketing agency for our ensemble. (Those taking part have had some introduction to business and run a school store). Four Nations doesn't know enough about them, their families and friends, and doubts if we can attract an audience to our programs of music. Their job is to get to know our product (classical music), get to understand the market (through surveys and interviews in their school), and develop an advertising campaign for classical chamber music that appeals to the market.

"There is never any pressure to 'appreciate' the music, only to observe and describe it. At the end of the school year, they present Four Nations in a concert. Tickets are available at the school store. The concert hall is managed by the students with the help of the chief staff. Every aspect of presentation, from box office through stage lighting to program design, is handled by the students. This year, they will select, from a list of pieces, the music and order they feel is best for the presentation. This business aspect is possibly the most unconventional part of the program.

"We have regular business meetings during the year to discuss the writing of copy and interpretation of the survey results. Here we can work on verbal, written, and math skills. This is an important argument for the viability of the program. Posters, art, and copy are discussed as if we were employees of a major advertising firm. You might imagine that I offer lots of input. But, mostly I try and clear away the thicket of resistance to imagination. Decisions and materials must come from the students so that they can recognize themselves in each final product.

"Concurrently, we begin working with other students in all grades, from K–9. There are regular mini-concerts (15 to 20 this year), at which time we introduce them to the chosen repertoire. Our sessions include performances and then the sharing of responses, from emotional to creative. All the pieces on the 'big' concert program are heard throughout the year. In this way, students enjoy the pleasure of recognition—one of the most important in the appreciation of concert music." (See http://www.fournations.org.)

▲

Children's Programming Beyond Schools

There are other great venues for children's educational programming, some with fewer bureaucratic and scheduling hardships. There are summer camps, after-school programs, community music schools, and preschools. For the pre-K crowd, check out the Fischoff Association's program for introducing great books to preschoolers through musical reenactments by chamber groups. The performers use their instruments to represent the story's characters, emotions, and ideas. Musicians narrate the story and often use props for additional drama. These interactive programs incorporate music, reading, art, storytelling, drama, and imagination. (See http://www.fischoff.org.)

Getting Hired   ◆

Over the past fifteen years, U.S. orchestras, opera companies, festivals, and concert series have invested heavily in the development of community education programs. Many opera companies have young artist programs that focus on touring children's operas and other educational community presentations. Orchestras offer contract work for players doing chamber music as teaching artists in their communities. The New York Philharmonic, Philadelphia Orchestra, and the San Francisco Symphony all hire outside teaching artist specialists—in addition to their own orchestra members—to do residency work. See the companion website for a selection of links to orchestral community engagement programs.

Many musicians make a significant portion of their income from residency work. The national organization Young Audiences contracts 5,200 teaching artists (musicians, dancers, and actors) to present educational performances in schools in thirty-three state chapters in the United States (http://www.youngaudiences.org). Also, state arts agencies (funded by state taxes) typically provide funding to subsidize residency work in public schools. Musicians also independently book their own residency work and create partnerships with community organizations.

But employers generally want to hire people with experience. If you're just getting started with residency work, rest assured that there are places in your community now where you could be developing residency skills and valuable experience. And some may even be able to pay you a modest honorarium while you develop your skills.

In looking for venues to present residency programs for adults, think about your own community connections. Ongoing residencies are built on partnerships, on relationships between the musicians and a partnering organization. Start with your network as you explore leads. Do you have colleagues, friends, or family connected with any local organizations? Make a list of possible venues and contacts, and then, just as for booking concerts, prepare a pitch and appropriate marketing materials. Do some reconnaissance visits to check out possible venues. You want to be familiar with the institution, the site, and your potential audience.

The Huntington Brass Quintet first honed their residency skills during a year-long grant-funded program that brought them to Stephenville, Texas, to perform, teach, and live in the community. The grant was the former Rural Residency program funded by the National Endowment for the Arts and administered by Chamber Music America (CMA). Though the NEA program no longer exists, CMA continues to offer its own residency grant program with flexibility about locations, community partners, and time commitment (http://chamber-music.org)

Subsequent to its Stephenville experience, the Huntington Brass Quintet (HBQ) went on to hold shorter-termed residencies at several Boston-area churches. Their residency work involved performing for special church services and holidays, and in exchange, the churches offered the HBQ their own concert series. Having their own "home" series allowed the quintet to grow their local audience base and gain visibility.

Church music residencies are not usually aimed at aesthetic education or hearing distinctions and specifics in music. Church residencies instead focus on linking music, faith, and community. Whether performing in a church, temple, or mosque, musicians are being heard in a context that helps listeners open their hearts to music.

In addition, the HBQ performed residency programs in schools, libraries, and other community settings. They found that presenters appreciated not just their good playing, but also their ability to talk with audiences and design interactive programs. Trumpeter Mark Emery attributed the group's frequent return engagements to their residency skills.

So yes, you can create your own ongoing residency. Partnering organizations may include concert series, after-school music lesson programs, and summer festivals. Start with one event: a concert, a fundraiser, or a master class. If the event goes well, you can explore the possibilities of creating a small series of events there and develop an ongoing relationship with the organization.

Possible Community Partners for Residency Work

Libraries	Hospitals
Festivals	Correctional facilities
Churches	Senior centers
Synagogues	Civic organizations: Kiwanis, Lions, Rotary
After-school programs	Hospice
Museums	Preschools
Boys and Girls Clubs	Parks and recreation departments
Public schools	Rehabilitation centers
Private schools	Shelters
Historical societies	Colleges/universities

Where to Find Residency Bookings

Beyond looking for residency work on a case-by-case basis, there are also a number of organizations that hire musicians or subsidize residency work:

Your state arts council most likely has an arts-in-education program that helps fund performances and short-term residencies in schools. Look up the website, and investigate the possibilities in your state.

County and city arts agencies are funded in part by their state arts councils. These smaller local agencies often fund a variety of community arts projects. To find what is available in your community, call or e-mail your state arts council for referrals to the appropriate organizations.

Young Audiences is a national nonprofit organization that arranges performances and residency programs in schools. There are thirty-three chapters and affiliate organizations nationwide. Find the one nearest you at http://www.youngaudiences.org.

Local organizations devoted to music performances in schools. To find other organizations that fund work in the schools, ask a reference librarian at your local public or university library. And ask local K–12 music department chairs and local parent-teacher organizations.

VSA Arts is a national organization that works to make the arts accessible to people with disabilities. The organization has network affiliates in forty-nine states (see http://www.vsarts.org).

National Funding Sources for Residency Projects

Chamber Music America, http://www.chamber-music.org

Association of Performing Arts Presenters, http://www.artspresenters.org

Meet the Composer, http://www.meetthecomposer.org

American Composers Forum Continental Harmony project, http://www.continentalharmony.org

Marketing Your Programs ◆

Concert presenters are becoming more sophisticated in terms of their expectations for residency activities. The work can be fairly well paid and competitive. So in order to market programs effectively, you need promotional materials that represent you well. Typically, experienced teaching artists have a separate flyer or brochure for their residency work that can be included in their promotional kit or sent separately. Even if you're just getting started, you can still come up with a simple and effective *one-sheet* with a compelling detailed description of your background and what you have to offer.

Residency Flyers

What to include:

- Contact information for the artists and how to get more information (website, e-mail, phone).

- Brief bio including where you've presented residency work.
- Testimonials, ideally with quotes from presenters who have booked your group.
- Concise and compelling description of the programs you offer: for each, describe the *benefits*, what the audience will get from each; appropriate age group for which each program is tailored; and recommended audience size.
- For in-school performances, describe how the program is tied to the curriculum. This is essential for principals and teachers in order to justify the class time given to the activities. In order to get the funding for residency work in schools, there needs to be a clear and specific educational value.

Effective K–12 Residency Materials: Study Guides for Teacher Preparation

One way to ensure that your residency program has some real impact is to create supporting materials for teachers to use before and after your visit. The best materials are those that teachers and students can immediately put to use.

Here are tips for K–12 residency materials from Brooke Thompson, a music teacher in the Chicago Public Schools, and Catherine Larson, music education faculty at DePaul University:

1. Keep materials and instructions brief, because teachers have little time.
2. Keep these user-friendly for non-musician teachers (who may be intimidated if they have little familiarity with music).
3. Offer relevant activities that teachers can do with their students before and after your program.
4. Include brief but clear instruction on how to do these.

Read others' teacher study guides. For example, see http://www.quad cityarts.com/studyguides.html and on http://www.ums.org (click on "education & community").

Quality Control: Evaluating Programs ◆

Getting objective feedback is necessary to improving your teaching artistry. If you're breaking in a new program, do several trial runs with friends, family, or colleagues as your audience. Let them know in advance that you welcome their specific and critical feedback. Tell them you are looking for comments such as, "I didn't quite follow the explanation about . . ." or "I'm not sure your audience will understand these terms you used: . . ." or "The balance of talking to playing was generally good but I thought you went on a bit too long about the third movement" or "I'm not sure why you demonstrated . . . or what it had to do with . . ."

When you present the actual residency work, ask a member of the host institution's staff in advance to observe your residency work. When people know you are open to hearing critical feedback and you really do want their input, they are more likely to give it. Sometimes non-musicians feel unqualified to give feedback, so make clear the questions you want to answers to, such as the following:

> In the presentation, when did the participants seem most engaged?
> When were they least engaged?
> Was there anything you noticed that would help me improve the
>   session?

The school or institution that hires you for this work will need concrete evidence of the effectiveness of the program. This is used in reporting to funders who support residency work. And evaluating yourself allows you to improve and develop better programs. The evidence of your effectiveness is also important for marketing purposes for future bookings and media attention, which is essential for your continued career growth. You can gather comments, quotes, and letters of recommendation, along with the constructive feedback for improvement.

For extended residencies in K–12 schools, portfolio assessments can work well. Have the children keep a journal in which they write about what they experienced in each residency session. For younger students, the journal may include drawings of what they worked on during each visit. Older participants can write about what they did with the visiting musician, what they liked most and least and why, as well as what they would like to do next with their musical interests and skills.

Evaluation information can be collected in a number of ways, some more formal than others. Get written thank-you notes or e-mails from participants, teachers, and staff, and use photocopies or excerpts of these when submitting your evaluation materials (these testimonials can also be useful for marketing purposes). Try to capture the informal verbal feedback you get from participants, staff, parents, and teachers. You can simply write these comments down or, when possible, record them.

Take photos; these are good for documenting your work and capturing audience reactions as well as for publicity. You can also videotape your program (ask a friend to not just film you but to try to catch audience reactions and response as well). But note that, to take photos or video, you must get permission from the partnering residency institution in advance. This can be particularly tricky in schools, because parents need to sign release forms.   ⸀

And of course, you can design a brief evaluation form for participants and guest observers, administrators, and teachers. Tailor the form to fit your program, but keep it concise because teachers and administrators are busy (so an online survey with only five or six brief questions is best).

Summary

Residency work is ultimately about creating connections and community. Helping others connect with the music you love is gratifying. Developing residency skills and opportunities takes time and effort, but the rewards are many: engaged audiences, additional performance opportunities, and the possibilities of grant and other institutional support. But the biggest reward is often personal: residency work can help remind musicians why they fell in love with music in the first place.

▼ ───────────────────────────────────────

Career Forward

Answering the following residency-related questions and writing down your responses will help you enhance your skills and opportunities.

Brainstorming for Residency Programming

1. Imagine that you have been hired to perform for a group of business people at an awards luncheon honoring the retiring president of the company. Choose one piece from your current repertoire that you would like to perform for this group. Imagine that because most people in the audience will be unfamiliar with this work, you have decided to introduce the work verbally. What could you say in a two- or three-sentence introduction to help the audience connect to this work?
2. Same piece, new audience. Now you are performing this work for a hospital's cancer unit in-patient audience. How would you introduce it?
3. Same piece, new audience. How would you introduce the work to a class of 25 fourth-graders?

Brainstorming for Finding Residency Work Partners

4. Where in your local community might you be able to offer residency work? Write down the names of three facilities or organizations. Forget about traditional concert series and halls, and instead think about places where there are regular groupings of people, possible new audiences for you. Perhaps they have an unusual performance space, or a particular membership base that

might also be interested in your music. For ideas, read your local newspapers, talk to neighbors, and search online. Think broadly and creatively: consider science museums, historical homes, and civic organizations.

5. Research the three community organizations. Find out about their resources, programming, and any current partnerships. Visit the organizations, and read their printed brochures and websites. Look at staff and board listings to see if you have any networking contacts connected with the organizations. Check with your alumni office. To make an initial contact, it is especially helpful, though not necessary, to start with a personal connection.

6. Take a piece of music in your current repertoire and design an initial program offering for an organization. Find the appropriate person at the organization, and make an appointment, hopefully with the help of an introduction from someone you both know. During the appointment, present your program idea for a single performance presentation. If the initial performance goes well for all parties, there may be interest in developing this work into a small ongoing series.

9

Performing
at Your Best

▼

▲

What Is Peak Performance? ◆

Performers sometimes describe their best performancee experiences as *peak*. In describing their state of mind during such performances, musicians report that they are free from distraction and that the performance seems to happen on its own, without interference. Time seems suspended, and the body works easily while the mind remains calm and receptive. Athletes describe this as being *in the zone*. Similar to meditative states, this involves a loss of self-consciousness. Psychologists describe this as *flow*, a state of optimum concentration and creativity.

To be clear, a peak performance is not necessarily a technically perfect performance. What makes it peak is not a lack of flaws but *the quality of the performer's state of mind*. In fact, when musicians focus on technical perfection, paradoxically, they may actually shut down the essential element of peak performances, which is a freedom from controlling thoughts.

Peak performances can be elusive, rare occurrences, impossible to predict or to make happen. But we can be physically and mentally prepare for them. The idea is to work to create the optimal environment to achieve peak performance, whether it happens in a phrase, a work, or an entire concert.

What does it take to perform at your best? Of course, preparation is paramount. But assuming that a musician is well prepared, the quality of the performance experience itself is a fascinating balance of physical, emotional, and intellectual factors. This chapter focuses on how musicians can use their bodies and minds to most effectively communicate their musical ideas to audiences. The specific topics in this chapter are stage presence, performance anxiety, and performance health. The vast majority of musicians experience difficulties in each of three areas at some point in their careers. Many musicians do not seek help, and many struggle in isolation. This is unfortunate, because there is so much that can be done to help, with access to good information, coaching, and specific interventions.

Developing Your Own Creative Voice

The Grammy award–winning composer and jazz bandleader Maria Schneider regularly speaks to musicians about ways to develop their individual creative voices. In two terrific talks she gave at the Eastman School of Music and the Berklee College of Music, she offered these five tips, paraphrased here:

1. *Don't follow the crowd.* Find your own artistic role models. Don't be overly influenced by your peers. Just because others are raving about particular musicians and constantly listening to their recordings doesn't mean you have to. Follow your own taste and inclinations: explore the creative works of those you are genuinely drawn to. Stay true to your own artistic sensibilities.

2. *Remember: the commodity of most value that you possess is your own individuality, your distinct perspective and sensibility.* So, even if you think you don't come from a dramatic background, an exotic place, have endured unthinkable hardships, or had an extraordinary education at a young age, you still have your own uniqueness that is in endless supply.

3. *Spend some time each week investing in yourself.* Spend time away from your own music, doing something alone that nurtures your creativity. This might mean a trip by yourself to an art exhibition or museum, going to a concert of music outside your specialty area, attending a play or an art film, or even taking a long hike in the woods. Give yourself this quiet time away from others in order to explore and cultivate your imagination.

4. *Read for inspiration.* In her presentations in 2009, Maria Schneider highly recommended a book by the artist and educator Robert Henri,

titled *The Art Spirit*. Though intended for visual artists, everything in the book is immediately transferable to musicians. The book offers perspective on how to stay motivated and how to approach creating work; it's thought-provoking and inspiring.

5. *Turn off your cell phone and PDA.* Do this for at least two hours each day, preferably for longer. Give yourself a break from distractions, find out what is going on in your own head, and listen to your thoughts. Solitude and contemplation are essential to creativity.

What Is Stage Presence?   ◆

In considering your performance experience, let's start with stage deportment—how you come across to others. In *Stage Presence from Head to Toe*, author Karen Hagberg defines the topic quite broadly, as the total "visual aspect of a live performance: everything from a performer's walk, bow, facial expression, and dress, to an ensemble's portrayal of a single, unified entity; from the condition of the chair, music stands, and piano, to the mechanics of smooth stage management."[1]

Some musicians have a natural charisma and a physical ease that translates immediately to their stage presence. That's fine for those few folks, but for the majority of musicians, things don't come so easily. The good news is that there are specific tips to retool your stage presence to become more at ease, both onstage and off.

Think about an artist whose live performances you have seen a number of times and whose stage presence you admire. How would you describe the impression this artist makes when she or he walks on stage and bows? Confident, austere, energized, humble, or preoccupied? Think about how *you* want to come across to your audience: what you want to convey about who you are and what your music is about.

The ideal is to create the right environment for your performance. This means your *stage presence and demeanor should invite the audience in to your experience with the music.* Hagberg describes good stage presence as a clear expression of a musician's "respect for the music, for the audience, for other musicians and for himself."[2] Working on obstacles to this is what improving stage presence is about.

▼
───

True Story

Hands down, the worst stage presence I ever witnessed was a concerto soloist (who shall remain nameless) who exhibited an extreme case of what I would call "stage arrogance." When he strode on stage, he barely acknowledged the applause, giving just a perfunctory nod in the manner of a cocky high school athlete about to compete in a sports competition. During the orchestral introduction, he appeared to be both bored and impatient. After he would finish a solo passage, he either nodded to himself, as if he approved, or he would shake his head from side to side and frown. With his body language and facial antics, he gave the audience a kind of blow-by-blow commentary on his own performance. The visuals were so exaggerated that it would have been amusing but for the fact that the musician was not a child but an adult professional. Either no one had taught him that this behavior was unacceptable, or else, if someone had told him, he simply did not care about the impression he made. As for his playing, he also sounded arrogant, even when I closed my eyes to blot out the visual distractions.

▲

Some performers convey their nervousness and unease, forecasting an unsure performance to the audience before they even start. Others have unconscious physical habits or facial tics that the audience may interpret as anger or discomfort. Most musicians are not such extreme cases, but then, most of us do not actually know how we come across in performance. Which brings me to the first recommendation.

Have someone videotape your next performance, including your stage entrances and exits and your bows. It can be very hard to be objective when you watch yourself, so view the video with a trusted mentor and discuss it together with the sound turned off in order to really focus on the stage presence. As you watch, ask yourself, am I conveying the image of a professional who welcomes the opportunity to share music with the audience? Or do I appear uncomfortable, tortured, nervous, or angry? Many performers have mannerisms and habits that are unflattering, but these can be overcome. This is worth working on because it is such a big part of the audience's experience.

Many of the specific pointers below come from the noted stage director and coach Janet Bookspan, from the workshops and seminars for musicians she has given at numerous conferences and schools of music. It can be especially helpful for musicians to work with an experienced stage director or acting coach because having an objective third party is often the fastest route to identifying problem areas and making improvements.

Take a Bow

The purpose of an entrance bow is to greet your audience and to acknowledge their applause. A bow is the equivalent of a handshake and a greeting when you meet someone new. When you walk out from backstage, walk straight to your performance position, with your head and chin up. Then, turn to the audience and make eye contact, not fixing on any one individual, but catching eyes as you let your eyes sweep over the crowd, and smile. The eye contact conveys your sincerity. And what you think about translates to your facial expression and body language. Focus on positive self-talk. Thinking, "I'm so happy to see you here!" may help to put you and your audience at ease.

Next, bow from the waist to about forty-five degrees, with arms relaxed at your sides—it is fine to let them fall forward. Do not clasp your hands in front or in back of you as you bow. Hands clasped in front is sometimes referred to as the "fig leaf" pose because it can appear that you are protecting your most vulnerable area. Look down as you bow; this is a sign of humility. When you come up, again make eye contact with the audience. Hagberg writes that when you do not complete all these components of the bow, it is the "equivalent to meeting someone and shaking hands without making eye contact, or turning to walk away before the handshake is finished—either of which would be dismissive and rude."[3]

Pointers
- Remember to smile! Check your posture. .
- Page turners should enter unobtrusively after the performers and should bring music to the stage. If entering the stage on the usual side, stage left, the page turner should walk behind the piano.
- If the audience applauds between movements, do not frown, glare, or roll your eyes. Instead, if you simply lower your head a bit, you can wait until the audience quiets, then proceed with the performance.
- After performing, bow and acknowledge the audience: convey that you appreciate their thanks and smile, *no matter how you feel the performance went.* When returning for curtain calls, return to center stage to bow.
- If you're given flowers, accept them graciously and bring them backstage. If there is another curtain call, leave the flowers backstage—do not bring them back on stage with you.
- Orchestral soloists make their stage entrance before the conductor, and walk to their intended spot and wait for the conductor to get to the podium. Then you both can acknowledge the applause (this shows respect to the conductor who is considered the bigger "star"). As a soloist, make sure you appear interested and involved during the orchestral tutti sections. When the performance is done, shake hands first with the conductor, then the concertmaster, and say thank you to the orchestra before taking your own bow, and then take the conductor's hand and bow together. For the first curtain call, simply shake

hands with the concertmaster. For the second, shake hands with the conductor and let her or him signal for the orchestra to stand (it's not your job to do this). Audiences, orchestras, and conductors all appreciate good manners.

- For stage exits, it always looks better if males let females go first. For entrances, however, if it is an ensemble performance, enter in the order your group will be arranging itself on stage. If you are a male recitalist and your pianist is female, you should enter first because it is your recital, but exit second (demonstrating that though you're a star, you're still a gentleman). Chivalry looks good on stage.
- About encores: should you announce these or simply launch in? This depends on the size of the hall and your ability to project your voice. Have a colleague come to your run-through and stand at the back of the hall to listen to your speaking voice and tell you frankly what will work best.

Just for Ensembles

1. All the ensemble members should move roughly at the same speed during exits and entrances. Pick a leader to cue the beginnings and ends of bows and to signal the stage entrances and exits. Clarify this before each performance. This can mean the difference between looking like a cohesive professional group and looking like a bunch of freelancers who have just met to sight-read a gig. When returning to the stage for curtain calls, return to stage center, in front of stands and chairs (as long as there is enough room to do this comfortably).
2. Figure out a tuning order and do it quietly, quickly, and accurately. If possible, take care of your tuning off stage.
3. Be careful of the way you sit so that all ensemble members' faces can be seen—the audience wants to see your expressions, your eye contact with each other, and all the nonverbal communication.
4. Look at your partners during their solos—show your involvement in the music. Do not "tune out" and simply count rests—audiences can always tell if you're not involved in the music.

Concert Attire

What you wear needs to be appropriate for the performance site and occasion. For a morning residency at a middle school, you would wear something different than at the formal evening concert on a traditional presenter's series. Get objective opinions on your concert attire from people who go to and who give lots of concerts. We all think we have great taste and that we know what is most flattering on our bodies, but the proliferation and popularity of television makeover shows would argue the contrary. We have all been to concerts in which the performer's choice of attire was less than optimal and made a less than favorable impression. The ideal is to wear concert attire that makes you feel confident, that you know for sure is flattering on you, and that shows well even from the back of the hall.

Dress for Success

- Make sure your concert attire allows you to move and breathe freely and looks good when you are moving in performance (musicians often wear concert clothes that are too tight or constricting).
- Pay attention to the quality of the fabric, and the design and line of the garment (how it falls on your body), because all this is very apparent under stage lights. Watch out for bargains that look second-rate on stage. Even wearing all black, it's possible to look elegant, distinctive, and attractive.
- Keep the distracting accessories to a minimum: no watches or dangling earrings. The exception is for female vocalists who can get away with more showy necklaces to highlight the face and neckline.
- Shine your shoes! And because onstage your socks and/or hosiery are usually partially visible, make sure you're not flashing bare shins or odd-colored socks or stockings. For men: your jacket should be buttoned when you enter and exit the stage. If you perform seated, unbutton the jacket after you bow and as you take your seat.
- For ensembles: consider how your group looks together. You don't necessarily need to wear the same suits or colors, but you need to create, with the help of your clothing, an impression of a cohesive unit. For men in ensembles, consider purchasing suits of the same design, label, or fabric. Otherwise, slight variations in shades of black and fabric can make a group appear amateurish.
- For everyone: watch out for hairstyles that hide your features—the audience wants to see your expressions.

Just for Women

Remember, your performance is not a fashion show. Your attire should help the audience focus on you and your music, not your clothing. The line and drape of a gown or trousers can help accentuate the positive and minimize the negative of any figure. Shop for your potential concert gowns with a colleague you trust, someone who will be brutally honest *before* you buy anything. Consider using a personal shopper; upscale department stores offer these services. There are also upscale resale shops where you may find high-quality, affordable gowns. Again, make sure you get good advice.

It's usually best to stick to a solid color because it's less distracting and will help elongate your line. The color, of course, should be flattering to you but should also help make an impact (for instance, dark reds and greens can look wonderfully rich on stage).

Be careful about lengths of dresses for daytime concerts: mid-calf may be the safest. If you sit to perform, choose fuller skirts. Cellists and harpists need full skirts full length or pants with a flattering drape. As for shoes, women do best with those that match the color of their gown (shoes can be dyed), pairing these with flesh-colored stockings.

Many women, young and old, have jiggly upper arms. If you do, avoid sleeveless gowns; instead, wear loose fitting sleeves that cover the upper arm. Make sure your audience can concentrate on your music making and not on the knees, legs, or thighs you may be flashing or the bodice out of which you may be falling!

Just for Men

In terms of formal concert attire, men have it easier. There are fewer ways to go wrong, because a dark suit, well cut and tailored, and made of quality fabric, is great. A good suit can be expensive, but it is an important investment. There are always end-of-season sales and outlet stores for purchasing high-quality suits at a discount. Ask a salesperson for help finding the right size, and have your suit tailored if needed. It is especially important that your suit jacket is cut so that you can move easily. You want lightweight natural fabric to stay comfortable under hot stage lights. Check the necks of your suit shirts also, so that your movements are not restricted. Make sure your suit is cleaned regularly, your shirt pressed, your shoes polished, your socks black and matching, your pants the right length, and that you have an appropriate tie.

Pre-performance Checklist

- ❏ Check the stage lighting carefully so that spotlights do not blind you or create too much heat on stage. Check that the lighting is flattering to performers.
- ❏ In your dress rehearsal, carefully arrange the chairs and stands the way you want them in the performance. Make sure your setup allows the audience to see all ensemble members and that all performers can see each other and have enough space to perform. If the stage crew

needs to move any of the chairs and stands before the concert, have the floor marked or "spiked" with tape so each setup can easily be redone. Do whatever you can to help make smooth stage transitions and to minimize the time between your stage entrance and the first note.

❑ Make sure all page turns are workable (photocopy, cut, and tape pages as needed).

❑ Pianists: if at all possible, arrange the bench height *before* you walk onstage, to spare the audience an extended display of bench adjusting.

❑ For ensembles: use folding metal stands adjusted low because these will neither block sound nor obstruct the audience's view of you and your instrument.

Remember that the audience experiences the performance as a totality, including your bows and facial expressions, any speaking from the stage, your clothing, and even your attitude at the reception. From the audience's point of view, the "concert" is much more than just how the music sounds, so make sure that their total experience is a good one.

Managing Performance Anxiety ◆

If you have performance anxiety, rest assured that you're not alone. Seasoned professionals, as well as rank amateurs, can experience debilitating performance anxiety. Pianist Glenn Gould retired from performing to the recording studio because of stage fright, and Barbra Streisand is reported to suffer from it as well. Every musician experiences performance anxiety to some degree. But the *way* each person experiences it is unique. The extent to which anxiety interferes with any performer's abilities is as individual as the combination and range of symptoms experienced.

In coping with performance anxiety, what works for one person may be useless to the next. What your studio teacher or coach recommends may not work for you. And musicians report that their performance anxiety changes over time, so the coping skills that worked for one phase of their career may not work for the next.

Unfortunately, there is no such thing as a quick fix because individual symptoms and coping skills vary so widely. Finding the right treatment strategies or intervention takes time and experimentation, and often works best in conjunction with a trained performance coach or therapist. Many musicians are too quick to dismiss a treatment method that they may have tried only once. Even the use of beta blockers (a prescription drug used to treat anxiety symptoms) is not an automatic fix because musicians typically need a few trial performances to determine whether or not the drug or dosage is effective. My first suggestion is to have patience. Adopt a neutral curiosity about your performance anxiety, and be willing to give treatment options a thorough and complete trial.

The Basics: What Is Stress?

Stress can be understood as the mental, physical, and emotional reaction to events and situations in our lives. Stress can be caused by negative as well as positive events, by the loss of a job or a loved one, as well as by a marriage, birth of a child, or a new job. Stress is basic to life; without it, existence would be predictable and boring. Stressors—the events and situations we react to—make life challenging, exciting, and memorable.

Experiencing stress before a performance can be positive: it means you care about the performance and are excited about it. Stress gives performances energy, the "edge" that can be lacking in studio recordings. So, stress is not the problem, but the *way you react to stress* may be problematic. The base level of general, underlying stress in your life—as well as your habits and methods of coping with it—plays a critical role in performance anxiety.

19 Stress-Busting Tips

To help better manage your overall "general life" stress:

1. Exercise every day (and no, practicing music does *not* count as exercise).
2. Get enough sleep.
3. Eat healthy; take real breaks for meals.
4. Notice the beauty and nature around you.
5. Identify pleasurable non-music activities that do not take a lot of time; *do* these regularly.
6. Exercise your sense of humor.
7. Be aware of daily stressors, and choose how to react to these.
8. Know yourself; pay attention to the physical and mental clues you get that signal you're on overload.
9. Use a daily planner, and keep your to-do lists short and reasonable.
10. Learn to say "no." Do not overcommit; delegate when you can.
11. Don't isolate: get feedback, suggestions, and encouragement from family and friends.
12. Don't be a slave to your cell phone, text messages, or e-mail—schedule downtime to return messages.
13. In a stressful or emotionally charged situation, dial back to being observant about the situation instead of letting your emotions immediately take over. This can buy you time to choose your response.

14. Meditate and/or use progressive relaxation exercises.
15. Dump your stress: on your way home each day, or when you pack up from a practice session, pick a symbolic spot where you can, in your imagination, dump the day's stress. You want to make sure that when you leave work, practice, or rehearsal, you let go of your stress.
16. Know your own core values, and make sure you are living in sync with these.
17. Remind yourself why you like your work and why you love music.
18. Own your successes, give yourself credit and celebrate the small achievements and daily pleasures.
19. Remember that you deserve to be treated well, so take good care of yourself.

The Mechanics of Performance Anxiety

"If you can do a piece in a practice room—efficiently and well—then you have the technical abilities to do it," says sports psychologist and performance expert Don Greene. "But then if you go on stage and are not able to execute the piece, it's not a technical issue. It's a mental issue, an issue of how you deal with stress. A lot of people then will go back to the practice room to work on a problem that wasn't there, namely their technique, when the problem wasn't their technique—it was their response to stress."[4]

Our body's extreme reaction to stress is called the fight-or-flight response, an instinctive reaction that includes an increase in heart rate and blood pressure, and a rush of adrenaline. Biologically, humans are programmed to react with the fight-or-flight response in life-threatening situations. But unless you are performing in a war zone, a concert is not a life-threatening situation.

When a musician reacts during a performance with the fight-or-flight response, this produces a chain of physical, behavioral, and cognitive reactions. The perception of fear can trigger sweaty palms, dry mouth, trembling hands, and distracted thoughts, all of which may lead to memory slips, missed notes, forgotten text, and other mishaps. Performance anxiety can be broken down into four groups of symptom types, but anxiety can manifest itself with any one or any combination of these:

1. *Physical symptoms* include shortness of breath, dry mouth, sweating, increased muscle tension, rapid heart rate, trembling, nausea, and/or dizziness.
2. *Cognitive indicators* are thoughts or worries that dwell on a negative assessment of the situation and negative thoughts about the performance and oneself.

3. *Emotional indicators* may include feelings of inadequacy, fear of disapproval, fear of the fear itself, and/or an irrational exaggeration of the performance situation (a concert becomes a test of one's worth as a person, a do-or-die situation).

4. *Behavioral changes* occur in response to the symptoms above, such as avoidance (canceling an audition, postponing a recital), or denial (procrastinating the planning, practicing, or rehearsing for a performance).

People who experience high levels of performance anxiety tend to concentrate on their symptoms. This in turn causes more worry, more negative thought patterns, more feelings of inadequacy, and an increase in the severity of these symptoms. Musicians can get stuck in a performance anxiety loop or a downward spiral.

The Sam Q. Story, Part 1

A talented flutist, Sam Q. found that his performance anxiety had increased over the past four years and it was becoming disabling. Before a performance, he would typically find his hands trembling and his mouth so dry it became nearly impossible to start a performance. The weird thing was, once he got started, the symptoms usually subsided and he was able to perform adequately—not as well as he could in a practice room—but better than he feared he would before the performance.

Treatment Starts with Self-Assessment ◆

Self-assessment entails exploring what kinds of conscious and unconscious thoughts and feelings are contributing to the anxiety. Your attitude matters, as in your attitude toward yourself (your confidence and self-esteem), toward your instrument (is it a love/hate relationship?), toward performing in general, and toward your audience. These are all important factors that contribute to how you experience performance anxiety. There are specific thoughts, associations, and feelings that can cause the range of symptoms any musician develops.

First off, perfectionism is a trap. Jeff Nelsen, the hornist with Canadian Brass and faculty member at Indiana University, points out that *flawlessness* should not be the primary goal in performances. Nelsen advises instead, to "Focus on what you want to convey, over and above the technical qualities of your performance, and trust your preparation to keep your errors to a minimum."[5] (See http://www.jeffnelsen.com.)

If you realize that perfection is not for humans and that mistakes are inevitable, you may give yourself the leeway to take risks in your performances. Be able to recognize what is good, what is valuable in your performances, and what your strengths are. We are far too good at analyzing our deficiencies and are often unable to articulate or appreciate our positive qualities. Give yourself permission to fail, and you may surprise yourself and feel a new freedom in your performances.

Attitude Toward Audience

The foundation of performance anxiety is fear of public humiliation. In competitive environments and professions, the festive aspect of performance can all but disappear. It's easy to get caught up in worrying about being judged. It's easy to forget why people come to hear performances in the first place. Audiences are not there to judge. They come to hear you and to be moved by the music. Even in competitions and auditions, the adjudicators *want to be moved*. Jeff Nelsen recommends shifting your thinking: "Sell the story, not yourself." Instead of focusing on wanting the audience to love you, "make them an audience that loves what you love."[6] Don't project your fears and negative thoughts onto your audience—they are on your side.

Examine Your "Self-Talk"

Distorted thought patterns typically result in negative self-talk. Think about what actually goes on in your head during a performance. Negative self-talk often comes in predictable flavors:

> "I can't believe I just f#&%d up that passage" or "Well, that was a disaster, and there's no excuse. It went great in the last rehearsal. I'm a wreck!" (*This is polarized thinking, critiquing what's past instead of focusing on the present.*)

> "Who do I think I'm fooling? I can't play this piece!" or "This is going really bad; this whole performance is going to suck." (*This is overgeneralizing, catastrophizing, personalization.*)

> "I can tell the audition committee hates me. I don't stand chance. This is so unfair!" or "Oh my God, here comes that passage I always screw up . . ." or "Yikes, here's where I had that memory slip last week." (*Anticipating disaster often makes for a self-fulfilling prophecy.*)

These thoughts are often lurking just below consciousness and may be long-standing habits that undermine our self-esteem and therefore our performances. We may not be aware of these messages at all. Self-talk is a backdrop to our daily activities that exerts a powerful effect. These negative thoughts produce negative feelings of worry, fear, a sense of inadequacy, and these feelings in turn incite the physical symptoms of performance anxiety.

▼

The Sam Q. Story, Part 2

When flutist Sam Q. started to self-assess, he noticed his thoughts in the practice room—what specifically went through his head while he prepared for his next quintet concert. He started to keep a practice room journal, and during each practice session he would spend part of his time imagining that he was in the warm-up room backstage with his colleagues and they had only five minutes before the stage call. He visualized everything, from seeing himself in his concert attire to hearing his colleagues warm up, to feeling the excitement and energy start to surge, along with his stomach acid. Sam noticed his self-talk and wrote it all down. His thoughts tended to center around worry over particular passages. He anticipated all kinds of disasters and obsessed over certain phrases, even though most of these passages had gone fine in the last rehearsals. His thoughts raced with frantic statements such as, "The third movement is no good, that fast passage is a mess!" or "What if I screw up that cue?" or "My intonation sucks!" As for what Sam was thinking about himself and his audience, he noted that right before walking on stage, he felt like he was unqualified, that he was a fraud and had no business giving the concert. He thought that the audience was going to "see through him" and judge him as incompetent. Sam wrote all this up in his journal. He was surprised at how negative and extreme the thoughts were. He was discouraged. His negative self-talk seemed so entrenched that he doubted he could find relief.

▲

Interventions and Treatment Methods ◆

Though there's no quick fix for performance anxiety, there are a range of methods and coping techniques that can be extremely effective. Changing our ingrained habits of how we react to stress takes time, patience, and experimentation. It also takes a willingness to explore our self-talk, underlying feelings, and emotional baggage.

A range of coping techniques and methods is included below. Keep an open mind, and experiment with these suggestions to find a combination or adaptation that works well for you. Consider your practice room as your laboratory. Try out the ideas and coping strategies below, incorporating them into daily practice to build new habits in the coming weeks and months before your next performance.

Treatment should address the specific symptoms and issues you face. For instance, if you physically tense up before a performance, you may need to work on specific muscle relaxation exercises and prompts. If you tend to become distracted, exercises to help you center and focus your thoughts may be helpful. If your perfectionism is plaguing you, there are affirmations and thought-stopping and resiliency exercises to explore. If you have a hard time quieting the critical voices in your head, there are also exercises to alter these ingrained "tapes." Here are a dozen suggestions:

1. *Find a counselor.* Seeing a professional counselor can be tremendously helpful. Consider those who specialize in working with performers and/or those who treat anxiety disorders. The purpose of working with a skilled therapist or consultant is to get objective feedback and perspective from a trained professional, someone who can help tailor a treatment program to your specific needs. Always get referrals; you may need to meet with several therapists before finding the best match.

2. *Check your community resources* and reach out to others for help; don't isolate. Find out what stress management courses or anxiety treatment programs are available in your area. Many community centers and hospitals offer these services. Whether or not they are specifically for musicians doesn't matter, since to some extent, anxiety is anxiety, and you may find excellent treatment and support.

3. *Preparation* for your next performance or audition will do a lot to increase your confidence. Create a plan for the months and weeks preceding the performance. Include a schedule of practice time and deadlines for completing work on each piece. You may want to schedule lessons with mentors to make sure that you are fully prepared and do not have concerns over your objective abilities to perform.

4. *Desensitization* is the process of gradually building up resistance and increasing tolerance to stress. This is the same technique used to treat allergies, social anxiety, and panic attacks. The idea is that you start with lower stress performance situations, such as playing a casual mini-concert in a less-pressured atmosphere, and gradually build up to the "real" performance. Start with just playing a small part of your program for one or two friends. Then you can "raise the stakes" regularly, systematically increasing the number of people and the level of stress in each performance situation. Arrange to perform at a local church, elementary school, or senior center.

The object is, in part, to learn more about what is going on in your thinking as you perform, and, most important, to become more accustomed to handling your symptoms as you experiment with various coping strategies. "Powerful performance is not about being relaxed," says performance expert Don Greene. "You have to accept that when you perform, you might be feeling some extra energy, and the more accustomed you can get to feeling that energy when you play your first few notes, the better."[7]

The reality is that most musicians simply don't get enough practice performing. Don Greene cites a basic mistake musicians make in their approach. They

> never switch over from practicing practice, to practicing performance. And then they go out on stage—where the environment is very different—expecting to do something they've never adequately practiced. All that time they've been practicing doing something they're not going to do. They're not going to go out there and rehearse, stopping and starting and correcting. At some point, a musician should start practicing performance—making an entrance, playing the piece straight through regardless of what happens, and then getting up to make the exit.[8]

So, you need to create more performance situations for yourself. A good place to start is by arranging for lower-stress performances in your community.

5. *Visualization* is the technique of creating detailed mental images that can influence your thoughts, feelings, and actions. Visualization is a powerful tool, a mental skill useful for performances, but like any skill, it demands practice. Below are three different visualization exercises. To find more, see the terrific book *Musical Excellence: Strategies and Techniques to Enhance Performance*, edited by Aaron Williamon, as well as the other recommended resources in this book's companion website, http://www.oup.com/us/beyondtalent.

A. *Re-creating a performance.* Think back to a performance of yours with which you felt satisfied. Using your imagination, re-create this performance experience in every detail. Remember what you saw, smelled, heard, and felt. How did your arms and legs feel as you were performing? What was your breathing like? What thoughts were passing through your mind? What feelings were you aware of? You can re-create this state of mind in your practice sessions, gradually increasing the amount of time you can stay in the remembered state, in the re-created sense of calm, focused concentration. With practice, musicians learn to bring back this desired state of mind and body at will, so they can use this technique in performances.

B. *Direct your own movie.* In your mind, you can create a movie of your own ideal performance, the way you best perform a particular passage, movement, or piece. Make sure that you are not just replaying a favorite CD or DVD in your head—this visualized performance has to be your own, based on your current best performance abilities.

Detail all of your sensory experience. You may want to close your eyes as you do this. How do your fingers, neck, shoulders, spine, and feet feel? In your ideal performance of a particular passage, what would you see? The conductor, a colleague, the music? What would you smell? How are the acoustics in the hall? What exactly do you notice about how the first passage sounds? Start first with just a phrase, then build up your movie-making ability to a complete work. When you create such a movie in your head, you are teaching your mind and body how to re-create this performance in reality.

C. *Circle of excellence.* In his article "Performing at Your Best," Michael Colgrass describes this exercise. Draw or mark a circle on the floor using chalk or removable tape (on a tile or linoleum floor), or in a carpeted room, you may be able to simply "draw" your circle in the carpet's pile with your finger. Now step into your circle of excellence. Michael Colgrass writes,

"Inside the circle is your own personal excellence, what makes you unique. If even for a split second you feel less than your best, you step out of the Circle, quickly do what's necessary to regain your optimum state, and step back in again. The Circle is like a force field made of your own energy, and it's impenetrable. You can visualize the Circle anywhere you need it—on stage, in the practice room, at auditions—and it's always with you because you carry it in your head. Performers claim they feel an almost electrical power in their Circle of Excellence, a feeling very like their peak performance state." Remember, you need to develop this skill over time in the practice room before trying it in performance. (See http://www.michaelcolgrass.com.)

6. *Keep a performance journal* to keep track of your preparation and performances. Record your self-talk and emotions in practice sessions and rehearsals. Record whatever visualization techniques you use and how they work. This way you can track your progress and your use of various techniques. After performances, write down how you felt before, during, and after the concert. Write what people said to you about your performance. It's important to be able to appreciate what's good and what is actually working well. Writing down these positive comments should help to let them sink in.

7. *Thought stopping* is the technique of consciously stopping the negative and replacing it with the positive. For this to be effective, you have to be vigilant, because most of us are unaware of our own self-talk. Negative thoughts kick off the cycle of performance anxiety symptoms. Cognitive therapy is based on the theory that your thoughts determine your feelings and there-

fore your behavior. So, when you replace negative self-talk with positive, you trigger positive feelings of confidence and reduce the physical reactions to stress. The main point is that you can control the self-talk and choose which "voices" to follow, the negative or the positive.

For instance, if you find yourself thinking things like, "I can't do this" or "There's no way this is going to be good" or "Oh my God, my hands are starting to sweat again," you need to quash these thoughts. You may need to shout in your head, "Stop!" and then replace the negative with positive talk, such as "I have prepared well," or "I have a good performance waiting to unfold," or "I have a story to tell through my performance and I want to share it with this audience." Self-talk is powerful; it determines our emotional states. If you want to change your emotional state, you need to change your self-talk.

8. *Learn to let go.* During your performances, are you able to stay in the present? If you make a mistake, can you let it go and not dwell on it? Can you stay focused on the now? Are you able to appreciate your performance in the moment?

Improvising is all about being in the present. I have often noticed a difference in the general attitudes that jazz and classical musicians have toward performing. Jazz musicians, because of the nature of their art, don't chase after a fixed version of perfection. So if you don't improvise now, consider taking a class or some lessons with a musician who does. Or take a theater class in improv. This can be a great way to start feeling more comfortable in your body and with the experience of being—and performing—in the present.

9. *Take a deep breath.* Better than any pill is using the technique of deep abdominal breathing. It is the best antidote for the fight-or-flight response. Slow diaphragmatic breathing will calm your racing heart, help regulate the surge of adrenaline, and help you calm down and focus. Make it a habit to practice this breathing twice a day. Start by practicing for two minutes at a time, and gradually increase your capacity. The practice will pay off: your body will adopt the *relaxation response* as a habit, a routine that you can "turn on" as part of your performances.

▼
The Relaxation Response

This is a simple practice that, once learned, takes ten to twenty minutes a day and can relieve stress and tension and help you toward a healthier, more satisfying life. The technique was developed by Herbert Benson, M.D., at Harvard Medical

School, tested extensively, and written up in his recommended book *The Relaxation Response*. Regular elicitation of the relaxation response has been scientifically proven to be an effective treatment for a wide range of stress-related disorders.

On the website for the Massachusetts General Hospital's Benson-Henry Institute for Mind Body Medicine, there are resource listings as well as this basic introduction to the Relaxation Response:

1. Pick a focus word, short phrase, or prayer that is firmly rooted in your belief system, such as "one," "peace," "The Lord is my shepherd," "Hail Mary full of grace," or "shalom."
2. Sit quietly in a comfortable position.
3. Close your eyes.
4. Relax your muscles, progressing from your feet to your calves, thighs, abdomen, shoulders, head, and neck.
5. Breathe slowly and naturally, and as you do, say your focus word, sound, phrase, or prayer silently to yourself as you exhale.
6. Assume a passive attitude. Don't worry about how well you're doing. When other thoughts come to mind, simply say to yourself, "Oh well," and gently return to your repetition.
7. Continue for ten to twenty minutes.
8. Do not stand immediately. Continue sitting quietly for a minute or so, allowing other thoughts to return. Then open your eyes and sit for another minute before rising.
9. Practice the technique once or twice daily. Good times to do so are before breakfast and before dinner.[9]

_____ ▲

10. *Meditation.* Many meditation exercises begin with slow breathing. The relaxation response above is a form of meditation and can be learned and practiced either alone or with a group. Yoga and Tai Chi are disciplines that are based on meditation and both can be tremendously helpful for musicians. The basic idea of meditation is to consciously empty the mind of thoughts in order to aid in relaxation and focused concentration. People practice meditation by focusing on their breath or on just one thing, such as a single syllable mantra or visual image. When you regularly practice meditation, you train your mind and body. Performance itself can be a kind of meditation, as being in the zone or being in flow are kinds of meditative states. So by practicing meditation, musicians can exercise the same state of mind they need for peak performances.

11. *Memorization.* Knowing and performing a piece of music by heart can be an aid to performers. It can ensure that the piece is thoroughly learned

and can give a performer a sense of ownership in his or her interpretation. Unfortunately, fear of memory slips can contribute to performance anxiety.

If you are preparing to perform a piece from memory, there are strategies that can help both the quality of your performance as well as your memorization. In our long-term memories, we store music using multiple representations:

- Conceptually—you know the piece's structure, so that in the midst of playing, you know where you are in the piece (such as at the exposition or recapitulation, or first verse, chorus, or bridge).
- Auditory—you can hear the music and what comes next.
- Visual—you can visualize the printed sheet music or score in your mind's eye.
- Kinesthetic—your body memorizes the motions, the fingerings, the position, the physical "dance" of the work.

You can work on each of these memorization strategies, taking small sections of a piece one at a time and working through them silently. For instance, you can play though a section or a movement, "hearing" the work in your mind, to work on your auditory skills. For visualization, you can also go through a section without performing it but instead "seeing" the score in your mind's eye and "reading" it through as you perform it in your imagination. As for your kinesthetic practice, you can perform the work again silently but while imagining all the physical sensations involved. And conceptual memorization is best worked on by analyzing the piece, to thoroughly understand its structure and organization (how the sections fit together). Because these practice techniques are worked on away from the instrument, this is not only good practice for memorization, but for concentrated and focused work without the concern of overuse or performance injury.

The most secure memorization relies on more than one method, so that, for example, if you momentarily can't hear what's coming next, or can't see the page in your imagination, your body knows the motions. In *Musical Excellence: Strategies and Techniques to Enhance Performance*, the memorization strategy recommended by contributor Jane Ginsborg is to first analyze the music so that you can use conceptual memory of the structure of the work as your overall framework. This is the metaphorical equivalent of being able to see the forest for the trees. Ginsburg next recommends you "chunk" the music and practice it in small structural sections, gradually increasing the size of the chunks as you become more familiar with the work. Then use rote, kinesthetic memory, along with either visual and/or aural memory, to enhance the security of your memorization.[10]

12. *Medication.* Beta blockers are prescription drugs that stop the body's response to adrenaline. Inderal, commonly prescribed to musicians for performance anxiety, is also used to treat high blood pressure, angina, certain heart conditions, and migraines. However, beta blockers treat physical symptoms only (they can reduce the sweating and slow down the racing heart). They do not address the feelings and thoughts that cause performance anxiety. Beta blockers may be psychologically addicting. They also have varying side effects, and there are possible drug interactions with other medication you may be taking. Because of this, don't *ever* use someone else's prescription!

Some musicians rely on beta blockers only for special occasions, for important auditions or particularly stressful performances. The problem with occasional and first time use is that you need to know in advance how your body will react to the drug in a stressful performance situation. If your performance anxiety is such that you feel the need to try medication, have a thorough medical exam first and then try taking the medication in several lower stress performance situations so that you can gauge your response.

Goal Setting ◆

In working on a performance anxiety management plan, it's essential to have concrete and reasonable goals so you can benchmark your progress. For instance, setting a goal to be free of all performance anxiety at your next performance two months from today is *not* a reasonable goal. Learning how to cope with your performance anxiety is a process that takes time and practice. In thinking through and devising appropriate goals, many coaches and consultants use the acronym SMART :

Specific—For example, you might set a goal to perform three low-risk "warm-up" performances at a local church, elementary school, and retirement home in advance of an upcoming formal recital to be performed four months from now.

Measurable—Your goals might be quite basic, such as getting through the three programs. But to help you measure how well you manage the anxiety, have a friend or mentor attend each performance. Tell this person in advance what you're especially concerned about, and tell them what to watch and listen for, so that you get useful feedback. Arrange to have the performances videotaped for study and comparison. With objective feedback from a mentor and the evidence from the video, you can measure your progress.

Adjustable—The performances will be organized in conjunction with the community venues, so the time, dates, and length of program will all need to be adjusted according to the venue. The goals for each performance may also need to be adjusted based on the experience and feedback after each performance. That's okay; it's all a process.

Realistic—Depending on what your performance anxiety symptoms have been, your goal may be to "stay in the present" while performing so that you notice what goes well. After each performance, stay and speak with the audience members. When you get home, write in your journal what went on in your head during the performance and what you noticed about your focus and concentration. Also write down all the comments you received from the audience because this can be an important reality check as to how the performance actually went.

Time Sensitive—The three performances might be scheduled for the month before the formal recital (with each one a week apart). The scheduling, programming, rehearsal times, and travel all need to be worked out well in advance and confirmed a few days before each performance. This will help to avoid any last-minute logistical worries.

Sam Q.'s Story: Final Installment

Looking for answers, Sam Q. read several books about performance anxiety. Although he found these interesting and informative, he felt he needed some individual assistance, tailored to his specific difficulties. He worked with a therapist and a performance coach and was able to analyze what was going on in his head around the start of the performance. He worked on thought stopping, meditation, and visualization techniques, and he developed a specific routine for pre-performance preparation.

In order to work on this program, Sam booked performance opportunities for himself in low stress situations, by offering to perform both for the local middle school and a nearby hospital. Sam now reports that he's managing his performance anxiety, feels much more in control, and often finds himself enjoying his performances in a way that is brand new for him.

Putting Performance Anxiety in Context: The Bigger Picture

Celebrate your daily successes and small joys: a productive rehearsal, a useful new contact, a good afternoon of teaching, a beautiful sunrise, or a friend's smile. You should feel good about how you choose to spend your time; if you don't, that's a clear indication that you need to make some changes. Benchmark your progress toward your goals by acknowledging the daily progress you make.

You will need to experiment with a range of techniques to find the answers to your own situation. This self-assessment and experimenting can lead to more satisfying performances and to a deeper understanding of how music can best fit in your life.

Performance Health ◆

To achieve peak performances, your body—not just your mind—needs to be in excellent working condition. Musicians spend countless hours and years training their bodies in very intricate, precise musculoskeletal movements and positions, much the way athletes do. Unfortunately, musicians do not usually give their bodies the same care that professional athletes do. Preventive care for musicians is paramount. Taking good care of your body is essential for peak performances as well as your career itself and quality of life.

▼ _____

Performance Health Quiz

1. Do you warm up carefully each time you practice, rehearse, or perform?   Yes ❑   No ❑
2. Do you take frequent breaks during practice sessions?   Yes ❑   No ❑
3. Do you evaluate your technique regularly?   Yes ❑   No ❑
   (Check if your playing or vocalizing is tension-free. Are you using unnecessary tension or force? Are you straining in any way while you practice?)
4. Do you videotape your practice sessions regularly?   Yes ❑   No ❑
   (Practicing in front of a mirror is not equivalent. You need to see your playing objectively, in action. Watching yourself on video can make it easier to spot areas of tension.)
5. Do you have good nutritional habits?   Yes ❑   No ❑
   (You need to fuel your body with a balanced diet.)
6. Do you smoke?   Yes ❑   No ❑
   (Consider a smoking cessation plan.)
7. Do you have a plan to manage your stress and performance anxiety?   Yes ❑   No ❑
   (Take special care during high-risk times for developing injuries, such as in preparing for an important audition, or when adjusting to a new instrument, repertoire, or technique.)
8. Are you getting plenty of sleep?   Yes ❑   No ❑
9. Do you exercise regularly?   Yes ❑   No ❑
   (Practicing does not count as exercise. Take a walk every day! Include stretching and strengthening as well as cardiovascular exercise in your routine.)

10. Is your attitude toward your music positive?   Yes ❑   No ❑
    (Perfectionism and ambition can cause too much stress and tension.)

▲

Musicians' performance injuries are, unfortunately, common. Musicians are a special risk group for repetitive motion injuries. Studies have shown that as many as 82 percent of musicians have performance injuries. Of instrumentalists, the most frequent performance injuries reported are among pianists, violinists, cellists, and guitarists, but every musician is at risk. So, if you are experiencing discomfort or pain, know that you are not alone. Many instrumentalists and vocalists go through performance-related difficulties—once you start asking around you'll find many colleagues who have had injuries and many who have gone on to make full recoveries.

What you experience as a performance-related discomfort may be caused or aggravated by other activities. For singers, a day job that involves a lot of talking can be a liability. For instrumentalists, computer and PDA use is often a problem, but sports, hobbies, carrying children, and other daily activities may also be contributors. Instrumentalists' injuries are often the same as computer overuse injuries. Carpal tunnel syndrome, tendonitis, and trigger finger or thumb are particularly common among pianists, guitarists, flutists, and string players. Singers may be at risk for vocal nodes and other difficulties. Overuse, in combination with an inefficient technique, is often at the root of these problems. Incorrect posture, excessive tension, and poor support can contribute to chronic injuries and disability. Again, the good news is there are preventive measures as well as effective treatment methods.

Warning Signs

Any kind of discomfort, muscle or joint pain may signal overuse or a need to re-examine your performing posture and your technique. The first symptoms may be a slight twinge, a dull ache, a sharp pain, a weakening or slowing of dexterity, numbness, or a "pins and needles" sensation. Vocalists may notice a limit to their range or an inconsistency in tone color.

If you experience any of these while practicing or performing, it is a signal. Your body is sending you a message, so pay attention. You need to stop and to temporarily suspend all practice, rehearsals, and performances, and *call your doctor.*

Sometimes the diagnosis is a simple matter of overuse, and all you need is to rest your muscles, vocal chords, tendons, or joints for several days or a few weeks. When you can start again, you may need to warm up more carefully and limit practice time, and cut down computer use and text messaging.

If it is not simple overuse, the problem may stem from your performance posture, the basic way you hold your body when you sing or play. Minor adjustments can make major improvements. You may need to change your posture to allow for more freedom of movement, more balance of weight and muscle tension. However, sometimes the pain or discomfort is a signal of something more serious. You will not know unless you get it thoroughly checked out by a doctor. It is very important lay off practicing and performing until you can get the difficulty sorted out.

Unfortunately, many musicians who develop injuries wait before seeing a doctor. Injuries often develop at the least convenient times (while preparing for important auditions or concerts), and musicians typically try to play through the pain and "tough it out." While a musician delays seeking help, his or her injury only gets worse. Some people minimize or even deny the fact that there *is* a problem. Or they assume that it's simple fatigue, so they continue to practice, which only compounds the problem. Do not wait and worry; see a doctor. *Early intervention is the best route to a quick recovery.*

Your general physician is fine for starters. She or he can either determine what the difficulty is or at least rule out some possible causes (vocal strain or simple overuse, as opposed to more complicated issues of vocal nodes, focal dystonia, carpal tunnel syndrome, or bursitis). Your doctor may refer you to a specialist, and you may want to get more than one opinion. When being referred, it's important to consult with people who treat musicians, who will understand your particular concerns and difficulties. There are medical clinics for musicians' injuries in many cities; see Performing Arts Medicine Clinics in the United States at http://yourtype.com/survive/clinics_for_performers.htm, and there's a terrific resource in the Musicians and Injuries site, http://eeshop.unl.edu/music.html. In addition, check out the Performing Arts Medicine Association (http://www.artsmed.org) and the journal *Medical Problems of Performing Artists* (http://www.sciandmed.com/mppa).

In addition to performing a thorough exam, a good doctor will take a detailed history of your practice and performance habits, and ask about which specific movements cause you difficulty. It's important that your health-care professional watch you play or sing. Your doctor should also ask about your nutritional and exercise habits, your emotional state of mind, your sleep patterns, and any other physical exertions beyond making music that may affect or contribute to your injury. Your doctor may prescribe anti-inflammatory medicine to reduce swelling and pain. Reducing swelling will aid your body in repairing the injury, by improving circulation to the injured area. So, even if you generally refrain from taking drugs, it is essential to follow the doctor's protocol of anti-inflammatory medicine. Typically, doctors also prescribe a period of rest in order to allow your body to heal and also to be able to gauge the severity of the difficulty. Then, depending on the nature of the injury, your doctor may recommend a range of treatment methods.

10 Suggestions for Preventing Musician Injuries

These are from Dr. Michael Charness, director of the Performing Arts Clinic at Brigham and Women's Hospital, Boston, and associate professor of neurology at Harvard Medical School. Dr. Charness (who is also a pianist) recommends the following:

1. Avoid playing more than twenty-five minutes without a five-minute break. Try taping the last five minutes of a session, and use the five minute break to listen critically. You may need to use a timer to make sure you take breaks regularly.
2. Stretch, warm up, and work gradually into practice sessions.
3. Compensate for increased playing intensity (recording sessions, preparation for an audition or recital, difficult program, stress, new instrument, altered technique) by reducing total playing time.
4. Intersperse repetitive rehearsal of individual passages throughout a practice session to avoid overworking one set of muscles. Learning and safety may be enhanced by playing a passage five times every ten minutes, rather than thirty times in a row.
5. Begin to increase practice time weeks to months in advance of recitals or auditions.
6. Return to work gradually after a layoff.
7. Begin slowly, and increase gradually any unaccustomed use of the hands (e.g., gardening, typing, sports).
8. Avoid unnecessary muscle tightness when you play. Excessive shoulder elevation or neck twisting may lead to muscle spasm and reduce the fluidity of movement in adjacent muscles. The burden of supporting the weight of instruments can be reduced by straps, posts, pegs, shoulder pads, and chin rests. Violinists and violists should adjust their supports so that the instrument can be held without *any* elevation of the left shoulder.
9. Be attentive to posture. Slouching in a chair for hours daily will eventually take its toll in back and neck problems. Good posture will reduce the work of small forearm and hand muscles by enabling larger shoulder and back muscles to support the combined weight of the arms and/or instrument.
10. Don't neglect your general physical and mental health.

Alternative Medicine/Treatments

Below is a range of treatment methods and practices that musicians have found helpful. Remember, what works well for one person may not work well for the next. Also, any treatments you consider must be checked with your doctor so that you do not aggravate your condition. In general, most musicians in recovery from a performance injury use a combination of Western medicine and alternative treatments:

- Alexander Technique
- Chiropractic
- Feldenkrais
- Rolfing
- Reflexology
- Massage therapy
- Acupressure
- Nutrition
- Exercise
- Tai Chi
- Acupuncture
- Swimming
- Yoga
- Physical therapy
- Occupational/hand therapy

"Musicians tend to jump from a path of treatment before giving it time to work," says Judith Ciampa Wright, occupational therapist and certified hand therapist in Massachusetts. *Your recovery demands your patience!* Judith explains:

> Too frequently, musicians seek treatments that involve their passive participation (like massages) without addressing posture, strength, flexibility, and activity modification—all of which are necessary for effective long-term injury management. A multifaceted treatment approach is often the most effective. For example one might combine a "bodywork" technique (such as massage therapy) with a direct treatment technique (such as Physical Therapy or Occupational Therapy) and also a great whole body exercise program (such as yoga or swimming).

Keep your doctor informed and thoroughly discuss ALL the treatment methods and kinds of activities you engage in that might affect your injury. If you jump from one treatment plan to another, experimenting with all kinds of traditional and non-traditional treatments, you may never know what is helping and what is actually adding to the problem.

Depending on what your doctor advises, you may need to take a break from playing for a period of months and then resume practicing only at very short intervals, five to ten minutes at a time, paying close attention to what specific movements cause pain. You need to be a detective, finding clues to what is not working right and searching for ways to perform without strain.

Reworking Your Technique

Most musicians, in order to recover from a performance injury, find they must rework parts of their technique, change their practice habits, and adjust their performance posture. This is the part of healing that you are most in charge of. Your doctor and a teacher may be able to assist, but ultimately, it is up to you to find out what works best for your body, because only you have direct body feedback. Think of the practice room as your own mini-biofeedback lab. You'll need to develop a finely tuned "body awareness" as you experiment with ways to reduce tension in your performing. Patience and a positive, open, and inquisitive attitude are necessities for the healing journey.

About Recuperation

Typically, performance injuries are compounded by the accompanying worry and stress. Musicians often feel as though they will never perform again, that the injury signals the end of their career. Sometimes musicians feel ashamed, as if they have done something "wrong." In other words, we can be our own worst enemy by becoming depressed and anxious, which typically intensifies the pain. Talking to others about your situation is important—get advice and counseling. It's essential to have a support system during this difficult time.

You can also use your imagination, dreams, and visualization to help in your healing. Before falling asleep, when your body and mind are very relaxed, you are in a suggestible state. You can say to yourself, to your subconscious, "I'd like to know how it feels to perform with ease, without stress or tension or pain." Imagining the new improved method and "memorizing" these kinesthetic sensations can help you reach your goals by creating a sensory image to work toward.

Take care of yourself in this challenging time by getting enough sleep, eating well, getting exercise, and keeping a positive attitude about your recovery. Because you cannot practice much, work on your inspiration. Expand your imagination by going to performances and listening to recordings of music beyond your own repertoire. Get a sense of renewal from the other art forms—visit museums, go to dance and theater performances—explore the other arts as a way to enrich your music making.

Summary

In all three areas—stage presence, performance anxiety, and performance health—the common denominator is the body/mind connection. Musicians do well to cultivate their own awareness and curiosity about these issues, to get reliable feedback and accurate assessments, and to be open-minded and resourceful in looking for solutions to the challenges they may face. Take care of yourself so you can have a lifetime of satisfying music making.

▼

Career Forward

Write down your responses to the following to work toward more peak performance experiences.

1. Describe how you want to experience your next performance. Imagine walking on stage: How do you want to feel physically? What kinds of thoughts do you want to be having? What emotions do you want to experience?
2. How would you like to come across to your audience? What image do you want to convey through your stage entrances, exits, and bows?
3. Have you recently videotaped a performance and later watched it with a mentor to discuss your stage presence? If not, when might you be able to do this?
4. How do you experience performance anxiety? Describe your specific symptoms:
    a. physical
    b. thought patterns (self-talk)
    c. feelings
5. Of the interventions described for handling anxiety in this chapter, which do you plan to work on?
6. Have you ever experienced discomfort during or after practice? What have you done as a result of feeling this discomfort?
7. How often do you take breaks during practice sessions? How long are these breaks? What do you do during these breaks?
8. To help ensure a lifetime of healthy music making, what else (beyond taking breaks) can you do to help safeguard your performance health?

▲

10

Freelancing
for Success

▼

In this chapter:
  To Specialize or Not?
  Networking for Referrals
  Researching to Get Work
  Marketing for Freelancers
  Musician Unions: Strength in Numbers
  Negotiating Fees
  Contracts

▲

The majority of musicians spend at least a portion of their careers as self-employed professionals, as freelancers. Being successful as a self-employed musician means being in charge of your destiny. As a freelancer, you are, in effect, running a small business. Freelancing can make for an exciting and varied work life, with each week bringing new projects and collaborators. However, not being a salaried full-time employee means doing without a steady paycheck, benefits, paid vacation time, or a regular schedule. So freelancers need to be organized and professional in their transactions.

For many, developing freelance work can be made easier with information, perspective, and networking. This chapter is intended to help musicians avoid making blunders that could hurt a reputation or a career. The following offers you a range of ideas and tips to try out.

▼

The Tale of Joan V., Bootstrapping
in the Freelance World (Part 1)

Trombonist Joan V. started freelancing while in graduate school. It started with her teacher and friends recommending her for orchestral gigs. Joan also played brass quintets with buddies and they gigged together, playing four weddings and a funeral, plus a party for a local political bigwig. But once she graduated, Joan found that this sporadic work was not enough to pay the bills. So she auditioned for the sub lists of several regional orchestras. She also asked her former teachers for the names of local contractors—the people who contract freelance musicians to play pick-up orchestra gigs. Joan called these contractors, sent them her résumé, and two of them asked her to audition. *Things were looking good.*

However, Joan was struggling to pay her bills, including her student loans. Some weeks and months there was plenty of work and money coming in, and she could afford to go out with friends. But at other times, she was doing what her Aunt Lil called the "starving musician, ramen noodle thing." To make matters worse, Joan's aging car had twice stalled on the way to performances and she couldn't afford a new one. *Now things were now* not *so good.*

Joan realized that though she was building her reputation and getting established as a professional, it would still be a while before she could manage solely on her freelance work. So she looked into getting private students, coaching the brass sectionals for a local youth orchestra, and teaching in the community music schools. A friend referred several students to Joan and told her about a part-time opening at a music instrument repair shop. Joan got the job, and found that it came with an added perk: she regularly met other freelancers and teachers who could refer more students to her. With the income from her day job and teaching, Joan got her car overhauled and started saving for a new one. *Things were looking up again.*

To Specialize or Not? ◆

Freelancing can be extremely varied, from orchestral and choral concert work to session work and background music for social functions. Freelancers perform as substitute players or guest artists with various ensembles. They may also play weddings, corporate parties, restaurant and hotel gigs, musical theater, and festivals.

So one approach is to think broadly and to diversify your skills, because the more you can offer, the more work you may be able to get. Do you perform only music of a particular period, style, or genre? For wind players, doubling (being able to play several instruments) is an important consideration, especially for those seeking recording and musical theater work. For jazz players, do you know enough cover tunes to play a gig for a four-hour corporate party? Can you write arrangements? For vocalists, what is the range of repertoire you can offer? Do you sing gospel, musical theater, and/or perform early and twenty-first century music? Flexibility and versatility are good things for freelancers. But don't overstate or promise what you can't deliver—offer the music you are skilled in and comfortable performing.

The other approach is to specialize in a particular niche area, a specific period, style, or repertoire. If you offer something distinctive and marketable, it differentiates you from the competition and can help establish your reputation. The catch is that your specialty area needs a niche market, an audience. For instance, for a group that plays early American music, it makes sense to seek bookings at historical societies and house museums. And a group specializing in Swing may do well playing corporate holiday parties, cruise lines, hotels, and wedding receptions. And some musicians try to get the best of both worlds by having a specialty area but also being flexible enough to perform a range of other music. There's no right answer here, just what's right for you, and it's important to think through your intent and approach.

Networking for Referrals   ◆

For any musician seeking freelance work, it eventually comes down to networking. It's a matter of who knows you and your playing. What is your reputation as a performer and collaborator? Are you known to be easy to work with?

Talk to your colleagues and teachers, find out who is playing where, and get to know the players who may be in a position to refer you. For instance, for classical pianists looking for vocal accompanying work, it makes sense to network with voice teachers, choral and opera conductors, and to investigate work opportunities with voice competitions and festivals. In other words, the kind of work you seek should determine your networking strategy.

One of the best things you can do to jumpstart your freelance work is *take a lesson or coaching session with a top freelancer in your area, someone in a position to refer work to you.* This can be a great opportunity to get feedback on where you stand in relation to other freelancers, and to ask for suggestions on where to audition and how to get more work. What's more, when veteran freelancers need a last-minute substitute, you want to be the one they think of to call.

You can also get to meet and know other musicians—and those who hire them—by attending local and regional (sometimes national) conferences and professional associations (there are membership organizations for flutists, organists, string teachers, and many others).

▼

The Tale of Joan V. (Part 2)

In her first freelance years, Joan noticed several things. She saw who got the calls and the gigs, and who did not. At first she was surprised that it wasn't always the best players getting the work. But the more she freelanced, the more it made sense. Some of the people not getting calls for more work were friends from school. Though these were top-notch players, Joan realized that some non-musical issues outweighed how well they played. Some of these friends had shown up late for a rehearsal or two. One was a bit of a slob; even in concert attire, he looked disheveled. And another one could be a "difficult" personality; he came across at times as extremely opinionated, even argumentative. Joan saw that this behavior was hurting her friends' ability to get work.

Joan also paid attention to the folks who *did* get the work. Some of these "A" list freelancers were also contractors for gigs. These pros got to gigs early, were always prepared, and somehow handled their busy schedules well. They all seemed to know each other and were generally pleasant, no matter what happened in rehearsals or performances. No big egos or temper tantrums, even when a conductor might be having both.

She asked one of these experienced freelancers for pointers, and was told, "Never argue with the section leader. As a section player, your job is to make the leader and the conductor look good." *Joan took note.*

▲

Timetable for Building a Freelance Lifestyle

Be patient. It takes time to build your reputation. For classical musicians doing orchestral and small ensemble work, below is a rough timetable for "getting connected" in a large culturally active city. This ballpark time frame assumes that your playing and networking skills are excellent. Keep in mind this is simply an estimate, and life doesn't usually unfold according to schedule.

> One year to get your "sea legs," to get started building a reputation and getting to know key contractors, conductors, and directors
> Three years to get hooked up in the new environment (paying your dues)
> Five years to get enough work to be in control of your life
> Ten years to be subcontracting other musicians and to have stability

Researching to Get Work ◆

Think about gig opportunities in your local area. Listed below are general occasions, locations, and organizations that hire musicians for their events. Use the list to brainstorm specific prospects in your area. What local institutions sponsor events that need music? Develop a targeted list of local prospects that might be interested in hiring you or your ensemble.

Next, look over your list of network contacts—especially non-musicians. Where do these people work? What civic organizations are they involved in? Look for personal connections to your list of targeted local organizations.

Occasions for Gigs	Organization That Hire	Places to Perform
Anniversaries	Chambers of commerce	Convention centers
Association Meetings	Civic clubs (Elks, Lions)	Churches/synagogues
Bat/Bar Mitzvahs	College student groups	Coffeehouses
Expositions	Country clubs	Cruise lines
Fairs	Government agencies	Military bases
Fundraisers	Hotels/motels	Museums
Memorial services	Local corporations	Private parties
Political conventions	Summer camp programs	Private schools
Trade shows	Teen clubs	Public schools
Weddings	Private clubs	Radio stations
Holiday events	Women's clubs	Resorts

Once you have identified these key contacts, call or e-mail, reconnect, and ask whom they know at specific institutions. Ask if you can use your contacts' names when e-mailing or calling. Send an introductory e-mail with basic information about your music, your ensemble, with links to your website and sound clips (or Facebook or MySpace musician's profile). Follow up with a phone call or, better yet, schedule a face-to-face meeting, during which you can offer additional marketing pieces. People like to hire by word of mouth and like to know the people they hire, so it's good to get out and meet other people.

Here is a sample e-mail message to Julia Plotkin, your contact in the human resources office at the HappyCamper Company. Your friend Mary Smith knows her and told you that Julia helps organize special events for the company.

Subject line

Mary Smith suggested I contact you re: special events at the HappyCamper Company!

E-mail text

Dear Ms. Plotkin:

Mary Smith suggested I contact you about your organization's need for live performances at special events. I am a local musician, the leader of the Bergman Jazz Quartet (BJQ). We play a wide range of music, from well-known standards and cover tunes to Latin jazz and blues. The BJQ has performed locally at the Willow and the Potomac Jazz Clubs and for corporate functions sponsored by the United Way and Kiwanis. Here is a link to our site with more details: http://www.bergmanjazzquartet.com; and to hear our sound clips: http://www.bergmanjazzquartet.com/sounds. I will call next week to speak with you about your music needs and how we might be of service to you at the HappyCamper Company.

Cordially,

Diane Bergman

Marketing for Freelancers ◆

Do you have the appropriate marketing materials for your freelancing? THe rule of thumb is to tailor your materials to the potential employer's interests and to the situation. When auditioning for conductors and contractors, have a performance résumé that emphasizes your freelance work first and foremost. Singers need a résumé with photo and a bio. For everybody's day-to-day networking and gigging, an online presence (with your bio, sound clips, and photo) and business cards are essentials.

▼

Beware of Bridezilla

Think about it from the prospective client's point of view. A bride looking to hire a string quartet for her wedding is not interested in the same details as a presenter who books a subscription concert series.

For wedding work, ensembles' online profiles should include photos, a bio, and a menu of appropriate repertoire with sound clips. In addition, it's a good idea to provide prospective clients with details on the booking process: discussing special repertoire and requests, handling deposits, and contracts. The idea is to emphasize the professionalism and helpfulness of the group, how you can make the wedding planning easier, by "enhancing the couple's special day with just the right music" (or words to that effect). Look online at how other groups tailor their marketing materials to wedding clients: borrow creative ideas, and adapt them to fit your own site.

It can also be helpful to have a postcard or an inexpensive one-sheet for your wedding work. This can include a photo, brief bio, a list of appropriate repertoire, and a few quotes from satisfied customers. One-sheets can be used for networking and mailings to wedding planners, caterers, church music directors, and function room managers.

"People booking music for weddings often need a lot of help in understanding what they want. This is an important part of a musician's service," says veteran freelancer John Steinmetz. "Some clients know what they want but can't describe it. Others think they know what they want and are asking for, when in fact they may be mistaken. Others are confused, conflicted, or unsure. The musician's job includes helping clients feel confident about their choices. It's a lot like the work architects do to help clients clarify their priorities."

And once the gig is booked, make sure it goes smoothly as planned. Guitarist Bob Sullivan recommends arriving extra early for wedding gigs, because clients are typically stressed and nervous about all the arrangements. At wedding gigs, Bob arrives early, checks in with his contact, and reviews with them where they want the musicians set up, as well as the timings and cues for performing during the ceremony. The idea is to help keep things calm and on track to make the event a success.

▲

Performance Résumés

Performance résumés are used to request auditions and in applying to competitions and grants. Résumés should provide the reader with a blueprint of your most relevant qualifications, skills, and experience. Detail the highlights of your background that are specifically relevant to the situation. The one-size-fits-all approach won't do. The challenge in writing a résumé is to write it from the perspective of the *employer's needs*. Try to take on the point of view of the person you are addressing. If you can understand what that person needs and values, you can better show that you are the person to meet those needs.

Most musicians have several versions of their résumé—different ones for performance, teaching, arts administration, or "day" jobs. Generally, performance résumés should not include teaching or arts administration experience because it's usually not relevant to the employer or situation. However, if you're seeking an orchestral or opera audition and the organization has an extensive community education program, then listing your outreach experience may be useful.

Résumé Construction

1. *Keep it short and simple.* Studies show that employers typically spend less than ten seconds reading a résumé, so the design and format should allow the reader to take in your most important credentials at a glance. Limit your résumé to one page (multiple page résumés and CVs are used only for college-level teaching). Your résumé should not include everything you've done—it should include only what's most relevant to the reader in this particular situation. Keep in mind that your résumé is always a work in progress. As you gain more experience, you will add new listings and delete the less impressive.

2. *Make it easy on the eyes.* Use an eye-catching, professional-looking typeface in your letterhead design (see chapter 3). For the body of the text,

use an easy-to-read, standard serif typeface such as Palatino, Garamond, or Times New Roman. Keep the eye distractions to a minimum. Use these very sparingly: underline, parentheses, bullets, bold, all caps.

3. *Divide and conquer.* Organize your information into categories, and use bold to highlight the headings. The category titles you use should be determined by the job for which you are applying. For instance, if you have performed a lot of early music or contemporary repertoire and this is relevant to your intended reader, these would be categories to include. Place the category sections in the order that reflect the *employer's* priorities. For instance, if you want to be considered for an opening with a string quartet, don't send in a résumé with the first category listing Orchestral Experience.

Typical résumé categories for listing performance and composition experience are:

> For classical vocalists: Full Roles, Partial Roles, Musical Theater, Choral Experience, Solo Recitals, Church Positions
> For jazz musicians: Clubs, Other Venues, Jazz Festivals, Has Performed with . . . , Recordings, Ensembles
> For classical instrumentalists: Orchestral Experience, Chamber Music Performances, Solo Performances, Soloist with Orchestras, Community and Education Performances
> For composers: Original Works, Selected Compositions, Premieres, Selected Performances of Original Works, Current Projects, Arrangements/Transcriptions, Commissioned Works
> For pianists: Solo Recitals, Soloist with Orchestras, Chamber Music Performances, Collaborative Performances with . . . , Accompanying Positions, Church Positions, Premieres

4. *To date or not to date?* Dates (years only) are used when listing roles for vocalists, ongoing church or accompanying jobs, orchestral experience, degrees, scholarships, and awards. In using dates, items should be presented in *reverse chronological order,* meaning list the most recent first and work backwards in time.

5. *It's all about the details.*

- For solo and chamber music performances, list *where* you performed: the name of the venue (the performance hall) or the concert series (if well known), the city, and state (or country, if outside the United States).
- If you have performed with impressive individuals, in chamber music performances or in a jazz ensemble, you may want to list these names

in a separate category titled "Has Performed with . . ." or "Ensemble Collaborations."

- For orchestral experience, include your position (principal, section player, substitute) after the name of the orchestra and before the city and state (or country).

6. *References anyone?* Your references are the people who have agreed to provide feedback about your skills and abilities to prospective employers. You can add a line at the bottom of your résumé page, "References available upon request," to signal that you have a contact list of these people and are ready to send the list when asked.

7. *Proofread!* Before sending it anywhere, have someone else proofread your résumé carefully. Spell-check is not enough. Double-check the spelling of the names of teachers, conductors, and awards. There's nothing worse than finding an embarrassing mistake in your résumé after sending it out.

8. *E-mail it right!* When e-mailing your résumé as an attachment, the software program you use matters. Your recipient may not have the same program or format and may not be able to open your document. Moreover, some of your formatting and typefaces may become altered, depending on your recipient's computer and software. The safest way to ensure that the reader will see what you intend to present is to send your résumé as a PDF attachment.

The examples on the following pages are performance résumés geared toward freelance work, both instrumental and vocal. These examples are composites of various musicians' résumés, and are designed to illustrate a variety of formats and styles. Notice on each example what is emphasized, what details are provided, and the order of the categories and the listings. Instead of following these as templates and trying to make your résumé look like someone else's, use these as suggestions for rethinking your own résumé. Get feedback on your draft from qualified professionals, particularly those who hire musicians regularly.

Musician Unions: Strength in Numbers ◆

Musician unions exist to protect your rights and interests. The primary work of unions is to negotiate collective bargaining agreements (CBAs) between employers (such as orchestras or opera companies) and workers (the musicians) to establish equitable levels of compensation, benefits, and working conditions. Union membership is typically required for the better paying ongoing freelance gigs, from opera and chorus work to orchestras,

Ippei Takahashi, Violinist

100 Canadian Terrace Ste. 3 • Toronto, Ontario A1A 2B2 • (647) 555-1234 • ippeitaka@Email.net

Orchestral Experience

Tanglewood Music Center Fellowship Orchestra, 2011
Schleswig-Holstein Symphony Orchestra, Concertmaster, 2010
Isabella Stewart Gardner Museum Chamber Orchestra, Boston, 2010
Boston Modern Orchestra Project, substitute, 2009
Boston Philharmonic Orchestra, 2008-09
Hartford Symphony Orchestra, substitute, 2007
Columbus Philharmonic, IN, 2006, 07
Evansville Philharmonic, IN, 2005-06

Solo / Chamber Recitals

Merkin Concert Hall, NYC
King's Chapel Concert Series, Boston
Longy School of Music, Cambridge, MA
Ichigaya Lutheran Center, Tokyo, Japan

Education

New England Conservatory of Music, Boston, MA
Graduate Diploma in violin performance, 2011

Indiana University School of Music, Bloomington
Bachelor of Music in violin performance, 2007

Principal Teachers	Coaches	Masterclasses
Malcolm Lowe	Eugene Lehner	Miriam Fried
Stanley Ritchie	Louis Krasner	Michèle Auclair

Honors

Fellowship, Asian Cultural Council Award, 2008
Prizewinner, Japanese American Association Music Award, 2007

Completely fluent in both Japanese and English; International student with legal permission to work in the U.S. under the curricular practical training program.

Example: Orchestral performance résumé. Note: for international students seeking work in the United States, it can be helpful to include extra information in the résumé and cover letter about both your language skills and visa status. This can help relieve a prospective employer's concerns about any difficulties in hiring you.

James Fortunato, Guitarist — Flamenco, Jazz, Classical

6435 21st Ave. NW, Seattle, WA 98195 cell: (206) 555-1234 jfortunato@hotmail.com
sound samples at: www.jamesfortunatoguitar.com

Solo Performances
Zeitgeist Gallery, Cambridge, MA
Peabody-Essex Museum, Salem, MA
Museum of Fine Arts, Boston
First Church Congregational, Wellesley, MA

Ensembles
Amaya, Flamenca Sin Limites, flamenco
dance troupe
Hankus Netsky Klezmer Ensemble
Carlos Campos Afro-Cuban Ensemble

Flamenco Performance Venues
Boston College, MA
Palace Theater, Manchester, NH
University of Massachusetts, Amherst
Boston Ballet
Boston Center for the Arts
Westbrook College, Portland, ME

Jazz Performances
Middle East, Cambridge, MA
Ritz Carlton, Boston
Copley Plaza, Boston

Dance Class Accompanist
Boston Conservatory, MA
Dance Complex, Cambridge
Walnut Hill School for the Arts, Natick, MA

Education
New England Conservatory of Music,
Boston, MA
Bachelor of Music in Contemporary
Improvisation, 2011

Principal Teachers	**Master Classes**
Robert Paul Sullivan	Eliot Fisk
Hankus Netsky	Sharon Isbin

References Available Upon Request

Example: Performance résumé geared toward solo and ensemble work

Janet Park, Pianist

14 Pinckney St. Boston, MA 02108 (617) 534-1112 jpark@hotmail.com
performance video clip: www.janetparkpiano.com

Solo Recitals

Gardner Museum, Boston
Kings Chapel Concert Series, Boston
All Saints Episcopal Church, Salt Lake City, UT
Harvard Musical Association Concert Series

Concerti

New England Chamber Orchestra, Boston
University of Utah Symphony Orchestra

Chamber Music

Brookline Public Library Concert Series
First Presbyterian Church, Salt Lake City, UT
All Newton Music School Young Artists Series

Accompanying

Studio pianist for Lucy Chapman, violin faculty,
    New England Conservatory, 2010–11
Studio pianist for Russell McKinney, trombone faculty,
    University of Utah, Salt Lake City, 2007–09

Recording

Music of the Baroque, Educational DVD, for Oxbridge Records, 2009

Awards/Honors

Scholarship, New England Conservatory, Boston, MA, 2010–11
Prizewinner, Harvard Musical Association Scholarship Award, 2010

Education

New England Conservatory, Boston, MA
Graduate Diploma in Piano Performance, 2011

University of Utah, Salt Lake City
Bachelor of Music in Piano Performance, 2009

Principal Teacher

Patricia Zander

Master Classes

Stephen Drury, Wha Kyung Byun

Coaches

Irma Vallecillo, Kayo Iwama

Example: Performance résumé for solo, chamber, collaborative work

Vicky Vocalist, Soprano

4444 W Walton St. #2
Chicago, IL 60622
(773) 773-7349
michelle@michellesantiago.com
www.michellesantiago.com

Insert
Headshot
here

Performance Experience

Roles Performed

Pamina	*The Magic Flute*	Utah Opera	2012
Adele	*Die Fledermaus*	New England Conservatory	2011
Jenny	*Down in the Valley*	Boston Lyric Opera	2010
Laeticia	*The Old Maid and the Thief*	New England Conservatory	2009
Witch	*Hansel and Gretel*	Milwaukee Opera Theater	2008
Celie	*Signor Deluso*	Lawrence University	2008

Scenes Performed

Polly	*The Threepenny Opera*	New England Conservatory	2009
Donna Elvira	*Don Giovanni*	New England Conservatory	2009
Belinda	*Dido and Aeneas*	Lawrence University	2008

Musical Theater Roles

Maria	West Side Story	Papermill Theatre, Lincoln, NH	2006
Meg	Little Women	Papermill Theatre, Lincoln, NH	2006
Anne	Anne of Green Gables	Papermill Theatre, Lincoln, NH	2006

Concert Performances, Boston Area
Handel *Messiah*, Trinity Church
Mozart *Requiem*, St. Paul's Episcopal Church
Solo Recital, Federal Reserve Bank Concert Series

Education
New England Conservatory, Master of Music in Vocal Performance, 2011
Lawrence University, Bachelor of Music in Vocal Performance, *Cum Laude*, 2008

Principal Teachers	Coaches	Masterclass
Patricia Misslin	John Moriarty	Martin Isepp
Susan Clickner	Dale Morehouse	

Awards/Honors
Prizewinner, Rose Palmai-Tenser Scholarship Awards Competition, 2007
Second Prize, NATS Southern Regional Competition, Graduate Division, 2007

Special Skills
Fluent in German and Italian; 14 years of piano, 7 years of dance training

Example: Performance résumé geared toward opera auditions

touring musicals, radio, TV, and recording work. Union members pay annual dues, and with membership comes guaranteed wage minimums, protection against infringement of contracts, and legal assistance in the case of contract disputes. Musician unions also offer members various benefits such as health and instrument insurance, and a pension plan.

There are several musician unions, specialized by type of work. The primary union for instrumentalists and the largest musicians' union is the American Federation of Musicians (AFM). But for vocalists doing opera or musicals, and for all musicians working in recordings, television, film, radio, or nightclubs, there are other unions, described below. Many musicians join the appropriate union once they win an audition for an organization that hires union musicians.

Some musicians note their union membership on their résumés, signaling to contractors and conductors in the audition process a certain level of experience.

Musician Unions

AGMA, the American Guild of Musical Artists, primarily represents singers and singing actors in opera, ballet, oratorio, concert, and recital work. Musicians join AGMA when they have been offered a contract with a production requiring AGMA membership. See http://www.musicalartists.org.

AFTRA, the American Federation of Television and Radio Artists, covers live and taped TV programs, taped commercials, radio shows, and recordings. AFTRA is for all performers in these areas except instrumentalists. See http://www.aftra.org.

SAG, the Screen Actors Guild, is for feature film work, filmed TV shows, filmed commercials, or industrial films. See http://www.sag.org.

AEA, the Actors' Equity Association (AKA: Equity), is for performers in live theater productions, either musicals or dramas. A singer seeking work in musical theater must first win an audition for an equity show, apply to be an equity candidate, perform for the length of their contract, and earn credit toward their equity card and full membership. See http://www.actorsequity.org.

AFM, the American Federation of Musicians, is comprised of more than 90,000 members and 250 local affiliates in the United States and Canada. AFM publishes *International Musician*, a monthly magazine (available online) listing auditions worldwide for orchestral and other work. This is the union for most instrumentalists' work. AFM offers a number of benefits and services with membership, including a pension plan, instrument and health insurance, plus legal, travel, and financial services. Your local chapter of AFM can be an excellent networking resource. Local chapters often have their own publications with listings for local auditions, classifieds, and jobs, and some locals provide gig referral services as well. See http://www.afm.org.

Negotiating Fees ◆

For freelancers seeking to play "gigs," such as weddings and corporate events, it's important to establish an hourly rate per musician to quote to clients. Make sure the rate is appropriate and competitive with what similarly experienced musicians are charging in local area. Call the local AFM chapter, and ask other musicians what they charge. For example, as of 2010 the New England Conservatory Music Referral Service (the school's gig office) quoted clients the rate of $125 per musician per hour for wedding gigs and corporate events.

The rates in various regions differ and change over the years, so ask around. You can be flexible with your fee, but you should know what your absolute minimum is and stick to it. Don't sell yourself short. If you're traveling a distance for a gig, you should charge extra to compensate for the time and cost.

Clients hiring a musician for a gig may be unfamiliar with standard fees and may question your rate. You need to be able to handle these conversations diplomatically and professionally. It is helpful to have a sentence or two ready and to be able to calmly—without getting defensive—explain, "I'm an experienced performer, and my rate is based on the musician union's standard rate for professional work in this region." Sometimes this is all that is needed, but also having a website (or social networking site) to refer prospective clients to is especially helpful. This way they can easily hear your sound clips, read your bio, and look through the list of places you've performed.

Guitarist Robert Paul Sullivan has performed as a freelancer with the Boston Symphony Orchestra as well as with most of the New England area orchestras and contemporary music groups. A veteran freelancer, Bob plays acoustic and electric guitar, banjo, mandolin, mandola, and lute. He has performed in Irish pubs, hotels, jazz clubs, and for opera productions, weddings, and wine tastings—you name it, he's done it. In terms of negotiating fees, before quoting a fee or rate to a client, Bob makes it a point to ask a lot of questions. He asks about the location, travel, any special repertoire requests, and the performance site itself. He does this because it is the details that will, in part, determine his fee (the distance he will need to travel, and any special repertoire, arrangements, and equipment needed).

Bob doesn't haggle with clients. If a client doesn't like his price, Bob cordially says, "Let me give you the names and numbers of some other excellent guitarists, and maybe you will find what you are looking for with someone else." He gladly refers work to others, and they reciprocate.

Because he is in demand as a freelancer, Bob has had gig date conflicts occur a number of times. For example, he may get a call to do a wedding gig two months from now. It's nothing special, he's free, the money's okay, and he says yes. A few days later, he's offered a much better gig for that same date—in one case, the second gig was with the Boston Symphony at Tanglewood. What does Bob do? He makes it a point to honor his first commitment. He turns down the second gig because he had already given his word to the first client, and because his word is a big part of his reputation as a professional. What does he say to the second client, the contractor? Bob explains that he is already committed for that date and refers them to someone every bit as good, *if not better,* than he is. The contractor is the pipeline for future gigs. Bob wants to be remembered as reliable and professional, so that the next time around, the contractor will again call Bob.

It's All in the Details

A big part of being a pro is handling details. Once you have a client wishing to hire you for a gig, you need to clarify many details and then come to an agreement. To make sure you cover all the details, a checklist can be helpful; tailor one to fit the kind of music and gigs you perform. You can keep a copy of your list on your iPhone or PDA and fill in the particulars each time you book or confirm a gig by phone.

You and your client need to clarify the following:

- ❏ *Date and time of the gig* (for non-concert performances, clarify lengths of sets and stop times).
- ❏ *Repertoire:* make sure you are clear on the type and genre of music the client is expecting and any specific requests. If you agree to play repertoire that demands that you produce your own arrangements, you should charge extra for this work.
- ❏ *Dress:* make sure you know what the client specifically means by "formal" or "casual."
- ❏ *Breaks:* beyond a concert situation, it's typical for performers on a gig to need and take a ten-minute break for every hour played. Make sure your client understands this and agrees.
- ❏ *Lighting:* make sure it is adequate.
- ❏ *Seating:* is there adequate space for your ensemble and appropriate chairs (armless)?

❏ *Piano:* is it a grand, upright, or electric? Will it be tuned?

❏ *Acoustics:* will you need to be amplified? If yes, what equipment will you need to bring?

❏ *Extras:* do you need electrical outlets, extension cords, adapters? Are these available at the venue?

❏ *Satisfactory working conditions:* for outdoor performances, you may want to specify that the musicians will perform under a canopy or roofed deck to be in the shade. Here is contract language you may want to add: "The client shall provide adequate shelter to protect the artist and the artist's equipment in the event of inclement weather" and/or "The temperature in the performance area should not exceed *(85 degrees F)* or drop below *(65 degrees F)* , for the protection of the artist(s) and their equipment."

❏ *Contact info:* the client and performers need to know how to reach each other, so be sure to find out the phone numbers, e-mail addresses, and the correct spelling and pronunciation of names. Ensembles should elect one member as point person to handle dealings with clients.

❏ *Directions and parking arrangements:* get the street address and explicit directions to the gig. Always leave plenty of extra time for traffic. Double-check the directions online, and keep a detailed atlas with street index in your gig bag. A GPS system is a smart investment.

❏ *Payment:* agree on who will pay you, when, how, and how much. Consider the travel involved; if it's beyond thirty minutes, add a little extra to your fee. Most giggers prefer to get paid at the gig, directly before the performance. Specify in your contract if payment will be by check, cash, or money order. Most often, the client will pay the group leader, who then divides the total amount to pay each member. For government or other agency clients that must requisition funds, payment may be delayed. Make sure you discuss this explicitly in advance.

❏ *Deposit:* get a nonrefundable deposit from the client to secure the date (typically fifty percent of the gig fee). Have the client send the check along with the signed contract. Then, should the gig be cancelled, at least you are partially compensated.

Remember that the key is to discuss all of these details in advance by phone. Be explicit. Don't assume that the client will know to provide any-thing—from electrical outlets to advance deposits—unless you ask for it and they agree to it when you negotiate the deal.

Then, after you've worked all of this out by phone, you can create the written contract to confirm the agreement. The use of a contract is a sign of professionalism. It ratifies the details you have negotiated, and it assures both parties that the gig will go as planned, so that there will be no unpleasant surprises for either party.

The Tale of Joan V. (Part 3)

Another big lesson Joan learned in her first years freelancing was about using contracts. Joan found out the hard way just how important these are. She'd been called for a pickup orchestra gig: two rehearsals and a concert at a church in a nearby suburb. Bartok and Brahms—no problem. But two weeks after the concert, Joan still hadn't been paid. She called the contractor several times over the next month, and the check was always "in the mail." Joan never got paid, and, because there was no contract and this was not a union gig, there was nothing she could do about it. After this experience, she joined the AFM, and from that point on, whenever Joan booked her own gigs—whether for a wedding, a community performance at a preschool, or a memorial service—she made it a point to use a contract and to get a deposit in advance.

Contracts ◆

Once you have gone over all the details on your checklist with the client (usually by phone), you need to draw up a written contract to confirm your agreement. Using contracts for weddings and corporate events is especially important because often these clients are unaccustomed to hiring musicians, and they may need further explanation about the details of your prospective gig.

A contract is a musician's security for getting paid. With a properly executed contract, if a client refuses to pay, you can take her or him to small claims court and sue for the money you are owed. Without a contract, you have no proof of the agreement and no recourse. And although it's convenient to communicate by e-mail and phone, to make a legally binding agreement, both parties (you and the client) must sign the contract, and afterward each party needs to receive a copy of the fully executed contract. This can be done by fax, mail, or electronically by using a scanner and PDFs.

So, once you have agreed to play the gig and ironed out the particulars, you simply write the details into your contract template and send the client two unsigned copies (or you can e-mail a PDF). The client signs both copies and mails both back to you. Then you sign both and return one to the client. If you are producing the contract, make sure you sign both copies last, *after* your client does. This is to ensure that the client does not amend or modify the document after you have signed it. This business of who signs when is important because a contract becomes legally binding only after both parties sign.

Use the general simple performance contract below as a model for creating your own; it can be easily modified for each gig. The details added for each particular gig are those from your checklist (the client's name, date of the gig, the time, location, fee, special requests, and so forth).

Make It Easy on Your Client

To ensure that your client sends back the contract with the deposit promptly, you can send a note that subtly applies polite pressure. Maurice Johnson, the author of the excellent *Build and Manage Your Music Career,* recommends sending your client two copies of the contract with a self-addressed, stamped envelope and including a brief cover letter with something like this:

> Dear Ms. Smith:
>
> Thank you for selecting the Mirabeau Quartet for your upcoming event. We look forward to performing for your guests. When you have a moment, please sign both copies of the enclosed contract and return one copy along with your deposit check. I am anxious to confirm your event in our calendar as soon as possible. If you have questions, please contact me at (617) 534–9999.
>
> Sincerely,
>
> Jessica Smith
>
> The Mirabeau Quartet

With your contract signed, you are ready to play the gig. Before leaving home, what should you make sure you have with you? Instead of frantically grabbing things on your way out the door, how about having a "gig bag" ready in advance? Buy a bag to use specifically for gigs, and pack it in advance, the morning of every gig, using a checklist. This will help you stay organized.

▼ ──

Pack Your Gig Bag!

❏ Copy of the contract
❏ Street address, map, and directions
❏ Cell phone
❏ Client's contact phone number(s)
❏ Phone number of the place you're playing in case you get lost

Contract for Performance

_____, herein referred to as "the artist," agrees to perform
    musician or ensemble name

for _____, herein referred to as "the client" on _____
        client's name   date

from _____to _____at _____.
        time   time   location

The artist will arrive no later than _____.
                                                    time (AM / PM)

The client agrees to pay the artist $_____ per hour for playing time/time on site, and the

total fee will be $ _____. A deposit of _____%, or $_____, is

required_____days in advance, and the balance is due on the day of performance, payable

by money order, cash, or check.

Signatures:

_____
            Client

_____
            Musician

The agreement of the musician(s) to perform is subject to proven detention by sickness, ac-
cidents, riots, strikes, epidemics, acts of God, or other legitimate conditions beyond their
control. On behalf of the client, the artist will distribute the amount received to other
member(s) of the artist's group as necessary.

By executing this contract as client or artist, the person executing said contract, either indi-
vidually or as an agent or representative, has the authority to enter into this agreement, and
should she or he not have such authority, she or he fully and personally accepts and assumes
full responsibility and liability under the terms of this contract.

Sample performance contract. Your letterhead design with all your contact information
goes at the top.

❏ Appropriate performance attire

❏ Folding music stand(s)

❏ Any other equipment needed, such as keyboard, amps, adapters, extension cords

❏ Sheet music for all performers, plus extra emergency copies

❏ Music stand clips or clothespins for windy outdoor performances

❏ Clip-on stand lights (for poor lighting situations and emergency blackouts)

❏ Instrument repair basics (extra strings, reeds, valve oil)

❏ Tuning device

In sum, with a gig bag, a contract template, a performance résumé and any other marketing materials you need for your freelance work, you're ready to put your talents into action. With networking and research, you too can be a working professional musician.

Career Forward

Writing out your responses to the following will help you better manage gigs.

1. Who are three people you could contact to network with about freelance opportunities in your region? (Hint: these may be colleagues, former teachers, conductors, and/or contractors.)

2. List five organizations in your area that are likely sponsors or clients for your future gigs.

3. If you do not have an updated performance résumé, write one. If you have one, how might you improve the layout or the format to better highlight your experience and accomplishments?

4. If you have not been using contracts for gigs, create a contract template for upcoming performances, with your letterhead and any specifics needed for you or your ensemble. Have this handy template ready to use.

11

Balancing Life:
Managing Time
and Money

▼
In this chapter :
Time Management
Managing Projects
Effective Practice
Financial Management
Taxes 101
Special Issues for Ensembles
▲

There are some universal issues that apply to everybody, not just musicians. People need to manage their resources—their time and money. One way to think about this is to realize that when we manage our time and money well, it reduces stress. This plays an important role in our quality of life and the quality of our music. Life is short. Let's make the most of it.

Time Management ◆

There are many time management tools—day planners, scheduling systems, software calendar programs—but none of these will give you more time in the day. You still only have twenty-four hours. All of the time management methods get at one essential point: to manage time effectively, you need to make conscious choices about what you will and won't do. Most people make *unconscious* choices of how to spend their time. They may be busy all day but end up leaving important things undone because they tackled other, less important tasks first. The alternative is to choose what to do and what not to do.

Ultimately, time management is about planning—but planning based on your chosen priorities. Creative artists sometimes bristle at the idea of managing their time. It can feel restrictive. After all, inspiration doesn't come on demand and no one likes to live according to a regimented schedule. Don't worry; time management is not about policing your time. It's about being more effective. Composer/freelancer John Steinmetz says, "The most important thing is not the schedule itself, but *clarity of intentions.* What do you want to accomplish and how are you going to do it—clear intentions are needed for both."

▼ _____

The Time Management Quiz
How well are you managing your time?

1. Are you frustrated by frequent interruptions and distractions?   Yes ❏   No ❏
2. Do you constantly feel tired?   Yes ❏   No ❏
3. Are you often late for appointments or rehearsals?   Yes ❏   No ❏
4. Do you get enough practice time in?   Yes ❏   No ❏
5. Are you making time for your priorities, your most important projects?   Yes ❏   No ❏
6. Do you have enough downtime, to retool, recharge, and refresh?   Yes ❏   No ❏
7. Are you making time for exercise and other activities important to your well-being?   Yes ❏   No ❏

Be honest. Did you answer "yes" to any of the first three questions or "no" to any of the last four? If so, you may want to take a closer look at the way you manage your time.

_____ ▲

French hornist Jean Rife, freelancer and music educator, says this about trying to balance her busy life: "It requires being clear about your priorities, and these have shifted over the years. I used to do a lot more freelancing but just now, my sixteen year old daughter is my first priority." Jean also teaches yoga and found that this has been a big help to herself and her music students. Jean says, "Yoga teaches you to be in the present moment so you are always aware that you have a chance to choose." You can choose how to use your time, react to stimuli and stress, and ultimately, these choices determine how you live your life.

The larger question in all this is: *Who is the person you want to become?* What you do in the present determines your future. So how you spend your time this week has everything to do with what you may be able to accomplish next month and next year. Make sure you're investing time in working toward your goals.

▼

The Tale of Joan V., Continued (Part 4)

Our freelance trombonist Joan, from the previous chapter, found that as she got busier, managing her time became one of her biggest challenges. It was getting increasingly difficult to make time for her own practicing in addition to the freelance work, teaching, and her part-time job. Joan asked some veteran freelancers how they fit everything in, how they organized their schedules. An oboist meditated every day for thirty minutes to clear his mind and to focus; a percussionist reserved two hours each morning for practice—no matter what; and a soprano swore by a time management system programmed into her iPhone. All three musicians said they'd struggled with managing their time and balancing their work lives, and each had found a different method that helped.

▲

Reality Scheduling

Planning saves you time, energy, and worry. Instead of each morning thinking, "What do I have to do, and when will I fit it all in?" you can plan a realistic weekly schedule. With a schedule that works, you can devote your thoughts and energy to living, instead of constantly making lists in your head or rearranging your daily timetable. The idea is to schedule your regular, recurring activities (lessons, rehearsals, day job, perhaps your weekly laundry, groceries, exercising) so that you are able to choose how to use the rest of your discretionary time.

Dana Young, a time management consultant and organization specialist, presented a workshop at New England Conservatory years ago and offered a version of the exercise below, which is excellent for helping with scheduling.

Time in Four Quadrants

On the chart below, write down your regular weekly activities. The grid divides these into four quadrants. List your scheduled, fixed activities (nondiscretionary), as well as the as yet unscheduled (discretionary) ones you want to fit in. Be realistic! It's helpful to see your regular commitments and activities laid out, to see clearly what you can control in scheduling and what you need to schedule around.

Now with your activities down on paper, the next thing is to organize a schedule that accommodates these. On the weekly schedule below, write in

Nondiscretionary: Career/professional *(i.e., time determined activities:* *teaching, day job, fixed rehearsal* *times)*	Discretionary: Career/professional *(i.e., practicing, career projects,* *networking)*
Nondiscretionary: personal *(i.e., scheduled healthcare* *appointments, childcare, etc.)*	Discretionary: personal *(i.e., socializing, groceries,* *laundry, etc.)*

your fixed commitments, your nondiscretionary activities, both professional and personal. Dana Young suggests that you write these in ink. Next, add in the discretionary activities using pencil so that you can rearrange as you think best.

In fitting in your activities, think about your daily highs and lows of energy. When is your concentration best? What time of day is best for practicing? You may not be able to get in a three-hour block for practicing each day, but you can do an enormous amount of good work with a regularly scheduled hour of peak concentration. And to fit in the less challenging activities, like laundry and groceries, schedule these to fit your periods of lower energy and concentration. There's no need to schedule everything down to the minute, but by plotting out these basics, you can discover what extra time you actually have and make good choices about how to use it.

Good time management is like juggling tennis balls, keeping up with each area of your life. If you drop one, you feel out of balance. As in juggling, the trick is adjusting your attention so that you can see the bigger picture and keep track of all your priorities. So, if you're practicing six hours a day but neglecting exercise, friends, and your nutrition, things aren't in balance. Likewise, if you're taking care of all the basics but never seem to find the time to practice or to work on managing your career, you'll have very few opportunities to perform, and your longer-term goals won't be achieved.

	Sun.	Mon.	Tues.	Wed.	Thurs.	Fri.	Sat.
6 am							
7 am							
8 am							
9 am							
10 am							
11 am							
noon							
1 pm							
2 pm							
3 pm							
4 pm							
5 pm							
6 pm							
7 pm							
8 pm							
9 pm							
10 pm							

Avoiding the Tyranny of the To-Do List

Besides a weekly schedule of recurring activities, we all have specific daily errands to fit in, from family calls and visits to picking up the dry cleaning, handling household chores, and networking. This is the stuff of to-do lists, and the problem is that is they can quickly get out of hand. To-do lists have a way of becoming unmanageable, with dozens of items, none of them prioritized. Many to-do tasks are never completed, but simply transferred from one day's list to the next.

The best antidote is to keep your to-do lists short, specific, and doable for that day or that week. If you find yourself writing the same thing down list after list and never getting it done, either schedule a time for the task and complete it or decide consciously to let it go.

Urgent versus Important

An urgent task is one that requires immediate attention (such as paying the electric bill because the company has threatened to shut off the juice unless they get the check tomorrow). Or, my favorite, you need to do laundry because you've run out of clean socks and underwear.

Important tasks, on the other hand, are those nonscheduled activities that are necessary to achieve your career or personal goals. These are the things that you need to *make* time for, such as grant research, making booking calls for concerts, updating your mailing list and promo kit, and networking. These tasks are easy to push aside unless you make them a priority.

It's all too common to have your schedule spin out of control because you're constantly taking care of the urgent, and never getting to what's important. Take a look at your schedule, and make sure you have made time for taking care of *both* kinds of business—the urgent and the important.

▼

Time Management Tips

1. *Find a calendar system that works for you, and then use it!* This can be a handy paper or electronic date book calendar. Even with these, many people get into difficulties because their habit is to consult their daily or weekly schedule, and they fail to look further ahead. You may need multiple versions. What I found I needed—after much experimenting—was a weekly desk planner for the office, plus a smaller date book I could carry with me. But my big discovery was finding a wall calendar that displayed three months at a glance. This has enabled me to see the longer-term deadlines well in advance.
2. *Before making any new commitment, consult your schedule and look ahead to upcoming deadlines so you can avoid overload.* And once you agree to any new commitment, record it in your calendar(s). Build a reputation as a professional—be true to your word by showing up on time as promised, and arriving fully prepared!

3. Use the *first and last ten minutes of your day to your best advantage.* At the beginning of each day, it's helpful to look over your schedule and organize your plans, looking ahead at upcoming deadlines. Then, at the end of each day, review what you did and what you need to do tomorrow. Give yourself credit for your accomplishments, and give yourself a chance to rethink your schedule and your to-do list. This "bookending" of your day can help you stay on top of your commitments and reduce stress over deadlines.

Managing Projects ◆

Beyond scheduling, the other important element to time management is handling long-term projects. Whether it's recording an album, planning a tour, or applying for a grant, the trick to managing larger projects is to break them down into smaller-sized daily or weekly tasks.

Use "backward planning." This is a necessary technique (described in the first chapter) for all wedding planners and self-managing musicians. Start with the due date of a large project (an audition, performance, or commission deadline), and work backward from it to determine "benchmark" deadlines. The idea is to break down a large project into manageable pieces, each with its own deadline. For example, if the project is a performance four months from today, then, working backward from the performance date, plan specific intermediate goals with deadlines. When would you want to schedule a complete run-through of the program? By which date would you want to have the repertoire memorized? Figure out when to take particular pieces in for coachings, so that you can plan your rehearsal times accordingly. You can also set due dates for handling the promotion of the performance, for sending press releases and invitations. Instead of being overwhelmed by the pressure of a looming deadline, it's much easier to plan strategically and work steadily toward the smaller, more immediate goals. This way you can avoid procrastinating, having to cancel performances, or miss deadlines.

Dana Young suggests thinking of a project as a Tootsie Roll—you can break it up into bite-size pieces and deal with these one at a time. Keep things simple. Your daily or weekly to-do list should consist of the most strategic things that need to be done by a given date—so choose carefully. In terms of your career project to-do lists, I recommend for busy musicians writing a list for the week with no more than three concrete, specific career advancement tasks. These should be simple and practical, such as making particular phone calls, compiling or updating your network list, or scheduling time to research grants. Write down your weekly list, and tape it to your refrigerator, bathroom mirror, or dashboard—wherever you will notice it regularly.

Completing the tasks and crossing them off your list by the end of each week will feel great, and you will be energized to take on next week's tasks. Setting mini-deadlines, getting feedback and support along the way, and rewarding yourself regularly are all good ways to keep focused and productive.

The first hurdle is to get started, and then there's the sticking to it. Ask yourself, what's a reasonable starting point, a to-do item to accomplish this week? Schedule some time for this task, and write it down. Not sure where to start? Ask people who've done similar projects or simply start with your best guess—because the action itself will lead to more steps, and other people, information, and resources.

True Confession

Writing (and revising) this book has been by far my largest project to date. It has taken more time and effort than playing concerts, writing grants, or organizing conferences. The writing, researching, editing, and revising has taken many years and has taught me more than I ever wanted to know about managing projects.

Writing the book had been a long-term goal of mine, but having the goal as an idea was a lot easier than actually getting it done. My "day job" (running the Career Services Center at New England Conservatory) is busy and more than full time. So to get the writing done, I had to *make* the time for it outside of my job.

At first I tried writing in the evenings and on weekends. But after work I was often too frazzled to write, my mind cluttered with other concerns, or else my competing social plans would win out over the writing. The work was not getting done. I knew that in order to finish, I would need to write every day in small installments, just like practicing. Eventually, I realized that the only way this would happen would be if I wrote first thing each morning. So I got up at 5:00 A.M. (ouch!), Monday through Friday, and wrote for about an hour and a half. I'm not a morning person; I'm not good for conversation at 5:00 A.M. But my mind is clear, and my energy at that hour is better than it is after a long day at work. If I write at 5:00, it means that I can still fit in my morning walk before going off to work. Surprisingly, I have found that on the mornings when I missed doing either the writing or the walking, I simply didn't feel as good during the day. The regular pattern of writing *and* walking helped me start the rest of my day with less stress.

What else did I do to manage the book project and keep focused? The deadlines from my editor helped motivate (and scare) me into working. I also went to several writers' conferences—the equivalent of summer music festivals—to gain perspective and inspiration. Like practicing, writing is solitary, often isolating work. Without regular feedback and support from others, it's easy to lose all perspective on a project, to become discouraged and filled with self-doubt. So one of the best things I did was to join a local writers' group. We meet twice each month to critique each other's work and cheer each other on. To cope with the "overwhelm" factor of the project, I concentrated on just one chapter at a time (my bite-size piece of the Tootsie Roll) and set deadlines for completing each one. I had the added incentive of submitting each chapter to my writers' group, and I also sent chapters to my musician colleagues for more feedback. My reward for meeting these deadlines was the comments, advice, and support I got from others.

How might this apply to you? Perhaps early morning practice sessions would provide you with the consistent, concentrated work time you need. Perhaps finding colleagues or a mentor to play for regularly will provide needed feedback and support. And along with long-term fundraising or recording projects, you may need to work toward short-term goals and give yourself deadlines in order to stay focused and motivated.

Effective Practice ◆

The ultimate time management question any musician has to face is "Am I using my practice time effectively?" Practice time is elusive. We never have enough of it, and yet we're never sure we're using it wisely. Most of us are not actually taught how to practice and so we spend our careers trying to figure out how best to work at our playing.

Much of practicing is a kind of internal conversation. We imagine what we're going after in a given phrase or section, analyze what we hear ourselves perform, and devise ways to work on improving and refining our "output." When we practice, we are enforcing habits—physical habits, as well as habits of hearing and thinking.

Musicians spend a significant portion of their lives in practice rooms, so we imagine we should be experts at practicing. But by regularly examining how we're actually spending our practice time, we can improve the results we get.

12 Practice Room Questions: You're the Expert

Take a specific musical passage you're working on and ask yourself the following:

1. How do you want this phrase to sound? Can you hear it clearly in your imagination exactly the way you want it?

2. How does it feel as you play or sing it? Could you be more at ease?
3. Once you have isolated a particular difficulty in a passage, what do you do to solve the problem? If a passage isn't working as desired, do you have the patience and creativity to take it apart, find the specific stumbling blocks, and build it back up again?
4. In playing through this passage, what are you focusing on? Can you focus on one specific area at a time (intonation, rhythm, articulation, or tone quality)?
5. What is going on in your head? Is your attention wandering?
6. Do you really know and hear when the passage you have worked on has improved? Do you leave practice sessions with a clear sense of what you have accomplished?

Going beyond how you practice a particular passage, here are some bonus questions for considering your practice time in general.

7. How accurately do you hear yourself? Do you record your practice sessions regularly? This is one of the best ways to improve your listening skills and your music making.
8. When and why do you use repetition as a practice strategy? How conscious are you when you're repeating a passage?
9. How do you approach learning a new work?
10. What is your practice routine? How much of this is *conscious* work? What parts of your practice are being done on autopilot?
11. How are you managing your practice time? How much time do you spend on warm-up, sight reading, études, technical work, and problem solving of the toughest parts of your current repertoire?
12. Do you practice with specific goals?

Financial Management ◆

This next section explores how to manage money, an important concern for most musicians. On top of paying their living expenses, many musicians also cope with student loan payments and credit card debt. Managing money is not easily done on freelance income, because work from month to month is unpredictable and there's no steady paycheck. So it's important for musicians to have a workable system to manage their finances.

First, it's essential to know how much you spend and on what. This means tracking all of your expenses to get an accurate picture. Most people don't know where their money goes; it just seems to disappear. And people are shocked to learn how much they actually spend on daily "nothings," on lattés, small daily non-essentials, and on eating out.

▼

How Much Do You Spend?

The easiest way to track your spending is to make sure you get (and keep) receipts for everything you purchase. Each evening when you return home, empty your pockets of all your receipts and tally them in a notebook. It takes sixty seconds to do. If you do this for several months and add in your fixed expenses (from checks or automatic bank transfers), you will know exactly where your money is going. You can do this with paper and pen or with any financial software program, such as Quicken or QuickBooks (both offer free versions online). However you choose to track your spending, group the expenses in appropriate categories such as shown below.

Monthly Spending

Rent/mortgage   _____
Heat   _____
Electricity   _____
Water   _____
Internet connection   _____
Phone   _____
Cable   _____
Groceries   _____
Dining out .   _____
Movies   _____
Clothing   _____
Laundry/dry cleaning   _____
Home insurance   _____
Car insurance   _____
Car maintenance/repair   _____
Gas   _____
Other transportation   _____
Health insurance   _____
Health-care appointments   _____
Prescriptions   _____
Health club membership   _____
Loan repayments   _____
Credit card debt payment   _____
Retirement contribution   _____
* Music/scores   _____
* Recordings   _____
* Instrument maintenance   _____
* Lessons/coachings   _____

* Instrument insurance   _____
* Concert tickets   _____
* Professional dues   _____
Other   _____
Total =   _____

*Examples of music career-related tax-deductible expenses (there are many more).

▲
_____

Once you have tracked your expenses for three or four months, you should have a reliable monthly spending average. Beyond giving you an accurate tally of your spending, tracking serves to make you more conscious of your purchase choices, and that's good.

Take a look at your spending patterns. Most people are surprised to learn how much they spend on non-necessities: coffee, casual meals, and countless little "splurges." How often to you eat out? Do you really need another cashmere sweater or that extra pair of boots? These small-scale luxuries can add up to large-scale problems.

Now look at the amount of money you have coming in each month. Tally your income from freelancing, teaching, and any other work. Are you spending more than you make? If so, it's time to cut back on your discretionary spending. By bringing to work a brown bag lunch and a thermos with your morning coffee, you may save $6–$15 per day, which can amount to as much as over $3,700 per year.

Reducing Debt

If you're spending more than you make, the problem may be with your credit card use. A good rule of thumb is to *avoid using a credit card to buy anything you can eat, drink, smoke, or wear* because these are discretionary and are typically impulse purchases. To rein in your spending, only spend what you actually have in your checking account. Studies show that when people pay with cash or debit card (without overdraft privileges), they spend significantly less. Some people keep a credit card but don't carry it, keeping their card locked up at home or even frozen in a block of ice in their freezer (so that they'll think very hard about making any purchases with it).

If you're carrying debt on your card every month and making only the minimum payments, you can easily get into serious financial difficulties. Here's the problem with credit card debt. Say that you have a $1,000 balance at 17.99 percent interest, and you're making only the minimum payment of $20 per month. At this rate, it will take you ninety-one months (7.5 years) to pay it off and you'll have paid $802 in interest—nearly double the original debt. However, if instead you pay $40 a month, you can eliminate the debt in thirty-one months—five years sooner—and you'll pay $239 in interest, saving $563. Again, the best thing is to spend no more in a month than you make.

If you're not sure about your total debt and credit card interest rates, find out. Unfortunately, introductory rates are designed to lure in new customers, and it's all too easy to have one late payment result in a substantially higher interest rate. See if you can transfer your balance to a credit card with a lower rate, but read all the fine print and be careful about transfer fees.

For debt-reduction advice on consolidating loan payments and negotiating reduced payment plans with lenders, visit the National Foundation for Credit Counseling at http://www.nfcc.org or the American Consumer Credit Counseling site at http://www.consumercredit.com. Financial guru and television advice show host Suze Orman also has an extensive online resource listing, with information and links for a wide range of financial questions, at http://www.suzeorman.com.

Checking your credit history and score periodically is also important. This is to make sure that you have not been the victim of identity theft. But also check that there are no mistakes in your credit report that might jeopardize getting credit for future large purchases, such as a car, home, or instrument. You can get a free copy of your credit report each year through http://www.annualcreditreport.com.

To understand your options and to create a plan for your long-term financial health, it can be very useful to meet with a financial planner. This can be a one-time appointment or a yearly financial "checkup." At the meeting, the planner can review your financial situation and map out a plan for budgeting expenses, reducing debt, and/or handling savings and investments. If you meet with an independent, *fee-based* financial planner, you will be charged an hourly rate for the appointment to get a professional assessment and unbiased recommendations for how to handle your money. Financial planners who work on *commission* for investment companies recommend only those stocks or mutual funds for which they receive a commission. To find a fee-based financial planner in your area, ask your friends and colleagues for recommendations. You want to find an excellent financial planner through reliable personal referrals.

Savings

With limited income, the idea of *saving* money may seem impossible. But even if you have to start small, the essential thing is to start! The best way to make sure you start saving is to arrange for it to be automatic. If you get a regular paycheck, have your bank set up an automatic payroll deduction. This will divert funds to a savings or investment account. This way, you won't be tempted to spend the money because it won't show up in your checking account.

If you're just starting to save now, your first goal is to set up an *emergency fund*. Suze Orman, the financial expert mentioned earlier, recommends keeping such an account funds for eight months of living expenses. For many, the thought of being able to raise this much can seem impossible. But it can be built up incrementally. Your emergency fund should be deposited in a safe place with easy access, such as a money market account or "liquid" certificate of deposit (CD). Once this starts to accumulate, you may be tempted to use it on a vacation or a special project. Don't. You need to save this for actual emergencies.

After you've got your emergency fund saved, the next goal is to start on a long-term savings plan, again using an automatic deposit system. Many financial planners recommend saving at least 10 percent of your income. If you hope to own a home, pay for your children's college education, and be able to retire, then saving more than 10 percent is necessary. Each month you want 10 percent or more going into a long-term investment account. You might want to start with a Roth IRA or a no-fee mutual fund account— something you cannot easily make withdrawals from. If you start the habit *now*, and your earnings are compounded and invested well, you will be able to reach your goals.

Record Keeping

We've discussed tracking all your expenses for a few months in order to get a handle on your budget. But beyond this, freelance musicians need to keep ongoing income and expense records for tax purposes. Why do this? For musicians who keep good records and are tax savvy, there are significant tax savings. And for those who do *not* keep ongoing, accurate records, there's the threat of being audited. The Internal Revenue Service (IRS) can and does ask citizens to produce their records and receipts as evidence of their financial situation. The IRS will also, if necessary, examine bank accounts as part of the investigation. If found in the wrong, you have to pay not only a fine plus the back taxes owed, but the interest on these as well. The IRS can garnish wages, taking money directly from your account in order to get what is owed. If you are having difficulties with your tax payments or bills, see the taxpayer advocate service at http://www.irs.gov. This is a free and independent service for individuals and businesses experiencing hardships resolving tax issues.

Taxes 101 ◆

How much do Americans pay in taxes? For many, their total federal and state taxes amount to roughly a third of their income. To keep this in perspective, tax dollars pay for roads, schools, national parks, social service programs, welfare, Medicare and Medicaid, Social Security benefits, national and state defense, federal and state arts programs, and more. A third of your income is plenty to pay Uncle Sam, but many musicians—because they don't understand the deductions they're entitled to—actually *overpay* their taxes. Don't let this happen to you.

Tale of Joan V. (the Final Installment)

Our freelance trombonist Joan did her own taxes that first year as a freelancer, and she got clobbered; she found she owed the IRS a thousand dollars. So she asked friends about handling finances. That's how she first learned about making a budget, keeping receipts for business deductions, and visiting a recommended musicians' accountant for help with her taxes. That next year, her "day job" boss, the music instrument shop manager, added bookkeeping duties to Joan's workload, and consequently Joan became more skilled with handling her own finances. The payoff came years later, when she was able to afford a new instrument, buy a new car, and even put a down payment on a condo. Joan's first years were tough, but she figured it all out and has since done well.

How do taxes work? Every April 15 in the United States, federal and state taxes are due on income earned during the previous calendar year (January 1–December 31). If you have a full-time job or an ongoing orchestra or opera contract, most likely you receive paychecks with some taxes already taken out. When you started the job, you filled out a *W4* form that included your Social Security number and the amount in taxes you wanted withheld from each paycheck.

Each year, sometime during the month of January, the employer mails you (and the IRS) a *W2* form, which states the total amount you were paid in the previous calendar year and how much was withheld in state and federal taxes. You use the W2 to fill out your taxes. Because musicians typically have multiple employers and jobs, you most likely will receive multiple W2 forms.

Besides the W2 income (which has taxes withheld), freelance musicians typically work a variety of shorter-term freelance gigs, and for these, they receive pay with no taxes withheld. If an employer pays you $600 or more for freelance work during the calendar year, the employer is required to submit to the IRS (and send you a copy) a *1099* form stating how much you were paid and the fact that no taxes were withheld.

So every January, organizations file with the IRS the appropriate W2 or 1099 for each worker paid the previous calendar year, and they send copies to the worker to be used for tax filing purposes. What you are taxed on is your combined total income, from 1099s, W2s, and any other income received in cash and personal checks.

▼

The Musician's Tax Quiz
Did you know?

1. You are obligated to file a tax return if you made at least $400 after expenses as a self-employed individual.
2. You need to declare the income from *all* your gigs and teaching, whether or not you received a 1099, because the employer may have notified the IRS even if you did not receive the copy.
3. The IRS may audit you up to three years after the fact—and charge you three years' interest and penalties in addition to the taxes owed—so make sure there are no mistakes on your tax return.

▲

Tax-Deductible Receipts = Substantial Savings!

How much you pay in taxes for your freelance income has everything to with the records you keep. Here's how it works: the IRS considers freelance work to be self-employment, and you—as a musician—are an independent contractor or small-business owner. The IRS recognizes that self-employed individuals must invest in their businesses, that they need to spend money in order to make money. Consequently, the IRS allows musicians to *deduct* necessary business expenses form their reported income and pay taxes only on the remaining amount. This includes all music career-related expenditures, such as music equipment, scores, recordings, and the cost of traveling to gigs and auditions.

However, you cannot take these tax-deductible expenses unless you keep records and receipts, and fill out the correct tax forms. You can deduct these business expenses from your taxes only if you use the 1040 (long form) with Schedule C for self-employed workers. Tracking business expenses means keeping receipts and records, but the savings are well worth it.

Help from an Expert

Because these forms can be complicated and the rules about what you can and cannot deduct are confusing, it's best to have your tax return prepared by a professional *who specializes in working with musicians*. The folks who work at the large chain tax preparation firms are generally not aware of all the deductions available to musicians. The fee for getting your taxes done by a musicians' tax specialist is a good investment, because you can save tens of thousands over the course of your career. The accountant can also advise you on how best to track your income, expenses, and deductions (and yes, your tax preparation fee is also deductible).

To Declare or Not?

Many musicians mistakenly think they can get ahead by not declaring all the income they earn. If they are paid in cash for lessons, they may avoid declaring this. But the musician tax specialists at Donahue and Associates in Boston report the downside of this. Musicians who fail to declare parts of their income are typically the same musicians who fail to declare many legitimate expenses as deductions, either out of ignorance or poor record-keeping habits. In order to take all of your deductions, you need self-employed income to declare against it. You are better off avoiding tax audits by keeping accurate records and reporting all of your income so that you can declare all your deductions. Your tax return should reflect that you are a professional musician. It should show your full income and full deductions, whether or not you also do any other non-music work. Without declaring all your music income, the IRS may question whether your music is a hobby—as opposed to a profession—and this may have dire tax consequences.

And there can be even worse consequences for not reporting (or under-reporting) your actual income. Eligibility for retirement and disability benefits is based on your work history and reported income. Taxpayers qualify for Social Security benefits by earning credits based on their reported income each year. As of 2009, each credit is accrued when $1,090 is earned and reported, with a maximum of four credits awarded per year. You need at least ten years and forty credits to be eligible for full benefits (disability, retirement, Medicare, etc.). So for those just getting started, *not* reporting in the first years of your career, say in your twenties, may cost you eligibility for full benefits—should you need them—in your thirties. Don't risk it! (See http://www.socialsecurity.gov.)

▼ ──

Musicians' Business Expenses

Tax-deductible items include the following:

Membership dues/fees for professional organizations and associations
Instruments, repairs, and supplies
Music scores and parts
Books on music: history, biographies, theory, career guides (*this* book, for
    example)
Home office supplies: computer and repairs, software, printer, toner, paper,
    plus domain name, ISP costs
Music-related journals and magazines

Publicity: photos, brochures, promo kit materials, flyers, posters, website design

Concert attire and cleaning, along with stage cosmetics

Recordings: CDs and downloads

Recording equipment and studio stereo equipment, iPod

Agent/management fees

Union dues

Accompanist fees, substitute fees

Tickets to concerts (for professional development)

Recording fees, CD manufacturing, printing, design, promotion

In-home studio expenses (percentage of rent, utilities, repairs, insurance; this is for those who teach and/or practice in a dedicated portion of their home—this space can only be used for your music).

Meals (during which professional music career issues are discussed and/or while on tour)

Travel (air, bus, taxi) to your gigs, auditions, concerts, festivals

Self-produced concert expenses (hall and equipment rental, promotion, printing, reception costs)

Telephone (percentage of your bill to cover music-business-related long-distance calls)

Postage, mailings (of promo kits, press releases, postcards, recordings, grant applications)

Business gifts (thank-you gifts to accompanists and colleagues)

Lessons, coaching, workshops, classes, seminars (these are considered professional development for established professionals). Note that undergraduate tuition is not deductible as a professional development expense, nor is graduate tuition unless you established a professional career after a bachelor's degree and then returned to school. However, there are other specific tuition tax credits; see a professional tax preparer for help with all this

▲

It's in the Bag

For tracking expenses, musician tax specialist Ed Donahue recommends the beautifully simple "paper bag in closet" technique. This involves saving receipts for *all* business-related expenditures each day. At home at the end of the day, empty your pockets and wallet of receipts, and write a short explanatory note on any receipts that do not list details. Then, put all of these business-related receipts in an open paper bag on the floor of your bedroom closet. At the end of each month (or year), you can sort the receipts into categories by purchase types using a file folder system. Come tax time, your life will be much, much easier.

All this is necessary because if you're audited, the burden of proof is on you to substantiate your declared income and deductions. You should also save credit card records, but note that these do not suffice for receipts because they do not detail what specifically was purchased, so you absolutely need to get and save store receipts and print and save your online purchase receipts.

Checks

Cancelled checks can be used to document your professional expenditures. Keep your monthly bank statements, so that if requested, you have a record of the expense in question. Some musicians open a separate bank account (or use a separate credit card) strictly to track their business purchases. This is certainly the route to go if you are handling the finances for your own ensemble.

Date Book

For expenses where you do not receive a receipt, such as tolls, gas, parking, mileage, or business meals under $75, your calendar date book may suffice for keeping records. Simply enter the amount you spent, or number of miles driven on the appropriate day, with an explanatory note. If you keep accurate records of these small expenses in your date book, you will be surprised at how fast they can add up to large deductions and substantial tax savings. Whatever system you use for tracking, you need to be consistent with it, and if it's an online system, you'll need a backup.

Ledgers

The purpose of keeping records is so that you can know where you stand financially—what you're earning and what you're spending. A ledger is a simple way to track your business expenses and income. Programs such as Quicken and QuickBooks can be used for this purpose, a simple spreadsheet, or the old pen-and-paper method.

For tracking expenses, set up a basic expense sheet ledger (or spreadsheet). This can be a chart with columns to record the date, an explanatory note about the purchase or expense, and the amount. This way, you can track your business-related spending by the week, month, and year. To determine the appropriate categories for your expense sheet and history, see the list of deductions earlier in this chapter and list the ones that apply to your spending habits.

Income Records

Next, set up an income spreadsheet or chart to record all the music-related payments you receive. With a tracking system, you'll know what you can afford to buy and do, and be able to make better decisions about savings or investments. Include columns that reflect the types of income you have coming in (lessons, gigs, recordings, royalties, or commissions). Simply record the date received, from whom, the type of income, and any special notes.

A good reason to keep records of your income is so that you can track any seasonal patterns in the ebb and flow of your freelance income. For many freelance musicians, there are certain predictable months (August and January) with little work. With a tracking system, you can reliably forecast the leaner months to help manage your finances and time to best advantage.

Special Issues for Ensembles ◆

It can be helpful to have a separate bank account and credit card that you use exclusively for an ensemble. In addition, here are some specific tips for ensembles from jazz bandleader Lucinda Ellert:

- Set up a database to record all of the band's finances: deposits, expenses, revenues, and payments to band members.
- Use a written ledger as well as a computer backup.
- Include tracking of all revenue made from sales of recordings.
- For leader-driven groups, the bandleader should take a leader's fee as compensation for handling all of the management. This may be "invested" into supporting band expenses (it's your prerogative).

Groups eventually need to decide about incorporating as a nonprofit, a limited partnership, or as a type of corporation. The time to decide this is once the group is stable, committed, and performing regularly. As for choosing which legal entity is best for an ensemble, this depends on the group's existing finances and its future plans. There are tax and accounting ramifications for each choice, so it's essential to get good legal advice for your particular situation.

In some cases, the corporate formalities can be eliminated entirely with the use of a "Band Members Agreement." This is a contract among the ensemble members, to clarify questions such as how the ensemble is managed, who owns the ensemble's name, how any royalties from recordings or publishing should be distributed, and under what basis the ensemble can write checks or borrow money. At the start of a new ensemble, when everyone is getting along well, it can seem strange to draw up a formal contract. This is not unlike a prenuptial agreement, in that its purpose is to safeguard against possible future claims or disagreements. In the event of a member leaving, or a new member joining, or a dispute over payments, there needs to be a written agreement in place. To draw up an ensemble contract, you need qualified advice from a trained entertainment lawyer. Consult with the national service organization Volunteer Lawyers for the Arts (http://www.vlany.org) to inquire about pro bono or reduced-fee legal help in your area.

Overall, the best resource for ensembles of all genres is the national service organization Chamber Music America (CMA; see http://www .chamber-music.org). CMA membership includes professional development consultations and resources, an annual national conference, access to and discounts on instrument and health insurance, subscription to *Chamber Music* magazine (which covers all aspects of the field), as well as access to grant programs for commissioning and residency work. You can call or e-mail CMA for contacts, resources, and ideas. The professional staff knows the field—the ensembles, presenters, managers, and how the business works—and can either provide you with the advice you seek or connect you with others who can.

Conclusion

In managing time and money, musicians need to pay attention to both the small details and the big picture. In the end, it's all about the direction you want to take in life and the everyday actions you take to get there. In organizing your schedule and tending to your finances, make sure you're heading toward your goal, to be the person you intend to become.

▼

Career Forward

Writing out your responses to the following will help you manage your time and your money.

1. What challenges have you had in managing your time? What are you spending too much time on? What are you spending too little time on?
2. Write out your schedule for next week. Put the fixed scheduled items (nondiscretionary) in ink, and use pencil to organize the discretionary activities. Make sure you have reserved time for your top priorities. Pay attention to when you schedule in the work that demands high energy and concentration.
3. How might you make your practice time more effective? Remember, it's not about the hours you put in, but what you're actually accomplishing during the time you have.
4. Track your spending this week. Save receipts from every purchase you make, and add these to your expense ledger. At the end of the week, calculate the amount you're spending on average each day. Do you see ways you could be saving money?

▲

12

Funding for Music Projects

▼

▲

Charlotte's been accepted to a prestigious overseas festival and needs
    funds to cover travel and living expenses.
Matt is recording a CD and needs money for the graphic design and
    studio time.
Rachel needs to buy a new instrument.
Casey's ensemble wants to commission a new work from a young
    composer.

Musicians often have great plans and ideas for projects, but just as often
lack the funds to complete them. The good news is that there are ways to
raise money for projects and many musicians are successful doing this. The
bad news is that raising money takes more time and effort than most people
realize.

There are generally two routes to pursue when seeking money for projects: you can either apply for grants or raise the funds from individual donors. For any particular project, one route may be more appropriate than
the other. But most often, musicians use a combination of the two.

Mapping Your Project ◆

No matter how you pursue funding, the recommended first step is to "map" the specifics to help organize your project and your thoughts. A project map is a detailed description of your intended venture, with your goals, qualifications, timeline, and the resources needed. The more concrete and detailed you are with this, the easier it is to get and stay organized, and to successfully complete your project. You can map your project by answering the following questions. Write your answers down because this can serve as the framework needed for grant proposals and fundraising efforts.

1. *What is the goal of your project?* Why are you seeking funds? What *specifically* do you want to accomplish?
2. *Why are you doing this project?* What need or problem does your project address? Who will benefit from this project? If the grant is for your own studies or for a recording or instrument, then you'll need to describe why the project is essential to your career development and your long-term career goals. If your project is for an ensemble or an organization, then you'll need to also include how the project will benefit others and how it will impact the community.
3. *What specific activities will take place as part of your project?* With this funding, what will you be able to do? The more concrete and detailed you are, the more you will enable others to imagine it and be inspired by your vision.
4. *What is your "track record" so far?* Detail what you have done in the past that demonstrates your ability to succeed with this project. List relevant awards, honors, degrees, performances, and teaching experience.
5. *Who will help or participate in the project?* Include details of your collaborators' backgrounds and credentials (short bios), and explain the nature and level of their participation.
6. *When will it be completed?* Include a timeline: make sure that what you plan is feasible given your schedule.
7. *What is your desired outcome?* Explain how you will measure the success of the project (how you will know that you have succeeded).
8. *How much money is needed?* Write out a detailed budget listing all anticipated expenses. You may need to "guesstimate," but do some research to be as accurate as possible. Some needs may end up being covered as *in-kind* donations or bartered services, such as the use of performance and rehearsal spaces, or services such as printing, editing, and catering. But include these in your budget anyway so that others can understand the full requirements of your project.

▼ *Money Talk: Clarifying Terms*

Development: the cultivation of relationships—the process of building others' involvement and commitment to your project.

Fundraising: the organized activity of soliciting and collecting funds for a project, organization, or cause. The success of any fundraising effort depends entirely on the development work that precedes it.

Grant: a sum of money given by an organization for a specified purpose or project. Grants are awarded by national and local foundations, community, civic, and religious organizations, as well as federal, state, and local governments, and by corporations. Grants are used to fund arts education and research projects, as well as recordings, commissions, and residencies. Grants are typically awarded through a competitive process, and usually require an application, proposal, and supporting materials, such as letters of recommendation and recordings.

Nonprofit organization: the nonprofit (or not-for-profit) status is a specific legal and tax designation, also referred to as 501(c)(3) status. Nonprofits are mission-driven organizations; they exist to improve communities. Nonprofits are structured with a board of trustees and a director who work together at determining the mission, goals, and long-range plans for the organization. Most performing arts organizations and music schools are nonprofits. They depend on charitable donations and grants because ticket sales and tuition cannot cover all the expenses of running these organizations. ▲

For Ensembles

There are many foundations that fund only nonprofit organizations. So ensembles often struggle with whether or not to incorporate as nonprofits in order to be eligible for grant funding. Becoming a nonprofit takes time, effort, paperwork, and, more often than not, a lawyer. If your ensemble is just starting out, it's probably best to first get some experience before incorporating.

In the meantime, ensembles can access grants restricted to nonprofits if they partner with a *fiscal agent*—a nonprofit organization that agrees to submit a grant on the group's behalf and then turns the awarded funds over to the group, often for a small administrative fee or percentage of the grant. Think about your network, your mentors and colleagues who work at nonprofit organization. They may be willing and able to help. Also, the arts service organization Fractured Atlas (http://fracturedatlas.org) regularly serves as fiscal agent for artists. To investigate these options, check out Volunteer Lawyers for the Arts (http://www.vlany.org), a national organization with regional offices. The VLA offers helpful publications and "To Be or Not to Be" workshops on the issue of nonprofit status.

Note that some grant programs for ensembles stipulate that groups must be together for a certain length of time at the point of application, because they're looking for stability and a track record of success. Research carefully to find the grant programs for which your group is eligible.

What's Next?

With your project mapped, the next step is deciding whether to apply for grants or to raise the needed funds from individuals. Most people imagine that applying for grants is the easier way to get funding, but this is *not true*.

There is limited grant funding available, and yet there are always many worthy applicants, so grants are highly competitive. Foundations have specific priorities, requirements, and deadlines. Researching to find an appropriate grant takes time, and then the writing of the proposal also takes considerable time.

The types of projects that may be grant eligible include the following:

- Undergraduate or graduate study in the United States and abroad
- Research projects, such as studying original manuscripts, the traditional music of a particular culture, or a specific music education methodology
- Technical support for arts organizations and ensembles (consultation assistance on topics such as marketing, management, Web design, and strategic planning)
- Commissioning new works
- Producing a recording
- Creating a concert series, festival, or after-school lesson program

Researching Grant Opportunities ◆

There are specialized grant research libraries across the United States. These libraries house the most detailed, current information on funding opportunities. The Foundation Center is the main headquarters for a network of cooperating grant research libraries. It publishes helpful guides for grant seekers and, along with its cooperating libraries, hosts workshops on grant writing. (See http://www.foundationcenter.org.)

As for searching online, the New York Foundation for the Arts (NYFA) has an extensive database of artist resource listings nationwide (see http://

www.nyfa.org). For scholarship funding for undergraduate and graduate study, see http://www.fastweb.com and http://www.finaid.org. Note: you should never pay for grant or scholarship searches because there are plenty of free resources and databases available.

Grant databases and directories typically list each grant program's priorities for funding, the amounts awarded, geographic or discipline restrictions, requirements, deadlines for applications, and contact information. You can search grant programs by areas of interest. You can use both broad search topics such as music, education, arts, as well as more specialized categories such as music performance, recordings, ethnomusicology, composition, and so forth. Beyond the area of interest, each grant program has specific criteria for the kinds of projects it funds. These program restrictions are based on the mission of the grant foundation. Some programs are open only to applicants from a specific region or state, or to individuals of a particular ethnicity, nationality, or age range. Pay close attention to the restrictions. Read carefully to know whether or not you and your project are eligible.

Hot Tip #1

Searching online is too often like looking for a needle in a haystack. Consult with a search expert: visit your local public or university library and ask a professional librarian for help. There's no charge, and this will save you much time and stress. Librarians can teach you some of the secrets to conducting a more targeted and productive online search, as well as help you gain access to specialized databases. Having the help of a skilled librarian is like having a professional detective on your side.

Don't overlook the possibility of funding options in your local community and your family's hometown. Civic groups and community associations (such as Rotary, Kiwanis, and Lions clubs) often have scholarship programs and may fund special projects. Local religious associations may also fund community projects. So your research might include checking with your local hometown library and the chamber of commerce as well.

Hot Tip #2

Be on the lookout for grants mentioned in other musicians' bios. Keep a running list—a tickler file—of the names of these grants, and then look them up.

Narrowing the Field: Finding Your "Best Bets"

After researching your options, you should have a list of possible grant programs that are potentially a good match for your project. The next step is to get complete program and application details for each grant. Some of this may be online, some not. You can call or e-mail to request needed information.

Once you have the guidelines and the detailed program restrictions, read them carefully. If your project seems like a viable match, but you're not absolutely sure, call or e-mail the funding organization. Briefly outline your project, and ask specifically about its eligibility. Grant administrators can be very helpful to you before submitting your application. After all, they want to get appropriate applications, so talking to you beforehand helps them, too. Having this conversation will make your proposal more memorable when it is submitted; the grant administrator will have that positive "Yes! I spoke with her" moment. Just don't call the day before the deadline when the foundation staff will be swamped! And don't waste your time—or theirs—by applying for programs that are not the right fit.

Research all your leads. You may find more than one program for which your project is appropriate. Applying to several may improve your odds of getting funded. However, a few highly targeted proposals carefully tailored to each grant program will get you further than using a shotgun approach and sending out multiple one-size-fits-all proposals. Keep in mind that grants are highly competitive. Professional grant writers consider one proposal acceptance out of every five submitted to be a good success rate.

Grant Applications ◆

There are some benefits to applying for grants regardless of whether or not you receive the funding. In the highly recommended book *Art That Pays,* authors Adele Slaughter and Jeff Kober offer this perspective: "Grant applications require you to define yourself and what you do, as well as how you plan to spend the money you're requesting. This process can be extremely useful and even cathartic. It can serve to clarify your goals and objectives, open your mind to new and different ideas and introduce you to resources in the community you did not know existed."[1]

Successful grant writing is a straightforward process of making a clear and detailed case for the legitimate match between your proposed project and the funder's mission. A successful grant proposal is essentially a compelling, well-reasoned case for *why* the granting organization should fund *your* project. To be effective, a grant proposal should describe a need or problem and then outline the proposed project that provides the solution. And your proposal should clearly explain who will benefit from the project and how. The basic idea is to present the *problem,* the proposed *solution,* and the anticipated *impact.*

Whether you're applying for a grant to study abroad or one to fund a local after-school program, there are essential components to all grant applications. To be convincing, a proposal should answer the questions below. (This is where the earlier project mapping exercise comes in handy.)

- What specifically do you plan to accomplish through this project?
- What are the expected outcomes: for you, for others, for the community?
- What evidence do you have that you are qualified to succeed with this project?
- What specifically do you need in order to complete the project? (Detail the needed funding, resources, assistance, and projected timeline.)
- How does this project match the interests and priorities of the funding organization? The challenge here lies in seeing your proposal from the *funder's* perspective. Throughout your proposal, emphasize the ways in which your project goals line up with the funder's priorities.

Organizational Grants

Grant applications for community projects, ensembles, or organizations are more detailed than those for individuals. Typical organizational grant proposals include the following:

1. *Summary:* a concise statement of the project. (Best written after the rest of the proposal is completed.)
2. *The need:* what is the societal or community need that your project will directly address? Who will this project serve, and how will they benefit? For example, with a project to start an after-school music program in which students learn to compose, perform, and record their own music, the need may be to address a specific low-income community's lack of after-school options and mentoring and arts programs for teens.
3. *Project description:* the details of the project, complete with goals and objectives. This includes the details of what the funding will be used for and how the project will be implemented. The review committee needs to understand exactly how a project will unfold.
4. *Background:* the credentials of all those participating in the project.
5. *Budget and timeline.*
6. *Outcomes:* the measurable indicators for successful results, such as numbers of students taught or coached, performances, audience members, or publications of the project research. More difficult to

measure are the qualitative results, the value of a performance, workshop, or recording in terms of emotional and intellectual experience. Grant programs typically require an evaluation process, which may include an evaluation portfolio with video clips, testimonials, and thank-you letters from project participants.

Warning: Thoughts to Avoid

Musicians sometimes think that grant writing is some mysterious or intimidating skill demanding professional training, that is beyond their reach. It's not, so don't let this fear prevent you from trying. Grant writing demands carefully following the program guidelines and employing your clear thinking, organizational skills, and attention to detail.

On the other end of the spectrum, some novice grant seekers make the mistake of thinking, "Oh, this application is simply paperwork: I'll just whip this sucker off. Besides, it's the recording and letters of recommendation that really count." *Wrong!* Don't underestimate the importance of having a well-written and compelling project statement. For funders, it's essential.

Nitty Gritty

A grant proposal is not a term paper. There's no need to be overly formal or to use a three-syllable word when a single-syllable one will do. Write naturally, as though you're explaining the project to a potential donor, because you are. Be concise; volume and verbiage will not win you points. Keep in mind that not everyone on a grant selection panel will be intimately familiar with your specific area of interest. Don't use technical jargon—describe your project in a way that an intelligent nonspecialist would understand it and find it compelling. Remember that your proposal will be one of hundreds, so be detailed and persuasive but concise.

Grant applications often call for supporting materials, such as letters of reference, demo recordings or DVDs, and scores. If the application states that you should submit a certain number of copies of your recording, or that the recording be labeled a particular way (for ease of evaluation and to guarantee impartiality), *follow the directions.* Supporting materials are crucial, so take pains to represent yourself well. Make sure that what you send to the selection committee meets all their specifications. Each grant program has its own application format, so read the details and follow the directions carefully.

▼ *Top Five Reasons Grant Applications Are Rejected*

1. Project is inappropriate to the funder's stated priorities and interests.
2. Late! Didn't meet deadline.

3. Unconvincing project description. The need, the solution proposed, and the projected outcomes all must make a compelling case.
4. Didn't follow directions with either the written portion of the proposal or in preparing the supporting materials.
5. Incomplete: missing one or more of the required support materials.

▲

How Are Grants Awarded?

Most grant programs use a panel process to select winners. The granting organization invites qualified, impartial professionals to serve as panelists. Each panelist receives copies of the applications and supporting materials to review. If there are too many applications, then these are divided into sets and each panelist reviews and presents her or his set of applications to the entire panel at the selection committee meeting. At these meetings, panelists present and discuss each application one at a time, and then votes are cast to select the awardees.

A grant program makes an *investment* with each award. Panelists have tough decisions to make, because there are always many more deserving proposals than there are awards.

So, if your proposal is not selected, don't take it personally! Wait a week or so to get over your disappointment, and then call the grant program officer and ask for feedback on how you might improve your proposals in the future. Program officers are generally very willing to have these conversations, but you need to park your ego and any lingering defensiveness. This is your chance to learn how to make a better case for the next proposal you write.

True Confession

I've written a number of grants for various projects, and each grant had its own lessons to teach me. But here's my Fulbright grant story. As a grad student, I wanted to study in Paris with the cellist Roland Pidoux. The Fulbright application requires two essays; one asks the applicant to describe the project plan in detail; the other, to cover one's background in detail. I wrote my essays and thought I'd done a fairly good job of covering all the points. I asked a friend to read my draft. He was a Ph.D. candidate in musicology, a smart, experienced writer, and I valued his opinion. Because I'd always done well with writing in school, I expected him to be supportive and encouraging.

Boy, was I wrong!

He calmly told me that my proposal was lousy (although he did this in more colorful language). He said it was unconvincing, that my plan of study wasn't specific enough, and that I hadn't detailed my qualifications. He said the writing was unfocused and that no one would fund a project described this way. For me, this was a harsh wake-up call for which I will always be grateful. Up until this point, I had never really considered how important writing could be to a performer, or that written communication skills could affect a performer's career opportunities.

I didn't get the Fulbright and was very disappointed. And I would not have tried again if my friend hadn't encouraged me. So, the next year I wrote a new proposal. My revised essays detailed what is specific to the French school of string playing and how this would enhance my American training. I detailed the repertoire I planned to work on and listed possible performance venues in Paris where I could give recitals. I described my specific long-term career goals and how a year of study in Paris would provide essential experience. I also included my relevant background credentials—festivals, repertoire, degrees, and concert venues where I had performed. The good news is that I got the Fulbright the second time around!

Lessons Learned

1. For your drafts of grant proposals, get detailed, critical feedback early on and be prepared to revise!
2. Yes, the "paperwork" really matters. The way you describe your goals and project will have a big effect on the outcome.
3. If you don't succeed at first, try again!

Fundraising 101 ◆

What can you do if there is no grant program for which your project is eligible? Or if your project is rejected and you cannot afford to wait to re-apply? Or the application deadlines and your project timeframe are not in sync. The good news is that you are for more likely to be successful raising money from individual donors—from supporters close to you—than by "gambling" on the competitive grant process.

People are typically resistant to the idea of doing their own fundraising. Most are horrified at the thought of asking others for money. They think of this as "begging." But talk to any experienced fundraiser and you will hear a very different perspective. Fundraising work is all about connecting with people and building relationships. It's helping people put their interests and values into action for a cause they care about. Like music itself, fundraising boils down to creating community. A grassroots fundraising campaign can rally individual supporters into a close-knit community galvanized by a project.

Why Do People Give?

Think about your own behavior. If you've ever participated in a walk-a-thon, put money in a church collection plate, tutored a child, donated blood, or contributed to a political campaign, ask yourself *why*.

People give for a number of reasons. For some, it's because they have a personal connection to the cause, the organization, or the person making the "ask." People are also inspired to give when the project or organization connects with their own ideals, their personal values. And some people contribute in part for social reasons. They may want to be acknowledged as a valued partner in a worthy endeavor.

When you have contributed to cause, how did it make you feel? You probably felt good! People like to help, and they like to see positive results. So when the student you tutor passes an exam or the church you played the benefit concert for meets its fundraising goal, most likely you felt proud that you were a part of this process.

When people give time, money, or expertise to a cause they care about, they get something important in return. They get to feel good about themselves. *This* is the real return on their investment. Self-worth is a great reward. As you imagine your future fundraising campaign, remember that fundraising is an exchange. When you ask people to contribute, you are offering them something valuable in return.

Hot Tip #3: Think Beyond Cash

In-kind donations are noncash contributions, such as equipment (computers, pianos, PA systems); space for rehearsals and performance; or services such as printing, graphic design, and website development. Think about the people in your network who might help with your project on a noncash basis. If you have an e-newsletter, this can be a great medium for requesting in-kind donations or asking for volunteers. Newsletters are also great places to acknowledge and thank your growing circle of supporters.

It's Personal: People Give to People

The first reason that people would contribute to your fundraising campaign is because of their relationship with *you*. Arts consultant Steve Procter explains what will motivate people to contribute to your project, "your exciting and valuable artistic 'product'; a compelling idea, bold vision, and credible plan; and a feeling of connection with the project and the people involved."

Who are your prospective supporters? They are people you share common interests with, who have similar values, ideals, and goals. They are people with a capacity to give and an inclination to help. This is not about being fake or kissing up to people you hardly know. This is about genuine relationships. The more you and your project matter to a prospective donor, the more they will be willing to give.

As you read this, you may be thinking, "But I don't know any rich people. The people closest to me either don't have anything to give or won't." The truth is that the vast majority of people in your network have some discretionary funds, money they use on a variety of nonnecessities. There are people in your network who could contribute $500 to a cause they believe in without it adversely affecting their finances. For some people, $50 is the limit of their comfort zone; for others, it may be $5,000. The bottom line is that people won't give unless they're asked. Nothing ventured, nothing gained!

The Quickie Campaign

Nick and Nora each needed to raise $1,000 to participate in a summer tour with an orchestra going to South America. They had a deadline of one month to raise the money. Their immediate families couldn't help, so Nick and Nora started thinking about their network, the family friends who had shown interest in their musical development over the years. Nora thought of her family doctor and dentist, who both were avid music lovers. Nick thought of his high school band director—with whom he'd kept in touch—and knew he was a generous fellow who contributed to community charities. These potential patrons were not rich, but all three were certainly well off. Nick and Nora had a reasonable expectation that these people could afford to and might want to contribute at least a part of the needed funds.

Nick and Nora each called their potential patrons to set up lunch dates, explaining that they wanted to catch up and to discuss an opportunity they had been offered. They practiced these conversations beforehand. Initially, they both felt awkward and nervous about asking someone directly for money, but once they practiced describing the orchestra tour opportunity and visualizing talking with these family friends, they both felt more confident. As for how they made out, the conversations were much easier than they had imagined. Their donors were enthusiastic. Nick and Nora got the funds they needed and had a terrific tour!

Your best prospects are people already in your network, those closest to you and your family, who already know you well and who can easily be brought up to date on your project and plans. It's easier to ask two people (with good potential) for $1,000 each than to raise your total in $20 increments.

Do It Right!

There's an old saying in fundraising: you have to have the *right* person ask the *right* prospect for the *right* amount for the *right* reason at the *right* time. In other words, if you haven't written to or spoken with your Aunt Ida in ten years, and she gets a phone call or letter from you out of the blue asking her to cough up $5,000, it probably won't go over well. This doesn't mean you shouldn't ask her at all, but you need to first reestablish a relationship with her.

Success Factors: The Five "How's"

The success of your fundraising campaign depends on these factors:

1. How much money you need to raise
2. How much time you have to raise it
3. How compelling your project is (how appealing it is to the people in your network)
4. How you present your project
5. How (and how often) you interact with the people in your network

The Development Continuum ◆

To put this in perspective, people contribute in proportion to their sense of involvement. The more invested they are in you and your project, the more likely they will be to invest financially. The development continuum below is a useful way to graph the level of involvement of your supporters. And the continuum illustrates the process—the how, why, and when people become patrons. This concept comes from workshops that fundraising gurus David Bury and Steve Procter have presented for the Chamber Music America and Arts Presenters conferences.

On the chart below are headings representing the possible relationship stages between you and members of your network. Farthest to the left is "ignorance," which is the category for people who are as yet unaware of you, your music, or your project. Development work is essentially about moving people, over time, from left to right along the continuum—from awareness or lukewarm interest in you and your project to involvement, commitment, and finally "ownership." Don't be put off by that last word. It doesn't mean people in this category "own" your project or you. Rather, this is the category for your strongest supporters and allies, your advisory board. These are the people who will feel a sense of partnership, pride, and identification with the success of your project.

Your Development Continuum

Using the chart below as a worksheet, write in the names of those in your network's inner circle, placing each name under the category appropriate for the current state of your relationship. You probably have twenty to twenty-five good contacts, people who have expressed some degree of interest in you and your future. Include your extended family, former teachers, and anyone else who cares about you and your career. Think about family, neighbors, colleagues, and old friends.

Levels of Relationship

Ignorance → Awareness → Interest → Commitment → Ownership

Not sure where to place members of your network on the continuum chart? At the awareness stage, people have attended one or more of your concerts, or bought your CD. The need to collect e-mails at every performance should be apparent, because without a mailing list to alert folks about upcoming performances and other news, you cannot move them along the continuum.

At the interest stage, you're getting to know these people and they're interested in your music and potentially in getting involved with your project. They may be interested in helping out with future concerts. If you don't ask, you'll never know. You can announce in the program, on your website, and from the stage that you're looking for people to assist with organizing the next concert or perhaps with the next recording project.

The most important way to move people along the continuum is to get them to your performances, talk to them afterward, and invite them to participate in support activities appropriate to your level of relationship. It's all about getting people actively involved. Once you have your strategic network contacts listed in the appropriate spot on the chart, the next step is to plan what development activities will help you develop these relationships and move people further toward the right.

▼

Hot Tip #4: Want Money? Ask for Advice!

(And if you want advice, ask for money!)

With your list of closest supporters, choose a few to have individual meetings with. Ask to take them out for coffee or lunch, and explain that you want to get their advice about a project you have in mind. It's best to do this in person, so you can get their full attention and response to your project.

Be prepared—have your project mapped out in a concise written form, and practice your verbal presentation in advance. It's not a speech, but you do need to feel comfortable describing it to your potential donor. Part of the development process is educating your network about your career plans. Non-musicians are often unaware of the costs and procedures of producing concerts, recordings, or advancing a music career. They most likely don't know why it's important to go to festivals or why you might need a better instrument. Your presentation should include a summary of your career path, your successes so far, and a description of how this project fits into your overall career plan. Include a detailed budget of all anticipated costs plus a listing of the resources you already have in place.

The goal of these meetings is to gather support and ideas, and in doing so, to deepen the level of involvement of your supporters. Be prepared for advice and suggestions, and be open to these. You don't have to necessarily act on any of the advice, but you should be receptive to considering new ideas and perspectives. Fundraising projects are most successful when they are a group effort, when you pool the talents and expertise of your network.

The best-case outcome is to have your advisor listen to your project description, get interested, take out a checkbook, and say, "How much do you need?" That's wonderful, but it doesn't always happen like this. Instead, your advisor may suggest changes to your project or plan, or may refer you to others for additional advice. Or your conversations may yield volunteers for hosting and organizing a benefit house concert. But in order to have any results at all, you need to have the in-person meetings.

▲

Fundraising consultant Steve Procter writes, "Beyond inviting supporters to lunch, the other powerful development tool is your artistry in action. Everything you do—concerts, school programs, coaching of ensembles—is a development opportunity. The surest and most powerful way for people to get on board is to see you doing your work. All that's required is that you make a personal invitation."

Consider organizing a series of house concerts for your inner network circle, and have them invite their friends. What about master classes, lecture demonstrations, or clinics in your hometown? You could also perform a benefit concert for a local community charity. You would benefit by having your concert announced and promoted to the entire mailing list of that organization. The concert could be good exposure, generate potential media coverage, and yield useful networking contacts.

Consider creating an event that pairs great music and great food. This could be a recital program of musical bonbons with an elegant catered dessert buffet-reception. Local caterers might participate, or you could do this as a local competition for most elegant dessert. Or it could be a musical "feast" with pieces performed between courses of a fabulous dinner. Use your imagination.

Making the Ask ◆

In the course of your "advising meeting," you should get a sense of the level of interest of your potential patron. If she or he does not volunteer to contribute, you need to "make the ask." Have a specific amount in mind to ask for that's appropriate to your supporter's income and to her or his level of interest in your project. The amount should be specific because if you say, "I'd be grateful for whatever you can give," people may give $20 or $50 instead of $200 or $500.

Do some research in advance of your meeting. Ask your family and friends—people who know your prospective donor well—what they think an appropriate amount might be. If your potential donor is well off and regularly contributes to community arts organizations, this should inform your thinking. You can look at donor lists of other arts organizations. They often have tiered giving levels with specified amounts, so you may be able to determine whether your prospect gives elsewhere and at what level.

Practice first. Practice your presentation with a mentor, teacher, or family member. A run-through will help you feel more comfortable in talking about yourself, presenting your project, and in "making the ask."

Let's say that you plan on asking ten people from your network for donations. Where should you start? Start with whomever you feel most comfortable. And keep in mind that the more you do this, the easier it gets.

In your presentation, after you outline your project for your potential donor, answer questions, and talk about the budget and how the project will benefit your career in the long run, you need to actually ask for their financial support. You can say something like, "I'm hoping you can assist me with this project. As my budget shows, the total cost is $3,000 and I've already raised $800. I would really appreciate a contribution of $ [appropriate amount]." Then PAUSE . . . and this is crucial . . . *don't* fill in the silence! Out of discomfort, you may be tempted to fill in the silence with "But actually, whatever you can manage is fine" and end up undermining your own efforts. Give your supporter a chance to think and respond. They may take out a checkbook or tell you it's too much but that they *can* give X amount. Or that they need to think it over and get back to you. Whatever the answer, thank them for their time, advice, and interest.

Keep in mind that no one "owes" you anything. It's their money to do with as they choose. Essentially, you are presenting a kind of investment opportunity to which your supporters may say yes or no. If the answer is no, it doesn't mean that the potential donor won't say yes to future projects. So if you're turned down, let go of feeling resentful. In the end, your deepening relationship with supporters is what matters. It's all about relationships. Fundraising and development, when it's done right, is not about a quick fix for funding one project. It's about your long-term career, about having a community of friends and supporters with you for the long haul.

Why Are These Meetings Done in Person?

You may imagine that this would be easier—or less awkward for you—if done by phone, e-mail, or letter. But fundraising is by far most effective when done in person, because you get more time and the full attention of your supporter. In-person meetings allow you to "read" the response of a potential contributor—facial expression, body language, and tone of voice. What's more, people find it much harder to turn someone down in a face-to-face meeting, especially when they know you and you've just presented a compelling invitation for their support.

The Art of the Thank-You

When is the last time you received a handwritten thank-you note? These days, it's so rare that getting one is a special occasion and you think very positively of the person who sent it. That's exactly why you *should* send them. E-mail, phone, and even in-person thank-yous just don't pack the same punch. Send thank-you notes to everyone who helps with your project. This includes the people with whom you had networking and advising meetings, those who helped you organize or cater the post-concert reception, and any others who contributed time, expertise, or money to your project.

Write more than simply the words *thank you*—explain how much you appreciate the help and the helper. Make it personal. This is part of cultivating relationships with people in your network. Any thank-you letter is an opportunity to deepen a relationship, so include reminders about upcoming performances or projects and any planned future get-togethers.

If your ensemble or organization has nonprofit status, donor contributions are tax deductible. Because the letter may be used for tax filing purposes, a more formal, typed thank-you letter is recommended (although adding a handwritten note is always a good idea). Below is an excerpt from a sample donation thank-you letter, which appeared in an article by Laurie Shulman, "The Power of Thank You," in Chamber Music America's *CMA Matters*, 2006. It's a letter from the general manager of the fictitious ABC chamber ensemble, a group that manages its own performance series.

Dear Mr. and Mrs. Johnson:

We were so pleased to have received your donation of $50.00. It comes at such a great time for us! As you may know, we're just about to embark on our [significant Anniversary/Composer] celebration, and your contribution brings us that much closer to achieving our goal . . ."

[The letter continues with an opportunity and invitation for the Johnsons to get even more connected, to move them along the development continuum.]

We are planning a pre-concert event to give friends of the ensemble an inside peek at preparations and planning. We want you to hear guest artist John Doe in conversation and musical demonstration with our artistic director, Jennifer Miller. Please mark your calendar [or: save the date] for Tuesday evening, 17 October. We'll be in touch as soon as we have details. As you know, the performance itself is scheduled for 19 October.

Thanks again for your help in making our forthcoming celebration possible. Your support is crucial to our success, and we are lucky to have you among our supporters.

Yours cordially,

Susan Brown
General Manager, ABC Ensemble

Send your thank-yous out right away—the day after the meeting, the concert, or when you receive a check. Your donors will appreciate your thoughtfulness.

You can also acknowledge and thank supporters in your printed concert programs and CD liner notes. But ask them how they would prefer to be listed, as "Dr. and Ms. John L. Smith," as "Jane and John Smith," or if they prefer to remain anonymous. If a local business provides you with in-kind donations, ask whether they would like their logo in your concert program or on your posters. If you keep your supporters happy and interested, they will want to continue to invest in you.

Thinking beyond Your Current Project

The development continuum is an ongoing process. Development work takes time because relationships are built over time, through shared experiences and one-on-one meetings. As you add new people to your mailing list, you will want to find ways to move them along the continuum. Think about what might help potential donors get to know you better and how you might draw more interested people to your concerts. Use occasional informal newsletters and e-mail updates to keep your network informed and connected to you and your work. Engage them with stories about your latest project or upcoming concert. Keep the long view—consider your current project in the context of your long-range career plans so that your actions set the stage for both immediate and future possibilities.

Benefit Concerts 101

An undergraduate, soprano Charlotte T. received an acceptance and scholarship offer to a summer program in Italy. She was thrilled but didn't have the funds needed—$2,000 to cover the travel, room, and board. Charlotte received the acceptance notice in May, and the festival began in July. Time was short.

Charlotte decided to give a benefit recital back home, in the small town in Maine where she'd grown up and where her family had strong ties in the community. Charlotte thought she could offer the concert in early June at the town's high school auditorium, a small venue with good acoustics. Needing help, she talked by phone with some key people back home first, to get ideas and support. The help of her former teacher, friends, and family was essential because Charlotte was planning this at a distance.

Charlotte made a list of people to invite, people who knew her and her family well, and who were interested in her development as a singer. She sent personalized, handwritten letters to everyone on the list a month before the performance, updating them on her accomplishments so far and outlining the festival opportunity in Italy. In the letters, Charlotte explained the importance of this experience, how the training and performances would contribute to her education and future career. Charlotte included the specifics, explained the budget total, how much she needed to raise, how much she'd gotten as scholarship, and how much she was covering from her savings. She wrote that she looked forward to seeing her friends and family at the recital and how much she appreciated their encouragement over the years.

To promote the concert, Charlotte's mom wrote and delivered press releases to the small local newspapers and submitted listings to local church bulletins. The whole family helped spread the word about the event: they made posters, sent e-mails, and, most important, they invited people personally.

Charlotte had a great turnout—about 100 people came, and this worked well for the venue. Charlotte's former teacher graciously welcomed everyone at the start of the program and spoke briefly about Charlotte's opportunity to attend the festival, reminding people of the call for donations. Charlotte sang a terrific program and verbally introduced each piece, engaging the audience throughout the concert. Afterward, there was a reception that her family and friends had organized.

Many people contributed at the reception, placing donations in envelopes in a basket. Many others sent checks in the week following the performance. All totaled, Charlotte raised close to $3,000 and exceeded her goal!

After the recital, Charlotte sent thank-you notes to everyone who contributed and assisted. Then while she was at the festival, she sent e-mail updates with photos and descriptions of the performances and her training. After the festival, she sent another e-mail newsletter, again thanking everyone and detailing all that she got out of the experience. Her net gain from the benefit concert was far more than the dollars: Charlotte now had a circle of supporters invested in her future.

Fundraising Letters ◆

We all get direct-mail appeals asking us to contribute to a wide range of causes, from local homeless shelters to the Red Cross, to cancer and AIDS research organizations. If you imagine that it would be much more effective to write a fundraising letter and send it out—think again. Direct-mail campaigns have a very small return rate (1–4 percent), whereas personal, face-to-face meetings have a much better rate of return. In person, you get an even shot at succeeding, a 50 percent chance of scoring a "yes."

That said, cultivation letters may be very useful tools to reconnect you with your existing supporters and friends. Letters can be sent to prepare people for in-person visits and to invite them to benefit concerts (as Charlotte did, above). When the potential donor is too far away, a very personalized letter can be tailored to the situation. Below is an example of such a fundraising letter. But note that this letter was appropriate because there was both a strong family connection and a recent one-on-one meeting. And the $500 "ask" was based on what Rachel's family thought would be appropriate for these supporters in this situation.

Crowdfunding

As discussed in earlier chapters, musicians are harnessing the power of their fan bases to help fund recordings and organize concerts. On the website http://www.kickstarter.com, you can read about projects that were successfully funded by various individuals and ensembles. The way Kickstarter works is that you create a profile with information about the project you're seeking to fund, including an engaging video invitation to participate. You send e-mails describing your project with a link to direct people to your Kickstarter page. Each project has a goal amount and a deadline. Donors pledge the amount they choose, but no donor's credit card is actually charged until the goal is reached.

April 10, 2011

Dear Jane and John,

Thanks so much for coming to my concert last week—it was so nice to see you again! I'm glad we had a chance to visit during the reception and to catch up a little. I was happy to hear Emily's doing so well in Chicago.

I appreciate the interest you've shown in my music, and I wanted to fill you in on my current plans. As you know, at the Conservatory I have a wonderful teacher, Donald Weilerstein. He has been very encouraging and is suggesting I apply to several prestigious festivals and competitions next year, including the Young Concert Artists competition in New York City this fall. He also tells me that I need a better violin. I've grown past the stage of having a "student" instrument and I need a professional-quality violin that will allow me to compete successfully in competitions and orchestral auditions. Unfortunately, these instruments are expensive.

The good news is I have found an excellent Italian violin made in the mid-19th century. It costs $11,000, and I have raised $4,000 so far (savings from part-time jobs and contributions from my family). I am contacting close family friends, such as you, to participate in my "new instrument campaign."

In June I will be back home and I'm planning a "new instrument" benefit concert for Sunday, June 20, at 3 pm at the Unitarian Church. I'd love to have you come, and I'd love to list your names in the concert program with the others who've contributed to the fund. Would you consider a contribution of $500 toward the purchase of a professional-quality violin?

I very much appreciate your encouragement and support! And I look forward to seeing you both, along with Emily and Kate, this summer. I will be in touch in the next few weeks.

Best Wishes,

Rachel

Commissioning New Work ◆

Commissioning new work is one of the best kinds of projects that musicians can take on. Commissioning projects can attract media attention and can help connect performers and composers with new audiences. In collaborating with composers, performers are often rewarded with an expanded musical perspective. It can be liberating to premiere a new work, to be the first interpreter, because there's no history or tradition against which to measure one's performance. For the composer, the benefits of working closely with performers include the chance to experiment and refine their ideas.

Which composers should you approach with a commissioning project? Many emerging performers, when they imagine commissioning new work, think only about commissioning "name" composers, imagining that the composer's name might cast luster on their own. And the project idea rarely goes anywhere, because the emerging artist can't afford to commission a celebrity composer.

Think differently—start locally. Go to the websites of the new music ensembles and series in your area. Sign up for their mailing lists, and start going to their concerts. It's a terrific way to become connected to the new music scene in your community. Attend the post-concert receptions, and network with the composers and the performers who champion their work. This may lead to future collaborations as well as information and ideas for funding the commissions.

In "shopping" for a composer, you want to find one whose music moves you—you need to either be in love with it or perhaps infuriated and fascinated by it. You need to be energized and enthusiastic about this composer's work because you'll need to engage others in wanting to fund the project.

Beyond your immediate community, you can use the searchable databases on the American Music Center (AMC) site (http://www.amc.net) and on the American Composers Forum site (http://www.composersforum .org). Online you can browse composers' scores, listen to sound samples, and read bios. The databases allow you to search by ensemble type or instrument, composer name, title, and duration of work.

Another option, through AMC and ACF, is issuing a *call for scores*—a notice that you, or your ensemble, are looking for scores (naming whatever instrumentation you have and an approximate length of piece). Composers will send you their works, but be prepared for the deluge! This can be a good way of finding out about composers you wouldn't otherwise meet, and from this pool of works you may find a great collaborator.

Funding for Commissions

Assuming that you've now found a composer whose work you love and whom you'd like to commission, there are a number of possible routes to funding. Chamber Music America, Meet the Composer, and the Association of Performing Arts Presenters offer commissioning grants, as do many state arts agencies. In addition, many presenting series, festivals, orchestras, choruses, opera companies, schools, and competitions commission new works. Individuals also commission music, sometimes to honor a loved one or commemorate an anniversary. You may have friends and family who would want to contribute to your commissioning project—they may just need to be brought on board and have a chance to get to know your chosen composer's music and to share in your excitement about the potential new work. Meet the Composer has a terrific online brochure, "An Individual's Guide to Commissioning Music," to give you great ideas (see http://www .meetthecomposer.org).

Consortium funding is a form of crowdfunding, with multiple contributors participating. Bang on a Can's People's Commissioning Fund allows folks to contribute $50 to $1,000 to become members, and this entitles them to a range of benefits, from tickets to the annual People's Commissioning Concert to bound scores of their commissioned pieces.

The publicist Amanda Ameer suggests reaching out to your community and offering people the opportunity to invest in portions of a new work. One hundred dollars might buy you thirty seconds of a new piece, or perhaps a certain number of measures. The participating contributors could be credited in concert programs and on the published scores. Just think, an individual can make possible a particular favorite phrase!

Violinist Jennifer Koh was able to commission composer Jennifer Higdon to write a concerto with the funding support of a small group of university presenting series. Jennifer approached presenters who knew her work and found they were enthusiastic about participating. The result was not only a terrific piece, but each of the partnering presenters had the opportunity to host his or her local premiere of the work. This model not only helps defray the burden of the cost of the commission by sharing it among partners, but it also ensures that the new work has multiple performances and the possibility of multiple reviews and audiences. Think about the presenters you know well and ask for their advice!

An alternative approach is the brainchild of saxophonist Ken Radnofsky, who founded the World-Wide Concurrent Premieres and Commissioning Fund, a nonprofit organization that selects individual composers to write a new work and then helps coordinate same-day world premieres of the new work by multiple performers in different locations worldwide. The costs are shared and logistical tasks are delegated among the participating performers, and this has made it possible to commission works by Chris Theofanidis, Michael Colgrass, Gunther Schuller, John Harbison, and many others. The idea is that the new work doesn't get just one premiere, but many.

And the piece has a much better chance of becoming part of the repertoire if it's being performed at forty or seventy premieres. For the performers, they don't have to raise the entire commissioning fee, just a fraction of it. And the story of the consortium effort often helps attract media attention to each individual premiere. With this model, everyone wins. (See http://www .kenradnofsky.com.)

As for the logistics for commissioning: the cost depends on the length of the piece, its size (whether its for solo harmonica, bassoon quartet, or full orchestra and chorus), and the reputation and career level of the composer. For mid-career composers, the going rate is often $1,000 per minute for smaller chamber works, and more for full orchestra and opera scores. Emerging composers may be willing to negotiate far lower fees, depending on the opportunity for performances and recording.

Once you have a composer willing to write for you, confirm your agreement in writing. A contract for a commission should include at least the basics, as detailed in "The ABC's of Commissioning New Music," by Amanda MacBlane (in *Chamber Music* magazine, October 2003). These basics are "identification of the parties involved, description of the prospective work [length and instrumentation], delivery dates for work and parts, fee and method of payment, commitment to perform the work within a specific time period, and cost allowances for part extraction and/or recording production." Typically, composers are paid 50 percent at the signing of the contract and the balance at the completion. It can be good to use a lawyer in arranging the contract, but it's possible to do without. A written agreement is an absolute necessity; for more pointers on these, see "Commissioning Music: A Basic Guide" on the Meet the Composer site (http://www.meetthe composer.org).

Corporate Sponsorship ◆

In some ways, corporate sponsorship lies halfway between grants and fundraising. According to HighgateGlobal arts consultant Liam Abramson, author of the recommended e-book, *Writing the Perfect Sponsorship Proposal*, corporations invest in projects for three main reasons: identity, ideas, and involvement.

Identity: most corporate giving is dependent on "identity return." The corporation wants to invest in your concert or project in exchange for publicity, standing within the industry, or its reputation among the company's clients and customers. Abramson writes, "The return the sponsor wants for their financial assistance is some form of 'signage' in order to promote their business to a particular sector of the market." So, a corporation that chooses to sponsor a sports franchise or the building of a theater will typically have its name on the building and in all the associated publicity. The corporation chooses either the sports franchise or theater based on which audience demographic it wants to reach. On a smaller scale, local businesses might buy ad space in a concert program, or a print shop might agree to produce the posters, tickets, and programs for a concert series, and in return the company will be acknowledged as a sponsor in all the series' press releases, in the program, and on the posters. But again, the business needs to perceive value in reaching that particular audience.

The second reason that corporations sponsor arts projects is to be associated with good *ideas.* The good idea might be an arts project that provides access to musical instruments, lessons, and ensemble experience to schools in an underserved community. Or the idea might be an ensemble's preconcert lecture series that pairs business and arts leaders to discuss creativity. By being associated with good ideas, the business enhances its reputation with the public and its customers.

The third reason Abramson cites is personal *involvement:* individual company leaders may be classical or jazz music lovers and may already be attending your concerts. You can get to know these people at post-concert receptions. Because these folks like feeling connected to the music making and to musicians, some might feel honored to be asked to serve on an advisory committee for your project. Involvement of key individuals—such as the managing director of a corporation—can help open the door to that company's sponsorship.

The preparation for approaching a potential corporate sponsor is similar in some ways to preparing a grant proposal (although there may or may not be guidelines and application formats). The smaller the business or corporation, the less likely it will be to have a formal process. Instead, you can write out a corporate proposal using the mapping exercise at the start of this chapter. Key components to include are as follows:

- Information about you and your experience
- Description of the music project or event
- Benefits you are offering to the particular corporation
- The financial investment sought in exchange for these benefits
- Ideas for furthering the sponsorship relationship in the future

Abramson advises to make sure that you promise the sponsor only what you can actually deliver. Benefits might include free tickets to employees, access to a special reception or house concert for VIP donors, signage on all the programs and posters, as well as mention in all press releases. But promised benefits should not include reaching a particular number of audience members, newspaper readers, or radio listeners, because you cannot control how many people will actually come to the concert or which news media outlet will print or broadcast your press releases.

The process of cultivating a relationship with any corporate contact is exactly the same as described in the development continuum earlier in this chapter. So don't pop the question too early in the relationship. If you have not done the necessary development work, it's the same as proposing on a first date—it's not recommended.

Lessons Learned

Lack of money or resources need not stop you from succeeding with your projects. Whether you write grants, raise funds from individuals, or do both, you'll need to be organized, resourceful, and creative. And you'll be far more likely to succeed if you enlist others to help. Brainstorm for fund-raising ideas with the people in your network inner circle. Host a brain-storming party—make it fun!

▼

Career Forward

By writing down your responses to the following prompts, you can prepare to successfully raise funds for your project.

1. What project needing funding do you most want to work on? If you have multiple projects, prioritize. Choose the one that makes the most sense to tackle now, at this point in your career. If you're stuck on which project to commit to, make an appointment with a mentor or advisor and talk it over to clarify your goals and priorities.
2. Map your project—write out your answers to the mapping questions at the start of this chapter.
3. Research grant programs appropriate for your project. Use online resources or those at a nearby public or university library. Get expert help from a profes-sional librarian.
4. Make a list of your supporters, the inner circle of your network. Where would you place these people on the development continuum chart shown earlier in this chapter?
5. Of the people on your list, choose the person you'd feel most comfortable asking for advice about your project. Write out a sample "script," an outline detailing how you would describe your project to this person in a face-to-face meeting. Then call and schedule your meeting, and go for it!

▲

13

Getting It Together:
Your Career, Your Life

▼

In this chapter:
  Portfolio Careers
  Transferable Skills: What Musicians Have to Offer
  The Day Job Dilemma: Five Key Considerations
  Teaching Opportunities
  Arts Administration Opportunities and Music Industry Jobs
  Long-Distance Job Search

▲

The previous chapters have focused exclusively on the specifics of moving ahead with your musical goals and projects. But these goals and projects do not exist in a vacuum. It's essential to consider these goals in the context of your total life experience. This includes your social and family life, health, finances, as well as your living situation. The focus of this chapter is on that bigger picture, putting together the total package.

Developing a career in music takes time. As you develop your career, you still need to put food on the table, pay rent, and take care of yourself, body and soul. How do musicians pull it all together? The majority of professional musicians do not make their livings solely from performing. Unless you win a full-time position with a top orchestra or chorus of a top-tier opera company, your performance work—especially as an emerging artist—will most likely be part-time. The good news is that musicians are multi-talented and that there are many ways to use your talents to do good in the world.

Portfolio Careers ◆

Almost all musicians have what can be described as "portfolio" careers, meaning that their professional work is made up of multiple strands of jobs and projects. There's an amazing variety in the ways musicians combine freelance work with teaching, entrepreneurial projects, and various day jobs. This diverse work package can tap into a musician's full range of talents and skills to make for a satisfying life.

How do musicians create niches for themselves in the professional world? How do they end up with satisfying careers? The answer is typically through experimenting. Musicians try out various music-related and non-music projects and part-time jobs. Through trial and error, luck and calculated risks, they explore and test themselves in the professional world. The more exploring they do, the more options they uncover.

Career Profile

Vic Firth, the legendary Boston Symphony Orchestra timpanist, retired in 2003 after fifty years with the orchestra. Conductor Seiji Ozawa said Vic was one of the two musicians in the BSO from whom he'd learned the most. Five decades with the same employer sounds like a very traditional career, but this same Vic Firth has had a "side" occupation. His drumstick manufacturing business (http://www.vicfirth.com) has evolved into the leading percussion equipment company in the world.

Vic started making drumsticks because he was dissatisfied with the available equipment. He began by modifying drumsticks, then experimented in making his own, fine-tuning the process to make superior sticks, perfectly balanced and precision matched in pairs. His products are now used and endorsed by classical, jazz, and rock musicians, and his company employs more than 140 people. With its manufacturing facilities in Newport, Maine, the company produces 85,000–90,000 drumsticks per day. As reported on the CBS Sunday Morning program, Mar. 29, 2009, "Vic Firth offers four hundred different models of drumsticks, all made from Appalachian hickory from Tennessee, dried in Firth's own kilns, shaped and molded and measured to his own strict specifications, then computer-matched by weight and pitch, and shipped all over the world."

As for the secret of his success, "The key word for me is persistence," he said. "Whatever you set out to do, you have to have a magnum passion for it, and you've got to work beyond what you ever dreamed you're gonna work to succeed at the level that you want to succeed at." What else? Vic adds, "Persistence, persistence, persistence!"[1]

Project-Based Career Advancement

As detailed in earlier chapters, music career exploration typically takes the form of projects, from various recording projects to forming or joining different ensembles, launching concert series or festivals, commissioning works, or starting a private teaching studio. Musicians' careers are often a series of such projects, one leading to the next, through collaborations and freelance work. These projects may last days or years, overlap or conflict, but they are sustained by the interest and enthusiasm of the musician. From month to month it can seem—to both the musician and others—that there's no big plan or career direction with these projects. It's usually only in hindsight that a musician can look at a series of projects and trace a path and a progression. The connecting threads of interests and skills that run from one project to the next are a kind of through line, a sustaining passion. The accumulation of talent, skills, experience, and contacts help musicians advance in their projects and create satisfying portfolio careers.

▼
Building a Portfolio Career

Stephen Beaudoin is a multi-talented and entrepreneurial young tenor. While completing his bachelor's degree, he served as an administrative intern for the Gay Men's Chorus of Boston, working on grant writing and fund-raising projects—a real education for an undergraduate! Stephen then used the skills he developed as an intern to find funding for his own project. He collaborated with a colleague, composer Martin Near, to write an opera dealing with the AIDS epidemic. Stephen applied for a grant from the American Composers Forum and was able to produce the opera at both Roxbury Community College and at the Boston Center for the Arts.

After graduating, Stephen juggled several part-time jobs. He performed with a professional choir, wrote classical music articles and reviews for two small Boston-area newspapers, and worked both at Starbucks (good benefits, flexible schedule) and at the American Composers Forum. He then went on to a full-time day job doing development work at a local cultural alliance. This allowed him to hone his skills in grant writing, event planning, donor development, and project presentation. The skills he has developed in his day jobs have helped him with the performing side of his career.

Stephen also performed regularly in the area with a classical guitarist, handling the duo's booking and promotion. The duo started a concert series at a local historic mansion. How'd they do this? They made an appointment to visit the director of the mansion. They presented their concept for starting a series, offering their proposed programs and their promo kit. The director loved the idea, gave them an extremely reasonable rental fee for use of the hall, and promised to help with the publicity.

Stephen found ways to knit together his varied interests and skills to make a busy and satisfying career path. Staying flexible and being open to possibilities brought him new opportunities.
▲

Making It Work

If you're building your repertoire, launching a new ensemble, and/or preparing for auditions and competitions, then most likely you will need to consider ways to earn money while you pursue these projects. Many musicians struggle with trying to balance the need to make a living with the need to pursue their passion. There is no easy way around it. The process of developing your professional career and earning income as a musician takes time. So most musicians, at some point in their careers, work "day jobs." As you network, ask musicians what kinds of work they have done outside of performing and composing—you'll be amazed. Ask them what work they liked or didn't and why. Ask what jobs fit well with their musical pursuits, and ask what they might recommend you explore.

Transferable Skills: What Musicians Have to Offer ◆

Music training builds a wide range of skills and abilities that have practical applications in many professional disciplines. In other words, musicians have *transferable* skills. Below is a list of the assets that trained musicians typically possess. This is what comes with music training, what a music education provides:

Skills

Communication	Listening
Analytical	Creative problem solving
Arranging/synthesizing	Teamwork/collaboration
Leadership	Interpersonal
Organizational	Presentation
Critical thinking	

Abilities

Analyze/interpret ideas and emotions	Work well under pressure
Assess/synthesize large amounts of data	Attend to details
Concentrate/work intensely for long periods	Develop ideas
Conceptualize/work with abstract concepts	Relate to people of varying backgrounds

▼
_____

Hornist Debbie Engel has played with the Delaware Symphony for more than twenty-three years. Her career "package" has also included working as both the orchestra's and opera company's librarian and director of education, overseeing an extensive community outreach program. She's had all this plus three (now teenage) children! How did she manage? Ms. Engel pointed out four key factors: her supportive family, extreme organization, her faith, and her positive attitude.

▲

The Day Job Dilemma: Five Key Considerations ◆

In looking for the right fit for your work/life balance, there are some important questions to consider:

1. *Do you want to work at a day job within the arts or beyond?* Some musicians want to have all of their working hours connected to the arts, to be around others who think and talk as they do. These musicians look for day jobs with various arts organizations, within the recording industry, or with music retailers, publishers, or music schools. For networking and feeling connected, this route can be a plus.

Other musicians prefer non-arts-related day jobs that give them some distance from music. They want to explore other skills and interests, or they find that with a non-music day job, they can conserve their creative energies to be used on their own time. There's no right answer here. Do what's right for you.

2. *What skills, experience, and interests do you have?* What skills would you like to develop? If you're going to spend a significant amount of time working a day job, it probably ought to be doing something you find interesting, satisfying, or meaningful. What are you curious about? What are your hobbies? For clues, think about courses you have found interesting, organizations you belong to, the kinds of books you read, and the type of news stories you follow. Musicians find meaningful and satisfying day jobs in all types of settings, including religious institutions, political campaigns, and grassroots community organizations. Some musicians choose day jobs in which they can gain specific skills useful to their music careers, such as positions in fund-raising, marketing, or public relations. What sort of work have you already done and found interesting? Summer and part-time school jobs can often lead to other opportunities.

Of course, some musicians prefer to find work that's stable and pays enough, but that also provides enough downtime on the job to allow for studying scores, or memorizing or writing new work. This might be a security position or receptionist work. Again, there's no right answer here, but it's important to weigh what you get out of any job (money, benefits, and more) against whether the job leaves you with time and emotional energy to work on your music.

3. *What kind of schedule, hours, and flexibility do you want?* Do you need certain nights free for rehearsals and performances? Do you need early mornings for practicing? Many musicians seek work with maximum flexibility, and this leads some to start their own services and side businesses. These can range from dog walking to recording, editing, massage therapy, catering, day care, website design, or tutoring. Other musicians find jobs that dovetail their music schedules. And depending on the work involved, a company or organization may be able to offer flextime as a benefit. But whatever the situation, in order to balance a day job with a music career, excellent time management skills are required (see chapter 10).

4. *What about health insurance?* The main reason most American freelance musicians take day jobs is for the health insurance. Some part-time jobs offer prorated benefits, which can turn a not-so-hot salary into a very good deal. If your spouse or partner can cover you on her or his health plan, that's great. If not, you need to get your own coverage. Without it, even a minor hospital visit or unexpected health issue can mean a debt of tens of thousands of dollars. Everyone needs ongoing preventive health care, but especially musicians, whose bodies need to be working well in order to perform at their best.

Freelance musicians often try to make do without health insurance, relying on "free care" programs at local hospitals and clinics. But many musicians are unaware that by law hospitals have to provide the uninsured only the most basic emergency care, not ongoing rehabilitation. This means that without insurance, the hospital will stabilize you, treat you until you are out of immediate danger, but that's it, even if you have a serious, life-threatening illness.

For freelance musicians, there are various associations that offer members preferred group rate health insurance. Some of the music service organizations that offer health insurance rates are Chamber Music America (http://www.chamber-music.org), ASCAP (http://www.ascap.com), Early Music America (http://www.earlymusic.org), and the Music Teachers National Association (http://www.mtna.org). For additional ideas, check the Artists' Health Insurance Resource Center (http://www.actorsfund.org/ahirc), the Freelancer's Union (http://www.freelancersunion.org), and eHealthInsurance (http://www.ehealthinsurance.com).

5. *What about the money?* How much income do you actually need each month? To make good choices about work, you need to know how much you

actually spend each month (not how much you *think* you spend). If you haven't written out your detailed monthly expenses, it's not too late (see chapter 10). Track your spending for at least three months to calculate a reliable monthly average.

Thinking through the questions above should help you explore and consider your work options. Consider your priorities to find a day job that works for you. The rest of this chapter details the two most popular categories of musicians' day jobs—teaching and arts administration / music industry work.

▼ ────────────────────────────────────

Tips on Shopping for Health Insurance

Jack Garrity is an insurance broker who specializes in working with musicians and other independent contractors. The musicians' union in Boston regularly refers their members to Jack, and here's what he recommends for people who're looking for insurance on their own:

> Shopping (and that's the key word—*shopping*) for health insurance isn't brain surgery but does require some patience and organization. Listed below you'll find what I (try to) do with everyone who contacts me.
>
> Do your homework. Get prices from three companies (if possible). You might start with major national insurers—Aetna, Cigna, and United. Or get quotes through any of the musicians' service organizations or associations. Compare the following nine items:

1. Primary Care Physician (PCP) Visits—how much per visit? What about for a specialist? Referrals needed?
2. Emergency Room (ER)—how much per admission?
3. Prescriptions (Rx)—co-pay for generics/name brands/rare name brands?
4. Outpatient Surgery (OPS)—covered 100%? Or must a deductible be paid first?
5. Hospitalization—see OPS.
6. Maximum Payout—is there a limit or cap per accident or policy? Massachusetts HMOs, for example, are unlimited.
7. Coverage Area—worldwide for emergencies and crisis care? What happens if you are injured outside of your resident state?
8. Network—are the doctors and hospitals offered in the network acceptable to you?
9. Monthly premium—and of course, and how long is the rate fixed for?

> See if you can reduce the monthly premium by dropping the Rx, if not needed, and taking a deductible and co-pay on the OPS/hospitalization coverages.

Please note that health insurance is regulated on a state-by-state basis, and so the procedures, coverage, prices, and applications can vary widely. In Massachusetts, being a small business gets you "business/commercial/ group" rates that are much better than non-business rates. Ask if this is true in your state, too.

Jack Garrity, Diamond Benefits

1–888–635–4402 (Mass. only)

1–781–477–9048 (outside Mass.)

Teaching Opportunities ◆

For many musicians, teaching is a satisfying and rewarding complement to their performing or composition work. Musicians often report that teaching helps make them better performers. At its best, teaching is challenging and creative.

Annie Fullard, violinist of the Cavani Quartet, relates how her group balances performing and teaching. She describes Cavani as "equally committed to performing and teaching chamber music, as we feel one directly enhances and influences the other." In an article in *American String Teacher* (November 1998), Fullard says, "Teaching is one of the world's oldest art forms. The more you teach the more you learn—it's a very simple thing."

There is a range of possible teaching opportunities available. These are private studios, public and private schools, community music schools, colleges, conservatories, plus teaching artist work in a variety of settings. Some musicians find they work particularly well with certain age groups or in teaching master classes, group lessons, or in the classroom. Part of exploring to find your niche may involve sampling a variety of teaching experiences. Below are suggestions for either starting or expanding your teaching options.

Private Studio Teaching: Attracting Students through Referrals

The most efficient way to recruit students is through referrals. These can come from local schools' band, orchestra, or choral directors, and from other teachers—and especially from your satisfied students and their parents. If you don't already have such contacts and you're interested in teaching children, research the schools in your area. Find the ones with strong music programs. Ask your colleagues, and call the schools: get the names and telephone numbers of the music directors. Then call the directors and introduce yourself with something like this:

Hello, my name is Janet Smith. I'm a local flutist and I perform regularly with the ABC Chamber Orchestra and have a master's degree from XYZ School of Music. I'm looking to add more private students to my teaching studio. I've heard very good things about your program from parents in the neighborhood. I was hoping to set up a time to come in and meet you. It would be great to hear your students in rehearsal. I'd be happy to offer a sectional or coach an ensemble and for you to get to know my teaching a bit, too!

School music directors are far more likely to refer students to you if they have actually met you, observed your teaching, and like what they see. Beyond referrals, there are other smart ways to attract students. Mimi Butler is the author of a series of recommended books, including *The Complete Guide to Running a Private Music Studio* and *The Complete Guide to Making More Money in the Private Music Studio* (see http://www.privatemusicstudio.com). She advises carrying and using business cards, and sending letters each May to local school music teachers about your summer studio. It's also wise to get involved in local music camps and youth music ensembles, to join professional music organizations, and to advertise strategically. See the companion website http://www.oup.com/us/beyondtalent for more resources.

Home Studio or Not?

If you plan to teach out of your home or apartment, consider whether your teaching space is appropriately comfortable and professional. Is your place in a safe neighborhood, and is parking or public transportation an issue? If you do use a portion of your home strictly for rehearsing and teaching, note that you can claim a portion of your rent and related costs as a deductible business expense. Consult a musicians' tax specialist to make sure you take all the appropriate deductions (see chapter 10).

An alternative to teaching out of your home or apartment is to travel to your students' homes. But travel time and scheduling complications usually make this a last-resort option. Instead, there may be a local religious, community, or civic organization open to your using the facilities for a teaching studio. Many public schools organize after-school lesson programs and hire local instructors. Check out your neighborhood, and ask everyone in your network.

A mezzo-soprano with a regular church job, Beatrice H. needed a place to teach but could not afford to rent a studio. She was friendly with the church choir director and asked whether it would be possible to use the church basement rehearsal room two afternoons a week to teach voice. It worked out well. Beatrice bartered for the use of the space, agreeing to handle some the

choir's performance library and scheduling duties. Because of the good relationship she built, Beatrice is now also co-presenting a recital series at the
church and starting a children's choir as well.

Have a Studio Policy

As a trained musician with performance and teaching experience, you are a
professional. If you want to be treated as such, you need to represent your
teaching as a *business*. To avoid frequent cancellations of lessons and late
payment, you need a written studio policy.

Having a studio policy that clearly details a payment schedule and cancellation guidelines will save you many headaches. Private teachers often
use monthly or six-week "semester" systems, with students paying in advance for each new block of lessons. A typical cancellation policy requires
two weeks' notice in order to have a lesson rescheduled. The teacher may
schedule an extra week of make-up lessons every three months or so, with
one makeup lesson offered to each student. When a parent and student come
to meet you initially to discuss private study, that's the time to explain your
studio policy and hand the parent a copy.

How Much Should You Charge?

Find out the going rate for lessons in your area. Ask other musicians and call
local community music schools to find out their rates. You should charge an
amount that's appropriate to the local rates and to your level of experience.
In the Boston area, excellent young musicians with little teaching experience may charge $40 per hour, whereas some members of the Boston Sym-
phony Orchestra charge more than $150 per lesson.

How to Develop and Expand Your Teaching Skills

Most performers learn to teach on the job, with little or no formal training in
pedagogy, music education, or developmental psychology. Typically, performers simply repeat the way *they* were taught. But not all of your students will be
like you were as a youngster. A narrow repertoire of teaching methods limits
your ability to meet the needs of your students. You can do better! It's important to develop a variety of tools and strategies for teaching students with various learning styles. Below are four ways to expand your skills.

1. *Observe.* Find the most experienced, creative, and successful teachers
in your area. Call to introduce yourself, and explain that you're a new teacher
hoping to develop your skills by observing excellent teaching in action. Ask
if you can observe them teach for an afternoon. People are generally flattered and willing to help. It's good to observe experienced educators working with a range of ages and abilities, and to observe teaching in a variety of
situations—in lessons, coachings, and master classes.

Look to see what a teacher focuses on with each student and how this instructor tailors her remarks to each student's personality and stage of development. Most likely, the educators you observe will spend some time with you afterward, answering your questions and discussing their approaches. And ask for recommendations of teaching books and videos.

2. *Find a mentor.* If you hit it off with any of the teachers you observe, you may be on your way to having a longer-term connection—to having a mentor. If you're learning a lot, ask to continue. Later on, you might ask this person to observe *you* teaching a few of your own students, to get feedback and coaching. Mentors may refer students to you when their own schedules are full, or they may ask you to do some substitute teaching. Eventually, a mentor may take you on as her or his teaching assistant. This can lead to added experience on your résumé as well as letters of recommendation, helpful when you apply for teaching jobs.

3. *Attend master classes.* Take every opportunity to attend master classes so that you can observe a diversity of teaching methods and approaches. Is there a conference for your instrument or specialty area? Organizations such as the National Flute Association (http://www.nfaonline.org), the International Trombone Association (http://www.ita-web.org), and the annual American String Teachers Association conference (http://www. astaweb.com) offer master classes with world-class artist teachers. Observing great teaching is an opportunity to see how master teachers approach an array of student abilities, issues, and repertoire. When observing someone else's master class, ask yourself, what would *you* focus on with this student? What would you say? And what would you ask the student to do?

4. *Take a class.* Effective music teachers are constantly improving their skills and experimenting with new approaches. Don't get into a routine or a rut. If you stay curious about teaching, you'll continually seek out new approaches and methods, and your students will benefit.

Find out whether there are pedagogy courses for music educators in your area. Some music schools offer specialized summer courses on methodologies such as Kodaly, Orff, or Dalcroze Eurhythmics. Or take a course in developmental psychology or a general education class to find out more about how to deal with students at different ages.

▼
Music Teacher Resources

American Choral Director's Association, http://www.acda.org
American String Teachers Association, http://www.astaweb.com
College Music Society, http://www.music.org

Kennedy Center's Arts Edge, http://www.artsedge.kennedy-center.org
Music Educators National Conference, http://www.menc.org
Music Teachers National Association, http://www.mtna.org
National Association of Teachers of Singing, http://www.nats.org
National Conference on Keyboard Pedagogy, http://www.francesclarkcenter
.org
National Guild for Community Arts Education, http://www.nationalguild
.org
Suzuki Association of the Americas, Inc., http://www.suzukiassociation.org

▲

Types of Teaching Positions

Outside of setting up your own private studio, there are teaching opportunities at various types of institutions, from community music schools to private and public schools, and colleges and universities.

Community Music Schools

These institutions offer after-school, weekend, and evening music instruction to children and adults. Community music schools hire teachers to give private lessons, coach ensembles, and teach theory, ear training, composition, and other classes. Most instructors are hired part-time and paid hourly rates with no benefits. The majority of such teachers are paid $25–$40 per hour. Parents pay tuition by the semester, and the school takes a portion of these tuition fees to cover overhead costs for the facility, advertising, and program management. The advantage to teaching at these schools is that the organization handles all the scheduling and billing, and provides the facilities. You can find listings of these schools at the National Guild for Community Arts Education see http://www.nationalguild.org.

In major metropolitan areas where teacher supply is great, community music schools often have their pick of qualified candidates, hiring only experienced teachers with proven track records. These schools often do not advertise openings, so musicians apply directly, sending a cover letter of introduction and résumé. Having good letters of recommendation from respected teachers can be a big help in getting hired.

Public Schools

Public K–12 schools hire music teachers to direct band, orchestra, and chorus, and to teach group lessons and general music classes. Teaching in the public schools demands abilities beyond musicianship skills. Public school teachers need to have effective teaching methods, an understanding of child development stages and learning styles, and classroom management skills. In addition, the work demands the ability to create and implement lesson plans that meet the school's and the state's education requirements. These are all skills that musicians can develop through coursework, including evening and summer workshops.

Public music school teachers can earn fairly good salaries, with excellent benefits and summers off. Starting salaries in the more affluent states are in the low $30,000s, and salary raises can be substantial with experience and additional training. Maximum salaries in some states can go to over $70,000. Because of the recent shortage of music teachers (especially in strings), public schools hold substantial opportunities for musicians.

The experience of teaching in public schools can vary widely, depending on the size of the class, grade level, and the school's funding, facilities, and administration. To explore the possibility of teaching in the public schools, it's best to observe at least five music teachers working with a variety of grade levels in different schools. Ask people in your network for contacts. Observe classes and rehearsals and talk with the teachers to get a sense of what these jobs are actually like.

To be hired by a public school, you must have teacher certification, a license to teach in a particular state. Because of the shortage of teachers, many states have streamlined the certification process to make it easier for people to enter the profession. To find out the current specifics for certification in your locale, contact your state's department of education. For job listings, check the Music Educators National Conference, http://www.menc.org, and the sites for your state department of education, any specific school districts you may be targeting, as well as the best local online job listing service.

Private Secondary Schools

Unlike K–12 public schools, which are funded by tax dollars, at *private* schools, parents pay tuition fees. Private schools include college preparatory or *prep* schools, parochial, and other specialized schools. They are generally for grades 9–12, though there are K–8 programs as well. Some prep schools offer both *day* and *boarding* options. Boarding students live in dorms on campus, whereas day students commute from home.

Private secondary schools hire musicians to teach lessons, coach and conduct ensembles, and sometimes to teach music appreciation, theory, and music history classes as well. Most private school music teachers work part-time and are paid at an hourly lesson rate, generally $30–$60 per hour. Classroom instructors are paid on a different scale, on a per-course and semester basis. The full-time positions typically include non-music assignments as well. At boarding schools, some faculty may live on campus as resident counselors in exchange for free room and board in addition to their teaching salary. There are teacher placement companies such as Carney, Sandoe and Associates (http://www.carneysandoe.com) that help private school job seekers and employers connect. See also The Education Group and the National Association of Independent Schools. Note that private secondary schools do *not* require teachers to have state certification, the way public schools do.

College-Level Teaching

Teaching positions in higher education can also be extremely varied. Musicians teach at community colleges, at liberal arts schools and universities where music is an elective, as well as at colleges and conservatories where students earn degrees in music. Colleges hire musicians to teach private lessons, to coach or conduct ensembles, and to teach courses in music appreciation, theory, history, pedagogy, and more.

These teaching positions can range from full-time, tenure-track positions (with full benefits and lifetime job security), to adjunct or part-time teaching for low pay and no benefits. Most full-time college music teaching positions involve more than private lessons. Typically, a faculty load will include ensemble coaching, master classes, and, depending on the number of studio lessons assigned, teaching one or more classroom course.

Where to Find Listings for College-Level Teaching

Bridge: Worldwide Music Connection, the New England Conservatory's online database of over 2,800 music listings of teaching, performance, and arts administration openings, plus grants, audition, and competition info. Available by subscription: http://www.necmusic.edu/bridge

Chronicle of Higher Education, http://www.chronicle.com/jobs

College Music Society's music vacancy listings, http://www.music.org

Higher Ed Jobs, http://www.higheredjobs.com

Generally, the job openings for full-time positions at universities list "doctorate required" or "doctorate preferred." Search committees may consider candidates without the doctorate if they have extensive and successful college-level teaching experience and/or extensive professional performance experience. At conservatories and highly competitive schools of music, search committees seek artist-teachers with significant national or international reputations and the ability to recruit advanced students.

Tenure-track jobs at universities are full-time positions with multi-year, renewable contracts leading to tenure—guaranteed permanent employment. Candidates in these positions are typically hired as assistant professors, and if successful, they may, over a number of years, advance in salary and status to the position of associate professor, and full professor, and may be granted tenure as well. Starting full-time salaries (depending on the location and budget of the school) are often in the $40,000–$70,000 range, although the better funded schools sometimes compete to hire "star" faculty at much higher salaries.

College-level music teaching positions are highly competitive, with many more qualified and experienced candidates than there are openings. A posting for a desirable job can attract 100–200 applicants. The less competitive opportunities are the part-time "adjunct" and "lecturer" positions, which are often not well-paid. These positions may be filled by people without doctorates. Working part-time at a college or university is an excellent opportunity to gain valuable experience and therefore become more marketable for full-time positions elsewhere. Part-time university teaching work can also serve well to complement a portfolio career.

Violist Kenneth Martinson is an assistant professor of music at the University of Florida. Earlier in his career, as a member of the Rackham Quartet, he took part in a Chamber Music America rural residency program—living and teaching in King City, California. In "Flying Together," a February 2002 article he wrote for Chamber Music America's *CMA Matters*, Martinson describes the effect of his early teaching experience on his subsequent career:

> Teaching 64 string instrument beginners certainly proved to be an immensely valuable experience for me. That year of teaching provided me with enough patience to deal with any student, at any level, for the rest of my life! The experience also forced me to re-evaluate every aspect of my technique from scratch . . . because of my residency experience, I have a rare combination to offer my students: highly developed performing skills and the knowledge I've gained in music education.

Teaching Résumés

An effective résumé can get you in the door for an interview. It's typical and recommended for musicians to have several versions of their résumé—one each for performance, teaching, and arts administration, or other "day" jobs. Each one should be geared specifically for that type of work.

The challenge in writing any résumé is to tailor it to the *employer's needs*. Your résumé should highlight the qualifications, skills, and experiences *relevant to the particular job to which you are applying*. Put yourself in the employer's shoes. Think about what he or she would want to know about you as a candidate. Use the job description to tailor a version of your résumé to the particular job.

Statistics show that employers typically spend less than ten seconds reading a résumé. So the design and format is important. It should be one page only. Longer teaching résumés and CV's are used only for college-level teaching.

Details

In applying for teaching jobs, the most important portion is "Teaching Experience." So it's a good idea to include more details here than in other areas. In listing your teaching experience, include a bulleted list underneath each job listing to detail your teaching accomplishments and convey what is distinctive about your teaching. Specify the age range and level of your students; describe any of their accomplishments, such as winning competitions, attending festivals, or winning scholarships to music schools; list the range of repertoire you teach; and describe what you emphasize in your teaching. Without these details, an employer has no way to distinguish your teaching from the other applicants. Consider including a "Professional Profile" or "Skills Summary" at the top. This works as a brief commercial for the package you have to offer the employer.

After teaching experience, your performance experience is the next most important thing an employer will want to know about. In one page, you may be able to list only selected credits—make sure you emphasize the range of your performance experience and impressive venues where you've performed. See the example on the next page.

Note that in some countries, it's common to list age, marital status, and photos on résumés, but the United States is generally litigious, and employers must be careful about any potential appearance of discrimination, so it's best to leave these items off your performance, teaching, and arts administration résumés. The exception is for classical singers, who use photos on their performance résumés (to aid in casting for roles), and sometimes also include these for teaching résumés as well.

Arts Administration Opportunities and Music Industry Jobs ◆

Beyond teaching, many musicians gravitate toward arts administration and music industry jobs. The term *arts administration* covers a wide range of administrative, management, and leadership roles with arts organizations. Most often the term is used in conjunction with nonprofit arts organizations such

John Doe, trombonist/teacher

1 Anonymous St. #2 ❖ Brighton, MA 02135 ❖ cell (617) 555-1212 ❖ johndoe@yahoo.com ❖ www.johndoe.com

Profile

Teaching experience includes private lessons, beginners to intermediate, ages 10-37; lessons emphasize ear training, applied music theory, & development of independent & critical thinking skills. Has coached mixed chamber ensembles (strings & brass), conducted choir, & arranged works for choir & instrumental chamber groups. Performance experience includes diverse musical styles from classical to funk & soul.

Teaching Experience

Private Trombone Studio, Salt Lake City, UT, & Boston, MA, 2006 present
- Beginners to intermediate, ages 10 to 37
- Lessons incorporate applied theory, ear training, and improvisation
- Emphasis on students' development of critical thinking skills by analyzing their own playing
- Variety of styles of music including big band, concert band, solos, & etudes

Choir Director, Church of Jesus Christ of Latter Day Saints, Cambridge, MA, 2010
- Conduct amateur, volunteer choir, SATB, 15 voices
- Prepare for monthly performances; select & arrange music
- Emphasis on balance, blend, & diction

New England Conservatory Summer Festival Youth Orchestra, Coach, Boston, MA, 2008
- Coach brass section and chamber group daily (repertoire included Mozart's *Musical Joke*)
- Emphasis on group interaction, communication, & intonation

New England Conservatory of Music, Teaching Assistant, Music History Dept., Boston, MA, 2007-08
- Presented selected lectures on music of Stravinsky and neo-classicism to undergraduate classes
- Tutored students in Romantic & 20th century music in preparation for exams
- Students who attended review sessions increased test scores by 10-25%

University of Utah Marching Band, Field Assistant, Salt Lake City, UT, 2005-06
- Coached trombone & low brass sectionals twice weekly

Selected Performance Experience

Orchestral	*Concerto Performances*
Utah Symphony Orchestra	Philharmonia, University of Utah
Rhode Island Philharmonic	Wind Symphony, University of Utah
New Bedford Symphony Orchestra	
Chamber Music Performances	*Non-classical Performances, Salt Lake City area*
Casals Festival, Puerto Rico	The Zephyr Club (Ska, Salsa)
Boston Public Library	Utah Arts Festival (Ska)
Boston University	Green Street (Funk, Soul, Ska)
Longy School of Music	Utah State University (Jazz)

Education

Longy School of Music, Performance Diploma, Trombone, Cambridge, MA, anticipated 2010
New England Conservatory, Master of Music, Trombone Performance, Boston, MA, 2008
University of Utah, Bachelor of Music, Trombone Performance, Salt Lake City, UT, 2006

Principal Teachers	Conductors	Chamber Music Coaches
Norman Bolter	Gunther Schuller	Charles Schlueter
Russell McKinney	Stanislaw Skrowaczewski	Donald Palma
Larry Zalkind	Keith Lockhart	Anthony Plog

as music schools, orchestras, opera companies, festivals, and foundations. The term *music industry* typically refers to the for-profit sector, including the recording industry, music publishing, technology, and retail markets.

Arts administrators and music industry professionals are the people who make things happen. They run concert series, performing arts organizations, music software companies, and online music businesses. They include the people who handle publicity, marketing, fund-raising, and programming. Many musicians work these part- or full-time jobs because they want to contribute to a larger effort—beyond their work as individual performers—to help the arts grow in their communities. Many musicians value the opportunity to use the full range of their skills and abilities in service of a larger cause.

Types of Organizations with Music Industry and Arts Administration Jobs

- Performing organizations (symphony orchestras, opera companies, choruses)
- Presenting organizations (concert series, jazz festivals, performance venues)
- Arts service organizations (such as ASCAP, BMI, American Music Center, Chamber Music America, Opera America)
- Foundations (state and regional arts councils, private and corporate foundations)
- Arts education institutions (community music schools, conservatories, college music departments)
- Arts research and consulting organizations (groups that work on audience development, marketing, assessment, and management issues for arts organizations)
- Music publishing companies (such as Belwin Mills, Schirmer, Hal Leonard, and Carl Fischer)
- Radio/TV (includes programming and research work)
- Recording industry (major and indie labels)
- Music technology (including music software development, online music services and distribution systems)
- Music retail (instruments, accessories, scores)
- Music instrument design, building, and repair
- Artist management firms
- Media relations companies

Typical entry-level positions are administrative assistant jobs. Employers seeking to hire for such positions generally look for candidates with communication, teamwork, computer, and organizational skills, the ability to multitask, and a knowledge of music and the arts. Entry-level, full-time position salaries can start (depending on the region) in the mid to high $20,000s. As people develop skills and experience, better pay is available. At the high end, top executives at leading symphony orchestras, record labels, and major service organizations routinely earn six figure incomes.

To explore arts administration opportunities, check for job postings on the websites of any of the arts organizations in your area. Your state arts agency may provide lists and contacts for these organizations. You can then arrange for informational interviews (described in chapter 2) with staff members at these organizations.

Where to Find Job Listings

ArtJob, http://www.artjob.org

Arts Presenters, http://www.artpresenters.org

Bridge: Worldwide Music Connection, http://www.newenglandconservatory .edu/bridge

League of American Orchestras, http://www.americanorchestras.org

New York Foundation for the Arts: http://www.NYFA.org

Also, check your state arts agency's website and your alma mater; many music schools offer job listing publications/online listings

Whether you're exploring a day job to pay the rent or to gain specific skills, you need to know your priorities, explore your options, and keep an open mind. Talk to lots of people, and gather ideas. Keep in mind that we cannot always see how the work we do today will benefit us in the future.

What Can Come from a Day Job?

Just out of college, French hornist Jean Rife took a clerical position in the textiles department at the Smithsonian in Washington, D.C. The important thing about that job was that it was down the hall from the musical instrument collection. Jean became friends with the department members, played their horns, and when they started an early music ensemble, she was right there. Thus began a career-long interest in early music and in playing the natural horn.

Jean moved to Boston, taught part-time at the Weston Public Schools, and took a part-time job at the MIT music library. There, she became friends with violist Marcus Thompson, who would stop by to talk. During one of their discussions, he mentioned that the woodwind chamber music coach he had hired couldn't come that semester after all. Jean was there to say, "I'll do it!" Marcus hired her, and she's taught at MIT ever since. These days, Jean's career package includes freelancing and teaching chamber music and horn part-time at MIT, New England Conservatory, and at the Longy School of Music.

What makes Jean's career especially interesting is that she is also a yoga instructor and has combined yoga practice with her horn teaching and coaching. Jean first found that yoga was incredibly helpful in her own playing and then as she incorporated it in her teaching, found it was also a great learning tool for other musicians.

Musicians are often multi-talented, but Jean has found a productive and creative way to connect her wide-ranging interests and skills.

▲

Opportunities

This list below includes job titles from a range of music-related jobs. Some of these jobs require additional specialized training, whereas others are appropriate for musicians who get on-the-job training. There's a world of opportunities if you think broadly about how to use your music training and knowledge.

Architectural music consultant	Festival manager
Music software programmer	Concert series presenter
Music retail store manager/owner	Instrument builder/designer
Royalties broadcast monitor	Instrument repair specialist
Music licensing specialist	Piano tuner-technician
Copywriter/clearance administrator	Media relations coordinator
Film music editor	Fund-raiser
Lyricist	Music publicist
Record producer	Orchestra/opera company manager
Recording engineer	Ticket services director
Copyist	Director of orchestral education
Music publisher	Music librarian
Tour coordinator/road manager	Concert hall manager
Radio show host	Music therapist
Artist manager	Music journalist/critic
Booking agent	Arts researcher

Below is a sample arts administration job description and following it a cover letter and résumé used in applying for the position. Note how the cover letter and résumé specifically address the *employer's* needs as stated in the job description.

ABC College of Music

1 Fictitious Ave.
New York, NY 10020

Administrative Assistant wanted for the Recording and Video Conferencing Department at ABC College of Music.

9-5 M-F plus occasional evening and weekend hours as needed

Job Description
Assist in daily running of busy office;
Interact with students, faculty, staff;
Schedule of special events and equipment use;
Handle questions/customer service;
Schedule repairs and equipment updates

Duties
Front office work, reception duties, handle correspondence, scheduling of equipment, troubleshooting

Qualifications
Knowledge of classical and jazz; Bachelor of Music preferred; customer service and office administrative experience; computer skills and technical abilities; organization and communication skills.

Send materials to:
George Pinkerton, Director
Human Resources
ABC College of Music
1 Fictitious Avenue
New York, NY 10020

Jane Doe

cell (617) 555-1212 jdoe@email.com
Temporary (good until May 30, 2010): 33 Gainsborough St. #714, Boston, MA 02115
Permanent: 1 Main St., Irvington NJ 07111 (973) 555-1212

May 7, 2010

George Pinkerton, Director
Human Resources
ABC College of Music
1 Fictitious Avenue
New York, NY 10027

Dear Mr. Pinkerton:

      I read with interest about the Administrative Assistant position opening for the Recording and Video Conferencing Dept. at ABC College of Music in the May 3rd Sunday edition of the *New York Times* (found on http://www.monster.com). Enclosed is my résumé in support of my application. I am very enthusiastic about the possibility of working at the ABC College of Music because of its fine reputation and because this position seems to be a good match with my background, interests, and experience.

      My relevant computer skills include MS Word, MS Office Windows, Excel, Clarisworks, and Finale Windows. I am well acquainted with work in music school environments and have held two work-study positions at the New England Conservatory in Boston, where I will receive my bachelor's degree in Jazz Performance later this month.

      Outside of the Conservatory, I work part-time as an Administrative Assistant at the Algonquin Club, an exclusive private social club where I have handled a wide variety of administrative responsibilities. Through this work I have developed excellent customer service, organization, and communication skills, and I learn quickly. I have acquired a broad knowledge of both jazz and classical music through my studies at the Conservatory, and I am interested and motivated to learn more about distance learning, video conferencing, and audio technology.

      Although I now live in Boston, I am planning to move back to the NYC area this summer. I will be traveling back and forth in the coming weeks and would be happy to meet with you to discuss the position. Thank you for considering my résumé. I will call next week to follow up.

Sincerely,

Jane Doe

Jane Doe

Enc. résumé

Jane Doe

cell (617) 555-1212 jdoe@email.com
Temporary (good until May 30, 2010): 33 Gainsborough St. #714, Boston, MA 02115
Permanent: 1 Main St., Irvington NJ 07111 (973) 555-1212

Profile

Office experience with excellent organization, communication, and customer service skills. Computer skills: MS Word, MS Office Windows, Excel, Clarisworks, Finale. Broad knowledge of jazz, classical, popular music. Motivated team player with willingness to learn.

Arts Administration Experience

Bindery Assistant, work-study position, New England Conservatory, Spaulding Library, Boston, MA, 2007-10
- Assisted in the repair of damaged books and scores
- Processed books and scores for shelving
- Organized and sorted catalogued scores and parts for processing

Audience Service Assistant, work-study position, Jordan Hall, New England Conservatory, Boston, MA, 2006-07
- Assisted with ticket sales
- Fielded customer service complaints and concerns

Telemarketer, New Jersey Symphony Orchestra, Newark, NJ, summer 2006
- Sold season ticket subscriptions

Related Administrative Experience

Administrative Assistant, Algonquin Club, Boston, MA, 2007-present
- Revised and updated daily and weekly function schedules
- Compiled weekly staff timecards and monthly inventories on spreadsheets
- Managed busy switchboard and all reception duties
- Handled office billing and communications

Program Assistant, Boys and Girls Club, Boston, MA, summer 2007
- Assisted in supervising 7 high school student counselors
- Taught folksongs
- Supervised 40 six-year-old children for field trips and all program activities

Computer Skills

MS Word, Clarisworks, Finale
MS Office, MS Excel

Education

New England Conservatory of Music, Boston, MA
Bachelor of Music in Jazz Performance, Voice, 2010

Honors/Awards

Scholarship, New England Conservatory 2006-10

References available upon request

Long-Distance Job Search   ◆

If you are considering a move to a new city or region, the key to making an easier transition is researching and establishing contacts in the target area in advance of your move. The site http://www.findyourspot.com provides an online survey to help identify cities that match your needs, interest, and lifestyle preferences. The survey assesses your preferences as to cultural amenities, public transportation, climate, recreational activities, housing costs, and more, to arrive at a list of suggested cities. These are issues to re-search and consider no matter where or why you are moving, because your quality of life matters!

Once you have a target city, you can get lots of preliminary information about your potential new location online. You can use the city's chamber of commerce and its travel/tourism sites, as well as Wikipedia, to find a wealth of information about the community as a whole and its arts offerings. You can find online cost-of-living comparisons and salary surveys and you can always read real estate classifieds to get a sense of housing costs. For relocat-ing abroad, do an online search for the target country's ministry of labor, embassy, and immigration sites.

Based on your research, create an estimated monthly budget of your anticipated expenses. This information will help you make decisions about the type and amount of work to seek in your new community.

To find relevant music organizations and venues, search online for the city's arts calendars. Contact the city and state arts agencies to get a list of music organizations and performance venues. Find the local chapters of relevant national arts organizations, such as the Music Teachers National Association (http://www.mtna.org), Suzuki Association (http://www.suzukiassociation.org), or the American Composers Forum (http://www.composersforum.org).

Beyond the online information, make good use of your network con-tacts. Ask family members, colleagues, and friends for contacts and leads in your target city. Check your school's alumni office for names and e-mails of the alumni living there. You want to find out about freelance opportunities, the local rates for teaching, and the names of conductors and contractors in order to inquire about auditions.

By doing your homework in advance and establishing contacts, you can make the transition to your potential new home much less stressful.

The Big Picture in Focus

The healthiest approach is to look at the whole of your life as a journey. Life is more than a series of achievements and accomplishments. My friend and colleague Derek Mithaug, former director of career development at the

Juilliard School, has a perspective on this. He writes, "You can avoid years of frustration by focusing now on how to create a journey that will allow you to combine all of your talents and interests. People who create their own paths become the directors of their careers and lives; they are in a position to choose the types of paths they wish to travel."

Keep your values and goals front and center. Gather your courage, your persistence, and patience for the journey ahead. You are ready!

▼
Career Forward

1. Write out the types of work you have considered doing to support your music career.
2. What other interests would you like to investigate for possible supplemental work opportunities? (Do you like to cook, garden, mentor kids, repair cars, or help with political campaigns?) Where can you get more information about these options?
3. Make a list of the skills and experience you have now that might lead to supplemental work.
4. Do you know musicians who have "portfolio" careers? Have you talked with them in detail about how they put it all together? Invite people out for lunch so you can learn from hearing their stories. It's fascinating and inspiring to hear musicians talk about how they got started, overcame challenges, and created their own paths.

▲

Postlude:
Five Career
Counseling Secrets
Revealed

With the information from the previous chapters, you have a great advantage over most musicians—you have the tools to build your success. Of course, information isn't all that's needed. As an added boost, here are five professional career counseling "secrets," some of what I've learned over the years, that you can use on your own.

I typically spend a fair amount of time during an advising session listening to and watching the client. This is part of practicing the first career counseling secret:

1. *Look for the light in the eyes.*

In most advising sessions, career counselors encourage clients to talk about their accomplishments and the choices they're considering. The trick comes in watching the clients talk, noticing when their eyes light up, when they are charged with energy and enthusiasm. It's obvious when clients are talking about a career direction or opportunity they really find engaging. The light in their eyes is the clue to their passion.

Although it's not easy to watch for the light in your own eyes, your friends and colleagues can give you valuable feedback. You can also listen for the enthusiasm in your own voice when discussing career issues that capture your imagination—you'll "hear" your eyes light up.

Once a client identifies areas of interest, the next thing is to figure out an action plan. Unfortunately, many people get stuck in the process right here because of all the "stuff" that's in their way—the *should*s, *but*s, and *if only*s. This brings us to the second career counseling secret:

2. *We often create our own obstacles.*

Identify your baggage—the actual and perceived obstacles that are blocking your path. Getting a client to acknowledge or discover what is standing in the way can be difficult. Sometimes I simply ask, "What's preventing you from moving forward?" The answer may be a litany of rationalizations and extraneous issues. The actual obstacle may be depression, or unrealistic expectations, a lack of information about the industry, or the client may be chasing someone else's dream (a spouse's or a parent's). You may need to do some soul-searching to identify your obstacles, but once you can see them clearly, you can devise strategies to get around them or get over them.

After identifying obstacles, it can be relatively easy to figure out the next logical action steps needed, and this leads to the next career counseling secret:

3. *With any goal, the first steps are the most important.*

Making a good start is key. Break down your goal into small practical action steps. To avoid becoming overwhelmed, use short weekly to-do lists, and keep your action steps simple, measurable, and practical. What needs doing next? It's important for your motivation to succeed in your first action steps and feel the resulting sense of accomplishment.

How can you tell whether your action steps are appropriate for your goal? Feedback from people working in the field is helpful. Get connected to get the information you need. Networking and researching will help inform your goals and plans.

Although it's very important to get the best information to make the best decisions, you also need to trust yourself and your intuition, which underlies the fourth secret:

4. *You already have the answers.*

That's right, your mentor or a career counselor is not the one who supplies the answers. It's you. Talking through your ideas and plans with professionals can help. But in the end, you are the person who determines what is best for you. Make sure you're acting in your best interests. Your daily small decisions—about how to spend time, what projects to focus on, and with whom to network—*these* determine your career.

And although career counselors always look for ways to motivate their clients and keep them pushing forward, when push comes to shove, the truth is . . .

5. *People move ahead when they're good and ready, and not a moment before.*

Clients may look and sound like they're ready for action steps, and they may have a great plan, resources, support, and opportunity. It won't matter. If they're not ready emotionally or psychologically, they won't budge. To move forward, you have to be ready and willing—no one can do it for you.

So with these do-it-yourself techniques, do you really need a career counselor? My best advice is to tap all the resources and support available to you. Check out what's low cost or free in your community—the local job resource center, public library, or college career center may all offer great services, including career advising. And armed with these career counseling secrets, you can make better use of whatever resources you do have. It's your future, go out and make it happen!

Notes

Chapter 1

1. http://www.oxingale.com, March 2009.
2. The Orchestra Musician Forum, Virtual Discussion Panel: "Entrepreneurs in Music" (March 24–April 4, 2008), http://www.polyphonic.org.
3. Roger Chaffin and Anthony Lemieux, "General Perspectives on Achieving Musical Excellence," in *Musical Excellence: Strategies and Techniques to Enhance Performance,* ed. Aaron Williamon (London: Oxford University Press, 2004), 20.
4. Malcolm Gladwell, *Outliers: The Story of Success* (New York: Little, Brown and Co., 2008), 50.
5. Ibid., 50.
6. National Association of Schools of Music, *Higher Education Data Service* report (Data Summaries, 2008–2009), chart 1–4.
7. The International Conference of Symphonic and Operatic Musicians, http://www.icsom.org/pdf/orchestrasalaryfacts.pdf
8. National Association of Schools of Music, Ibid., chart 2–11.
9. Statistics from Sarah Lee, arts researcher at the Cultural Policy Center at the University of Chicago, who compiled data using 2005 records from the U.S. Census County Business Patterns and the U.S. Census Non-Employer Statistics (which counts self-employed musicians).
10. http://www.wordlessmusic.org, March 2009.
11. U.S. Census Bureau newsroom press release, June 25, 2007.

Chapter 2

1. Mike Jolkovski, "How Bands Die," http://www.musiciansatlas.com/newsletter/ju107/howbandsdie.asp, March 2009.
2. Ibid.
3. Janice Papolos and Howard Herring, *Can This Marriage Be Saved? Interpersonal and Organizational Guidelines for Ensembles* (Chamber Music America, 1986) 17.

Chapter 3

1. Artist's bio, http://www.joshuaroman.com, March 2009.

Chapter 4

1. "Sex, Drugs and Updating Your Blog," *New York Times,* May 13, 2007, http://www.nytimes.com/2007/05/13/magazine/13audience-t.html.
2. "ArtistShare Taps Web, Fans to Earn Its Musicians Money, Grammy," *Wall Street Journal,* Feb. 7, 2008, http://www.livemint.com/2008/02/07233946/ArtistShare-taps-Web-fans-to.html.
3. Joan Jeffri et al., *Taking Note: A Study of Composers and New Music Activity in the United States* (New York: Research Center for the Arts and Culture Teachers College Columbia University, 2008), 31–32.

Chapter 5

1. "Second Life Finding New Life," *ABS-CBN News,* Mar. 16, 2009, http://www.abs-cbnnews.com/technology/03/16/09/second-life-finding-new-life.

Chapter 6

1. Robert Besen, "The Quest for Management," *CMA Matters,* October 2007
2. Ibid.
3. Ellen Highstein, *Making Music in Looking Glass Land* (New York: Concert Artists Guild, 2003), 160.
4. Bradley Sowash, "Self-Marketing for Artists," http://www.artjob.org/cgi-local/displayPage.pl?page=article_template.html&sid=PUT_SID_HERE&article_number=3.
5. Ibid.

Chapter 7

1. Paul Somers, "Getting Ink," *CMA Matters,* August 2004.
2. Ellen Highstein, *Making Music in Looking Glass Land* (New York: Concert Artists Guild, 2003), 138–139.

Chapter 8

1. David Wallace, *Reaching Out: A Musician's Guide to Interactive Performances* (New York: McGraw-Hill, 2008), 20.
2. Ibid, 17.

Chapter 9

1. Karen Hagberg, *Stage Presence from Head to Toe: A Manual for Musicians* (Oxford: Scarecrow Press, 2003), 2.
2. Ibid., 5.
3. Ibid., 15.

4. David Templeton, "Stressed for Success," *Strings*, October 2003, No. 113, http://www.stringsmagazine.com/article/4/4,82,BodyandMind-1.asp.

5. "Ten Tips on Becoming Fearless," Indiana University, January 3, 2008, http://newsinfo.iu.edu/web/page/print/6937.html.

6. Ibid.

7. "Stressed for Success."

8. "Stressed for Success."

9. Benson-Henry Institute for Mind Body Medicine, "Eliciting the Relaxation Response," Massachusetts General Hospital, http://www.mbmi.org/basics/whatis_rresponse_elicitation.asp.

10. Jane Ginsborg, "Strategies for Memorizing Music," *Musical Excellence: Strategies and Techniques to Enhance Performance*, ed. Aaron Williamon (London: Oxford University Press, 2004), 137.

Chapter 12

1. Adele Slaughter and Jeff Kober, *Art That Pays* (Los Angeles: National Network for Artist Placement, 2004), 70.

Chapter 13

1. *CBS Sunday Morning* television segment, "The Beat Goes On," March 29, 2009, http://www.cbsnews.com/stories/2009/03/29/sunday/main4901084.shtml.

Index

Music Organizations by Abbreviations

ACDA	American Choral Directors Association, 331	
ACF	American Composers Forum, 219, 316, 323, 341	
AEA	Actors' Equity Association (AKA: Equity), 266	
AFM	American Federation of Musicians, 266–67, 270	
AFTRA	American Federation of Television and Radio Artists, 266	
AGMA	American Guild of Musical Artists, 266	
AMC	American Music Center, 132, 316	
APAP	Association of Performing Arts Presenters, 219, 316	
ASCAP	American Society of Composers, Authors, and Publishers, 93, 103, 113, 114, 149, 175, 188, 326, 338	
ASTA	American String Teachers Association, 331	
BMI	Broadcast Music, Inc., 93	
CMA	Chamber Music America, 38, 43, 119, 157, 212, 215, 217, 219, 294, 316, 326, 335, 338	
MENC	Music Educators National Conference, 332, 333	
MTC	Meet the Composer, 219, 316, 317, 318	
NAPAMA	National Association of Performing Arts Managers of America, 156	
NASM	National Association of Schools of Music, 6, 349n8	
NEA	National Endowment for the Arts, 10, 144, 217	
NYFA	New York Foundation for the Arts, 298, 339	
PAS	Percussive Arts Society, 195	
SAG	Screen Actors Guild, 266	
SESAC	Society of European Stage Authors and Composers, 93, 113, 114, 175	

Aaron Copland Fund, 109
Abramson, Liam, 318, 319
accomplishments
    promotional use, 45–49, 86, 111, 181, 183
    success defined as, 2–4, 142–44
accountability, as success factor, 214
acknowledgements, including on CDs, 312
acoustics, during recording, 98–99
activities, time management of, 274–80, 326

administration. *See* arts administration
    opportunities
administrative assistants, 160, 338
administrators, networking with, 161, 215, 222, 300, 338
adult residency programs, 213–14
advance sales, of CDs, 109–10
advertising. *See* promotion *entries*
advisors, networking with, 24, 307